YOU ARE CORDIALLY INVITED TO JOIN

Dylan Jones, EDITOR-IN-CHIEF, BRITISH G

IN THE RALPH LAUREN MARQUEE
FOR AN EXCLUSIVE DAY OF TENNIS TO CELEBR
10 YEARS OF RALPH LAUREN OUTFITTING
THE CHAMPIONSHIPS, WIMBLEDON

Thursday, 2nd July, 2015

11.00AM: CHAMPAGNE RECEPTION
11.45AM: LUNCH
1.00PM: MATCHES BEGIN

*All England
Lawn Tennis Club*
WIMBLEDON, LONDON SW19

KINDLY RESPOND TO +44 (0) 207 535 4635 OR
ALEXANDRA.WALSHAW@RALPHLAUREN.COM

GQ

MW01133000

Butterry

*Grey Goose Le Citron, St. Germain
White Grape Juice
Basil, mint, lemon*

Peach Bellini
Soligo Prosecco, fresh peach

Soligo Prosecco, Brut N/V

Feudo Arancia, Grillo 2007

Primaterra, Primitivo 2007

Jone

Sir Paul Smith, Tinie Tempah & Dylan Jon
request the honour of the presence of

 Mercedes-Benz

at a private dinner to celebrate

**LONDON
COLLECTIONS:
MEN**

Wednesday 9 January 2012
Jpm cocktails, 8.30pm seated dinner

Sketch
9 Conduit Street, London W1S 2XG

RSVP
GQDinner@condenast.co.uk

Invitation is non-transferable. If after acceptance you find you
are unable to attend, please call 07721 077347

ESTATES & WINES
COLLECTION **BELVEDERE**
VODKA Veuve Clicquot

Sir Elton John, David Furnish
and Dylan Jones, Editor of British GQ

invite

to a private soirée at

CECCONI'S
West Hollywood

8764 Melrose Avenue, West Hollywood, CA 90069

Monday 6th April
Cocktails and cicchetti from 7pm until 9pm

RSVPs: mariella.kroll@condenast.co.uk

Dylan Jones

Editor of British **GQ**
invites

's 'NY JS DB 6.

'room,
SW1

.30pm

Connaught Hotel

a Mackay
3739

Chateau Marmont, 8221 Sunset Bou

& CHANDON
AMPAGNE

Sir Elton John, David Furnish

& Dylan Jones, Editor of British **GQ**

invite

to an evening hosted by Alfred Dunhill

at The Polo Private Dining Room, The Beverly Hills Hotel & Bungalows
on Wednesday 16th April 2008
Drinks from 6.30 until 8.30 pm

Please RSVP to:
Victoria Harvie Telephone: 310 358 1739
victoria.harvie@pmkhbh.com

dunhill

THESE FOOLISH THINGS

Also by Dylan Jones:

Loaded: The Unexpurgated Oral History of the Velvet Underground
Magic: A Journal of Song (with Paul Weller)
Faster Than a Cannonball: 1995 And All That
Shiny & New: Ten Moments of Pop Genius that Defined the Eighties
Sweet Dreams: From Club Culture to Style Culture
The Wichita Lineman: Searching in the Sun for the World's Greatest Unfinished Song
David Bowie: A Life
London Sartorial
Manxiety
London Rules
Mr Mojo
Elvis Has Left the Building: The Day the King Died
The Eighties: One Day, One Decade
From the Ground Up: The U2 360 Tour
When Ziggy Played Guitar: David Bowie and Four Minutes that Shook the World
The Biographical Dictionary of Popular Music
Heroes (with David Bailey)
Cameron on Cameron: Conversations with Dylan Jones (with David Cameron)
Mr Jones' Rules for the Modern Man
iPod Therefore I Am: A Personal Journey Through Music
Sex, Power and Travel: 10 Years of Arena (ed.)
Meaty, Beaty, Big & Bouncy: Classic Rock and Pop Writing from Elvis to Oasis (ed.)
Ultra Lounge
True Brit: Paul Smith (with Paul Smith)
Jim Morrison: Dark Star
Haircults
The i-D Bible (co-ed.)

THESE FOOLISH THINGS

A Memoir

Dylan Jones

CONSTABLE

First published in Great Britain in 2024 by Constable

1 3 5 7 9 10 8 6 4 2

A CIP catalogue record for this book is available from the British Library.

ISBN: 978-1-40871-985-5 (hardback)

Typeset in Kepler Std by SX Composing DTP
Printed and bound in Great Britain by Clays Ltd, Elcograf, S.p.A.

Papers used by Constable are from well-managed forests and other responsible sources.

FSC www.fsc.org MIX Paper | Supporting responsible forestry FSC® C104740

Constable
An imprint of
Little, Brown Book Group
Carmelite House
50 Victoria Embankment
London EC4Y 0DZ

An Hachette UK Company

www.hachette.co.uk

www.littlebrown.co.uk

For Sarah

'I never dreamt that I would get to be
the creature that I always meant to be'

Pet Shop Boys, 'Being Boring'

Contents

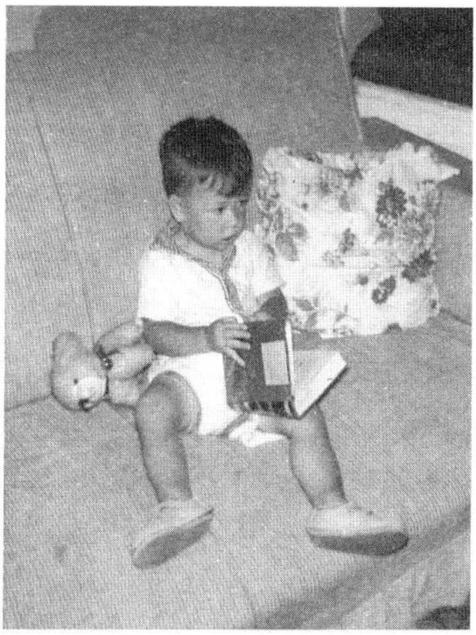

Boy with a book, Malta, 1963

WHEN I TOLD MY FRIEND Paul McGuinness I was going to write this book, he said any decent memoir had to involve a modicum of treachery – which is one of the reasons he said he was never going to write his – but here I haven't attempted to settle scores. This isn't a book about retribution. When Alex Bilmes, my old features editor at *GQ* who went on to edit *Esquire*, found out I was writing an autobiography, he sent me a note: 'Go easy on us. We were young and needed the money.'

I have, I think. Largely.

This is How I Remember it

The Greatest Show in Bow Street

The Men of the Year Awards, Covent Garden, 2014

TONIGHT, LIKE THE SECOND TUESDAY of every September, I felt like Captain Kirk.

It was 9.45 p.m. on 8 September 2015, in the Royal Opera House, London, and instead of the USS *Enterprise*, it was the *GQ* Men of the Year Awards coming in to land. Tonight was the result of nine months of careful, robust planning during which the entire team had been working to produce an event that we were duty bound to improve each year. That was the purpose. To have produced an event as good as last year's would have been not just a disappointment, in our eyes, it would have been a disaster.

Everyone was here. *Everyone.* The guests had arrived by a combination of taxi, limo, private jet and (whisper) commercial airlines. The caterers were primed, the gargantuan goodie bags were all packed (the winners received hampers worth £25,000, which had already been hand-delivered to their hotels), the flowers had arrived on time, and all the staff militarily briefed. I could tell a few of them were nervous, particularly the younger, newer ones. A couple had already had more than their regulation glass of champagne (I always suggested one glass before the event started, and then nothing until the after-party), while a few of the more seasoned members of the team I could tell had already visited the lavatories.

I was surrounded by five hundred people – from politicians and entrepreneurs to musicians, actors, sportspeople and – of course – legends, which was fundamentally what our event was about, celebrating the very best. Applauding legends. Our host tonight was Samuel L. Jackson, who was taking no crap from anyone; in fact, everyone was so scared of his withering rebukes that they were tremendously well behaved and were keeping their speeches respectively short. 'If you don't,' he had said from the stage, 'I will strike down upon thee with great vengeance and furious anger . . .' encouraging everyone else in the room to silently mouth the rest of his classic *Pulp Fiction* monologue.

Tonight, we had already celebrated the likes of Lewis Hamilton, James Corden, Blur, David Gandy, José Mourinho and, perhaps surprisingly at a Men of the Year Awards, Emilia Clarke ('It's a privilege to be recognised among all these talented, handsome men. So I'm going to turn my Tinder on: I'll be dragon baby mama if any of you are kind of looking for that'). We were gearing up to present Keith Richards with his big prize (Legend – seriously, how could he really be anything else?). Everyone was there in person, moving between the tightly assembled tables to the front of the opera house, to be venerated on stage. There was a policy that the presenters needed to be as famous as the winners, maybe more so. This year's were no exception: Elton John, Kate Moss, Bob Geldof, Naomi Campbell, Stephen Fry . . .

And now it was the turn of Will Farrell, 2015's Comedian of the Year.

'Thank you, I, ah, I feel a little emotional actually, partly because of this award,' he said, taking in the room, his eyes afire. 'I was afraid my speech would be too slow, because of Samuel's warning, that I did a little bit of cocaine in the bathroom, and when I do too much coke I cry, and um, [breaking down] and so I want to thank Dylan, thank you [sobbing]. You've been like a father to me [sobs]. We've had so many good times together, the time we buried that dead body and we said we'd never talk about it [sobs] . . . My heart's racing! I don't want to die tonight, I don't wanna die! Anyway, thank you *GQ* . . . *GQ* thank you . . .'

As he walked off to thunderous applause, Tracey Emin – an actual friend – leaned into me and said, *sotto voce*, as though she were reaching across the bridge on the Starship, 'That was very *GQ*.'

And I suppose it was.

It was a typically bonkers evening. As I looked across the room, at all these ridiculously fabulous people, I briefly allowed myself a moment of pride. It was hubristic, of course it was, as something awful could have easily been about to happen, but it was a rather special collection of people. Mad. Idiosyncratic. Eccentric even. Rich in texture. And – while it was likely to combust at any moment – very, very prescribed. I knew where everyone in the room was sitting, who they were sitting next to, and why they had been invited in the first place. I knew who was sleeping with who, who wouldn't want to be in someone else's eyeline, and who was likely to cause a scene or insult someone when they walked onstage.

Everything was coordinated, everything anticipated, even the bad behaviour. The mix was all. Celebrity. Sponsor. Hack. The trick was to make sure there was enough protein; too many carbs and the room started to slow. Too much fat and the room became toxic. You always needed protein, and tonight we were amino acids-a-go-go. Yet again we had made the magazine come to life, a magazine that – like all magazines, presumably – tried to catch lightning in a bottle, time after time after time. And tonight, we were letting the cork out, watching the lightning bounce around the room. In many respects the room was like my life – it was a court, all a game, a dance, going round and round and round.

And here I was, trussed up in a tuxedo on the captain's bridge, freakishly trying to control it all.

1977: Corridor Creeping

When Roxy Music met Dr Alimantado

New Kings Road, Chelsea, 1977

THERE WERE TIMES WHEN THE Ralph West Halls of Residence felt like one giant jukebox.

Sitting opposite Battersea Park on Albert Bridge Road, just 400 yards from the Thames and a ten-minute walk to the Kings Road, to me this modernist tower block felt like nothing but the centre of the world.

This was August 1977, and I had just moved in, fresh from High Wycombe, at the height of punk, and every evening as I walked along the fourth floor, back to my room at the end of the corridor by the fire escape, I'd be treated to a catena of musical treats, as a different type of music would seep out from under each door. As I made my way along the hard-tiled strip-lit corridor from the lift, I might hear the Clash, followed by Fleetwood Mac, which might be followed in quick succession by Talking Heads, Dr Alimantado, David Bowie and the MC5; on other nights it might be the Isley Brothers, Roxy Music, Al Stewart or Kraftwerk, and, from the room next to mine, very loudly, Patti Smith's *Horses*. Walking along the corridors of Ralph West was like being inside an enormous musical advent calendar, as out of the bedrooms there poured everything from Captain Beefheart to the Ohio Players, from Neu! to the Sex Pistols. It was as though you were turning a radio dial as you walked along the floors, as rhythms smashed into each other with complete disregard. There was some convergence, though little consensus.

As for myself, David Bowie's *Low* and Roxy Music's *Country Life* seemed to take precedence. My cheap little turntable entertained everyone from Van Morrison and Steely Dan to U-Roy and Glen Campbell, but for a while the second side of *Low* – the largely instrumental one – and the first side of *Country Life* appeared to be equipped with the right kind of glamorous dystopian top notes, music that seemed to mirror so much of what was going on at the time, from nascent industrial noise and spiky new-wave disco to DIY futurism and scratchy punk.

All human life lived in these halls, at least you'd think so walking along its corridors: along with the smell of spilled Lambrusco and burning Red Leb, music poured out from each compartmentalised disco. Sometimes, intrigued by what I heard, and not knowing what it was, I'd knock on a door, and then pad back to my room clutching a newly borrowed LP by Jonathan Richman, Big Star or the Congos.

When I got in from college – I had just enrolled on the foundation course at Chelsea School of Art and was having the time of my life – I usually worked my way through the first two Ramones albums, Culture's *Two Sevens Clash* and Wire's *Pink Flag*, although at night, after carousing around the punk clubs of central London, in addition to *Low* and *Country Life*, I'd fall asleep listening to John Martyn's *One World*, Steely Dan's *Aja* or Joni Mitchell's *The Hissing of Summer Lawns*, the eddies of the music slipping into the memories of the day, creating a torrent of images – from an unknown Los Angeles to an unknowable Scottish hinterland – right here in the heart of the city.

While it was assumed that when we baby punks made our way back to our flats or houses, we hastily put imported dub or hardcore industrial albums on our turntables, many of us listened to the music we were now being encouraged by the music press to unceremoniously dump. So while I would certainly listen to the likes of the Clash's debut album, Richard Hell's *Blank Generation* and various Throbbing Gristle bootlegs (horrible then, and horrible now), I would still wind down (what chilling out was called back in the day) listening to Neil Young, Isaac Hayes or one of the first five Roxy Music albums (Bryan Ferry's lyrics sparkling beadily amid the murk of the mid-seventies). For while I spent my evenings jumping up and down in sweaty West End venues, I was still dreaming of driving down Sunset Boulevard in a big fancy car listening to 'Virginia Plain' or 'Mother of Pearl'. My room may have been covered with Sex Pistols posters, but my heart (and my dream cocktail glass) was elsewhere, in the deserts of Arizona, on the west coast of Ireland, back in Notting Hill in the late fifties, or in a Belgravia townhouse in 1972, with the first Roxy Music album on the turntable. On the perimeter of sleep, I would lie there and imagine myself living the lives in those songs, believing my own life to be full of the same possibilities.

But then London was *alive* with possibilities.

That was the problem with punk, I suppose, if there was a problem at all. While I loved the rabid excitement, the music, the gigs and all the running around, in some respects it was a cartoon life, a riot of a life fuelled by amphetamine and cheap lager and the possibilities of change. In my heart I was still in love with the world painted by David Bowie and Bryan Ferry, the one where a piano was always tinkling in the next apartment. That to me felt like real change. After all, that was why I had bought so many velvet jackets back when I was fifteen. I had three – navy, black and burgundy – and would wear them over a T-shirt or, if I was feeling especially confident, over my bare chest, with a thin scarf knotted around my neck.

It seemed so important at the time. And maybe it was. It was certainly indicative of how I felt about my life. Because basically, I wanted someone else's.

The Ralph West building was a ten-storey Inner London Education Authority tower block overlooking the Ethelburga Estate on one side and Battersea Park on the other, a modernist, some might say brutalist building which housed all the first-year students at the big London art schools (Chelsea, St Martin's, Central, Camberwell and the London College of Printing). It was all glass, blond wood and straight lines, and looked like something from an architectural magazine. If you were from the provinces, and you were in your first year studying at one of those colleges, and you could afford it, or were poor or lucky enough to have a grant (like me), this is where you stayed. (The Clash's Joe Strummer stayed there in the early seventies when he was at Central School of Art – the experience inspired him to write 'Lost in the Supermarket' on *London's Calling* – as did the Pistols' Glen Matlock a few years later.)

Just a short walk from the Kings Road, Ralph West was like New York's Chelsea Hotel reimagined as a youth hostel.

From my window I could clearly see Battersea Power Station, and each morning when I woke up and opened the orange curtains, I fully expected to see Pink Floyd's famous pig miraculously flying between the white concrete chimneys.

There were around five hundred residents, all of us striving for some kind of individuality, a mass of seventeen- and eighteen-year-olds, defined by our mutability. Within weeks of moving in I was wearing make-up, inexpertly dyeing my hair (my love affair with peroxide would soon cause my hair to fall out) and had invested in a proper leather jacket (with a diagonal zip) from a shop opposite Kensington Market. It cost £45 and I wore it until it fell apart. Everything was new, every experience a novelty, whether it was going to hastily arranged gigs in the wilds of Willesden or sitting with my new fancy friends in Pucci Pizza in the Kings Road. These were worlds that were all new to me. One night I'd be at a house party in Greenwich or Hackney, struggling to find a night bus home; the next I'd be at a dinner in Chelsea, eating food I'd never heard of and listening to the kind of conversation it would have been impossible for me to anticipate. It was all exciting, all intoxicating, and there was nothing I didn't appreciate.

My desire to move to London was a mixture of escape and reinvention, although until I arrived, I had no idea how narrow my previous existence had been, how small, how provincial. London didn't suddenly feel like a new city, it felt like a whole world. Having been conceived and almost born in London (my parents had lived in Soho before temporarily moving abroad), I felt I needed to reconnect with it. Sometimes I'd get on a bus and sit right at the front of the upper deck and spend a day getting to know London, working out how Islington joined up with Archway, how the City joined up with King's Cross, and going all the way from the river to Finsbury Park and back again. Or else I'd jump on the Circle line at Sloane Square and just go round and round and round. I'd make the obligatory trip to Heddon Street to see the phone box featured on the cover of *Ziggy Stardust*, linger too long outside the flat Bowie had lived in on Oakley Street (just a five-minute walk from Ralph West) and go and see where Biba used to be. I couldn't believe how big London was.

If I wasn't going out to gigs or clubs, I'd go to one of the many late-night cinemas in Chelsea, or the Scala in Tottenham Street, or the Screen On The Green in Upper Street, happy to see John Waters's *Pink Flamingos*, Tobe Hooper's *Texas Chainsaw Massacre* or Nic Roeg's *The Man Who Fell to Earth* on repeat. And I think I was contractually obliged by the Inner London Education Authority to watch *The Rocky Horror Show* at the Kings Road Theatre at least once every six months. Weekends would be spent in Rough Trade, Record & Tape Exchange or Cheapo Cheapo, or in the basement of the Vintage Magazine Shop. Too often, I'd be trawling for clothes in Kensington Market, Acme Attractions, Laurence Corner (the army surplus store in Camden) or charity shops (knowing the right clothes to wear wasn't the same as being able to afford them). I was a cultural tourist.

Walking back home across Albert Bridge always made me feel special, almost as though my own life was being lit up with theatrical bulbs.

Everything involved some kind of discovery. I bought books I'd only ever read about and never seen, I devoured new trendy magazines, and I started making notes. I'd once read Charlie Chaplin had kept a dictionary in the bathroom at his hotel so he could learn a new word every morning, and – pretentious – I did something similar, writing down a word whenever I saw one I liked, or sometimes a phrase. If I saw a word I didn't know, I'd look it up. I wouldn't have dreamed of saying it, but I stored it away in case I wanted to use it in print one day. One of the few books I had in my room was a huge red Collins dictionary. Everything was banked, filed away for the future. Just in case.

I hadn't really learned much in school – as my father was in the Royal Air Force and we moved about so much, I'd been to a dozen schools by the time I finally left, and I didn't think any of them were any good – so I was going to start now. I spent my money on magazines, newspapers (I loved the *Evening Standard,* and regularly tore images out of it to pin to my wall. 'Standard! Standard!' – that's what I remember hearing outside every tube station on my way home) and concert tickets; sometimes I bought clothes and drugs, but not often. Art supplies were mainly courtesy of the college.

I also fell in love with George Smith, the hero of J. P. Donleavy's novel *A Singular Man*, the 'professional' human being who remembers all too well the perils of being an amateur. I loved the image of him on a train station, enjoying the admiration of those around him, as though he were an especially introverted rock star. Smith was a passive hero – written as a character to whom things happen rather than someone who causes things to happen – and yet he was instantly appealing. As one reviewer put it, 'The central concern of all of Donleavy's novels is the fortune of a single male protagonist isolated from family and country and pursuing a lifestyle that is improvised and erratic.'

He seemed like a pretty good approximation of a seventeen-year-old let loose in London.

In Ralph West, young love was everywhere, and one couple was having so much sex, usually up against the doors of their respective rooms, that the girl used to say she had forgotten what to do with her legs. There was a lot of sex at Ralph West, and the halls saw the flowering of my libido as well as that of every other seventeen-year-old who lived there. Sex suddenly seemed unimportant, casual, which was obviously brilliant. For the first time in my life, I met girls who found the idea of relationships ridiculous.

As for Chelsea School of Art, it was everything I wanted it to be, and more. New people, new horizons, a wardrobe change, everything. Essentially this was all about freedom. Unlike a lot of people I met around then, who appeared to know precisely what they wanted to do with their lives, all I really knew was that I wanted a life in the creative arts, which was why Chelsea's foundation course was such a superb primer, exposing me to painting, drawing, screen-printing, photography, sculpture, the lot. Each morning I would walk along the embankment to Bagley's Lane, in Chelsea Wharf, which housed the foundation course students. And most nights I'd wander off into Soho, taking the 11, 22 or 19 bus, destined to end up in a basement, exploring London on my own, disappearing into the 100 Club and the Marquee to watch the latest punk groups.

IN FACT, FOR NEARLY A year before I moved to London, I had already been exploring the city and taking the train up from High Wycombe, often by myself, to see gigs at the Roxy, the Fulham Greyhound, the Red Cow, the Nashville and the Hope and Anchor. Sometimes I'd just end up in the Marquee because I knew I could get in (the bouncers didn't seem to mind how old you were) and almost regardless of who was playing. One night it might be the Pat Travers Band, Widowmaker or Ted Nugent, another it could be Roogalator, Eddie and the Hot Rods or the Count Bishops, until the second division metal bands and pub-rock groups started to be replaced by the likes of the Clash, Subway Sect and Wire.

I particularly loved the 100 Club in London's Oxford Street as it always felt like a malevolent student bar; every time I went there a fight seemed to break out. The place was cursed. I saw Adam and the Ants play there in the summer of 1977 and as Jordan, the guest vocalist (was she a singer? Well, she had an ability to stand in front of a microphone, shrieking and looking vaguely intimidating), walked by me on her way to the front a pint glass went spinning across my face, landing somewhere near a speaker stack to the right of the stage. The Ants weren't what you would call accomplished – in 1977 no one was, and you would have been suspicious had they been – but they knew what to do on stage, namely create a din that spoke of every transgressive act one could imagine, be it sexual, political or cultural.

I also spent a ridiculous amount of time in a pub called the Nag's Head near my home in High Wycombe, which was run by a man called Ron Watts, who also promoted gigs at the 100 Club. Consequently, I saw dozens of punk bands, as he'd book them into both venues. I remember being in the downstairs bar as the Sex Pistols played upstairs. I was still at school, wearing a navy-blue velvet jacket and an orange scarf. I was only a kid and looked like a roadie from the Rubettes.

So, by the time I moved to London in the summer of 1977 I had been in love with punk for over a year, or, more specifically, I had been in love with the Ramones. I'd fallen for them since I'd first heard 'Beat on the Brat' at a house party a week after Nick Kent's review of their first album in the *NME*. ('The Ramones don't say much,' wrote Kent. 'They're pretty vacant. But they rock out with a vengeance.') The next day I decided to turn myself into Johnny Ramone, and for the previous twelve months had been walking around with a floppy, pudding-bowl haircut, drainpipe jeans, plimsoles, a matelot top and a (plastic) leather jacket, bought from an Oxfam shop in High Wycombe. Overnight I morphed from a lank-haired neurotic boy outsider in a velvet jacket, a secondhand Biba top and a hooded brow into an unconvincing Home Counties approximation of a Bowery punk. Four years previously, I'd done the same thing with David Bowie, although it had been a lot easier to adopt a Ramones haircut.

At 7.30 p.m. on 6 July 1972, I was sitting by myself watching *Top of the Pops* in our semi-detached pebbledash terraced house in Deal, Kent – which is where we briefly lived before moving to High

Wycombe – and couldn't quite believe my eyes. Back then, the show was regularly watched by 12 to 13 million people every week, almost a quarter of the population. A large percentage of viewers were teenagers, like me, who – having seen David Bowie strut about in his space-age onesie singing his new single 'Starman' – thought he was talking directly to them from the BBC studios. Bowie was ridiculously flamboyant and had a campness about him that was immediately appealing. I had already seen an ad for *Hunky Dory* in the *NME* but at the time thought he was just another singer-songwriter. On television, he was very different. He was wearing a multi-coloured jumpsuit and playing a blue acoustic guitar, and he looked scary. Essentially, he looked carefree in a way no pop star had ever looked before. His performance was colourful, risqué, transgressive and very appealing to an impressionable twelve-year-old. Previously, my pop consumption had been based around one-hit wonders and odd T. Rex records. Bowie, to me, was a complete revelation. For me, Bowie kick-started the seventies, as the decade turned from black and white to colour overnight. It was this performance that changed my world, that made me immediately obsessed with music. It was an obsession that I would carry with me, initially as an alternative reality, and thereafter as a continuous soundtrack.

His appearance had a sweeping effect on me; my way of pledging my allegiance was by trying to emulate his haircut. Having summoned up enough courage to call the various unisex hairdressers in the area, I made an appointment for the following Saturday, and duly turned up with a photograph of Bowie torn from a recent copy of *Disco 45*. The hairdresser looked at the picture, looked at my thin, dank hair, and slowly shook his head. After a valiant attempt to fashion my hair into something approximating Bowie's thatch, I left the salon with a fringe that made me look more like Dave Hill, the decidedly un-Bowie-like guitarist in Slade.

I had other interests – Alice Cooper and Lou Reed were (incongruously) replacing George Best and Manchester United, Joseph Heller and Tom Wolfe were starting to nudge out *The Goon Show*, and Bryan

Ferry was completely reinventing my idea of a role model – but Bowie was now very much front and centre. For my generation, Bowie acted like Google, introducing us to a motley collection of fascinating cultural oddballs. And if he liked someone like Lou Reed, for instance, then I was going to love him too.

Bizarrely, one day my father admitted he liked Lou Reed too. Being an incredibly violent man – he'd nearly killed a boy when he was at school and had spent much of my childhood taking his frustrations out on me – my dad was the kind of person it was best to be wary of. Mike had spent most of his career in the Royal Air Force, although every now and then his creative frustrations poked through, indicating he spent most of his time denying them. And in 1972, these frustrations started to manifest themselves in strange ways. Having previously shown no interest in sartorial matters, he began wearing brightly coloured peaked caps and cravats, and started sporting an equally garish shoulder bag. It was almost as though he was trying to tell the world he was gay (something I didn't think was possible), but probably pointed to a midlife crisis (he would have been in his forties). His transformation only lasted a few months, but it was disconcerting to say the least.

But nothing had prepared me for what happened next. As I came in from my secondary modern one day, he handed me a copy of 'Walk on the Wild Side', the first single from *Transformer*, brandishing it as though it were a fresh £10 note or a stolen book. I can't remember how he described it, but it was less a peace offering and more an over-eager display of his apparent hipness. I didn't have the heart to tell him I had already bought it – this may have resulted in a punch to the head – but it made me never want to bring the subject up again. Luckily, that was the last time he ever mentioned Lou Reed.

I'm not sure I'd heard of the Velvet Underground before Bowie's endorsement of Lou Reed, but after buying and loving *Transformer* I started to scour local record shops to see what other treasures I could find. In a junk shop in High Wycombe, one of those that still looked like it was supplied by the prop department in *Steptoe and Son*,

I eventually found a copy of the *Andy Warhol's Velvet Underground featuring Nico* double album (the one with illustrations of lips and Coke bottles on the cover that were meant to look as though they were painted by the artist), and shortly after, bought a secondhand copy of the first album – albeit with the British cover – in Kensington Market, on a rare trip to London.

At that age – I was an extremely precocious thirteen-year-old – I spent most of my spare time in record shops, hunting through the racks for rarities and bargains; these two purchases were both. One of the most appealing things about the process of discovering esoteric and idiosyncratic music was imagining what kind of lives the musicians had outside of recording and touring. What did they do during the day? Where did they live? Did they make this mad, crazy, intoxicating music because they were on drugs? Or did they take drugs because they made this mad, crazy, intoxicating music?

When I started listening to the Velvet Underground and the Stooges (another Bowie recommendation, obviously), I was not equipped to imagine what they got up to when they weren't playing music. Which made them even more alluring. They just felt so . . . urban. Two years later, before fully embracing butterfly-collared shirts, velvet jackets and Oxford bags, I even went through a period of rolling up my drainpipe jeans – skinhead style – worn with pink socks and black Dr Martens shoes in the vain hope of trying to advertise the fact I owned records by people who lived in New York. In my eyes, that city started to take on an almost mythical glow, reinvented in my imagination as an island peopled exclusively by the weird and the interesting. This was why I would initially lean more towards the New York punk groups, preferring the Ramones to the Sex Pistols, and Richard Hell and the Voidoids rather than the dubious and parochial delights of the Damned. If you were from New York, you were exotic.

Particularly if you were Andy Warhol. By 1972, I had already become quietly obsessed with Warhol. I'd read about him in newspapers and magazines, and occasionally seen him on TV. I'd already flirted with David Hockney and Salvador Dalí (the most obvious affiliations a nascent teenage art lover would make at the time), but Warhol was something else entirely. Earlier in the year, David Bailey had self-published a transcript of his controversial TV documentary on the artist, and which I had bought in WHSmith. In 1971, the media impresario Lew Grade had hired Bailey to direct a series of arts documentaries for the ATV franchise, despite his complete lack of experience in the field. He ended up making three films, on Luchino Visconti, Cecil Beaton and, infamously, Andy Warhol, which would go on to cause press outrage and legal action from moralising fanatics. The Warhol documentary turned out to be a portrait of the dying days of the Factory, with Bailey getting extraordinary access to both Warhol and the likes of Holly Woodlawn, Jane Holzer and Candy Darling.

It was. however, the transcript of the show, complete with Bailey's intriguing photographic glimpses of this secret New York world, that piqued my interest. I hadn't even seen the film. I didn't for one minute imagine I could ever somehow make it to New York, but my growing obsession with Warhol encouraged me to think about little else but going to art school. Precociously, American pop art became my thing, and I devoured anything I could find on Warhol, Roy Lichtenstein, Robert Rauschenberg, *Interview* magazine, and all those travel books I found in the library full of photographs of Main Street America, billboards, Coca-Cola signs, Las Vegas swimming pools, palm trees, traffic lights, backlit Perspex shop signs, and the cluttered skylines of Los Angeles and Detroit. Americana was what I was in love with, seen through the quizzical eyes of pop art, Tom Wolfe and Vance Packard.

THERE WERE MANY OTHERS I met at Chelsea School of Art in 1977 who had had their lives transformed by both Warhol and Bowie, and Bryan Ferry, come to that, including Tom Dixon, who would soon become a much-celebrated furniture designer (after being an uncelebrated pop star), and Jon Baker (known mononymously as Mole), who would go on to launch the Gee Street record label. Jon arrived on his first day looking like Keith Richards, while I still looked like a Ramone; in a matter of weeks, we were both approximating a punk orthodoxy. There was also a ridiculously cool chap called Martin Jackson, who looked like a cross between Ferry and a male model from a French fashion magazine: he had a wedge, Bowie pegs and a big, billowing raincoat. He even had business cards, and he was only seventeen!

You were only meant to stay at the Ralph West Halls for your first year in London, although I managed to extend my stay for another nine months, by which time there had been another intake. In August 1978, when I started on the graphics course at St Martin's School of Art, a new tranche of students moved in, including Chris Sullivan, all the way from Merthyr Tydfil (and whose life always seemed packed with incident), and Fiona Dealey, all dolled up from Southend. I got to know them both, with Fiona and I becoming fast friends. We spent hours in each other's rooms, moaning about St Martin's (she was in the first year of the fashion course), gossiping about the sex lives of people on our floor, and working out which parties we were going to gatecrash at the weekend (one Saturday she took me to a party in Basildon organised by the boys who would soon become Depeche Mode, and left me to freeze on the train station).

St Martin's was even more intoxicating than Chelsea. I'd applied to the college for three reasons: 1) I was chasing a girl called Lynda Shearsby, who was already on the graphics course, albeit in the year above; 2) it was close to all the music venues and nightclubs in Soho; and 3) it was St Martin's, the coolest art school in the world bar none.

Even though I was excited by being at St Martin's, it immediately felt old fashioned; far from immersing myself in its history, I wanted to subvert it. As I was doing graphics, I was obviously obsessed with design, with the way things looked. Furniture, magazines, posters, films, clothes and, saliently, photography. I look at my old scrapbooks now and they feel completely modernist, futuristic, almost sci-fi – my life drawing sketches are all angular, my graphics work looks suspiciously like Malcolm Garrett's work for the Buzzcocks, and the short, animated films I made all looked like the kind of things you might see accompanying a Mountain or Can track on *The Old Grey Whistle Test*. My photographs were mostly black and white, journalistic, harsh, unforgiving. I started photographing everything and everyone, usually using Ralph West as a studio: my friend Fiona, Corinne Drewery (later of Swing Out Sister), Stephen Linard (who would go on to massively influence John Galliano), the painters John Glenn and Peter Doig, the milliner Stephen Jones, and putative Blitz Kids like Richard Ostell, Myra Falconer and (Boy) George O'Dowd. I've still got contact sheets of dozens of pictures I took of Antony Price's Plaza on the Kings Road, a shop fetishised by those of us who loved Roxy Music.

Was I any good? Not so much.

College work was interesting, but not as interesting as my social life. Almost immediately the future started unfolding, and the extraordinary people I met there over the course of my three years only added to my sense of weird entitlement. We all felt the same. We weren't exactly smug, but we knew we had *something*. We thought we were special. I didn't think the world owed me a living, far from it, but I certainly had an irrational belief in myself. I was still going to gigs (they were so cheap, you could often get in for less than the price of a bus ticket), dashing out most evenings to the Marquee, the 100 Club, Hammersmith Odeon, the Hope and Anchor, the Moonlight Club and the Nashville to watch an increasingly disparate bunch of post-punk groups (Siouxsie and the Banshees, Joy Division, Gang of Four, Slits, Pere Ubu, Cabaret Voltaire, etc). There was such an air of impermanence about punk that, as well as rushing around to see anyone who was new, there was a sense that bands were going to implode on a regular basis. I saw many so-called 'final' gigs by the Jam, the Damned, Subway Sect, Sham 69 and the Slits. Fiona, meanwhile, would be dressing up to go out to nightclubs, which soon included Billy's.

By 1978, punk had started to flag, and many of those who had been there at the beginning were starting to tire of the relentlessly downward mobility of it all. One day in the autumn of 1978, Rusty Egan was chatting with Steve Strange about how the London club scene had become stagnant. After a brief conflab they decided to open their own club, alighting on Billy's just off Dean Street in Soho. Popular with local sex workers, it tended to be empty on a Tuesday, so the pair asked the owner if they could start a weekly club night. They printed flyers with the strap line 'Fame Jump Aboard the Night Train / Fame, Fame, Fame. What's Your Name?', and very soon they were full. It soon became known as Bowie Night, popular with a small group of clubbers who had briefly ended their affair with disco to embrace punk, but who had retreated when the scene became overrun by hordes of denim-clad rockers who nine months previously had been nodding their heads in unison to Thin Lizzy and Hawkwind. The club soon started to fill with other disenfranchised night owls intent on reinventing themselves, and the crowd followed Strange and Egan to the Blitz on Great Queen Street in 1979. Fleet Street soon took an interest, called them the Blitz Kids, and a new movement was born, as Soho became overrun by eighteen-year-olds wearing tartan ballgowns, pillbox hats, nun's habits and deathly white make-up. The Blitz generation took punk and dressed it up, giving it a twelve-inch remix in the process. They anticipated the style-obsessed eighties when the world became a global catwalk. Narcissism plumbed new depths as haircuts reached new heights. Here, everyone had an alias, an ambition and an aerodynamic haircut to match.

Steve Strange was a lot smarter than some gave him credit for, as he understood clubs were driven by people, not just music, and that while many of those he didn't let into his clubs thought he was just being spiteful, it was all about curation. Not that the lucky ones were exactly overflowing with empathy. To those left outside on the pavement (Steve delighted in telling badly dressed punters they couldn't get in), the lucky ones could appear snotty, the sort of people who might cut you dead if you saw them again in daylight. When I started going, I wasn't asked to pay as I'd slip in with the regulars, which obviously spoiled me; I was determined never to pay to get into a nightclub again. In truth, the denizens of the Blitz were adopting the modus operandi of Andy Warhol's Factory, of never responding to anything or anyone around them. The lesson learned was to never get excited about anything, and just stare instead. The mantra was simple: look at it and let the looking of it become the thing that you're doing. This was called the silent shrug, and it was employed by many of the lucky ones inside. Being one of the chosen few encouraged a certain unnecessary conceitedness.

On those nights when I wasn't going out, I'd sit in my room in Ralph West playing Iggy Pop and David Bowie records while Fiona would sit on the end of my bed, looking like a Bond Street Valkyrie, complaining that she had nothing to wear. I'd often ask her, in strong vernacular terms, what she thought she looked like, jokingly wondering aloud how she had the audacity to go out looking so extreme (she wore long leather skirts, lace bustiers and skyscraper stilettos). In truth I thought she was one of the most exotic creatures I'd ever seen, and became intoxicated by both her and the worlds she moved in. I found the whole thing fascinating.

I found the new clubs as exhilarating as the early punk clubs. Not that I was dressed for the part. I can still remember what I wore the first time I went to the Blitz: black studded leather jacket, black T-shirt, black skinny-legged jeans and black patent winklepickers. In hindsight, I could pretend that I was channelling one of the early sixties Warhol gang, or a Tom of Finland leather boy, but in truth I was simply wearing what I always wore. I would soon learn that this wasn't really good enough.

We would sometimes walk across the bridge and go drinking in the Roebuck on the Kings Road, which was where, in the upstairs poolroom, Malcolm McLaren had once forced John Lydon to audition for the Sex Pistols, changing the course of British music history in the process. Here, truant schoolgirls mingled with drug dealers and old rockers such as Phil Lynott and Gary Holton from the Heavy Metal Kids. Lydon still frequented the place, although it had got incredibly druggy upstairs and had started to be frequented by what we called 'weekend punks'. You could even buy heroin over the counter, along with your pint of Guinness.

The action appeared to have moved on, and the place that seemed to be the nucleus of this merging of punk and club cultures was the Cambridge, a pub that still sits on the northwest corner of Cambridge Circus in the West End. It was just a hundred yards from the Marquee, a hundred yards from the 100 Club, and only fifty yards from Saint Martin's. At the time, the Cambridge was the most important pub in Soho, and every band who wanted to leave an impression in the neighbouring venues usually ended up there, pumping money into the jukebox, drinking green and yellow bottles of Holsten Pils, and throwing shapes in their leather jackets.

The downstairs bar often felt like a Parisian brasserie – long, busy, everyone giddy with expectation, including the tourists – but the upstairs bar was where you went if you knew what was going on. It was always full of demanding people – punks, art students from St Martin's, pop stars and fashion designers – and so you had to be on your guard. Malcolm McLaren had his own stool, the Sex Pistols seemed to be there every Friday night, and whenever they were there, Siouxsie and the Banshees took up residency by the jukebox. The Pistols' record-cover designer Jamie Reid was the coolest man there. He always sat on the same barstool, staring straight forward, discouraging eye contact. He always wore a tight, thigh-length black leather suit jacket, his hair was always fashioned into this greasy, truck-driver quiff, and he always had a bottle of Pils seemingly grafted to his left hand. Pils was the only thing that anyone drank, making it seem as though it was the only thing they sold. The Cambridge was a punk-rock circus before it became a weigh-station for London club culture. You'd have Sid Vicious and John Lydon in one corner, and Steve Strange and Rusty Egan in another. You'd find Kim Bowen and Lee Sheldrick, Billy Idol and Tony James, Robert Elms and Chris Sullivan. It was a fancy-dress party every night of the week, month in month out.

Everything happened at the Cambridge: a girl was decapitated by a lorry after she bet her friend she could crawl underneath it before it pulled away; a St Martin's painter called Alan was beaten senseless because he persisted in dressing like Hitler (floppy fringe, jackboots, leather trench coat and tell-tale moustache). The first time we saw him we immediately took bets on how long it would take before someone kicked the living daylights out of him. And just two weeks later he stumbled into the Cambridge covered in the most fearsome bruises. Alan had, to quote an old Nick Lowe song, been nutted by reality, and soon left the college.

Most people congregated at the Cambridge before moving off into the night, to the latest tranche of nightclubs sprouting up all over the city. With the fancy-dress parade at its height, a generation of young entrepreneurs was taking over nightclubs for one night a week, installing their own DJs and creating a phenomenon out of nothing. While one of the biggest changes in London nightlife in the late seventies was the shift from the likes of the Marquee and the 100 Club to nightclubs such as the Embassy in Old Bond Street (which opened in April 1978) and Legends in Old Burlington Street – as we started going out to dance rather than going out to watch bands – so there was also a shift from pubs to cocktail bars, as the proto-Blitz Kids started wanting more glamorous places to drink.

And the obvious place to come was Mayfair. Yes, you could have gone to Peppermint Park or Rumours in Covent Garden, and yes you may have wanted to scoot all the way down to the Kings Road occasionally, but the most esoteric place to drink your Tequila Sunrise, your Singapore Sling or your Pina Colada (drinks which might sound incredibly naff today but were considered to be exactly the opposite back then) was the Beachcomber Bar in the Mayfair Hotel, which had once been the first London iteration of the American Polynesian restaurant phenomenon. It had plastic palm trees, rainstorms over a pond of caimans, parrots in and out of cages, and oceanic art all around. I first went there in the spring of 1978, and it was one of the most glamorous places I'd ever been. Ironic, but glamorous. As you sat sipping enormous pink drinks in extravagant glasses, life-size animatronic crocodiles crawled around the foliage and the pink plastic foliage beside you. It was a world away from the warm lager you'd find in the pubs in Soho, a world away from punk, and in fact a completely new world altogether.

THE BEACHCOMBER OPENED IN JULY 1960, while I had arrived six months earlier, barely two weeks after the start of the sixties, on Monday 18 January, in the RAF hospital in Ely, en route from London to a temporary home in Lincoln. Born into an air force family, I moved around a lot when I was young, and the first sixteen years of my life were spent in London and High Wycombe, in Cyprus and Malta, in Anglesey, and various places on the east and southeast coasts. We would spend nine months, maybe a year in each place, so it was like a conveyer belt of novelty. And as I spent much of my childhood on air force bases, and as many of these were American, I suppose it's no surprise that from an early age I latched on to the obvious manifestations of US pop culture – midnight-blue sharkskin suits and metallic tail-finned cars, Goober Grape and Hot Dog Relish, Archie comics and the records of Frank Sinatra and Dean Martin. The bases were full of American pilots and their beehived wives, who all appeared to wear pedal pushers, stilettos and completely opaque Jackie O shades (the wives, not the pilots). Even when they were picking up their children from the local school. From England's 1966 World Cup victory through to the moon landing in 1969, Frank and Dino were rarely off our turntable, and many of my early memories revolve around listening to 'I've Got You Under My Skin', 'My Kind of Town', 'Volare' and 'Under the Bridges of Paris'. For me, these songs were gaudily exotic but homely at the same time, and defined a certain kind of sophistication, no matter how ersatz it may have been.

I would stare at my parents' Frank Sinatra and Dean Martin singles for hours. They all had heavily stylised photographs of the singers on the picture sleeves (which, even back then, were so brittle they were in danger of cracking); both were hypnotically attractive figures – Frank looked like he swung because it was cool, while Dino swung not just because swinging was cool, but because it was easy.

Perhaps unsurprisingly I became quietly obsessed with fifties and sixties Americana.

These were probably mainly my mother Audrey's records (apart from Lou Reed, the only records my dad played were classical). Her favourite, Dean, blasted daily through the walls, and as I heard her singing along, even as a boy I could tell she was singing about a world that would never be within her reach, resigned instead to a life of compromise and domesticity. How she semaphored this, I don't know, but even when she was happily singing, occasionally a sadness appeared to define her. You pick things up as a kid. Especially when your parents are always fighting.

'Ah, Dino,' she would say, emphatically, as though she were wistfully remembering some romantic Sorrento holiday. 'What an old smoothie.'

She was being dismissive while at the same time taking a kind of ownership of him, but even she couldn't disguise the fact that she found him completely exotic. Imagine! She owned not one Dean Martin record, but dozens! Back in the sixties, to my parents' generation, buying a new record – be it single, EP or album – wasn't incidental, it wasn't like buying a pack of cigarettes. It was like buying a fridge or a television set.

I can still remember my mother saying to my father, on more than one occasion, 'Shall we listen to the new Dean Martin record again?' Swells, she called them, when she mentioned Dean and Frank, and that's what they were – swells.

Consequently, I loved them too, although it wasn't just the music, of course – it never was. The men pictured on the single, EP and LP sleeves lying around the house were like no men I had ever seen; you didn't get many Italian Americans swanning around East Anglia dressed in herringbone sports jackets, butterfly-collared shirts and polka-dot cravats. And certainly not in pink V-neck cardigans, white silk socks and black suede loafers. Not even on the US Air Force bases where I grew up. But then that was the point, I guess. Dino and Sinatra inhabited a world that wasn't easily accessible to an eight-year-old who was yet to buy his own trousers, let alone visit the Sahara Tahoe.

My parents' singles were the first pieces of vinyl I ever remember holding, racked in a vinyl-coated dark green box – with a cheap, goldish metal lock on the lid – just big enough to hold about forty seven-inch singles. There were all sorts of singles in there, most in thin, brightly coloured paper sleeves, and all looking as though they'd been imported from America. I've still got my parents' beautifully scratched 45 of John Barry's wistful 'Vendetta', still got an EP of various tracks from *Songs for Swinging Lovers*, still got Topol's 'If I Were a Rich Man' (from the 1964 musical *Fiddler on the Roof*). There was lots of Herb Alpert, too, and if history can be caught in a single breath, then there are few better ways of explaining the Populuxe aspirations of American suburbia during the late fifties and early sixties (when the advertising industry began to believe its own publicity) than by listening to the piercing yet sweet 'Ameriachi' sound of Alpert and his Tijuana Brass. Lying around the house was also a fair amount of Les Baxter, the soundtrack composer who, along with Martin Denny and Arthur Lyman, helped invent the hyperworld of exotica. How esoteric of my parents.

These were American tastes, but then at home we were steeped in Americana. Not only that, I almost *felt* American.

One song that I fell in love with at the time which was unmistakably American was Glen Campbell's 'Wichita Lineman'. For many years I thought I was the only person who liked 'Wichita Lineman'; the song was an important part of my childhood but I thought I might have been the only person from my generation to have heard of it, let alone actually heard the record. I eventually worked out that, like most of Glen Campbell's great songs, 'Wichita Lineman' had not been written by Campbell himself, but by somebody called Jimmy Webb, a songwriter nicknamed the Master of Sad – he wrote terrifically maudlin songs (Campbell called them 'hurt soul') such as 'By the Time I Get to Phoenix', 'Where's the Playground, Susie?', 'Galveston', etc.

Another obsession of my mother's was the Beatles. There was no generation gap between Dean Martin and the Beatles, as to her they were both examples of a new kind of freedom. In this she was incorrigibly plural. If the Beatles had boundless curiosity, Sinatra and his gang were simply exploiting destiny. To her, watching films of the Rat Pack performing in Las Vegas and Los Angeles was just as socially emancipating as hearing the beat groups from Liverpool and London; she was adamant that everything they did was some sort of billet-doux to life itself. Far from being bewildered by all this new activity in the sixties, she genuinely seemed to enjoy it, even if she knew she was never going to fully experience it. She felt she owned the sixties just as much as young women half her age. It was liberty, something genuinely different after the war. She saw the way the American women on the USAF bases conducted themselves, and she didn't see why she shouldn't have some of it for herself. She was properly smitten with the Fabs, and every new single would be lovingly bought and treasured, filed away in the dark green singles box. I didn't realise this until I was about seven, but I could see the joy they brought her, and there was a ceremonial aspect to the way they were played. This wasn't done indiscriminately and was more like a treat. *A Hard Day's Night* was also the first film I ever saw at the cinema, aged four, smuggled in by my mother at a matinee performance in a small cinema in Soho. I found it as infectious as she did and afterwards would clap along whenever she randomly sang 'Yeah, Yeah, Yeah' at home. A generation earlier, people just didn't say 'Yeah, Yeah, Yeah', which is why the Beatles were considered so brash (when Paul McCartney and John Lennon had just finished writing the song, in McCartney's childhood home in Liverpool, he ran into the living room to play it to his father; his response was to suggest dropping the 'Americanisms' and sing 'Yes, Yes, Yes' instead). She loved it, and loved them, and consequently I did too. My love for the Beatles would eventually be mirrored by my love for David Bowie, two objects of desire that would stay with me for the rest of my life. They weren't always fashionable, and weren't actually always present, but there they were, forever in the background – one a staple diet of British society, the other an oddity who turned out not to be an oddity at all.

My mother felt that by simply being a pop consumer she was part of a kind of revolution, a personal revolution. Therefore, she felt empowered by pop, and everything that came with it. She was in her thirties by the time the Beatles arrived, but then she was experiencing much of her life a little later than usual (she had had five miscarriages before I was born), and so she was initially giddy with the way the sixties had started, or so she said. Things would quickly change, though, as for both of us the decade quickly darkened.

My childhood was chaotic, and so I very quickly learned how best to try and control it. Control. It was all about control. If I couldn't control what was happening around me, the violence, at least I could try and control my environment. Consequently, everything became prescribed: how I talked, where I walked, how I dressed, even what I thought. I became very careful with everything I did. I couldn't trust anything around me so I had to trust myself. I didn't necessarily like myself – there are only so many times you can be called a piece of shit without believing it – but I could grow to trust myself. I was never going to be a casualty, so my life became about survival. And that meant control. This is how I needed to behave in order to make sense of the world. Control. I had to be in control. At first this manifested itself in drawing, because I could control what I drew, but then spread to every other aspect of my life – spotting danger and escape routes, controlling my environment and always being on my guard.

That old muckraker Albert Goldman once said that music was a way for us to keep young, not by trying to stay cool and relevant, but by an almost generational refusal to grow up. In his mind, pop stars were becoming surrogate parents, keeping us away from the horrors of growing up and the onslaught of real life. For me, the horrors of real life had always been at home, and they had been very real indeed. From an extremely young age, I was regularly beaten, smacked, punched by my father. He would hit me every day, hard. Very hard. So hard that I developed a stammer that made it impossible for me to say my own name until I was five years old. Looking back from a fifty-year distance, I think I became inured to this abuse fairly quickly. I certainly didn't let it define me, and in truth probably became quite dispassionate about it. I'm sure far worse things happened to other children. In fact, I know they did. Being knocked about wasn't so special back in the sixties.

I rarely talked about my childhood abuse and had certainly never written about it. But in 1995 the *Observer* wanted to run a piece on stammering, and a friend who worked there approached me about it. Having initially said no, and then having said no again, I was convinced to go and see a speech therapist, and eventually wrote a piece about the process. Of course, as I delved into the reasons for my stammer, I needed to explain aspects of my childhood, which in hindsight I regret (it now seems self-indulgent). But this stuff is out there now, so I can't really deny it. I'm not a huge fan of misery memoirs, but I hope the takeaway from whatever trauma I experienced is the simple fact that I didn't allow it to determine the person I am today.

If it wasn't me being hit, it was my mother, who was always jumping into her Ford Anglia, disappearing off to see her girlfriend and leaving me to fend for myself, allowing my father to practise more hours of unsupervised torture. Strangely, I didn't begrudge her this. My mother occasionally had relationships outside her marriage, with women, and specifically with a woman called Rita she'd met as a member of the Women's Auxiliary Air Force, who since leaving the force had lived on her own in a council flat in Chalk Farm, north London. When I was much younger, she would take me to visit her; my strongest memories are eating at what I thought at the time was a ridiculously sophisticated Italian restaurant in Swiss Cottage, and the sight of the Post Office Tower, newly built and looming over Rita's council flat like a benign Invader from *The War of the Worlds*. My mother's relationships obviously caused ructions at home, resulting in more fights, more black eyes for my mother, more desperate respite being sought at our neighbours. 'He's done it again,' was the refrain I remember most when my mum knocked on the neighbours' back door.

Audrey's clandestine behaviour could occasionally seem exotic – none of my friends had parents who were openly bisexual – until my father came home, of course, and started punching her again. My mother's disposition sometimes made me think that my father might have been gay too, but I never saw any evidence of this. And when, probably around the time I discovered David Bowie and Lou Reed, I found his stash of pornography, it was resolutely heterosexual.

But we were being punished, my mother and me. She for pursuing her freedom, and me presumably for curtailing his. Could the five miscarriages have had something to do with it? Who knew. Unnervingly, for both me and my mother, my father was unpredictable. He didn't get violent when he was drunk – he was never drunk – and didn't appear to work himself up into a state. He just all of a sudden flipped. That was his thing. Flip, smack! The unpredictability made both of us anxious. So, my mother would drink and I would just clam up. I couldn't really speak anyway. My stammer was now so bad that when I did attempt to talk my father would hit me again, simply out of frustration.

Consequently, I would disappear, sinking into music that offered a completely different experience from my reality. The music I liked was exotic, sophisticated, hinting at a make-believe world I was unlikely to ever see. If my mother could lose herself in Frank and Dino, then so could I.

And I did.

Often, the abuse was just verbal. My father's vocabulary was one forged in the forces, and he really knew his ABCs. When he was too busy to hit me, I would regularly be called a stupid fucking cunt, a long streak of paralysed piss, a useless fucking idiot, or, for purposes of simplification, simply cunt. Cunt, cunt, cunt. My father could be unusually tender sometimes, and full of praise, but then five minutes later I was a cunt again. A useless, stupid, fucking cunt. Misdemeanours could result in a smack, a punch, or just a couple of stupid cunts. In retaliation, my mother swore too, so the house would regularly shake with the noise of two people swearing at each other, in a bizarre kind of profane farce – white noise turning blue. God knows what the neighbours must have thought of us. Consequently, conditioned to this almost sophisticated way of communicating – it felt other-worldly, alternative, strangely modern, as I didn't hear my friends' parents being so open – I started to swear too, cramming as many profanities as possible into everything I said. I obviously thought it was clever, cool, and because the sweariest child in the class gets a special kind of kudos, I did it more and more. So I became sweary boy, the stupid fucking cunt who regularly added an unnecessary profane prefix to literally anything. I was a ten-year-old from a nice middle-class family and I was swearing like a fucking trooper. Of course, it was a form of chaos, but one I could control.

The only time he didn't hit us was at Christmas, when there seemed to be an armistice of sorts. My parents stopped fighting, they managed to be civil to each other, and all was temporarily at peace. I remember imploring my father to stay at home as long as possible after Christmas, in a bid to keep the family unit together for as long as possible, watching daytime TV, making SodaStream cola and pretending that all was right with the world.

He didn't, of course, and the beatings continued for both of us.

Falling in Love with Midnight

From the Cradle to the NME

Stephen Linard, Blitz, 1979

APART FROM THE FACT MY mother and I were hit all the time, home life felt quite normal – why wouldn't it? I had nothing to compare it to. We were usually never anywhere longer than a year, but yet again that felt normal. We were a nomadic family, and that's what we did. Both my parents were working class – although my father's family were already aspiring to be lower middle class – both Londoners, and towards the end of the war they had embraced the armed forces, choosing the RAF as a way to escape what they already knew, eager to confront the world and discover the future. My mother was a WAAF, while my father was one of the Brylcreem Boys, named after the glutinous hair cream the pilots and desk jockeys of the RAF used on their scalp. Both of them were very careful about the way they looked.

My grandfather on my mother's side was a greengrocer, while every summer the family went 'hopping' down in Kent, the annual pilgrimage made by London's working class to pick hops in the garden of England. She couldn't have been prouder of her working-class roots, and yet she wanted more. My parents met in Egypt, on an RAF base, just after the end of the war, and they married almost immediately. My grandmother on my father's side intimated that she thought he had married beneath him. My other grandfather had been a farmer (unsuccessfully), and then a draughtsman, and was already trying to escape the confines of his class. His son had sophisticated ambitions but entry-level tastes: his favourite things to eat were bread and dripping, cockles and black pudding.

Nevertheless, my parents were both 'up for it', engaging with the post-war opportunities of prosperity and travel. They were part of the generation that wanted to 'better' themselves, dedicated to making their children's lives better than their own. Becoming middle class, staying middle class, these were their goals.

My mother was perceptive about this.

'Everyone will hate you,' she said, almost in passing. 'The working class will hate you because you're trying to move on, and they can see what you're doing. The upper classes will hate you because they know you're trying to impinge on their world. And the middle classes will hate you because they can see one of their own.'

With the desire to better themselves came the inevitable disappointments – socially, culturally, financially. My parents' generation had no way of knowing that their petit bourgeois aspirations would collide with another generational push that wanted to put as much distance between the past and future as possible. And then there was us, a generation whose understanding of the war was traduced to school lessons, and whose life was informed largely by pop culture.

My mother always talked about the war with respect. You didn't make light of the war. You could make jokes about it, but you didn't diminish it. She didn't talk about it often, but when she did, she'd talk for hours.

She would talk about the Blitz, air-raid shelters, blackout curtains, sleeping in the Underground, rationing, going hungry, the dreams she'd have about bananas, the gas masks she treasured. She talked about hoarding coal (your own, not other people's), painting seams down the back of her legs so she looked like she was wearing stockings and how she would use gravy browning to tan her legs.

She also talked about being rescued by military firemen while she was having a (tin) bath, just minutes before a German bomb destroyed her parents' house in Neasden (precisely where IKEA is now). She would talk about the fear (unexploded bombs taking more lives than anyone ever remembers), the enormous collective community spirit and how the war divided people into the good and the bad. Most people behaved well, but the bad were treated accordingly.

My mother never romanticised the war, and she didn't think much of people who did, but she always said people generally were kinder during it. She talked about her father not talking for a year after he came back from the front; he was literally and metaphorically shellshocked. But mostly she talked about the men she knew who didn't come back, didn't come home, and who left distraught and bewildered families behind – children who were never going to see their fathers again, babies who would never see them at all.

She talked about the sadness. The war defined her, as it defined so many of her generation, so much so that when she was old enough, she joined up, became a military nurse and took herself off to Egypt. Working-class girls didn't tend to do things like that back then, but she wanted to see the world, even though much of it had been destroyed. When she came back, she drove cars for the government. She drove ambulances. She drove Winston Churchill and would drive celebrities to and from Downing Street, dropping them off right outside the door. She drove Laurel and Hardy there once, but she didn't talk about it much. They were famous, but they were only funny men in the films. The men she talked about were the brave men who didn't come back from the war.

My father didn't mention the war much at all. He had only caught the tail-end of it, but he had seen enough to sign up. His anger was a mystery to me, as there seemed to be no reason for it. That being the case, I accepted it, and it didn't seem so unusual: parents whacked their kids. I wasn't going to let it define me. I also had no intention of joining the family firm, even though I had been expected to. My brother Dan, born five years after me, was already being lined up to join the air force, but I had already flatly said no. Forcefully, too. By the time I was sixteen – and finally punching my father back – the idea was preposterous anyway, as there was just no way I was suitable for that kind of life.

There were only five years between Dan and me and yet it felt like a lifetime. The first time I saw him, in his pram, a few days after he and our mother had returned from the hospital, all I wanted to do was be rid of him. My mother, who was suddenly a lot thinner, was now someone to be shared, which didn't please me at all. Could I smother my brother and make it look like an accident? I was only five and yet I already had a malevolent streak. My brother was a far more benevolent soul – quieter, kinder, more amenable – but then he had nothing to be angry about. (Dan would join the RAF as soon as he could, married his childhood sweetheart Gill, and appeared to know from an early age what would make him happy.) As a child, the only time I saw him angry was when he tried to drown my talking Action Man (he never uttered another word, my Action Man, that is). And he only did this because my father had done what he occasionally did after he hit me – buying me an expensive gift that we as a family couldn't afford; his guilt only served to embarrass and anger the rest of us. For a while this became standard practice, his guilt manifesting itself either as bribery or praise, constantly being told I was brilliant having just been beaten.

I had already planned my escape route: art school.

I LEFT GREAT MARLOW SECONDARY Modern in the summer of 1976 with three O levels (Art, English and Technical Drawing) and no prospects, at the age of sixteen. At school, our career advice had consisted of a sole presentation from a mediocre woman from a factory that produced machines that made cigarettes in High Wycombe, a few miles away. I had already been suspended from school for a series of what I considered unworthy misdemeanours, including regularly flouting the school uniform. My own uniform at the time usually consisted of a butterfly-collared shirt on which was printed a French café scene, a pair of high-waisted pinstripe Oxford bags, a ridiculously expensive *Budgie* jacket (based on the jackets Adam Faith wore in the TV series, which appeared to be fashionable throughout the first half of the seventies) and a pair of beautiful oxblood spoon shoes; most of what I wore had been shoplifted from shops in High Wycombe. I looked like Jimmy McCulloch, the skinny guitarist in Wings, and this is what I was wearing when they briefly let me back in to take my exams.

My favourite item of clothing was a wide-collared, soft cotton polo shirt emblazoned with the image of Frank Zappa and the Mothers of Invention painted by Guy Peellaert for his 1973 illustrated book, *Rock Dreams* (they were drawn as Hells Angels, on big-gleaming bikes, like motorised horsemen of the Apocalypse). This, and my two-tone, three-inch platform shoes; I probably thought I looked like a cross between Bryan Ferry and Alex Harvey but, in reality, I'm sure I just looked odd. In 1976, my wardrobe was as confused as my record collection (where Alan Hull sat happily with Lou Reed and the O'Jays), with my faux-Kings Road clothes starting to be alternated with my new skinny jeans, winklepickers and plastic leather jacket – an homage to my new love, the Ramones.

I may have been the only person in the school who had ever heard of Guy Peellaert, but I guarded my pretensions fiercely. I was also probably the only person in the school who had ever read Tom Wolfe (and that included the teachers), and my precocious assumptions were what gave me the confidence to want more than I was supposed to want. I loved Wolfe, but it wasn't as though I was reading much else, because it wasn't something I often enjoyed. I liked Tom Wolfe because what he wrote about was real. He also looked really cool. And I liked people who looked really cool. Which was why I loved David Bowie and Bryan Ferry. Most of Ferry's songs seemed to fuse celebrity ennui with a celebration of the night, and to kids like me the world-weary, star-spangled existence he painted was beyond glamorous. It seemed like a world that, frankly, wouldn't be too much trouble to negotiate.

I had always found school difficult, as I wasn't able to focus my attention. I wasn't unhappy, but I always had a problem with learning, a problem retaining information. Later, much later, in my fifties, I would be diagnosed as dyslexic, which was news to me; but it made sense, as I found it much easier to create things rather than absorb them. I liked writing but wasn't especially good at reading. What I was good at, or at least what I was most enthusiastic about, was art. Drawing. Painting. Creating things which didn't exist. Again, I wasn't particularly good at drawing representations of things that already existed – I was certainly no draughtsman – but I could knock you out an alternative universe in twenty minutes. I had what would have been called, at the time, a vivid imagination. Not academically gifted, but 'imaginative'; which, in the sixties and seventies, was tolerated, encouraged even, but it wasn't necessarily rewarded.

Nevertheless, that's what I was: 'artistic'.

So, at school I took refuge in the art department. Moving schools every year wasn't conducive to making lasting friendships, and as I grew older, my defence mechanism revolved, unsurprisingly perhaps, around humour. I became a joker. Being funny meant you were more likely to be accepted, even if you were shy, which I was. My other way of ingratiating myself with my fellow thirteen- and fourteen-year-olds was through shoplifting, which I became extremely good at. Along with a friend of mine who I'll call Martin, because that was his name, every Saturday I would take a bus to Maidenhead, Reading, Slough, sometimes even London, and steal. We would also shoplift in High Wycombe, although we had to be careful not to advertise our expertise so close to home. We would steal to order: LPs, cassettes, eight-tracks, shirts, belts, booze, cigarettes, pens, kitchenware, anything we could shove under a jacket. It was brash and nerve-wracking, and for me showed a hitherto undiscovered entrepreneurial streak, but it was also incredibly exciting. There was almost no security in high-street shops in the seventies, and it was remarkably easy to slip a copy of *Led Zeppelin IV*, *For Your Pleasure* or *Aqualung* under your coat. When we weren't stealing to order, we would take things from department stores and then try and return them, for cash, or goods in kind. Eventually, this is what did for us, as we nearly got caught returning some ridiculously expensive hammers in a department store in High Wycombe. And we ran, nonstop, for twenty minutes before vowing never to do it again.

Around the age of fifteen, drugs made themselves apparent, and for eighteen months or so I experimented wildly. Dope, speed, acid, downers, the whole storefront. I took a lot, probably too much, but again the excitement outweighed the negatives. There were few things more thrilling than falling into someone's car, high as a badly made kite, and driving off into the night, usually ending up at the Nag's Head in High Wycombe, Skindles in Maidenhead or the Marquee in Wardour Street. I loved it. Of course, drugs at the time were so closely associated with particular lifestyles that it became obvious quite quickly which rabbit holes you were being drawn down. Consequently, I started using them more sparingly, and for purely recreational reasons.

As I wanted to go to art school, in my last year of school I applied to High Wycombe Technical College but (luckily) I was told I was too young. So I then spent a year doing part-time jobs. I worked in a local factory making Evel Knievel dolls, I worked in pubs, I flipped burgers in a Wimpy, picked rocks out of fields that were being developed for council housing and, when I had enough money, disappeared up to London to watch rock bands. Art school had been my only ambition since I was about twelve, and after a while I knew it had to be in London, as I was in love with the place. I felt giddy in the knowledge I hadn't been accepted in Wycombe. My intention had always been to use that as a stepping stone, but my rejection turned out to be my salvation. I applied for the foundation course at Chelsea School of Art in the spring of 1977. The circumstances of my application are lost to me – all I remember is that I knew St Martin's and Chelsea were the best places to go to, and that Chelsea's foundation course was meant to be the better of the two. Because of our financial circumstances I would get a grant, my mother would give me a little money to live on (my parents were now separated), and I automatically had a room in Ralph West.

And so that's what happened.

IT'S EASY FOR ME TO look back now and simply focus on what happened outside art school, and yet what happened inside it was, in its own way, crucial to what I would later end up doing. At Chelsea, I would largely study graphics and photography not just because I was interested in them, and wanted to learn as much as I could, but also because I thought in the back of my mind that a career in publishing was something that could be appealing. I wasn't going to be a painter or a sculptor, and the idea of doing textiles was absurd. What I loved was design, photography and the application of taste. I would do mock-ups of *NME* covers, *Time Out* covers, *Interview* covers.

I'd loved magazines for as long as I could remember, from *Tiger* (for Roy of the Rovers) and *Whizzer and Chips* to *Goal!*, *Mad* to *Popswap*, and finally Nick Logan's *New Musical Express*, which became my bible throughout my teens. I didn't read much, but I read the *NME*. It sold in excess of 250,000 copies each week and was probably the most influential music paper of the time. I started reading it in 1972, principally because of Nick Kent and Charles Shaar Murray, as they wrote about the kind of music I liked – Alice Cooper, David Bowie and Roxy Music. Not only that, but they were also often less than complimentary, which gave me the confidence to be more circumspect too. So, when Bryan Ferry released his first solo album, *These Foolish Things*, I felt better about not liking it as much as I thought I would. Of course, I loved the title track – why wouldn't I? I worshipped it – but why did I need a mediocre version of a Beatles song ('You Won't See Me') I didn't really like in the first place?

The *NME* was also the place I learned about William Kotzwinkle (*Doctor Rat*), Robert M. Pirsig (*Zen and the Art of Motorcycle Maintenance*) and, of course, Hunter S. Thompson and Tom Wolfe. I also occasionally read *Sounds*, another music weekly, but couldn't get on with *Melody Maker* as I found it too dry and pompous. *Street Life*, I liked, as well as *ZigZag*, *Rolling Stone* and *Let It Rock*. When I moved to London, I spent much of my free time in newsagents, browsing the aisles like I would in record shops. I could waste entire afternoons, and I couldn't believe the stuff I found. While I also bought design magazines, and old periodicals for projects, I started to devour *Interview*, *Frizz* and *Wet* (a magazine conspicuously and comprehensively ignored by media anthropologists); I loved the *Sunday Times Magazine* and the *Observer Magazine*, and bought secondhand copies of *Oz*, *International Times* and *Nova*. If I visited Rough Trade, I'd buy fanzines too, and I still have half-a-dozen original copies of *Sniffin' Glue*. The *Evening Standard* started to loom large in my life, and it became my newspaper of record. I would buy it every afternoon as it was the only place where you really found out what was going on. Even at my callow age, I also saw that it was politically agnostic, which was extremely powerful.

A lot of the magazine material baffled me, not that I was going to admit it. I just started piecing everything together, trying to work out how all these disparate worlds fitted together, trying to find out as much as I could about all these weird and wonderful people. I instinctively knew how magazines worked, who they were aimed at, and – even though these were alien worlds to me – how they appeared to create their own communities. Even though I wasn't a writer, I could tell good writing from bad and developed a design sensibility simply by exposing myself to so many magazines.

I would spend all my money on these magazines, having found them in the WHSmith in Sloane Square (which, back then, was almost as big as Sloane Square itself), small newsagents in Soho, secondhand bookshops along Charing Cross Road, junk shops and the college library at Chelsea. Many of them found their way into my music satchel (another Oxfam find) when no one was looking.

In truth, I was taking more interest in magazines than I was in my course work, which certainly wasn't something I'd planned. I just found them fascinating, especially the way in which they created their own worlds, their own very particular brands. What I enjoyed was the way in which they treated their readers, flattering them with the kind of inclusion you didn't always see in other forms of media. Before the eighties, before the UK had its own style magazines, our reading matter in this area was principally American, and our perceived sense of style largely came from magazines such as *Interview*, *New York* or *Punk*. People my age might have taken a lead from something in *Sounds* or the *NME*, or maybe *Tatler* or *Vogue*, but there was no magazine for the generation of young people who had been inspired by punk. Sure, there was a fanzine industry, a thriving independent sector responsible for some of the most passionate music journalism of its time; but there was nothing with a wider brief. The music papers had a huge demographic, and they were very much in their pomp in 1978, although there was also another, smaller and more particular set of magazines at the time that appealed to a more select group. Today they are long gone, available only in libraries, vintage magazines shops and in those dark corners of the internet where few dare to venture, gone to the great reading room in the sky.

And what wonderful things they were: *New Style*, David Bailey and David Litchfield's *Ritz*, *Midnight* and *Viz* – not the scatological comic, but a London-based monthly featuring what all these magazines featured: art (usually home-grown stuff by Allen Jones, Duggie Fields or Peter Blake), fashion (Antony Price, Claude Montana and a newcomer called Jean Paul Gaultier), furniture, sub-erotic photography, nightclub vox pops, arch celebrity profiles, restaurant reviews, gossip (back when gossip was a novelty, not a publishing genre), lots of articles about *The Rocky Horror Show*, and dozens of ads for long-forgotten Kings Road boutiques. *Midnight* was so large (four foot by three) it was almost like an art piece, a magazine almost as big as a roll of wallpaper. In these post-punk gazettes the motif was usually leopard skin, the cultural touchstone Biba (which had closed down a few years before, in 1975), the cool club always the Embassy, the Bond Street haunt that was Mayfair's answer to Studio 54. In broad brushstrokes, these magazines were a cross between *Tatler* and the *NME*, a mixture of uptown and downtown, of street life and park life, of toffs and commoners colliding in a giddy world of fashion, music, cocktails and lifestyle, before lifestyle became what we know it as today. I found them all intoxicating, even if most of the editorial was part of a steep learning curve. They included words I'd never heard of, people I'd never heard of, and places I'd never heard of. But I was determined to get to the bottom of all if it. I loved the *NME* and would devour it every week (one of the great things about living in London was discovering you could buy the *NME* late on Wednesday afternoon instead of having to wait until Thursday morning), but I was already starting to feel promiscuous.

One of the most impressive titles was *Boulevard*, a monthly large-format London-based style magazine that was launched at the end of 1978 by Baron S. Bentinck. Containing the usual *Ritz/Viz/New Style* mix, *Boulevard* also had about it a certain hi–lo punk pizzazz, a sense of what was right for the times, an energy that was missing from the others. The 'baron' managed to cajole a number of soon-to-be-important people to work for him, too, including photographers Helmut Newton, Terence Donovan and paparazzo Richard Young; fashionable illustrators Jean-Paul Goude and Connie Jude; and writers Nik Cohn (*Boulevard* published his seminal travel story '24 Hours On 42nd Street', which I later discovered had been licensed from *New York* magazine) and Craig Brown. Now the provost of Eton, and for years the bigwig at Condé Nast, Nicholas Coleridge wrote book reviews for *Boulevard*, and remembers the operation with understandable fondness. 'There was a very cool atmosphere in the office,' which, naturally, was situated on Sloane Street, albeit above a pub. 'There were all these friends of Duggie Fields and Andrew Logan lolling about on black vinyl desks making phone call to their friends.'

Kerry Sewel was a St Martin's student – we were in the same year – and she produced illustrations for *Boulevard*. 'It was the only magazine to work for,' she said. 'There was *Ritz*, of course, but *Boulevard* was the only magazine that was big and glossy, the only one produced on shiny paper. It might not have been the greatest magazine in the world, but it felt like it at the time. It captured something, whatever that might have been.'

These magazines didn't last long, as there was yet to be the critical mass to support them. They were too early. All were owned by entrepreneurs acutely aware of how easily new magazines (like new restaurants) haemorrhaged cash, and the stark reality of 'vanity publishing' was compounded by the fact that many of these magazines were such odd sizes that, unable to fit them on to their shelves, newsagents simply put them on the floor. Which was no place for a glossy magazine.

One day I turned up at *Boulevard* with my portfolio of St Martin's illustrations dressed in my black leather jacket, my skinny black trousers, winklepickers and Kensington Market T-shirt, and sat on a black leather sofa until the 'baron' came out to tell me the magazine was closing down. *Boulevard* managed just half-a-dozen issues, and though *Ritz* carried on well into the eighties, the other magazines were gone by the time the 'new romantics' arrived, when mass elitism, lifestyle careers and the commercialisation of youth culture became the defining elements of the early to mid-eighties. The big difference between the style magazines of the late seventies and early eighties was the fact *Viz*, *Boulevard*, *Ritz* and *New Style* were all exclusive – they were preaching to the converted and didn't appear remotely interested in adding to their flock. They were aimed at the 'Them' crowd, that hip, smart London set who all looked as though they were living inside a Roxy Music album cover. Art students, fashion designers, hairdressers and magazine journalists, they were the London equivalent of the Warhol New Yorkers – the women trying to look like Jerry Hall (even though most of them resembled Cruella de Vil), the men trying to pass themselves off as Bryan Ferry or Antony Price. If you picked up any of these glad mags they'd be full of photographs of Andrew Logan, Derek Jarman, Tchaik Chassay, Zandra Rhodes and Peter York. The congregation had a restricted membership, which is why these magazines – great though they were – ultimately failed.

Unlike *Nova*, the phenomenally influential sixties women's magazine, which eventually closed in 1975, and whose formula many of these publications tried to emulate, they were unable, or unwilling, to tap into public tastes. All sizzle and no sausage. All polish and no finish.

Boulevard's closing-down party was a riotous affair, with enough champagne to sink the *Titanic*. One wag, a staff writer who was a little peeved that he had just been downsized, felt he owed the owners a parting gift. And so, as he left the office that night, walking away from the boulevard of broken dreams, he called the speaking clock in Los Angeles (something you were still able to do in those days) and left the receiver off the hook. It's not known when it was replaced, but one wonders if the bill was ever paid.

Ritz was the real harbinger of change, and the magazine that made it possible for the launch of *i-D*, *The Face* and *Blitz*, as it kick-started celebrity and style culture in the eighties. In the early seventies, the legendary David Bailey had been briefly the photographic consultant on a magazine called *The Image*, which was edited by David Litchfield and focused on graphic design and photography. Bailey, though, was sick of working for other people and wanted to do something for himself – a magazine of which he could be proud. And *Ritz* was the magazine he came up with, a stylish fashion and photography magazine that 'evoked the style of Fred Astaire'.

I was already obsessed with Peter York, who I started to think of as Britain's answer to Tom Wolfe (as he no doubt did himself), and a man who was taking style watching to hitherto uncharted heights. His caustic way of pigeonholing people became the benchmark of what I really enjoyed about journalism, a way of looking at the world through the noise on the surface, the micro determining the macro. In his columns in *Harpers & Queen*, a magazine ostensibly aimed at posh women in Chelsea and the shires, Peter used social observation to interpret trends, traits and petit travesties. And he was very funny.

He was brazen about his unapologetic cultural analysis: 'When you get inside a literary novel you feel the author, more often than not, just doesn't know enough about things,' he wrote. 'They haven't been around enough – novelists never go anywhere. Once I discovered true books about real things – books like "How To Run a Company" – I stopped reading novels.' No one wrote like that in the late seventies, which made Peter special. He validated the rejection of orthodoxy in a completely original way, which obviously became extremely appealing.

Harpers & Queen and *Ritz* had started to take a keen interest in the Blitz's new romantic scene, and consequently pictures of us had started to appear in their society pages. The first magazine I ever appeared in was *Camouflage*, when I was eighteen, a small black and white photograph of me on the Kings Road, and I was beside myself with excitement. Someone had thrown a little stardust our way and of course we all loved it.

The Blitz lasted until October 1980, by which time other clubs had started to crop up, not just in London, but all over the UK. Chris Sullivan, Robert Elms and Graham Smith (who was developing into the scene's in-house photographer) had already had some success with a number of warehouse parties at Toyah Willcox's Mayhem Studios in Battersea, and so in January 1980 they partnered with an old friend of Sullivan's from Merthyr Tydfil, Stephen Mahoney, and opened a Monday club at St Moritz, a cellar in Wardour Street. Here, the music reflected the retro leanings of the Blitz crowd, being somewhat old-fashioned and camp. St Moritz lasted until March 1980, and two months later Sullivan joined forces with Strange and Egan in a new venture, Hell, in Henrietta Street, again in Covent Garden. This closed the same week as the Blitz, a month before Sullivan, Elms and Smith started another one-nighter at Le Kilt, where the tropes were tartan and funk (two things which were previously thought to be mutually exclusive). Nightlife was a world of subterfuge and nicknames: Fat Tony, Little Tony, Fat Sue, Big Louise, Big Liz, Big Pete, Paranoid Pete, Donkey, Barnsley, etc. You could know someone for years and not even know their surnames, or what they did during the daytime.

Club for Heroes was probably the final club to be labelled new romantic, as the scene was quickly morphing into something else.

Nestling next to an upmarket estate agent in Baker Street, it was one of the chicest venues Steve Strange and Rusty Egan had ever hired.

By this time, I was already seeing Kim Bowen, someone who – like Fiona Dealey, Michelle Clapton and Princess Julia – could legitimately call herself a Queen of the Blitz. You would have thought she could have just sidled up to me in Hell or Club for Heroes, but her chosen method of seduction was coming to pick me up after I'd just had a root-canal operation in a dental hospital opposite Stephen Linard's flat in Camden. Nevertheless, it worked. For a while. Our final night together occurred on the day of Charles and Diana's wedding in the summer of 1981. We had taken some MDA, a forerunner of MDMA, an early iteration of ecstasy, which we had both found somewhat bewildering. We had been at a house party near Tower Bridge, Kim dressed in a diaphanous white dress, and me with a zoot suit, braces and goatee beard. Later, in bed, Kim was more honest than she needed to be: 'I can't have sex with you tonight,' she said, with a look of horror on her face. 'You look like Peter Sutcliffe.'

I LEFT ST MARTIN'S THAT summer. My degree show consisted of an extremely meta (read: pretentious) sixteen-page teenage 'Love Story' magazine, some portrait photographs, and a series of pornographic pictures I had taken of Action Men having sex with each other. There were some fashion pictures in there, too, but none was really any good. I got more attention modelling in Stephen Linard's end-of-term fashion show. His collection, called 'Reluctant Émigrés', featured half-a-dozen deliberately moody boys (including Chris Sullivan and Christos Tolera as well as myself), modelling clothes that made us all feel as though we ought to be in a band; the thing was, half of them already were.

After I left, I spent the next six months working with many of the people I was going to nightclubs with – taking photographs (I've got hundreds of pictures of Cerith Wyn Evans, naked, in various religious poses), designing unsuccessful album covers (as well as designing covers for unsuccessful albums), and modelling . . . but to little avail. I was hustling, but my chosen profession – photography – wasn't really doing it for me, principally because, as I secretly knew, I wasn't good enough. Actually, I don't think it was so secret. Everyone I showed them to must have known this too.

Drumming was something else I wasn't much good at. One of the first things I did with my second grant cheque at St Martin's was buy a Premier kit from the huge music store in Soho Square. I fancied myself as a drummer and auditioned for various nondescript punk and post-punk bands. In 1978, I had joined a band that played sixties covers and original ska compositions, a kind of prototype Madness, but obviously nowhere near as good (I played 'Dancing in the Street' as though I was in the Glitter Band). A year later, I helped form a sub-Joy Division group whose only notable contribution to the narrative arc of pop was its appallingly pretentious name, The Timing Association. We made a self-financed single called 'It's Magic', which wasn't. On receiving our first copy, we took it down to Broadcasting House to wait for John Peel, in the hope we could convince him to play it on his radio show. As we approached him, he stepped back a couple of paces, and when we produced our record said, 'Jesus Christ, boys, I thought you were going to mug me.' He played it three days later, but the world remained on its axis. And then a year later, in 1980, I formed a synth duo with someone whose only musical expertise turned out to be owning a vast collection of Kraftwerk bootlegs.

Towards the end of the year, my friend Sean McGrath told me Steve Diggle had just left the Buzzcocks and was forming a band called Flag of Convenience and was looking for a drummer. Sean arranged a meeting, and so I met Diggle in a pub in Victoria one Sunday night in November, and without hearing me play, he offered me the gig. Why, I don't know, but my reluctance to say yes was driven by a) the fact that the Buzzcocks drummer John Maher was a genius and there was no way I could match him for style, power or aptitude, and b), the not unproblematic fact I'd just sold my drum kit.

Clubs for Heroes

Stalking the BBC

Boy George at the St. Martin's Alternative Fashion Show, 1980

BY THE END OF 1981, I was six months out of college, twenty-one, broke and, like Benjamin Braddock in *The Graduate*, a little confused about what I was going to do with the rest of my life. Since leaving St Martin's I had spent six weeks working with Tim Roth as a cocktail barman in a Brixton nightclub called the Fridge, helped run an African nightclub called the Gold Coast Club in Soho with Joe Hagan and club runner Christian Cotterill (directly underneath that goth haven of fishnet tights and smudged eyeliner, the Batcave), and been flown to Japan for two weeks to model for the fashion designer Takeo Kikuchi. At the show, I wore designer bondage trousers and was pushed off the catwalk by a female model on MDA. Mostly, however, I had been living in a flat in Peckham with sauce-encrusted bottle tops, a three-bar electric heater and too many clothes. I was getting up at midday, eating heated-up leftovers and drinking too much.

My life was not exactly distinguished. I wanted to work in the arts but had absolutely no idea how to go about this. My friends and I had already been to art school – the lucky ones among us, anyway – and we were plotting careers in the applied arts, in graphics, or photography, or writing, or something – anything! – that was going to flatter our taste rather than our aptitude.

Life was lived after dark, in nightclubs where we all masqueraded as other people. Futurism had slipped backwards, and we spent as much time trying to look behind us as in front – trying to escape the present by moving into the future by looking like the past. There was already a large student body in London that had started to dress like Frank Sinatra, or at the very least the kind of men who surrounded Sinatra when he burst into song on film. We were scouring charity shops and secondhand stores, looking for old demob suits and broken-in Oxfords, searching for the kind of clothes our parents had worn when they were our age. We were sick of dressing like punks, so we started dressing like film stars – OK, film extras – complete with double-breasted suits, kipper ties (many of which appeared to have floral patterns that had sunk into a jungle gloom, like very old wallpaper), old man hats and watch fobs. Cary Grant and Bryan Ferry had nothing on us.

I'm not sure where all this came from. Perhaps we were tired of looking poor, tired of looking like overgrown children, and wanted to look like grown-ups, but only in a way that articulated our ambivalence; we weren't sure we really *did* want to be adults, but we didn't mind looking like them for a while, until we worked out what we were really going to do with our lives.

I was one of these young men, someone who wanted to look like someone I wasn't. And by the end of 1981, which is when ABC released their first single, 'Tears Are Not Enough', like many of my compadres, I looked rather a lot like the members of ABC. Or rather, we all thought they had started to dress like us. Honestly, didn't they know we'd been dressing like this for *ages*?

ABC would leave a mark on my life, although not in the way I expected. As a boy, I'd often casually thought I'd like a little Action Man scar, a straight one-inch cut lying diagonally across the cheek. Nothing scary or particularly disfiguring, just a small battle scar, something to indicate I'd been around. Later, in my teens, I briefly considered a tattoo, but luckily realised that self-inflicted scars didn't carry the same cachet (while the girl who would have been the subject of my inking soon disappeared from my life). By the time I was twenty, I didn't want either.

Then, suddenly, I didn't have any choice.

It happened towards the end of 1981, on a cold November Saturday night (everything seemed to happen on a Friday or Saturday night back then) in a London dead zone just behind King's Cross, an area which at the time seemed resolutely immune to any kind of gentrification. Among us were my Belgian friend, Pascal Gabriel (who would soon become a successful record producer), Corinne Drewery plus our friends Jill, Rebecca and Stella.

It was around 11.30 p.m., chucking-out time. We'd just fallen out of the Hemingford Arms, where we'd been all evening, and were on our way to a party down the road. All night we had been playing ABC's 'Tears Are Not Enough' on the jukebox. We alternated between 'Tears . . .' and Elvis Costello, Dollar and Pigbag, as well as Roxy Music's 'Same Old Scene' (their rather wonderful last hurrah), but it was ABC who we found the most intriguing. They were modern (or at least had been relentlessly championed by the *NME*), they had soul (or what we were rapidly understanding was a new kind of European soul), and they appeared to understand fashion or, more accurately, 'dressing up'. How could a gang of fancy-pants Motown-friendly art students not like them? I've no idea whose party it was we were en route to – no one ever knew in those days; you just pitched up and clocked in, a six-pack of something or other swinging in a plastic carrier bag. As we strode along, five girls and two boys, searching for street numbers, seven or eight lads in their late teens came towards us, shuffling along the pavement. They were wearing training shoes, tracksuits and floppy fringes: soft shapes disguising hard fists, hearts and minds.

When they got parallel, one of them punched Pascal hard and full in the side of the face. I turned around and started towards him as the girls stood in fright. But before I'd taken two paces I was kicked from behind and pushed on to the road. Someone immediately jumped on my back. I was too drunk to be scared, and the adrenalin was pumping so much that I wasn't really aware what was going on. I knew the situation was dangerous, but the only logical thing to do seemed to be to punch and kick as hard as I could. Which I did.

But then I felt something sharp and wet in the back of my neck, swiftly followed by something similar in the middle of my back. I was being cut – slashed, stabbed, call it what you like – with what felt like a cut-throat razor (having never been stabbed before I wasn't sure about this – but I soon found out). I didn't feel pain, as such, just shock. Because I could tell that my skin had been broken in at least three places.

My mind raced as the actual attack seemed to unravel in slow motion. And the sounds from the pub kept whirling around my head – jokes, Pascal's command of the English language, the rush for last orders, words pouring out of the jukebox . . . tears, souvenirs . . . 'Tears are not enough . . .'

I responded immediately, jumped up, threw the tracksuited troll off my back and sprinted fifty yards down the road, following the girls, only turning round to make sure he wasn't following. And as I turned, I saw the razor dangling in his hand. He stood and stared at me, legs spread, chest pounding. Seconds later, I was running towards King's Cross with Pascal and the others, the pumping blood in my head blocking out the ricocheting plastic soul of ABC.

We ran for what seemed like ages, and then stopped. There was a fuss, of course, because no one knew if I was badly cut. I still couldn't feel much, and I didn't think I was in serious danger, but as I couldn't see the wounds, I began to worry.

Hell, Hunter S. Thompson had said it plain enough once: 'It is one thing to get punched in the nose, and quite another to have your eyeball sprung or your teeth shattered with a wrench.' Violence takes a great leap when it involves daggers, knives, barstools or, indeed, wrenches.

For me, being stabbed was enough. I was inspected: I had been slashed on the back of the head and right along my spine. The cuts weren't particularly deep, though the one in my back was bloody and long enough (six inches) to cause alarm. We eventually made it to the party, where I was inspected some more (it didn't seem so bad with half-a-dozen girls staring at my half-naked torso in a small kitchen), and where it was decided that I should be taken to hospital.

Although the stabbing had sobered me up somewhat, I was still drunk enough to be cavalier about the whole thing. I was wearing a brand new silver-grey zoot suit and made a big deal of the fact that it was ruined, and how it had cost me over £100. We had joked in the pub that I looked like a cut-price Martin Fry, as my suit wasn't a million miles away from ones he was wearing at the time. His was gold, and mine was silver, which I suppose had a certain logic to it.

And so we went to hospital. Pascal with his (considerable) bruise, the girls still with a Waitrose bag of Holsten Pils, and me with my torn suit, wounded ego and bleeding back.

As I sobered up in casualty, it soon sank in how potentially serious the situation had been. I should have been scared; if I had been sober, I would have been petrified, and frankly would have been worried if I hadn't been. I can't remember whether or not I gave the police a statement; I probably did, but none of us was under the impression that anyone would ever be caught, let alone prosecuted. I do remember getting a tetanus jab in the backside (which was inordinately more painful than anything else that night) and over a dozen stitches. Waiting to be discharged, I tried getting drunk again, but by now my heart really wasn't in it. When I thought about the attackers, it was in the abstract – I didn't know them, and certainly couldn't remember what they looked like. They were out for blood, and mine just happened to be in the vicinity. The attack was territorial and was in many ways predictable: we were walking through the wrong part of town at the wrong time wearing the wrong kind of clothes. Shit, as they say, happens.

I made a point of going out the following night, knowing that I was unlikely to get stabbed again or, come to that, have my eyeball sprung, or my teeth shattered with a wrench. Thankfully, I was right, although for years, that part of town remained one of my least favourite parts of London. And as for ABC, whenever I hear the synthesised strings, over-produced drums and plaintive, heartbreaking lyrics of 'Tears Are Not Enough', I think of running down a King's Cross backstreet in a silver suit, with blood pouring from my back.

THE SPECIALS WERE ANOTHER BAND who were having a tumultuous effect on the way in which pop was developing. Through going out, I got to know their leader, Jerry Dammers, and would regularly hitch up to Coventry to sit in sullen working men's clubs with him and his extraordinary circle of friends and acquaintances, discussing socialism (we often differed), the provenance of Prince Buster and the validity of Heaven 17. We went clubbing together, spent a few memorable New Year's Eves in Bristol (where Jerry's parents were from) singing our own versions of 'Ten Green Bottles', spent birthdays together, and once DJ'd together at a miners' benefit at the Wag Club with the comedian Harry Enfield and various members of Madness. I even sat through some of the tortuous recording of the *In the Studio* album by the Special AKA (which is what the Specials morphed into), containing Jerry's defining moment, the monumentally influential 'Free Nelson Mandela'.

This song ultimately led to the Mandela Seventieth Birthday Tribute concert at Wembley Stadium and helped add to the groundswell of support that led to Mandela's release from Robben Island. As a piece of agitprop, 'Free Nelson Mandela' was peerless, a political pop record that managed to achieve even more than it set out to do. Written as a call to arms, a marketing tool almost, it set in motion a chain of events that changed history. And you can't say that about most pop records. The music Dammers started recording with the Special AKA was uncompromising to say the least; their first single, 'The Boiler', was a first-person account of a rape, complete with actual screams, while the follow-up was called 'War Crimes'. Dammers famously told the

NME that pop music was about giving people what they want to hear. 'We're giving people what they don't want to hear.' But although 'Free Nelson Mandela' was part of a cause, the song itself wasn't a misery fest; rather it was exuberance personified, a joyous happy ending.

Dammers drafted in Elvis Costello to produce it (he had done the honours on the Specials' first album, after all), and he did a sterling job, roping in former bandmate Lynval Golding and the Beat's Dave Wakeling and Ranking Roger to sing its life-enhancing, relentlessly upbeat chorus. As proof that perhaps he wasn't the right kind of person to marshal pop hits from such unlikely material, Dammers started playing an indulgent piano solo towards the end of the recording, before, that is, Costello turned the tape off. Furious that his musings had been cut short, he said, 'Elvis, that's jazz!' Costello shot back with, 'It's bollocks.' Nevertheless, between them they created one of the most successful protest songs of all time. 'It ends with the thing of "I'm begging you" and then "I'm telling you",' Dammers said. 'It is a demand but in a positive way; it brought some sort of hope that the situation could be sorted out.'

LIFE WAS SCHIZOPHRENIC. THE NIGHTLIFE was intoxicating, and the daytime was often grim. When I left St Martin's in the summer of 1981, I was living above a greengrocers in Stamford Hill, and then started bouncing around housing association flats in south London. First was the Oval, then Herne Hill, then Peckham, before finally arriving in Brixton, where I would stay for five years, before moving to Shepherd's Bush. In the summer, these places were fine – the Brixton mansion flat in particular feeling not unlike a Manhattan tenement – but in the winter they were all bleak. Me and my flatmate Tom (he was at the Royal College of Art, although we lived separate lives) would huddle around a two-bar heater, watching television and eating soup. On the days we didn't leave the flat we would walk around in our duvets, arguing about who was going to go to the shop and buy milk. If anything was going to incentivise us to become successful, it surely would have been the dreadful places we lived in, but our ambition was somewhat tempered by the vicarious glamour offered by the nightclubs we went to each and every night. I seemed to live in the damn places at the time. Sometimes I would stay with friends in Islington, sometimes I might end up in the wilds of Notting Hill, and often I would walk four and half miles back to Brixton.

All around me, friends and acquaintances were starting to become famous. Spandau Ballet were already pop stars. Funkapolitan (featuring Tom Dixon, Nick Jones and Toby Andersen) had already been on *Top of the Pops*. Corinne Drewery and Jill Tattersall were making a success of their fashion company, as were Fiona Dealey and Stephen Linard, and Boy George was just about to become one of the most popular people in Britain as the lead singer of Culture Club. Bob Elms was working for *The Face*, and all those people I'd been seeing in clubs for the last four or five years were beginning to pop up in the media.

Even George Michael and Andrew Ridgeley had become famous, as Wham! These two soul boys hailed from Bushey, north London. If George was the suburban sonneteer, happy in his bedroom writing tear-jerkers, then Andrew was the quintessential party animal, the Liam Gallagher of his day, unable to leave a party without a bottle of Moët in one hand and a bottle blonde in the other. It was Andrew who realised George's pop ambitions, Andrew who acted the extrovert to George's shy loner. George might have written the songs – in four years, Andrew only gained three co-writing credits, for 'Wham! Rap', 'Club Tropicana' and 'Careless Whisper' – yet it was his partner who looked the part when they sang them. Andrew's image would crystallise on the twelve-inch version of 'I'm Your Man': a racing car is heard careering through a plate-glass window, followed by the sound of its driver cackling with laughter as he asks, 'Where's the bar?' Their coming-out party was the launch of their debut LP *Fantastic* (such confidence!) in a small suite of offices just behind Fulham Broadway tube station in London. While dozens of sneering music journalists and record-company bigwigs stood about, working at being brilliant, the two nineteen-year-old soul boys, dressed in

Hawaiian shirts, cutaway jeans and deck shoes, jived together on the dancefloor, jitterbugging along to their own version of the Miracles' 'Love Machine'. Rarely had I seen two men enjoying themselves so much. To be dancing to one of their own records! At their own party! In front of other people!

I started to DJ a bit, and did a bit of entry-level spinning at the Fridge, the Wag Club and various warehouse parties. I don't think I was very good, but like everyone else doing it at the time – and lots of people were – I learned you had to be performative to really make a mark; you had to look like you knew what you were doing. It was also a good way to get girls.

To supplement my dole money, in the spring of 1982, a friend of a friend suggested I spend a while being a film extra. There was always lots of work around, he lied, and with overtime you could earn more than £100 a day. You got free food and the chance to muck around with the likes of Harrison Ford and Jessica Lange. *Cool*, I thought. *Yes, I'll do exactly that.*

And so I became a film star. Sort of. I joined the suggested agency, pledged my allegiance to the silver screen and called up every morning to see if there was any work. Which, mostly, there wasn't. One of the first things I realised about being a film extra was that there were always more people than there were roles (or, more precisely, more crowds than there were crowd scenes) and that I had to be prepared for a lifetime of rejection and disappointment. Just like a real actor, in fact.

My first job, that summer, rather remarkably (for me) was *The Hunger*, the David Bowie/Catherine Deneuve/Susan Sarandon vehicle about vampires and the undead and stuff. The *LA Times* called the film 'Stylish! Explicit! It'll take your breath away!', though I can only assume the reviewer owed the director money because it really is a pile of dreadful old tosh, even if it was fantastically exciting to a twenty-one-year-old who had worshipped Bowie from afar for a decade. (The movie also has one of the worst taglines I'd ever seen: 'Nothing human loves forever', it proclaimed, bold as brass, as though people were actually going to believe it.)

This was to be my first exposure to the world of film. By chance, about a year earlier I'd been a 'friends and family' dancer in the pop promo for Spandau Ballet's 'Chant No. 1', filmed at London's infamous Le Beat Route (where my friend Fiona worked), but this was my first time 'on set'. The scene we were to film took place in Heaven, the gay nightclub underneath the arches in Charing Cross. It was a club scene and my contribution consisted of walking down a flight of stairs as Bowie and Deneuve walked up them. Bowie spent most of the time puffing away on a cigarette, leaning against the handrail, in between chatting to Deneuve, who was also leaning against the rail, although as we'd all been pointing out since we got there – to ourselves, not to her – Mr Protein Pill was leaning against it with a bit more conviction. After all, she'd already been in dozens of films, probably hundreds if you counted properly, and no doubt couldn't care less about leaning against anything, whereas this was only Mr PP's fifth feature film, and he was going to get as much leaning in as possible. His smoking was easily as good as his acting. But then he was smoking Marlboro Reds, so you would have expected him to be better at smoking those than Embassy Regal, for instance. Or Player's No. 6.

You can still see me if you freeze the film at a certain point, although I realise that watching *The Hunger* is about as likely as anyone listening to the collected works of the Thompson Twins. Or Hazel O'Connor. There I was, a callow new romantic barely out of my teens, dressed in a bow tie and silver suit, with a drink in one hand and a cigarette in the other, standing around enigmatically as the messianic rock god brushed by me. Oh, and they cropped my head out.

Brushing past Bowie would have been enough for me to brag about for months, but my anecdote moved up a gear around two o'clock that afternoon when Bowie marched up to me and asked me for a light for his Marlboro Red. Now, this may not be up there with watching John Travolta rehearse the dance scene in *Pulp Fiction* or Robert De Niro asking you to help him with the mirror scene in *Taxi Driver*, but it's the sort of thing that extras thrive on. Spend half an hour on a film set and you would hear that 'Sean Connery told me this joke' (translation: I was standing behind him when he told the director the joke) or 'Al Pacino practically congratulated me on the way I walked into the room' (i.e., he didn't even blink). Celebrity encounters, however fleeting, or indeed untrue, are the only currency extras have. Personally, I was just thrilled to be in the same room as the bloke who'd sung 'Life on Mars'.

Weeks went by before I got another job, this time on the James Bond movie *Octopussy*, which was being shot somewhere in the not-so-wilds of north London. Again, I hardly distinguished myself, and spent most of the day chatting to Roger Moore's stand-in (I can't remember his name but I'm fairly certain it was Brian). Around four o'clock, the director, John Glen, actually started to film something, a scene where a half-dozen Latin American baddies try and shoot down Bond's plane using an anti-aircraft gun. And I was the extra chosen to fire the gun, swivelling around on a concrete dais and pulling back the trigger as though I did this sort of thing all day. It wasn't an especially demanding role, but it meant that I joined a long-exalted line of evil Bond adversaries, including Oddjob, Dr No, Auric Goldfinger, Ernst Stavro Blofeld and Jaws.

And, like George Lazenby after *On Her Majesty's Secret Service*, that was pretty much the end of my film career. Until 1986, that is, when I would have a comeback of sorts. A friend was a production manager on the appalling Bob Dylan/Rupert Everett movie *Hearts of Fire*, and as they were filming for a few days in London, she asked me if I'd like to come down and see the car crash in person. On the day I visited they were filming a scene that involved a press conference and my friend asked if I'd sit in and pretend to be one of the hacks. We all had to perch there and ask His Bobness various questions, though the only thing I remember from the scene is the director Richard Marquand walking up to Dylan after every take and asking him if he could grunt with a little more conviction (Joe Eszterhas had written the grunts, after all). To his credit, Dylan complied and, on several occasions, even managed to string his grunts into three syllables.

Unsurprisingly my name isn't on the credits. I bet Dylan wished his wasn't either.

A few years later I very nearly appeared in a Steve Martin film when I was on holiday in LA. I was sitting on the dunes at Venice Beach with Robin Derrick, when an extremely flustered young woman came up to me brandishing a clipboard and a mobile phone. 'I'm really sorry to have to ask you to do this,' she said, without any attempt at sincerity. 'But you're directly in shot, so could you go and sit somewhere else?'

NINETEEN EIGHTY-TWO WAS ALSO THE year when I started to get serious about work. I started taking my photography more seriously – I took a series of pictures at Peter Gabriel's first WOMAD festival in Shepton Mallet and tried to sell them to *The Face*, and took dozens of interior shots on the opening night of the Haçienda in Manchester (for a couple of weeks I practically lived in the place). I started taking fashion pictures again, and pitched small stories to the *Evening Standard*, *New Sounds New Styles*, *Blitz* and the *Sunday Times*. I knew I needed to be proactive and made a decision to try and force my way into the industry. I even started pestering people in TV; I managed to get a meeting with Trevor Phillips, who was then a producer at London Weekend Television (I pitched him half-a-dozen ideas, none of which he wanted), and sniffed around various TV music shows, getting to know the likes of Jonathan Ross, Peter Edge, Alan Marke and Pedro Romhanyi, all of whom would go on to rule their respective kingdoms in film, music and TV. I began reviewing gigs and doing small interviews for the weekly music press, for the *NME* and *Record Mirror* (I was terrible but enthusiastic – I even feigned enthusiasm when I was commissioned to interview the rhythm section of Big Country), and basically started hustling. I was taking pictures, and even though I couldn't really write, generating story ideas too. European publications started to get in touch, eager for some bulletins from trendy London, and so I worked for *Manner Vogue*, *L'Uomo Vogue* and *Mondo Uomo* (as soon as one came, they all came). I was obsessed with dance music, but most of the music papers habitually marginalised it; they didn't think it was particularly interesting, and certainly didn't think it sold papers.

What did I have to offer? Like a lot of people my age and from my background, I was very opinionated. Confrontational. In hindsight I can't quite believe how judgemental I was in meetings with fairly senior TV people, executives who had decades of experience, and with whom I was lucky to be in the same room. I was wildly critical of any TV programme, magazine, newspaper or radio show that attempted to target the youth market, even though I had no idea practically how to improve them. I was a critic, but one decidedly without portfolio. What did I know? I must have seemed appallingly arrogant, and yet I think that was also my USP. It was certainly part of my DNA. I suppose it was all about choices and having the ability and the opportunity to make those choices. Like a lot of my generation, I felt sprauncy because I suddenly realised the people whom I assumed knew about stuff like this actually knew nothing at all. And that was empowerment. It meant we could do anything; all we needed was access.

With a friend of mine, Helen Gallacher, who was a junior producer on the BBC's flagship arts programme *Arena*, I even tried to develop a television magazine show. She was frustrated by her inability to climb the corporate ladder and, as I was obviously keen to get involved in the arts and was already fairly well-connected, we invented *Avid*. This, we thought, would cover music, nightlife, books and everything else that currently wasn't on TV. It wasn't meant to be a dreadful 'youth' show, but more of a metropolitan 'salon' where we would mix restaurant and club gossip with political sideswipes and antagonistic panels, combined with music, fashion and film. *Avid* (I was ridiculously proud of the name) was meant to be a TV version of a style magazine, but perhaps a bit more rarefied. It was supposed to be passionate and annoying in equal measure. We asked Peter York to get involved, which I remember being incredibly stressful (what if he didn't like me?), and another BBC producer, the lovely May Miller. We had a meeting with Peter in one of the *Arena* offices in the old BBC Television Centre in White City, and all I can remember is Peter asking if we were going to do anything on Kool and the Gang, with whom he appeared to be obsessed. Was he being arch? We couldn't tell. So we immediately created a segment in the first show about the semiotics of 'Ladies' Night' and 'Hi De Hi, Hi De Ho'.

Helen and I were developing the show with the great Paul Watson, who had produced the 1974 BBC series, *The Family*, directed by Franc Roddam. This was one of the first classic fly-on-the-wall documentaries, seen by many as a precursor to what would come down the pipe with reality television. It followed the day-to-day existence of a working-class family from Reading called the Wilkins family. Even I had seen *The Family*, and the Wilkinses weren't that different from many of our neighbours back in Deal. It was a massive critical and commercial hit, even though some people said it was the first time any BBC producer had actually met a genuine member of the British working class. Paul knew Helen and had weirdly taken a shine to me, which in itself felt like some kind of gift. I had no experience, no apparent aptitude, and I wasn't remotely like anyone else whom I met at the BBC (apart from Helen, perhaps). Nearly everyone I met was privately educated, and thought culture was opera, classical music and theatre. In hindsight, I must have seemed tremendously arrogant, but at least I was passionate. Paul was an inspiration, and showed me – for the very first time – how passion and integrity are disciplines at which you have to work. Paul appeared to have an innate sense of goodness, and yet I could easily see how it would be possible to be corrupted by the enormity of the world he inhabited.

Avid didn't happen – we made a pilot that crashed and burned – but it gave me a taste of something just out of reach.

i-D: Swinging London

The Dawn of the Style Magazines

With Caryn Franklin, Marion Moisy and Terry Jones,
i-D offices, West Hampstead, 1984

IN 1983, MY LIFE SEEMED to revolve around showing off. Living it large. I might have been spending every day in bed watching television, with only a two-bar heater for company, but at night I was a baby celebrity, a face who could be relied upon to turn up wearing something interesting, with a new story to tell. Every night myself, Corinne, Pascal, Joe Hagan and whoever else was around all made ourselves into a news item. A story. Forty years later, we would have defined ourselves by our Instagram posts; in the early eighties all we had to sell ourselves was, well, ourselves.

I was bouncing around between dead-end jobs – I worked at a marketing conference in Earls Court for a few weeks, and sold sex toys and dirty magazines in a porn shop at the top of Portobello Road

– in between attempting to break into the media. I was keen, and persistent, but I wasn't especially worried about what might happen. Even when I was living in a housing association flat in Peckham, eating one meal a day and spending my life in nightclubs, I weirdly believed in myself. I found myself doing entry-level or demeaning jobs rather than admit I didn't have a proper career. Although I was writing and taking pictures and starting to hassle people for jobs, in reality I was in denial. And yet I arrogantly knew I was somehow going to be all right. I had no reason why. It wasn't so much an inner strength as an inner confidence. I knew that all I needed was a bit of luck.

And then suddenly, in the autumn of 1983, it came my way.

ONE DAY I WAS CALLED by a well-spoken photographer friend called Mark Bayley who needed someone to interview a bunch of people he was shooting for *i-D* magazine, the fashion fanzine. I can't remember what the questions were, although, given the era, I doubt they were any more sophisticated than 1) Where do you buy your clothes? and 2) How much do you hate Margaret Thatcher? But the editor obviously saw something I didn't as he promptly called me up – well, as I didn't have a phone, he called one of my friends – and offered me a job. Would I like to be an editor on the magazine? Would I like to use my writing (and presumably my editing) skills to improve its quality? Even though my degree show at St Martin's had included a magazine, I certainly didn't consider myself a writer, as I'd had absolutely no formal training. I don't think I could actually write at all. So not only did he save me, he invented me, gave me a purpose, and gave me a sniff of a life I had previously only dreamed about.

Terry Jones was that man, a former art director of *Vogue* who had left the magazine when the punk explosion had suddenly made the street more interesting than the catwalk. He had started *i-D* in 1980, the year that also saw the launch of *The Face* and *Blitz*, two other magazines that would go on to define the eighties. I ended up working with Terry for four years, a period in which he became a close friend as well as my mentor. Terry always said he wanted to infiltrate the mainstream; in reality he created it, and like many of the other people he plucked from obscurity, not least Nick Knight, Edward Enninful and Kate Moss, I was given the keys to the kingdom and then told to hurry up and unlock it.

I wouldn't have got my foot through the door if it hadn't been for Terry, something I always go out of my way to mention whenever I'm asked how I got into the industry. No one does it by themselves, and someone always gives you that first piece of encouragement. Which is why mentoring is always so important.

i-D started, naturally enough, with a wink, which is often the way with relationships, particularly ones that last. A wink, a smile, and the promise of a great new tomorrow. The original idea was a simple one, something Terry Jones hatched while still art director of British *Vogue*. Terry was there from 1972 to 1977, only leaving when it became evident that his colleagues didn't share his enthusiasm for the fresh and exciting new direction in street style that exploded in tandem with punk (Terry also designed the logo for John Lydon's PiL). So, he left the magazine, eventually starting *i-D* in the summer of 1980. Initially looking like little but a punk fanzine, *i-D* was essentially an exercise in social documentation; a catalogue of photographs of 'real' people wearing 'real' clothes, what Terry liked to call 'straight-ups'. People on the street. In bars. In nightclubs. At home. And all of them on parade. Although the magazine developed into an internationally renowned style magazine, full of fancy photographers and the very fanciest models, this 'straight-up' element has never been lost. Above all else, *i-D* was always about REAL people.

Energised by the popularity of fanzines, Terry wanted to create a fashion zine dedicated to street style: unfiltered and fast, and it would look handmade. 'It was about the idea that you could do it yourself rather than have a fashion magazine dictate what you could wear,' said Terry. 'It was the time when post-punk, club life, and the music scene were all coming together. It was about DIY self-expression.'

When it launched, *i-D* didn't look like any other magazine on the shelves, and in many respects still doesn't. Turned on its side, the *i-D* logo resembles a wink and a smile, and every cover since the first issue has featured a winking, usually smiling face; a theme that has given the magazine an iconic identity as strong as that developed by *Playboy* in the fifties (which always included a bunny silhouette somewhere on the cover). I can remember where I was when I saw the first issue, in September 1980: it was on a friend's desk in the first-floor second-year graphics department of St Martin's. Having long been an avid reader of *New Style*, *Viz*, *Boulevard* and *Ritz*, it was refreshing to find something that plugged right into British subculture, a heat-seeking stylesheet which found room for every fledgling youth cult in the country – from punks, soul boys and new romantics to psychobillies, rockers and penny-ante trustafarians. Along with *The Face*, which had launched a few months previously, *i-D* was suddenly the voice of a generation: a generation with no name.

Terry felt that the best way to reflect the creativity he admired in street style was through 'immediacy', through visual imagery rather than just straight text, and so the magazine used a typewriter font, tickertape headlines and wild, often perverse graphics. And although this was a style born of necessity as much as any ideology, it gave the magazine an identity that it preserved for over three decades.

The magazine was A4 in size (slightly thinner than most glossies), though in the early days it was landscape as opposed to portrait and opened – somewhat annoyingly – longways. The first issue was just forty pages, stuck together with three rickety staples, and cost 50p. A bargain. 'Fashion magazine No.1' it said on the cover, and that was all you really needed to know. Inside were several dozen 'straight-ups' of various upwardly and downwardly mobile exhibitionists: Cerith Wyn Evans, some fairly dodgy-looking Blitz Kids, a rockabilly or two, a goth and some teddy boys from Brighton. A girl called Pennie, interviewed about what she was wearing, had this to say about her jumper: 'I got it from some shop in Oxford Street. I can't remember the name. I get so mesmerised when I shop along Oxford Street I never notice the names.' (For the first few issues, Terry only allowed photographers to shoot two frames per person – to save money – so the 35 mm contact sheets became works of art in themselves, a sort of sartorial police file.) There were also a few fashion ads from Fiorucci, Robot and Swanky Modes. It even had a manifesto of sorts: '*i-D* is a Fashion/Style Magazine. Style isn't what but how you wear clothes. Fashion is the way you walk, talk, dance and prance. Through *i-D* ideas travel fast and free of the mainstream – so join us on the run!'

Terry was keen to reflect the fact that street style was a democratic, amorphous process. And *i-D* wasn't ever, if truth be told, anything like a barometer of style. Even though the magazine originally branded itself 'The Worldwide Manual of Style', it has rarely been prescriptive. Sensibly, Terry always believed that it's important to like the bad stuff too. He was never particularly keen on drive-by journalism, not interested in ring-fencing people in arbitrary social groups. For the quintessential style magazine this was ironic, seeing that the 'style' magazines and newspaper lifestyle sections that came in its wake seemed devoted to the reductive. *i-D* was many things – irritating, infuriating, wilfully obscure, over-extravagant and often impossible to read – but it was rarely without substance.

SO, I'D BEEN GIVEN A job by Terry, but it was a job I didn't know how to do. I couldn't write. Not properly. Of course, I could *write*, but I didn't know how to write like a journalist. I'd written essays at college and the text for various projects – including one on the tepee people of south Wales, where I visited for a week one dark, cold December – and as well as the occasional review I'd obviously written the thing that Terry had liked so much, but I couldn't, as the saying goes, string two sentences together. When I needed to write something, I'd agonise over it for hours and get so stuck because I couldn't think how to express myself. Consequently, for a while I would just write headlines and then stick them all together. The problem was nobody noticed, and everything I wrote got published. From a writing perspective

I grew up in public, as there were no gatekeepers at *i-D*, no one to tell me what I was doing wasn't any good, no one to help me improve. Terry couldn't write, and we didn't employ sub-editors, so everything immediately went into the magazine, unfiltered. And a lot of it was pretty poor. I had enthusiasm, and I was well-read enough to pepper my copy with words and phrases I'd stolen from elsewhere, but I was a case study in amateurism. The other issue was productivity – I was writing so much of the magazine that a lot of it felt rushed.

One of the reasons I threw myself into the job so furiously was a) because I felt as though I was a couple of years behind everyone else in terms of finding a career and needed to catch up, and b) because it didn't feel like a real job.

I also loved the money. I wasn't paid much, but I was now able to buy more clothes and not worry about spending so much money in restaurants. I didn't spend more than I earned – I never had – but after being a student and then largely unemployed, even a little bit of money felt like empowerment.

As *i-D* was a magazine that seemed to thrive on chaos, my limitations didn't seem to matter very much, and my mad, often incoherent and wildly hysterical text appeared to dovetail perfectly with the cut-and-paste nature of the layouts, as well as the magazine's general inchoate sensibility (inchoate not being a word I would have known at the age of twenty-three). The magazine thrived on enthusiasm and a unique understanding that what we were doing was right. To outsiders, and to people who had no connection to this world, or who lived in Edinburgh, Toronto or Belgium, the magazine must have seemed mad, although to his credit Terry went out of his way to try and make sure that *i-D* reflected what was going on all over the place.

My confidence was such that I threw myself into any project with gusto, even though my dilettantish sensibility meant I was often underqualified. I would rush off to interview Ken Livingstone or Divine or Peter York (what a joy!) with a list of random questions and then write up the interviews as though they were surreal poems. At least that was what they looked like when they eventually appeared in print.

Nevertheless, it all seemed to work. After a while, the complex, knockabout nature of the writing in the magazine (and, I have to say, the editing) lent even more weight to *i-D*'s character. My bonkers writing and future *Clothes Show* star Caryn Franklin's incredibly inventive fashion meant that we were steering the magazine into waters that felt like they echoed the anarchic sensibilities of the sixties. Caryn was such an important part of the magazine, and her contacts and her editorial direction helped to give the title its DNA. Her visual flair was extraordinary, and we ran the magazine with a combined sense of (passionate) abandon. Of course, while she was spontaneous, I was precisely the opposite. I gradually learned that by being fastidious, and by controlling the elements on a page, I could steer the magazine in a way I found satisfying. We were both obsessives.

It was such a lot of fun. I'm not sure any of us did much more than work and go out to nightclubs. I didn't play sport, didn't go on holiday. I had a two-speed life.

I definitely wanted to get better at writing, though. My as yet undiagnosed mild dyslexia meant that I've never been able to spell and I have problems with sentence construction, but I was becoming obsessed with trying to improve, and so I practised. Wrote a lot. Rewrote a lot. Tried to write a sentence without cutting it in half with a comma or a clause. And gradually I got better. I wrote and wrote and wrote and eventually started to improve. Everyone who worked for the music press seemed to have had an extraordinary immersion in popular culture, and they all wrote effortlessly. I knew I would never be as good as any of them, and so I practised. I started freelancing again for the music press – *Smash Hits*, *Record Mirror*, *NME* – then, after a while, the likes of the *Observer* and the *Sunday Times*, who obviously thought my enthusiasm could be rewritten and subbed into material they could publish in some form. When I started writing for other people, I made up for the fact I couldn't really write by over-researching, doing enormous amounts of homework, which, I soon discovered, was what real journalism was about anyway. So even though I couldn't properly articulate what I was learning, I *was* learning. In terms of style, though, it was all about practice. Practice, practice, practice. I'm still not a great writer but I know how to do it and have found a style that works. I just need to keep practising. Which is what I do every day.

I also didn't learn to touch type. Everything I have ever written, including this book, has been typed with just my two index fingers. Maybe this has always affected the way I write, but it's what I've been doing for forty years.

As I developed as a writer and then as an editor, I developed my own passions, as well as finding a way to feed them all into the magazine. I wanted to bring those passions to life, mixing music and fashion and journalism and media and all forms of cultural insurrection. I was a classic autodidact with an obsessive nature, someone for whom culture – pop culture, style culture, counterculture, all the cultures – was like oxygen. It was literally all I cared about – I certainly cared more about it than family, personal relationships or initially, at least, my career. And now I was being given a magazine to muck about with. What fun. What a gift, what an absolute gift. I knew that it was culturally normative to treat 'culture' as incidental, or peripheral; national newspapers were extraordinarily good at minimising culture, just as they were exceptionally adept at minimising women (the *Guardian*'s women's pages, lifestyle sections, fashion stories). And I think all of us working on the magazine at the time – and that included Caryn Franklin and Alix Sharkey – were determined to treat culture in a completely different way.

Because *i-D* was a vehicle for art direction as much as journalism, the magazine found itself being haphazard, irrational and wildly pretentious. The readers understood this and somehow went along with it. Some of them, anyway. In the fifth anniversary issue various readers were asked how they'd sum up the magazine. 'You discover all the secret talents and mad scientists,' wrote Michael Odimitrakis from Kostas, while J. Dominic from Deptford compared the magazine to Marks & Spencer's Continental Biscuit Assortment (a rare accolade indeed). My favourite comment was sent anonymously and is nothing if not succinct: 'You are a stupid lot of wanking ignorant trendies.'

Charmed, I'm sure.

The magazine was put together on the top floor of Terry and Tricia's terraced Edwardian house in West Hampstead, north London. Tricia was Terry's beautiful wife, and *i-D*'s secret weapon. Even though *i-D* was run by Terry, it was Tricia's moral compass that helped steer the editorial direction, which was one of egalitarian bohemianism. She was the one who welcomed the six of us every morning, after we had made our way there on the Jubilee line, and it would be Tricia kicking us out at 9 or 10 p.m. having put in a good twelve hours, putting the magazine together with cow gum, scissors and Sellotape. Photographers such as Marc Lebon and Nick Knight would regularly traipse up and down the stairs, while we sat around and painstakingly tried to introduce some cohesion into a rather anarchic production process. Every now and then, we would be invited down to the basement kitchen, where Tricia kept a fridge that to our undernourished eyes looked like a capsule version of Waitrose. We were always eager to be fed. That was the duality of working at *i-D*. On the one hand we were running around the world thinking we were micro celebrities, and on the other hand we were near paupers, extremely happy to avail ourselves of free food.

As an editor, Terry's often total disregard for the printed word was, on occasions, supremely painful. I soon became victim to his vagaries. As a cub reporter on the magazine in 1983, I had just returned from an assignment – no doubt interviewing some equally artless fashion designer, club runner or nascent pop star – to find Terry laying out the next issue. As I glanced at the layout of one of my articles, I saw Terry cutting the bottom three inches off the galley, so my piece ended inelegantly, slap-bang in the middle of a sentence. Sensing my apprehension, he turned to me and smiled: 'Well, it won't fit.'

It was to be the first of many such arguments, most of which Terry won. The rest of us would occasionally get frustrated by Terry's wilful disregard for conformity, and whenever we saw something in the magazine that we thought could have been improved, we would give each other an *i-D* wink and say, 'It looks like a dog's arse with a hat on.'

*

IN A WORLD THAT SOON became awash with style magazines aimed at every different type of demographic, it was easy to forget that in 1980 magazines like *i-D* just didn't exist. *i-D* was the first street-fashion magazine, a pick 'n' mix grab-bag of punk fashion and DIY style, a pop-cultural sponge soaking up everything around it with inelegant haste. During a decade when the safety net of society was gradually folded away, *i-D* catalogued a culture of self-sufficiency, even if that culture was at times only sartorial. Sure, the eighties were the decade when 'designer' became not just a prefix but also an adjective, but it was also the decade of unreconstructed, and often rabid individualism. And even though it had an egalitarian ethos, *i-D* was obviously elitist, offering privileged meaning to a narrow, self-defined audience, offering lifestyle liveries for each and every member.

i-D was deliberately anarchic, both in tone and design, and its sensibility was echoed by the chaotic way it was put together. One of the most orthodox things we ever did was the celebratory portrait series we produced for the magazine's fifth anniversary in 1985. It was largely produced by myself and Nick Knight, and involved Nick shooting what we considered to be the 100 most important people who had ever appeared in the magazine. In essence, we thought they were the 100 most important people involved in our iteration of Swinging London, and included everyone from Leigh Bowery, Lynne Franks and Peter York to Katharine Hamnett and Steve Strange, from John Galliano and Tony Wilson to Morrissey, Paul Weller and Paul Morley. As I wrote – rather hysterically – at the time, it was a rogue's gallery, a beauty parade, a 'Gallery of Style'. We were a conceited bunch: fifteen of those included worked for the magazine in one way or another. To my knowledge, thirteen of our stars are now dead, and the further away we get from the mid-eighties, the more particular they all seem. Some are still operational – Jools Holland, Stephen Jones, Chris Sullivan, Marc Almond, Gary Kemp, etc. – some are still doing what they were doing in 1985, and some have fallen off the radar so it feels as though they were part of a time capsule.

We asked them all various asinine questions. When I asked Nick Logan what the most important event of the decade was, he said, 'Presumably this means "Apart from *The Face*"?' When I asked Cerith Wyn Evans what he would be in five years' time, he said, 'A 14-year-old Venezuelan prostitute walking the streets of New York.' The final portrait was of the maverick shopkeeper Tommy Roberts, the self-proclaimed 'most vulgar man in fashion', and the man behind Kleptomania, City Lights and Mr Freedom. He was used to long periods of indolence interrupted by short periods of creativity. Responding to my question about what he might be doing in five years' time, he said, 'I'll either be running a department store or dancing for a drink in Covent Garden.' Tommy would die of cancer in 2012.

As the magazine became more successful, so we began being courted by the big luxury advertisers. This was novel, and rather flattering, although initially I wasn't as equipped to negotiate these new worlds as perhaps I ought to have been. If I'm honest, I could have done with a bit of guidance, a helping hand, a concerned word in my shell-like. Like many young men, I was the dictionary definition of gauche: I didn't always know what to say, what to do or what to wear. Even in my early twenties I'd be in an alien social situation and just . . . sort of have to wing it. Sometimes I got by – charm helped a lot in these situations – and sometimes I sank, deep, deep into the murky, glutinous depths of very public embarrassment.

Once, when I had been at the magazine for about six months, I was taken to Caviar Kaspia, the tremendously smart Mayfair restaurant to which Princess Diana used to go. I was being taken to lunch by the MD of a French luxury goods company, who was all suited and booted in what I assumed to be top-dollar Savile Row. We both ordered gravadlax (smoked salmon to me), and as he waited for me to start eating (the man was nothing if not polite), I carefully took the gauze off the half lemon that had kindly been left on my plate, so I could squeeze the juice over my fish. Having never seen anyone do this before, I naturally thought this was the right thing to do. Until, of course, I saw my host simply squeeze his lemon through the gauze, making me feel like a jumped-up interloper. You could say that if he'd been truly polite my host would have copied me, but then as he no doubt knew everyone else in the restaurant, he wasn't going to embarrass himself by acting like a rube. That was my job. I felt about as comfortable as a donkey in a swimming pool.

WE STARTED TO BE ASKED to produce events, putting on fashion shows on the other side of the world, hosting club nights, promoting bands and even curating the famous ICA Rock Week. The 1984 week had been curated by John Peel, but the following year we were asked to get involved, and so we organised a week of events that leaned heavily towards club culture, electro and indie, building on the success of the Smiths and Prefab Sprout with bands such as 52nd Street and the Jazz Defektors, pop groups like Swing Out Sister and Curiosity Killed the Cat, and DJ sets from Jay Strongman, Fat Tony and Rusty Egan. Malcolm McLaren was in the audience most nights, as were half of London's A & R men.

At *i-D*, we weren't obsessed with innovation, but we were often embroiled in it. In 1986, Sigue Sigue Sputnik (named after a Filipino street gang) released their first album, *Flaunt It*, a wonderful exercise in style and marketing over content. Fronted by ex-Generation X mastermind Tony James (nice man) and glorified shop assistant Martin Degville, they were a triumph of vacuous eighties excess; they looked wildly brilliant but sounded as though they'd been created by an especially cheap computer (the record was produced by Giorgio Moroder). Which I think was sort of the point. Described by James as 'hi-tech Sex, designer violence and the fifth generation of rock and roll', his sub-Malcolm McLaren tabloid-baiting motto was 'fleece the world'. The album was unique in that the band sold advertising spots between the songs, a meta nod to the iniquities of rampant consumerism. They managed to secure ads from L'Oréal, Kensington Market, the pirate TV station Network 21, and of course from us at *i-D* (the ad was voiced by Alix Sharkey). James's defence of the ruse was cute: 'A lot of our records sound like advertisements,' he said.

Pop culture in the UK appeared to be obsessed with mixing the past with the future, perhaps because the present seemed to be so depressing. Elsewhere, pop simply became giddy with its own possibilities. Take the metallic reggae of Grace Jones. Grace acted as a kind of postmodern cypher, while her music was an animatronic fusion of exotic funk and brittle electronica, packaged to within an inch of her life by the French photographer and graphic designer Jean-Paul Goude. She was one of the strongest personalities to emerge from the period, a larger-than-life approximation of what a modern pop star could look and sound like, Goude's illusory style being perfect for Jones's assault on a pop audience still wary of emancipated soul divas. They met at Studio 54 in the late seventies, when Jones was still trying to make it as a performer. 'I always loved the mixture of threat and beauty, I just thought it was time for Grace to just stretch out,' says Goude.

As it was, the reinvented Grace Jones (she had been a model and a partially successful disco singer) was one of the most transgressive figures of the eighties. She made many of the small British electronic bands seem quite parochial.

For many she was an acquired taste – there are those who say that her voice has always had the animation of the Speaking Clock – but she quickly became the ultimate disco queen, a mirrorball icon who was completely sure of herself. I interviewed her at the time, at the height of her fame, and it's an experience I've never forgotten. She was in London to have a cast made of her body for Madame Tussauds, which obviously made it easy for me to accuse her of being self-obsessed.

'You think I'm narcissistic?' she growled at me. 'Well thank you very much. For a while I was terribly vain, but not any more. When I was modelling, I spent half my life staring at thousands of perfect reflections. It got to a stage where I was losing all sense of reality – so after I quit modelling, I took all the mirrors out of my house . . . That's why I started dressing like a bum.'

For journalists of my generation, an interview with Grace Jones was always a poisoned chalice, because while you would certainly come away with great copy, there was always the danger that she might belt you round the face or shout at you for being less than she expected. Only four days before my interview she had allegedly punched a French journalist for probing too deeply. When I arrived at her hotel suite that morning she acted as if she had already drunk half a bottle of champagne . . .

'I've had more misrepresentations than I can handle, and people have told the wickedest lies about me,' she said. 'A lot of them have taken their frustrations out on me, and I don't like that because it can wound . . . Journalists can be so bad.'

She was extremely beautiful, outrageously thin, with an Azzedine Alaïa waist and amazingly chiselled legs, although her voice was disconcertingly masculine, with an odd cockney lilt – 'Alroit?' She smoked incessantly, too, ate her club sandwich with both hands, and stirred her champagne with one of last night's dirty chopsticks.

I told her she had become renowned for being intimidating. Did she need constant recognition?

'No, not constantly. I like a bit of honesty every now and again.'

But not too much.

'But not too much.'

THE EIGHTIES HAD A LOT to live up to. If the sixties had been a decade of confrontational happiness, and the post-punk seventies full of agents of social change, the eighties were crowded with a generation devoted to self-empowerment and self-improvement. It was a decade that couldn't wait to get ahead of itself. Reinvention became almost a prerequisite for success as soap stars became pop stars, pop stars became politicians and politicians became indistinguishable from their *Spitting Image* puppets. Everyone was a party catalyst, everybody a star. When Andy Warhol said that in the future everyone would be famous for fifteen minutes, he wasn't simply talking about New York in the sixties or seventies; he was unwittingly describing London in 1985. A vortex of entrepreneurial hedonism, London hadn't swung so much since 1966.

And *i-D* was the first magazine to hold a mirror up to what it saw on the street, exploiting the boom in youth culture and London's burgeoning reputation as a crucible of transient young talent. In a way, the magazine made a genuine – if not always coherent – attempt to return control of the fashion world to those who actually inhabited it. It was Instagram on paper.

We were obsessive about the minutiae of style. I wrote an exhaustive and somewhat hysterical piece about the Italian youth cult, *paninaro*. The *paninari* were teenagers who dressed in bright Timberland boots and coloured puffa jackets, rode motorbikes and scooters, and spent their leisure hours hanging around sandwich bars. I had been told that the Pet Shop Boys had recorded their own paean to them, due to be released as a single, and which I duly put in my piece. They hadn't, of course, but when Neil Tennant and Chris Lowe read this in *i-D*, they liked the idea so much they went and recorded one, 'Paninaro'.

There was a lot of posing in the eighties, and a lot of it happened in Soho. One night I was in the Soho Brasserie, in Old Compton Street. There he was, this classic Neurotic Boy Outsider, all gaunt and secondhand, sitting by himself, surrounded on other tables by braying eighties would-be whizz-kids – colourful young things with gaudy clothes and short attention spans talking about money, magazines, travel and nightclubs. The NBO was reading a Penguin Modern Classic.

But as I passed him on my way out, I noticed his book was upside down.

I HAVE DOZENS OF FAVOURITE *i-D* covers, though the two I like best bookend my time at the magazine. The first is Nick Knight's photograph of Sade, which was produced at the tail end of 1983, not just because it was the first issue I worked on, but also because in one small wink it said more about the eighties than a thousand editorials ever could. Striking a defiant pose and offering an immaculate statement of intent, Sade looked as though she was about to conquer the world (and eighteen months later she did). The other cover I love is the last one I worked on, the 'smiley' cover from December 1987, which incorporated the *i-D* wink as well as heralding the advent of acid house. (There is a third cover I love, too, a Johnny Rozsa photograph of Leigh Bowery dressed as a pig, wearing three pairs of spectacles, six ears and three foam snouts. When Rozsa first met Leigh, wandering around Soho, he said he looked like 'Krishna on acid'.)

As he showed by giving Madonna her first magazine cover, Terry was always good at exploiting pop, but then during the first three or four years of the eighties, all publications were. Pop music was vital in disseminating this new visual culture of fashion and arrogance, and the emergence of the new pop groups such as Duran Duran, Frankie Goes to Hollywood, the Eurythmics, Spandau Ballet and Culture Club – who, in a move away from the punk ethos (more like a volte-face) began spending their vast royalty cheques in the designer boutiques along Bond Street and the Kings Road – gave rise to a newfound tabloid interest in anything to do with pop.

Suddenly the red-tops latched on to the idea that pop was fashionable again. The lives and loves of Boy George, Simon Le Bon, Annie Lennox, Holly Johnson and the Kemp brothers became front-page news. The pop stars believed their own publicity, too, and many – particularly Duran Duran – began living the life of dilettantes and new-moneyed aristocrats, poncing about on boats and dating catwalk models. They had taken reinvention to its natural conclusion. Five years before their huge success, they had looked as though they were made of money even though their pockets were empty; now the good life was theirs for the taking. And they took it, each with both hands. Greed was good, after all, and credit so easy to come by, while dreams and wishes seemed so easily obtainable. In a way, success became democratised, and worlds that had once been available only to certain sets of people became accessible to, if not everyone, then at least anyone with enough luck and tenacity.

I started to meet tabloid journalists, and my instinct was to be wary; they were never interested in cultural diversion, only personal transgression.

The pop world wasn't just fashionable, it was sexy, too, and the arrival of androgynous celebrities such as Boy George and Annie Lennox put a whole new spin on Swinging London (British pop was then such a potent export commodity that in 1983 more than a third of all American chart places were taken by British acts). Pop stars began hanging out with fashion designers and frequenting the many nightclubs that were springing up all over the capital; PR agencies were beginning to exploit this new confluence of art and commerce, and the high street began taking notice of all the new money.

Pop had replaced sport as far as the media was concerned. Back in the sixties, the *South Wales Echo* started a Saturday sports paper, requiring its writers to file more copy than usual. When it launched, one of the editors called the paper's star writer, Peter Corrigan, and asked if he could contribute a story for the first issue. On being told he needed to file his copy by Tuesday instead of Friday, Corrigan was understandably agitated. 'Look,' he said. 'What would you prefer? A piece of well-crafted, considered prose by Friday, or rubbish on Tuesday?'

The editor, echoing the thoughts and wishes of sub-editors everywhere, said, 'Rubbish on Tuesday.'

Pop stars were now the focus of newspapers' appetite: never mind the quality, never mind veracity, it was all about voracity: feed the beast with endless titbits about the stars.

LIVE AID WAS A POP tabloid moment, as was the Band Aid single before it, and it was also the first time I found myself as a media witness. On 24 October 1984, as Bob Geldof sat in his Chelsea home watching the BBC *Six O'Clock News* with his girlfriend Paula Yates, he saw a disturbing report from Ethiopia. This was in the days when the *Six O'Clock News* had an audience of around 10 million, or roughly a sixth of the population. They were watching BBC reporter Michael Buerk's second film on the Ethiopian famine, and it was harrowing. A long-term drought and warfare had caused the failure of most food crops in Ethiopia and Sudan, so a terrible famine had struck the area. As the summer of 1984 dragged on, crops had withered and died, and the human tragedy grew worse. Western Aid was organised immediately, but it was far too little to have any real impact. In particular, it was the sight of a young English Red Cross worker that really shocked Geldof, as she had to decide which of the starving children she could help with her limited supplies.

A few days later, I was invited to the launch of Peter York's *Modern Times*, his *Style Wars* sequel, at Heinemann's swanky offices in Grosvenor Street. As I was now at *i-D*, I started to be invited to everything – film screenings, restaurant and club openings, and of course book launches. And here I was at this one, along with various editors from *The Face*, *Evening Standard* and *Sunday Times*. At the event, Bob Geldof told me, and indeed anyone else who would listen, about the terrible images he had seen in Buerk's BBC report. The BBC's *Arena* arts programme was filming at the launch, as a segment of a modern-day *Pygmalion* they were producing, called *Ligmalion*, about making your way in the Swinging London of the eighties. Geldof was caught on camera describing the awful scenes, and that night – inspired by the party guests' apathy as much as anything else – he decided to make a record to raise funds for those affected by the famine. The next day he called Sting, Ultravox's Midge Ure and Duran Duran's Simon Le Bon, and proceeded to plan the Band Aid record. This in turn led to the huge Live Aid event the following year, and as I stood there at Wembley, the magnitude of this philanthropic exercise wasn't lost on me. I had been dragged in the opposite direction, being asked to contribute to *Ligmalion* as a progenitor of modern-day self-interest.

Ligmalion was the invention of my old friend Helen Gallacher, and had been developed after various late-night discussions in the Soho Brasserie, in Old Compton Street, where Helen listened to my stories about blagging in London, about bouncing between nightclubs and private views, between gigs and parties, and never paying for a thing. She was fascinated by the way that being on the staff of *The Face* or *i-D* gave us a kind of special dispensation in Trendy London, affording us the keys to the city. There was nothing we couldn't go to should we wish, nothing we weren't invited to, no one we couldn't get access to if we asked the right people. We felt gilded, and probably quite entitled, and *Ligmalion* was a picaresque, tongue-in-cheek guide to doing it yourself. So, having sold the idea to Alan Yentob at the BBC, Helen invited me to get involved, and asked me to get some of my nightclubs pals along for the ride. She also reached out to various boldface names, namely Sting, Tim Curry, Alexei Sayle and Peter York, along with Bob Elms, the Wag Club's Chris Sullivan and us, the Lig of Gentlemen – my *i-D* pal Alix Sharkey, Christian Cotterill and myself. Halfway through the film, we burst into song, having been asked to describe the best way to navigate the avenues and alleyways of Swinging London – without spending a penny. The music was written by Working Week's Simon Booth, and the lyrics, such as they were, were written by the three of us:

Hey you, you wanna move in a hipper groove,
Get your face in the fashion race?
Gain a free pass to the mobile class,
In the lane with the hottest pace,
But money gets tight,
When you're out every night,
So when you're queuing up at that door,
You need advice from the guys, sharp, shifty and wise,
Who've played this game a thousand times before,
We say we lig it, we live it, we love it, we dig it
Now listen while we lay down the score,
We don't flash the cash to get in White Trash,
We just walk right through that door.

We thought we were all very special at *i-D*. In that respect I think we were quite conceited. When we went out, we would be photographed. We would be in gossip columns. And we'd start to be on television. God knows what we said, but we were enthusiastic: we knew we were part of something. We knew that as well as cataloguing our own iteration of Swinging London, we were part of it.

And we loved the attention. Like the nymphs of Arcadia, we were eagerly pursued but easily caught.

THERE WAS A HUGE DISPARITY between the fuss that was made of us when we were out at night and the relative cottage industry of our day jobs. *i-D* remained absolutely chaotic. If you left anything lying around the office for long enough, it would probably end up in the magazine. Passports, address books, taxi receipts, Terry would find a use for them all. I once made the mistake of showing Terry some old family snapshots, only to come back from holiday and find they were in the magazine. Heigh-ho. If you couldn't get an original copy of a particular photograph then why not just photocopy the book you found it in? It was unlikely anyone was ever going to notice. It was a very democratic place to work, too, where a receptionist could be fired one day and hired the next as a features writer. One particular receptionist ended up being the television critic of the *Observer*. Which is just as well: she was a lousy receptionist.

I was there from the late summer of 1983 to the end of 1987, four years in which we tried – relentlessly, religiously and, I must say, with a modicum of success – to reinvent our own particular wheel. Using guerrilla graphics, cutting-edge fashion photography and tongue-in-cheek text ('Why did God make homosexuals?' asked one gay fashion editor in a particularly flippant editorial. 'To take fat girls to discos.'), Terry Jones's *i-D* quickly gained a reputation as the complete Situationist tipsheet and street-fashion bible. Terry not only gave a career to me, photographers Nick Knight, Marc Lebon and Juergen Teller and journalists Caryn Franklin and Alix Sharkey, but hundreds of other teenage and twentysomething wannabes including art director Robin Derrick, stylists Simon Foxton and Ray Petri, and writer Kathryn Flett.

But the real stars of the magazine weren't the contributors, they were the subjects, whether it be Leigh Bowery cavorting about in the depths of Taboo, a Japanese cycle boy in an Eisenhower jacket or some UK garage DJ whose name no one could ever remember. Or Sade, Madonna, Björk or Kate Moss, all winking as though their careers depended on it (often they did). Any fashion designer, photographer, stylist, hairdresser, filmmaker, actor, model, style journalist, make-up artist, club runner, DJ or pop star who contributed anything to what is laughingly called the Zeitgeist in the eighties was, at some point or another, profiled or photographed in *i-D*. 'How much do I spend on clothes?' Frankie Goes to Hollywood's Paul Rutherford told *i-D* in 1984. 'Is Jean Paul Gaultier a rich man?' The *i-D* story is the story of pop culture in the eighties, a roll call of the great, the good and the unseemly, a litany of bad behaviour and unhealthy diets. While *The Face* could claim to be no less influential, no magazine has produced such a rogue's gallery of achievement as *i-D*.

DAVID BOWIE WAS A CONSTANT influence in our lives, even when he wasn't present, and even when he was making bad records. I had spent a day with him backstage at his famous Milton Keynes concerts when he was promoting *Let's Dance* in 1984 – he made me blush by calling me his 'friend' – and then a few months later we ended up at the same party during the Notting Hill Carnival, at the home of a mutual friend, the Stiff Records alumnus Cynthia Lole (who was about to start work as a music coordinator on the film *Absolute Beginners*). The only details I can remember are that I had my head shaved over Cynthia's sink after losing a bet with my friend Robin, and that Bowie chain-smoked throughout the afternoon.

Like many other journalists, I was flattered by his attention, and at one point even considered that we might really be 'friends'. We weren't, and never would be, but I certainly got to know how his mind worked, and saw how he would size up people, situations and culture – books, records, films – and analytically disassemble them for his own benefit. Bowie was the quintessential cultural magpie, and nothing was safe in his company. If it wasn't nailed down, he would have it. Metaphorically speaking, of course. He would make contact at the most inconvenient times, luring you into his web and making you feel as though you were the most important person in the world. You knew you were sort of being conned, but you didn't mind as he was so unbelievably charming. He had the same thing George Martin had, an ability to talk to you for the first time and make you believe that not only had you suddenly bonded, but that everything you said was of paramount importance.

Having become a global superstar in the summer of 1983, with the release of *Tonight* in September the following year, Bowie's seemingly innate sense of cool evaporated, almost instantly. It was as emphatic as it was temporary, and yet it seemed almost inevitable. After *Let's Dance* Bowie was owned by everyone, and for a while there didn't appear to be anything special about him; so much so that I distinctly remember being in the *i-D* office in the spring of 1984 and being asked if I wanted to appear in the extended promo film, *Jazzin' for Blue Jean*, Julien Temple was making to support the *Tonight* album, and rather snottily turning it down. Implausible, I know, and absurd to think of now, but that's how uncool we (briefly) thought David Bowie was in 1984, when notions of cool were bestowed and terminated often within hours of each other.

I would meet my other teenage hero a year later, when Bryan Ferry was publicising his first solo LP since the seventies, *Boys and Girls*. Even though I was fast approaching my mid-twenties I still had a crushed velvet soft spot for the man who had turned an affected, withdrawn thirteen-year-old into an affected, withdrawn thirteen-year-old with an unhealthy interest in snakeskin jackets and fifties American kitsch. I might not have been able to copy his jet-black duck's tail quiff, but I could pretend to sing in French as well as anyone in my class ('Jamais, jamais, jamais!').

Rather annoyingly, it had been arranged that I would meet the ageing crooner at his Chelsea offices early one Sunday morning. I had co-hosted a warehouse party the night before in Lipstick Studios (with Caryn Franklin and Robin Derrick), over in east London, and as I had stayed at a girl's flat afterwards, I was still wearing a bright red velvet fingertip drape coat, a garish pink shirt with elaborate ruffles and a pair of voluminous custom-built trousers made from dozens of pieces of violently clashing tartan. These had been designed for me by my friend Toby Andersen, who had once written the songs and played keyboards in the west London band, Funkapolitan (one of the few acts whose record had actually gone down the charts after an appearance on *Top of the Pops*). At three o'clock in the morning I no doubt looked as presentable as anyone else in Lipstick Studios, but at nine the following day, stumbling down the Kings Road, I must have looked an absolute fright.

But dear old Bryan didn't think so, or if he did, he didn't let on. Oh no. He was sitting cross-legged, immaculate in black Comme des Garçons, sipping an espresso, a picture of enigmatic cool. After a few polite exchanges he looked down at the material covering my legs and said, in an incredulous whisper I have never forgotten, 'My God, those are the most amazing trousers I have ever seen.'

Now, even though I know that this could have been just another example of Ferry's notorious charm, I was quite shocked at my reaction. The singer had disarmed me so much that the interview was a mere formality. (Even by this stage of my career I had interviewed a lot of famous people, but Ferry was the only one who had caused the hairs on the back of my neck to spring up when he walked in the room.) There was no way I could ask him anything remotely challenging (Why had he bothered ruining John Lennon's 'Jealous Guy'? Why had he risked emasculating Roxy Music with *Avalon*?) as I was still beaming at the memory of these casually delivered words of praise.

Ferry had been another one who had fed my obsession with an art-school version of the past, with Roxy's music, clothes and 'cover girl' album sleeves, an unholy mixture of sci-fi aspiration and fifties Americana. Roxy were a modern-day love letter to an anglicised America, a seventies idea of fifties Populuxe nobility. They – we! – were conquering the new frontier. In silver jump suits! Playing guitars! In front of girls!

And now here was their leader, nearly fifteen years later, in a small management office in the Kings Road, complimenting another man's trousers. I, of course, found the whole thing fascinating, especially as it was such a contrast to the reality of my life – living in an unheated, dirty, first-floor housing association flat behind the Ritzy Cinema in Brixton, earning practically nothing, and whose sense of self was validated by not having to pay to get into nightclubs. And, obviously, I thought I was fabulous.

The Face & *Arena*: Boy George v. Tom Wolfe

The Publishing Inferno

With Gordon Burn, Nik Cohn and Tony Parsons,
The Academy Club, Soho, 1988

I KNEW NICK LOGAN LONG before I went to work for him. Having spent four exhausting years at *i-D* jockeying for newsstand positions and media attention, we were locked in a battle of attrition with *The Face.* The two magazines were wildly competitive, but we liked each other and, I think, respected each other.

Back in 1980, in the space of three months, three magazines launched that would define the decade. Nick Logan, Terry Jones and Carey Labovitch started a small publishing revolution by launching, respectively, *The Face*, *i-D* and *Blitz*. Logan, former editor of the phenomenally successful *NME* and creator of *Smash Hits*, and Jones both independently realised that style culture, or what was then simply known as 'street style', was being ignored by much of the mainstream press. Labovitch, an Oxbridge graduate, was thinking similar things, although *Blitz* was initially more of a magazine dedicated to culture. These magazines were launched not only to catalogue this new explosion of style, but also to cater for it. *i-D*, *Blitz* and *The Face*, which – unusually for the time – were aimed at both men and women, reflected our increasing appetite for street style and fashion, as well as for ancillary subjects such as movies, music, television, art and Zeitgeisty things in general – everything that was deemed to have some sort of influence on the emerging culture. They soon became style bibles. Cutting-edge manuals of all that was deemed to be cool. Fashion, nightclubs, art, pop – if it clicked, it went in.

Nineteen eighty was Year Zero in terms of independent British magazine publishing, in much the same way that 1976 was Year Zero in the music industry, the date when lifestyle suddenly became an end in itself rather than a by-product of success, and when magazine publishing houses started to realise that men and women might be able to buy the same magazines.

Of the three, *The Face* was initially the most orthodox, being a glossy monthly. In the space of a few months, it became the benchmark of all that was important in the rapidly emerging world of British and – in a heartbeat – global 'style culture'. It was a well-produced, well-designed and well-written monthly with music at its core but with expanding coverage of the subjects that informed it, from fashion and film to nightclubbing and social issues.

I bought the first issue from the corner shop opposite my first-floor flat (above a greengrocers) in Stamford Hill, northeast London. It was a Sunday, back when Sundays really were Sundays, when little was open but pubs at lunchtime. Having been a long-term consumer of the *NME*, and having spent a year at Chelsea School of Art and being halfway through a graphics course at St Martin's, I was a slam-dunk target reader.

I loved *The Face* immediately.

The man who started it, Nick Logan, was already a peripheral hero in my eyes, as he had reinvented the *NME* in the early seventies, making my adolescence, and the adolescence of 250,000 other like-minded music fans, a rich and vibrant time. The *NME* was how we discovered everything from esoteric pop music to galvanising politics and cynical OTT cultural criticism; it was our own national newspaper, a place where passion and cynicism were encouraged in equal measure.

When I was hired by him, *The Face* and *Arena* (the men's magazine that Nick would launch in 1986, and which would cause a tsunami of publishing activity, including *GQ*) both operated from a small, converted laundry in Ossington Buildings, just off Marylebone High Street. For a while, this was the citadel of London cool, a place where everyone from Robert Elms, Nick Kent and Tony Parsons to Ray Petri, Jean Baptiste Mondino and Boy George would congregate, all of them metaphorically tugging their forelocks whenever Nick himself appeared. Logan was, like Terry Jones, one of the least demonstrative people you could ever meet, and yet he had a very tight and exact idea of what was right and what was wrong.

Nick asked me to go and work for him at the perfect time, when he was starting to expand, and when he could tell I was getting restless at *i-D*. I had loved my time working for Terry, but I knew there was nothing more I could do to formalise the magazine. I was frustrated there were still spelling mistakes in the magazine and didn't understand why it couldn't become more professional while losing none of its innate cool. So, Nick took me for a coffee and asked if I wanted to move across. He wanted me to contribute to *The Face*, but was offering me a big job on *Arena*, one that would soon turn out to be an editorship. It wasn't easy telling Terry, as he had been the one who had rescued me, reinvented me and helped me find a career. But I think he knew it was time for me to go, too.

The Face's *raison d'être* was simple: what was the correct thing to do? We would all sit in the downstairs 'War Room' and discuss exactly that, on a daily basis. In the year leading up to the 100th issue in 1988 we spent many nights in there, excitedly compiling a list of the most important events of the decade, from the emergence of Go-Go to the proliferation of the Filofax. And having shouted at each other for an hour or four, we would then trudge down to the Soho Brasserie in Old Compton Street to drink expensive imported beer and carry on arguing late into the night.

What *The Face* invented was a new way of looking at the notion of cool. And though this wasn't initially prescriptive, after a while the contents of the magazine almost became self-selecting: you could look at a layout and know immediately whether or not it was 'right'. In a sense, this collective idea of what was the correct thing to do was not only a reflection of the decade, but also a product of it. Hey, *The Face* even had a trendy estate agent to find it some new premises in recently gentrified parts of London – David Rosen at Pilcher Hershman, who employed the magazine's superstar designer, Neville Brody, to design the agency's logo.

Logan could do everything – he had almost singlehandedly put out the *NME* week after week during a strike at the paper in the mid-seventies – and everyone who worked for him was expected to learn on the job. The entire staff of *The Face* were also resolutely left leaning, as anyone who expressed an admiration for the Tories was put into the toxic box quite quickly. Eventually, politics would play an enormous role in the magazine, and yet the editorials were socially liberal rather than particularly strident. The left would often criticise *The Face* for exemplifying elitism, yet this was a massive oversimplification of what it, and its staff, stood for. *The Face*, *i-D* and *Blitz* all espoused liberal sensibilities, they just did it with a certain panache.

Logan was exacting. While sitting in our repro house up in Kilburn late one night during the final week of production (this is where we finished subbing and designing the magazine before it went off to be printed), I watched him spend over an hour carefully editing the intro to a tightly worded column on the back page (written by Geoff Deane). Having worked his way through yet another packet of cigarettes, he passed the page through, sat back and said, with as much satisfaction and enthusiasm as I ever heard him muster, 'There. Now fifty more people might read it . . .'

Each month, I would spend two weeks working on *The Face*, and then start production on *Arena*, although the staff on both were largely the same. *Arena* was all about detail. Every caption was as important as a cover story, the only pictures we used were originals (no dupes), and text was ruthlessly edited. Hacks didn't last long; they were lucky to get in the front door. We didn't care if newspapers and other magazines would rip us off; the important thing was to do it first and to do it best. Early one evening, Nick sheepishly came into my office to tell me that he thought I'd finished a piece too quickly. I was mortified, and he was right. You couldn't take your eye off the ball for a second because, if you did, you would be severely reprimanded by one of the team. The exacting standards created a very particular kind of camaraderie. We were united in our obsession with aesthetic one-upmanship, and we'd learned it all from Nick.

He could be unreasonably fastidious, but then he had extraordinary taste. He was an old mod, and he disliked and distrusted things that were at odds with his worldview. If someone wore the wrong shoes, or persistently used the wrong adjective, or had an annoying habit, that was it as far as Nick was concerned. Stephen Fry met Nick once and he thought he was the funniest man he'd ever met. We didn't really get this as Nick wasn't publicly demonstrative. He was drier than a dry thing. And we all loved him.

Arena was where I learned my craft and started developing my own eye for detail. This is where I learned about paper quality, the importance of pull-quotes (the text that was enlarged on the page to break up the reading text), the power of colour, the tricks of the flat-plan (the miniaturised page plan of the magazine, which would be the guide for the layout of the issue). I think I liked having the ability to control a confined environment, having total control over the content, the structure and the nuance of a magazine. After a childhood where I was constantly looking over my shoulder, I loved the sense of autonomy.

I learned quickly. I started to understand how you denote class from the relationship between words and pictures, and the way in which typefaces could seduce a reader. The more I learned, the more I learned to subvert, too. So having inherited the chaotic sensibility of *i-D*, I applied that to the orthodoxy of *Arena*, and started to produce a magazine that looked beautiful, read powerfully, but yet had both a sophistication and an energy, a kind of street energy. Thinking about it now, it was a magazine version of Roxy Music – glamorous, but cool, smart and gritty. We would spend hours discussing the right juxtaposition of images in a fashion story; pictures weren't just randomly plonked down but pored over endlessly. We were obsessive. It didn't matter how the end consumer treated the magazine – we knew it was as good as it could be, and that was good enough for us. If the reader wasn't smart enough to grasp the blood, sweat and tears the layouts had involved, then sod them.

I developed a gut instinct for what was good and for what wasn't. Inspired and encouraged by both Terry and Nick, I learned to trust my own judgement, and to create ideas rather than copy other people's. Everything was about judgement: is this any good? Is this great? Is this, well, actually rubbish? Would it look better if it were green and upside down? Actually, why am I asking? Of course, it would look better if it were green and upside down. I was learning a science but also learning how to subvert it and ignore it.

Logan was also obsessive about only taking the right kind of advertising, advertising that would flatter the editorial as well as the reader. You might have thought that an independent publication would take any advertising it could get, but Nick was emphatic about this. We would only take advertising if we liked it, if it looked good, and if it fitted with the way in which the magazine was developing editorially.

Arena fostered an extremely good relationship with Armani, who saw us as the younger, slicker end of their men's market. In 1990, we co-hosted a party at their gigantic shop in Knightsbridge. As usual, the brand and media partner pooled their celebrity contacts and came up with a list of suitable invitees. Increasingly these affairs were being filled with 'brand ambassadors', boldface names who were paid to wear their sponsors' clothes, espouse them in interviews, and to turn up at events like this one. The events obviously always worked best, however, if the people who turned up actually wanted to be there, rather than because they had been paid. This night, there were no brand ambassadors, and no one on the payroll, just a lot of media, customers and 'friends' of the magazine.

There was a largish room at the back of the shop, which had been reserved for staff and for those celebrities who wanted to dip out of the party. Towards the end of the evening, when I had tired of encouraging people to have their picture taken in the magazine cover photobooth (which produced a Polaroid of your face with the magazine's logo across the top), I stepped into the ad hoc green room for a glass of wine. As soon as I walked in, I was struck by two things, or at least two people: two celebrities standing in opposite corners of the room, each completely oblivious to the other's fame: Paul Gascoigne and John Malkovich. I thought to myself that not only did this show the wide appeal of the magazine, but it also showed how celebrity was changing. The era of the superstar footballer was just beginning. The event taught me a lot about branding.

ARENA HAD A HARD SATIRICAL edge, not dissimilar to Graydon Carter's sassy New York version of *Private Eye*, *Spy*, and the team enjoyed coming up with columns and story ideas that were primarily designed to annoy those mentioned in them. In early 1989, we ran a column about 'Coasters', those well-known names who had taken their feet off the accelerator – 'Not so much the jet-set as a fraternity of gliders, of very easy riders.' This was social anthropology with a twist, snark with bite, and in essence these ideas were simply well-manicured excuses to insult people. For instance, the list of coasters accompanying the article included Marlon Brando, San Lorenzo (the restaurant), Malcolm McLaren and Wales. Oh, and anyone in a charity football team.

This may have been the decade of the power lunch – L'Escargot, Alastair Little, 192 – and the cocktail hour, but in the world of Wagadon (Nick's small publishing company), all hands were needed on deck at all hours of the day. We arrived, we worked, and then we left – many times we went out, gallivanting around town, but often we simply went home to finish an article we couldn't afford to commission anyone else to write. (This was independent publishing, and we simply didn't have the budgets newspapers did, so we had to be inventive.) With *The Face*, as with *i-D*, there was a certain amount of growing up in public, and our enthusiasm was often enough to get us from gun to tape. I think we all felt enormous privilege in being able – largely – to write about anything that took our fancy, whether it was an esoteric new nightclub, a beer bar in Barcelona, a hitherto obscure sixties movie or the contorted prose of a forgotten nineteenth-century hipster. What these magazines offered was a sense of freedom, for their readers as well as their contributors. People maybe look back upon the eighties and think that a magazine like *Arena* was full of clichés, whereas in fact we were obsessive about offering precisely the opposite. If anyone on the editorial team (myself included) suggested anything approaching a cliché (by using a weak pun, for instance), they were literally laughed at. We were ridiculously hard on ourselves, too, and if we discovered a mistake in the magazine after it had been printed, we would fret about it for days.

Covers, though, were different, as I wanted them to be generic. Covers were vitally important for letting the reader know what a magazine *wasn't* as much as telling them what it was. And at *Arena*, the better we got at this, the more commercially successful we became. If the reader, or potential reader, was in any way confused by what they saw, then you could forget it; they just wouldn't buy your magazine. This didn't mean the reader wouldn't accept variety – it just had to be the right kind. I wanted the covers of *Arena* to differ completely from those of *The Face*. The covers of *The Face* could be wildly creative; in fact, they were meant to be wildly creative. I wanted the *Arena* covers to have a similarity about them; I wanted them to be uniform, elegant and orthodox, in order to turn the magazine into a brand. Ignoring any cultural entropy, I wanted to codify things and put them in boxes.

The first cover star was Mickey Rourke, which, in 1986, was just about the perfect cover choice for a men's magazine, regardless of whether it was British or American. The original idea, however, had been something different altogether. When Nick Logan met Lynn Doughty, the marvellous COMAG executive who had been charged with shepherding the launch of *Arena* (COMAG was the distribution company co-owned by Condé Nast and the National Magazine Company, the British subsidiary of Hearst), he was hesitant. He knew what he was about to suggest went against all publishing wisdom.

When Lynn asked who the first cover star was going to be, Nick said, 'Well, it's going to be a black and white picture . . .'

'Ah,' said Lynn.

'Of a boxer,' said Nick.

'OK,' said Lynn, her heart sinking.

'A black boxer,' continued Nick. 'And it's going to be the back of his head.'

Nick was intending to use a recent Albert Watson photograph of the back of Mike Tyson's head. Admittedly, Tyson's head was one of the most recognisable in the world, even from the back, but the distributors weren't happy.

'It's a nice idea,' said Lynn, ever the pragmatist, 'but it's not very commercial, is it?'

At the time, editors, publishers and distributors were all convinced that magazines with black people on the cover sold considerably less than magazines with white people on them. Both Lynn and Nick knew this to be bunkum, but retailers were less enlightened. There then ensued a conversation that resulted in Tyson being sacked off for Rourke (in colour, from the front), a far more orthodox solution and one that almost set a template for what came after, when I inherited the magazine. With *i-D* and *The Face*, it was important to keep challenging the reader, to continually offer them something they probably hadn't seen before (two of *The Face* covers I was responsible for, Jean Paul Gaultier and Neneh Cherry, could not have been more different from each other), but with *Arena* I wanted the covers to be as *Arena*-like as possible. Another analogy would have been Roxy Music (again), developing an idea until it didn't just become sophisticated, it became the very personification of sophistication. I wanted every issue of *Arena* to sound like 'More Than This'. I wanted to define what the cover style was, and then refine it every time. Of course, what you needed to guard against was complacency. And that was where your skills as an editor came into play, offering the same thing but different, every single time.

After all, a good editor or creative director knew that after you had found your formula, getting each cover right took no time at all. By this stage, when you knew the exact components that contributed to a successful mix, you could design a cover in a matter of minutes. You instinctively knew which kind of photographs, which cover lines and which colours worked. I always liked tightly cropped head shots, making the heads as close to life-size as possible. I thought the reader would identify more with someone if their head was the same size. It was like painting by numbers, and I compared this process to Tony Visconti producing that great run of eleven T. Rex singles back in 1970–3, from 'Ride a White Swan' to 'Truck On (Tyke)'; having created a great formula, he and Marc Bolan repeated it time and time again. This kind of thing also semaphored confidence, which was crucial to success whether you were creating a magazine or a hit single. And as soon as you lost that confidence, the reader could smell it a mile off.

Unless the reader understood the architecture of a cover then whatever you were doing as an editor simply didn't work. And some editors and designers, while being perfectly good at editing and designing, had no concept of what made a good or bad cover, and whether or not that cover was appropriate for their readers. If you were good at your job, you could take over a title and transform it in one of two ways, either by radical transformation or by seamless transition. If you weren't so good at your job, you could destroy the brand in a heartbeat; there were countless magazines that lost their mojo during the eighties when a new editor would come in and completely destroy the cover policy, confusing readers and advertisers alike.

I also wanted our cover stars to be suitably generic. We instinctively knew who would make a good *Arena* cover star, even if we didn't like them personally. They included Arnold Schwarzenegger, Rutger Hauer, Terence Trent D'Arby, Gary Lineker, Gary Oldman and Sean Penn. We also mixed these figures up with the likes of Richard Rogers, David Lynch and Antony Sher, boldface names who nonetheless would normally never warrant a magazine cover. I couldn't really put my finger on who made a good *Arena* cover; I just knew. The third issue I edited had Michael Caine on the cover (interviewed, brilliantly, by Tony Parsons), although it was Neville Brody's idea to use a classic David Bailey shot of Caine from the sixties, a picture Bailey once told me was his favourite of the period. In the nineties, lots of magazines would copy this idea (especially *Mojo* and *Radio Times*) but, when we did it, it really hadn't been done before. I initially thought it was an incredibly lazy thing to do, using an old photo, but as soon as Neville mocked it up, we knew how iconic it could be. Plus, I don't think we actually had anything else. It was already an iconic photograph, and it was about to be an ironic magazine cover. We would repeat the idea with Marlon Brando, Jack Nicholson, Paul Newman and Elvis Presley.

WORKING AT *THE FACE* AND *Arena* was intoxicating and relentless fun. There was only half a dozen of us in the office most days – Nick Logan; the advertising manager Rod Sopp ('A face only a mother could love' was one of his many catchphrases); Neville Brody, our brilliant if lugubrious art director; Kate Flett and Sheryl Garratt, who generated features for *The Face*; Kelly Worts, our picture editor; and Christian Logan, Nick's son, who was ostensibly the office manager but soon became a foil for Rod's incessant stand-up routine. I don't think I ever laughed so much as I did working for Nick Logan. His magazines had an extraordinary global reach and were hugely influential; whenever we were visited by people from abroad – writers, photographers, fans –

they would walk in expecting to find an office full of Agnes B-wearing aesthetes. What they usually found was Rod telling a decidedly un-PC joke and Christian shouting abuse at one of his equally West Ham obsessed friends on the phone. It was like being a member of the Bash Street Kids; ponderous media editors would arrive to do an interview with one of us, expecting to meet Cecil Beaton, Anna Wintour or David Sylvian; what they found instead must have been confounding.

The contributors were the very best: Jon Savage, David Toop, Chris Salewicz, Gordon Burn and so many more. Boy George would pop in, as would the Pet Shop Boys, Paul Weller, Stephen Fry or Jean-Paul Goude. One unsung hero was my friend Debra Bourne, who worked diligently for Lynne Franks, the original inspiration for *Absolutely Fabulous*'s Edina Monsoon. For a few years, Debra's antenna was so acute she was responsible for at least six cover stories of *The Face*, including Neneh Cherry and Jean Paul Gaultier. Our social lives were content, and the rationale for both magazines was simple: if you went out, it went in.

Pride was what propelled us, a collective understanding that only the best would do. Often, decisions were made in seconds; other times we might spend all day on a caption. And the caption would have to be good. (Kimberley Leston wrote a small piece about the pros and cons of wearing evening dress, which was illustrated with a photograph of Bob Hoskins looking like he is about to tear someone's head off. The caption? 'Bob Hoskins spots a man failing to show an inch of cuff.')

We spent an enormous amount of time making every page of *Arena* look as beautiful and as easily digestible as possible, breathing down the necks of our designers, treating each spread, each story, almost as a work of art. Nowadays, in the era of the internet, this seems crazy, but at the time we were obsessive. Every issue of the magazine was an art object, and it was our job to make sure it arrived in front of the consumer in as perfect a state as possible.

Pride and dedication, however, weren't always rewarded. Robin Derrick, who had joined Neville Brody's design team from *i-D* a year before me, was so enthusiastic when he arrived, in his first week he spent all night designing a new font to be used in headlines; as he left at 7.30 a.m. for a couple of hours' sleep before going back to the office, he saw a near identical font on the side of a bus.

NOT LONG AFTER I ARRIVED, Gordon Burn walked into the office with the script of his interview with Tom Wolfe, a man who had been an inspiration to all of us. Wolfe had just published his first novel, *The Bonfire of the Vanities*, a brilliant episodic drama about the money and social ambition to be found in contemporary New York. Wolfe had poured all his laser-sharp talents as a documentarian into a roller-coaster of a book, an adjective-rich potboiler that didn't so much scoop out the barrel of modern Manhattan as perform major exploratory and investigative surgery. In terms of contemporary reporting, if we (as journalists) thought that the cultural waterfront was being covered successfully by *Vanity Fair*, *The Face* and the *Sunday Times Magazine*, this raised the bar more than a notch. It made for fascinating reading, and encouraged many journalists to believe that their socio-economic observations and obsessions could be played out on a larger canvas. We were in awe. Wolfe's book was originally conceived as a serial in the style of Charles Dickens and ran in twenty-seven instalments in *Rolling Stone*. Like most people, I hadn't read the extracts, but devoured the heavily revised text in book form while on holiday in Italy, and it had immediately become my favourite novel of the decade. It went on to be a phenomenal bestseller (and a deservedly maligned film directed by Brian De Palma).

For me, this felt quite major, suddenly going from an environment where the minutiae of London club culture was all important, to a world in which Wall Street Masters of the Universe ruled supreme. Wolfe let light in on magic, describing his working day and the effect his clothes had on how he wrote. He had become synonymous with his tailored white suit, and even wore formal dress when travelling with Ken Kesey during his infamous acid tests in the sixties. He said clothing was a wonderful doorway that most easily leads you to the heart of an individual: it was the way in which people revealed themselves. 'I take some solace in knowing that Balzac was criticized the same way – he was obsessed with furniture,' he said. 'Details are of no use unless they lead you to an understanding of the heart. It's no mystery; it has to do with the whole subject of status.'

Wolfe said that writers, whether they wanted to admit it or not, were in the business of calling attention to themselves. His own taste was counter-bohemian: 'My white suits came about by accident. I had a white suit made that was too hot for summer, so I wore it in December. I found that it really irritated people – I had hit upon this harmless form of aggression!' His white suit had also become something of a suit of armour. 'It has done me so much good,' he said. 'Not long after I published my first book, I quickly found I was terrible at being interviewed. But then I'd read the piece and it would say, "What an interesting man; he wears white suits." And so it was a good ten years where the suits were a substitute for a personality.'

He told Burn he always maintained that if anybody in an interview asked him what he wore in bed, he would say double-breasted pyjamas with big lapels and frogging. 'They're what people *should* wear in bed. And I do in fact own several pairs, but they're made of such wonderful, heavy material, and all houses and rooms in America are so hot, you can't possibly wear anything like that. So my *official* answer is that's what I wear, but in fact I like nightshirts and the best ones I have are made by my mother.'

The only thing you couldn't see in Gordon's piece was the way in which Wolfe's tongue was stuck firmly in the corner of his cheek.

AS THE DECADE PROGRESSED, FOR pop people it wasn't thought sensible to have your photograph taken unless you looked your very best, and this wasn't thought possible without employing the talents of a stylist. All over London, stylists were now working with photographers to form partnerships through which they could forge a recognisable, and commercially viable, style.

One such partnership was Buffalo, although it was less a partnership and more of a collective. In the early eighties, a loose-knit gang began congregating in photographic studios in west London and in the nightclubs of deepest Soho. Primarily they were friends, but friends with ambitions: there were singers (Neneh Cherry, Nick Kamen), photographers (Roger Charity, Cameron McVey, Marc Lebon, Jamie Morgan), stylists (Mitzi Lorenz) and their mentor, a quiet man from Dundee called Ray Petri, who became pivotal to the look of *Arena*. Ray was also a stylist, but he had the kind of magnetism that drew people to him, specifically young creatives. A shy man with something of a stoic resolve (he didn't get frazzled, didn't shout), he possessed an uncanny coolness. The Clint Eastwood of trendy London; even Petri's voice was square jawed.

Petri was slightly older than the rest of what became his gang. Born in Dundee in 1948, he left for Australia in 1963, where he formed and sang with an R&B group, the Chelsea Set. Back in England in 1970, he got involved in the antiques business before becoming embroiled in photography – first as an assistant, then as an agent and finally as a stylist. It was here, in the early eighties, that he was to make his mark most deeply. Working with the likes of Charity, Lebon and Morgan, Petri began producing seriously iconic fashion photographs, creating a glamorised version of street style which, after initially appearing in *Honey* magazine, began filling the pages of *i-D*, *The Face* and then *Arena*. He mixed high fashion with streetwear, vintage with ethnic, and was a keen advocate of Black models.

Petri had a very particular vision, one inspired by the photographs of Walker Evans, Richard Avedon and Bruce Weber, and by old black and white B-movies, Jamaican street style, classic rock 'n' roll, the books of Hubert Selby Jr and by the London nightclubs they all went to – an American vision seen through strictly European eyes. There was always something insular about Petri's crowd, and it was this gang-like mentality that underpinned their creative energy. Rather enigmatically, he called this amorphous bunch of image-mongers 'Buffalo', and – very Petri, this – its pretensions had solid foundations. 'Buffalo was started as an umbrella,' he said, 'collecting different people with similar ideas all in one place . . . What we wanted was a creative agency which would channel our work. If you work for other people you soon become sucked into the mainstream, but with a corporate title suddenly everything takes on a different meaning.'

'People tend to associate the word Buffalo with Bob Marley's "Buffalo Soldier",' he said at the time, 'but in fact it's a Caribbean expression to describe people who are rude-boys or rebels. Not necessarily tough but hard style taken from the street. It's the whole idea of boys – and girls – together, just like it was when you were a kid going around in a gang, looking cool. Buffalo can be anything – a movie, a car, a sound, whatever. But basically, Buffalo is a functional and stylish look; non-fashion with a hard attitude.'

Buffalo was also something of a code, as what Petri was doing was shooting far more Black male models than anyone in the UK had done before.

'We became a family,' says Neneh Cherry. 'We had real group intuition, and really fed off each other's creativity. We were always aware of how valuable that was, but it was still funny when everything started rolling so fast.'

Juxtaposition was the stylist's currency, and back in the mid-eighties few juxtaposed with greater aplomb than Petri. From 1983 until his death in 1989, his pictures became the cutting edge of fashion via *Arena* and *The Face*. He was at the epicentre of a so-called British street style that was starting to infiltrate the more corporate worlds of advertising and the global music industry. While his signature was a streamlined classicism, tough-edged and Brandonesque, he had a knack of producing gay, iconic images that were somehow instantly appealing to heterosexual men. In the fashion pages created by Petri and the Buffalo team, credibility shone through, lifting the images off the page. 'I start outside of whatever I'm doing and try to look on it with a new perspective,' he once said.

Models were almost always found through friends, and ideas were formed on the street, not in a fashion editor's office. The Buffalo look went beyond style into attitude. This, unlike the ideas, was beyond imitation, as it was all in the casting. 'If the face fits, then it's fixed,' Petri used to say, and you only had to look at his pictures to know what he meant. 'The important thing in good styling is the people; once you have the right face it all fits into place.' He discovered Nick and Barry Kamen, hired Naomi Campbell when she was just fourteen, and made glossy paper stars out of a host of gorgeous-looking creatures whose Christian names became their monikers: Cameron, Tony, Simon, Felix et al. His pictures didn't have much respect for tradition. Here was the debut of ski- and cycling-wear as street chic, boxer shorts worn with Dr Martens boots, day-glo dungarees and cashmere tops, muscle-rippling boys in jewellery, wild-eyed girls in Crombie coats. This seems silly written down, and yet these images became incredibly powerful symbols of a rejuvenated London. Heavily featured in Buffalo pictures were city cowboys, Olympic heroes, leather-clad biker-boys, T-shirt De Niros – a hard, forthright mixture of mythical America and European street life. He could make a pork-pie hat, a white T-shirt and a pair of black Levi's look like a military uniform ('I think the strongest fashion statement that America has produced is denim,' he said. 'You have to go a long way back to look good in anything other than jeans.') He even famously put men in skirts, acknowledging the Blitz dressing-up box, but making the idea far more masculine in the process.

Perhaps Petri's most visible success was the surplus-store garment – the black nylon US Air Force flying jacket, the MA-1, which not only became the most ubiquitous fashion item of the decade, but also replaced the leather jacket as a symbol of rebellion as it traversed the global fashion underground. Unsurprisingly, it didn't take the rest of the world long to notice and, while the other members of Buffalo found sporadic fame and fortune, Petri was soon being courted from every area of the image business. Captains of advertising and publishing soon began knocking on the Buffalo door, asking Petri and his team to overhaul their corporate images, their ad campaigns, television commercials, promotional videos and editorial pages.

Petri was hired to work on the Julien Temple promo video for the David Bowie single 'Day-In Day-Out' – a lamentable career low for the man who was largely responsible for the Blitz and much that came in its wake – but managed to fall out with him almost immediately. The first day on set, Bowie came out of his trailer and pointedly asked Petri just exactly what it was he was going to do to him. Petri, taken aback by Bowie's laddish and out-of-character demeanour, told him the first thing he needed to do was ditch his leather jacket and to stop looking so old-fashioned. Bowie fired him on the spot, although he was persuaded to relent and let Petri stay for the rest of the three-day shoot.

Petri was also one of the main forces behind the launch of *Arena*. Working often with the American photographer Norman Watson, it was in the pages of the early issues of *Arena* that he would produce perhaps his finest work. In Petri's hands, androgyny took on a new form, a masculine image that was feminine around the edges, the counterbalance to a world awash with gender fluidity, at least in a visual sense. He defined diversity before it became a cliché.

Towards the end of the decade, Ray contracted AIDS, and his decline was swift. He developed sarcoma, his face covered with lesions, and very quickly looked like one of the walking dead. I went with him to Paris fashion week in 1989, and the reaction of people around him was astounding. Some were kind and asked him how he was – 'I have good days, some bad days,' Ray would say in response, repeating this like a mantra – and others went out of their way to avoid eye contact. It was so unnecessarily cruel and was something I will never forget. His death signalled the end of the eighties.

BEFORE *ARENA* LAUNCHED IN 1986, there were no men's magazines in Britain. There were genre-specific titles (fishing, motoring, etc.), there was the style press, and then there was pornography, but there was no general interest magazine that covered fashion, food, film and literature as well as sport, politics, cars and the modern malaise. Since the demise of *Town* in the sixties, the general interest men's magazine had become, if not the holy grail of British publishing, then at least the Bermuda Triangle. No one could try it and survive. Until we proved them wrong.

Because we were the first, we had the run of the toyshop, commissioning anyone within earshot to go out into the big, bad, matt-black, post-feminist world and bring back stories on everything from the Colt .45 and nouvelle cuisine to skincare regimes and sartorial promiscuity; from the Foreign Legion and Mike Tyson to mountain biking and Robert Bly; from the perfect Martini to the perfect blowjob, the fastest cars to the fastest women, the strongest beers to the strongest chorizo. We sent journalists to Hollywood and Romania, to Milan and Leningrad, New York and Beijing. On one occasion, we even tried sending someone to the moon, though the nearest they got was Peckham.

It's possible to illustrate the mercenary tendencies of the decade by the simple fact that they were spent going to shop openings; not 'happenings', not art events and not always concerts. We collectively paid homage to consumerism. I went to hundreds of parties in the eighties in many parts of the world, but oddly many of the ones I remember most took place in shops – the openings of Tower Records in Piccadilly, the Katharine Hamnett store in Brompton Cross, the relaunch of Harvey Nichols, the relaunch of Way-In at Harrods . . . And the thing that these parties had in common is the fact that at each and every one of them I saw famous people thieving – walking off with magnums of champagne, CDs, jackets, bottles of perfume, silver trays full of uneaten canapés, other people's girlfriends. Everything was free in the eighties, even the things that weren't meant to be (especially the things that weren't meant to be).

During the eighties the media went fashion crazy as London became a crucible of self-expression, the centre of anything and everything. Everyone wanted to buy into the dream, even pop stars. Style culture became the binding agent of all that was supposed to be cool. Catwalk models were no longer simply clotheshorses, they were rechristened supermodels. Fashion designers were no longer just considered gay iconoclasts or hatchet-faced prima donnas. They became solid-gold celebrities to be fawned over and profiled. Designers who had previously been demonised for their outrageous abuse of models and staff were now being sanitised for everyday consumption. Pop stars were no longer considered to be council-house Neanderthals, they were suddenly elevated to front-page sex symbols, whose every word was copied down, amplified and endlessly repeated in the gossip columns of the national press. It was a sartorial melting pot, a visual mélange of crushed velvet miniskirts, high heels and lipstick. And that was just the men.

In previous periods of intense fashionability in London – namely in the sixties, when class divisions in society first began breaking down – the consumer aspects were largely confined to the female market: trendy women's magazines, trendy women's shops, trendy female icons. But in the eighties, it was different, and if the decade can be remembered for anything, it should be as the decade in which the post-industrial man finally became liberated. If women found their (supposed) sexual liberation in the sixties, men discovered their social mobility in the eighties – as consumers.

At *Arena*, it wasn't the moisturisers or the flat-fronted trousers that stirred our souls, nor the eight-button polo shirts or the modernist bachelor pads. No, the greatest satisfaction usually came from the features: What Makes Michael Portillo Tick? The Myth of Male Bonding. The Post Modern Dance. The Curse of the Pub-Human. The Problems with Essex. Auto-Erotica. Male Rape. What Women Really Want from Pornography. Heroes. Sissies. Cyberspace. And beyond . . .

We also reintroduced the 'At lunch with . . .' feature, which had been popular in various magazines back in the sixties, but which had been consigned to the dustbin of history, along with Baked Alaska, Peach Melba and the Waldorf Salad. One of the best subjects was Bryan Ferry, gently skewered by James Truman. 'Il Cantinori being no kind of cheap New York spaghetti joint, the waiters have at least ten years of drama school training to assist in the recital of specials,' wrote Truman. 'Though largely self-taught, Ferry's aria of gloom is no less polished; it slips in and out of irony so softly that it plays like an ambiguous combination of self-pity, self-mockery and artful put-on.'

IN THE SPRING OF 1992, we published a series of literary parodies ('Rare Proofs') of Truman Capote, William Burroughs et al. Here's a slice of my Bunyon spoof, 'From Broadway to Soho' by Demon Onion:

> The Slounge is a very high-class trap which is patronised only by the better elements of rumpots and general newspaper guys. There is no band or floor show to speak of, but a good enough selection of fair-looking dolls, even if they are often accompanied by ugly-looking scribes. In fact, The Slounge has just about everything a man can wish for a good time. Personally, I never go there much, because I do not care for such places, what with the liquor being nothing extra at all.

By then, my idea of a good time – and London's – was also changing. When I started at *Arena*, I bowed out of London clubland. Having dipped in and out of the Blitz to no great consequence, in 1979 I threw myself into clubland with something of a vengeance. I like to think I was fairly dedicated, and I lasted until 1988, when – in the space of a few months – acid house turned a cult into a custom. Suddenly my double-breasted Jean Paul Gaultier jacket didn't seem to fit in among the T-shirts, whistles and bandanas at Shoom. I had been having dinner in the Groucho with the journalists Rob Ryan and Jon Futrell, along with Andrew Hale (who was 25 per cent of Sade). We had heard about this new club at the Astoria, and so we ambled along there around midnight. As we approached the bar, it looked empty, although people were still serving drinks. Having each grabbed a beer, we made our way into the auditorium only to find a sea of eighteen-year-olds wearing T-shirts and bandanas and all holding little bottles of water. The music, while intriguing, sounded like a fax machine on the blink. Acid house had arrived, and pop culture had switched again.

During that time, I had many favourite clubs: Chris Sullivan's first warehouse parties, Le Beat Route, Club for Heroes, White Trash, the Dirt Box, the Wag, Taboo – probably too many favourites, actually. One night in 1984 in the horseshoe bar in Do-Do's, I turned to Robin Derrick (who was dressed – in the style of the summer – in a pair of patent leather shoes and a pale-pink zoot suit with windowpane checks that appeared to be bigger than the suit itself), and said, rather haughtily, 'You know, these are the good old days.' For some, and for many people at the time, they were.

Nightlife was part of *The Face*'s DNA, and we covered it relentlessly. For the magazine's 100th issue, which was planned like a military exercise for a year before publication, we decided to do an exhaustive retrospective of the important London clubs since Billy's in Meard Street in 1978. One of the main elements was a ridiculously complex chronology illustration depicting the way in which the various clubs had morphed, merged and transformed over the previous decade. It looked not unlike a London tube map, although I had based the idea on something I'd seen in *Vanity Fair*, which had attempted something similar a few months earlier. London after dark had far more equity than New York's, and far more characters. As if to prove this point, we commissioned Bob Elms to write an accompanying essay, and then asked Kevin Davies to photograph a comprehensive group shot of all the major protagonists from the period, from Rusty Egan (The Blitz) and Susan Carrington (The Fridge) to Chris Sullivan (The Wag) and Oliver Peyton (Raw). We invited around a hundred people (Philip Salon turned up dressed like an astronaut, obviously), while the only important person who didn't appear was Leigh Bowery – we had to photograph him separately, and then stitch him in afterwards. He arrived looking like a Fabergé egg.

London didn't just attract people like Leigh, it encouraged and sustained them. Leigh had run the infamous Taboo club in Leicester Square, a nightclub that tabloid journalists would probably say looked like the bar in *Star Wars*, full of weird, alien beasts with intergalactic haircuts and tinfoil tunics. This is what I imagined the last days of Rome had been like, if the Romans had had discos. Everyone dressed up, everyone danced, everyone had sex. Lots of sex. Fucking in the toilets, blowjobs at the bar, girls doing girls, boys doing boys, everyone doing each other. There was one infamous female journalist (who later turned into a quasi-pop star) who used to trade blowjobs for coke, and could regularly be seen traipsing off to the toilets accompanied by a boy with a hard-on and a rolled-up £10 note. Another night there, two famous fashion designers, one feted contemporary artist and the lead singer of an enormously popular rock band were huddled together in a cubicle in the men's loo, hovering up cocaine as though it was going out of fashion (fat chance).

Sex appeared to be everywhere in those days, if you looked for it. Every night after Taboo (which was held every Wednesday, for almost exactly a year), the truly heroic would retire to an unprepossessing hotel behind Marble Arch, where one night one of London's most notorious cover girls serviced nine men at once. Around four in the morning this is where you'd often find the six 'Daisy Chain girls', who would decamp from Taboo or the Wag Club, bringing with them any available DJ/minor pop star/journalist/club runner/dealer who had a bag of user-friendly coke. Their party trick was lying naked in a circle, giving each other head, writhing around to the beatbox strains of the Beastie Boys, Schoolly D and Soulsonic Force.

Leigh Bowery could often be found here, holding court, while looking as though he'd turned up to a fancy-dress party. Wherever he was, even in a den of iniquity – as my friend Alix Sharkey said – he stood out like an erection in a convent. More through serendipity than design, Leigh had turned himself into a performance artist, one who revelled in the scatological. Once, at an event at the ICA in the Mall (just a few hundred yards from Buckingham Palace), I witnessed Leigh perform his 'piss piece', which involved him spinning around like a Catherine Wheel, urinating in a circle.

You had to be there, as they say.

ONE OF MY FINAL JOBS at *Arena* was commissioning a photographer to shoot Sade for our cover, to publicise the release of the band's new album. I chose Albert Watson for the job, and suggested he shoot Sade naked, something she had never done before, at a time when magazines didn't really do this kind of thing. I wasn't sure she would do it, but I figured I had nothing to lose by asking. I had started to put women on the cover, but I always tried to make the images quite coy, parodying vintage *Playboy* covers, and always with a twist. I wanted the covers to look classic and classy, not tarty and trashy.

The pictures Albert eventually took of Sade were remarkable, although I didn't actually see the full results until one of them appeared on the cover of the album, *Love Deluxe*, a few months later. We had been royally done over. Instead of being given the photographs the magazine had commissioned and paid for, we were given a selection of rather anodyne, black and white headshots to choose from instead. While I was momentarily irritated, the photograph that was chosen for the album cover has become one of the most iconic pictures ever taken of her – it's also one of the few where Sade used her very obvious beauty to shuffle outside her traditional comfort zone. It would have made a stunning magazine cover; instead, it made a stunning album cover.

My final event as the editor of *Arena* was at the end of 1992, at the British Society of Magazine Editors Awards dinner, the print-magazine Oscars. Against all the odds, I won an award, and what had up until about 10.45 been a fairly uneventful evening suddenly took a turn for the worse. Congratulatory champagne was delivered to our table, more wine was ordered, two newspaper editors decided now might be a good time to unsettle their differences, and an unscheduled trip to the Groucho was now on the cards. We arrived in Dean Street around midnight, only to find that the eighties had finally turned into the nineties. Keith Allen was there, as was Blur's Alex James, Tracey Emin and at least three other YBAs (Young British Artists), as well as what appeared to be half of Fleet Street. I spent the evening clutching my award as though it was the FA Cup, immediately grabbing it back whenever anyone snatched it out of my hands. Around 2 a.m., cabs were ordered, and we hobbled out into the street. As I emerged from the revolving door, with a champagne flute in one hand and my glass 'Editor of The Year General Interest Magazines Non-Weekly' gong in the other, it slipped to the floor, smashing into a thousand pieces. All that was left was a two-inch chunk of brass, which I hastily shoved into my pocket.

So much for independent publishing.

The *Observer* & the *Sunday Times*: Madonna v. Gwyneth Paltrow

Growing Up in Public

More Blonde Ambition, 1992

BY THE EARLY NINETIES, I needed to move on. I was self-aware enough to know that in the grand scheme of things, as a journalist or editor you weren't really taken seriously unless you'd worked on a national newspaper. So, when Simon Kelner was relaunching the *Observer Magazine* in 1992, I went to work for him. He took me for lunch in Joseph Ettedgui's Joe's Café, in South Kensington (I took a biography of Dan Quayle to read on the tube), he doubled my salary, and I started six weeks later, at the comically postmodern Marco Polo Building, coincidentally on the other side of Battersea Park, even closer to the famous power station than Ralph West.

Even though we were nowhere near, these were the last days of Fleet Street. As soon as I started at the *Observer*, I was shocked by a) the fact no one ever appeared to do any work; b) the way some of the staff treated drinking as a military exercise (I remember one leaving party at the Danish Club in Knightsbridge – which was one of Simon Kelner's favourite venues – where the great sports writer Hugh McIlvanney was so drunk, he violently threw up in the urinal, and then went back to the bar to order another triple vodka and soda); and c) the staff's cavalier attitude towards expenses. Petrol was the only expense you didn't need receipts for, so whenever I was in need of cash to supplement some bad debt or kamikaze drinking session, I would, every three or four days, have to make a circuitous and totally fictitious car journey to interview a circuitous and totally fictitious young actress in Cardiff (which was a fairly plausible place to drive to). I was going so often, on paper at least, that the accounts department suggested I start paying council tax.

Another time, I saw Simon emerge from his office with a fistful of receipts and a bemused look on his face.

'Who did I have lunch with last Thursday?' he asked me. When I shrugged my shoulders and carried on reading my *A–Z* of Cardiff, his face lit up as he remembered someone he'd seen on the way to lunch that previous Thursday.

'A sighting's as good as a lunch,' he said, before wandering back into his office.

Simon was extremely good at managing upwards, which basically involved giving Donald Trelford, the *Observer* editor, a lot of attention. He would spend just enough time with Trelford to flatter him, but not bore him. Calibrating this was itself something of an art, and Simon did it brilliantly. Trelford wanted to know what was going on, but he didn't need detail; he wanted to know which members of the staff were plotting against him, and he liked gossip. And Simon delivered all of this faultlessly. Consequently, we were largely left alone.

A lot of the senior staff were simply indolent. They would dribble into the office on a Tuesday morning (everyone had Monday off as the staff worked on Saturdays) in time for the weekly eleven o'clock conference, at which the week's stories would be decided. Then, two hours later, they would rush off to lunch, and that would be the last you saw of most of them until Thursday or Friday, when they would be back at their desks, attempting to put the paper together. On the magazine, we worked Monday to Friday, and so were rather bemused by this abnegation of journalistic duty. I immediately knew why the *Observer* wasn't as good or as successful as the *Sunday Times*: the staff didn't work as hard. Trelford worked Tuesday to Saturday, and had a daily ritual with his secretary, Barbara (no one called them personal assistants yet). As he was leaving his office to go to lunch, he'd turn and say, 'Unless I get lucky, I'll see you around 3.30.' To which his secretary would reply, 'I'll see you around 3.30 then.'

This was in the days of copytakers, where you would call up from a phone box outside a football stadium, or near the lavatory of a pub, or (if you were lucky) in the middle of a crime scene, and dictate your copy while the somnolent bods on the other end would interject with, 'Is there much more of this?'

THE NEWSPAPER STAFF DIDN'T TAKE too kindly to us magazine people as they thought – correctly – that our budgets were bigger than theirs. We also tended to have a lot more fun than they did. But then we deserved to. We weren't indolent. Even though we were already in the nineties, pop culture didn't rear its head much in the *Observer*. The arts editor, a ridiculous woman called Gillian Widdicombe, was called 'the Opera Nazi' behind her back, as little else appeared to get in the paper. Pop culture was deemed incidental, and marginal at best.

Apart from the frivolities, the new magazine we were developing was genuinely different from its competitors, and while we certainly enjoyed ourselves, when we worked, we appeared to work with more diligence than anyone else on the paper. Simon was very much a 'work hard, play hard' leader, and the magazine reflected that. He didn't have such a clear eye for detail, but he was exacting in other ways, always wanting something that was slightly better than the thing he'd just been given to read. In fact, I soon got into the habit of telling him a piece of copy had already been rewritten before he read it. I liked his quick decision making; he wanted copy that was powerful, direct, funny. And he could tell after only a few paragraphs if something was any good or not. This chimed with the way I worked.

I wrote a lot for the magazine, and I also came up with an idea which was soon copied by most of Fleet Street: in December, doing a review of the year told through cartoons, especially political cartoons, rather than the usual round-up. It was relatively cheap, original, and soon became the traditional way to round off the year.

I've still got the original dummies of the magazine at home; the idea was to try and recreate the excitement of the first Sunday supplements of the sixties, a magazine which reflected the changing cultural nuances of society in a world dominated by every other form of media. I'm not sure we succeeded, although the magazine certainly felt different from anything else around at the time. Plus, people noticed; in 1992, if you hired a new columnist or ran a particularly challenging feature, it would be talked about. Today, not so much. One of our best hires was John Lanchester, who became our restaurant critic; his columns were as funny and as trenchant as the work he would go on to do for the *New Yorker*.

Our big coup when we launched was buying exclusive rights to Madonna's *Sex* book, with photographs by Steven Meisel, which we ran over twelve pages in our 11 October 1992 issue, for the magazine's relaunch. We commissioned Martin Amis to interview her in conjunction with the extract, but word soon came back from Madonna's people in New York that Amis was too famous. Nevertheless, his appraisal of the book was more than apposite. 'The fact that Madonna regards the book as essentially comic – even the S&M poses are "meant to be funny" – shows how overevolved and tangential her own sexuality has become . . .' he wrote, 'there is the feeling that *Sex* is no more than the desperate confection of an ageing scandal-addict who, with this book, merely confirms that she is exhausting her capacity to shock.'

Amis wasn't wrong. Her book was basically designer sex for a world where that prefix could be applied to anything from mineral water to entire lifestyles. In the same issue, I interviewed Philippe Starck, the maverick French designer, who appeared to negate Madonna's mission. 'Most design is like bad radio reception – buzz, buzz, buzz – too ugly and confused. We must make important design that makes people think. It's the same for me to design a toilet brush or an aeroplane. I have no dream. I just want to make my work better.'

A few weeks later, I interviewed Herb Ritts, another late eighties imagemonger who was adapting himself to the changes in the culture, and a man who had spent his life photographing the type of people who rebelled against nothing but personal discomfort. Ritts didn't just portray the famous in a flattering light; to be photographed by him meant you automatically became a member of an exclusive club. His style was instantly identifiable, so naturally the people he claimed for posterity were identified as celebrities, whether they deserved to be or not. Celebrities who didn't deserve to be famous would become part of our lives more and more. Generally, the culture was getting harder, more brittle, and you could feel it on both sides of the Atlantic, with music, and specifically with comedy. Towards the end of the year, I interviewed Denis Leary, whose targets were rock stars, fortysomethings, liberals, drugs, just about anything and anybody. The latest acronym to set Madison Avenue alight was Grumpies – grown-urban mature professionals – ageing baby-boomers who had become their parents. The fortysomething generation, who had come to prominence at the end of the eighties, were the first generation to have made growing old fashionable. And Leary hated them. He lampooned the young and made a point of trashing the new Care Bear decade. Leary was an example of the Pepsi Generation gone wrong. 'We snorted, drank, and rocked our way through the past 20 years,' he said, 'and now we wonder why our planet's problems haven't been fixed? Fuck us and the polyester pants we rode in on. I hate the pious – we should blame ourselves, not everyone else.'

IN THE SUMMER OF 1993, after months of speculation, the *Observer* was finally bought by the Guardian Media Group (when I did a search on Google to try and verify some facts about the sale, it came back immediately with: *Did you mean When did the Guardian bury the Observer?*), with almost all of the senior staff, myself included, being fired. The *Guardian*'s editor, Alan Rusbridger, had sat in on various editorial meetings and obviously didn't like what he saw; I think he thought we were too raw, or maybe too much fun. (A few of the female staff told me they found him creepy.)

I had long suspected this was going to happen, so when I negotiated my contract the previous summer, I had made sure there was some contingency. I had already spent several weeks talking to various executives at the *Sunday Times*, where I ended up a month after leaving, initially as associate editor of the *Sunday Times Magazine*. Culturally, the atmosphere could not have been more different, and the heightened sense of editorial urgency was invigorating. Andrew Neil, who was still the editor, was a difficult man to work for, but he was good. Efficient, brutal, and the least sentimental journalist I'd ever met, he was a brilliant editor. He was also more than adept at dealing with Rupert Murdoch, the ultimate Sun King. 'All Sun Kings have a weakness for courtiers who are fawning or obsequious,' Neil said a few years after leaving the organisation. 'But the wisest – among whom we must number Rupert Murdoch – know they also need courtiers with brains, originality, and a free spirit, especially in the creative media business. But independence has its limits: Sun Kings are also control freaks – and they are used to getting their way.'

After I eventually left the *Sunday Times*, I would grow to enjoy Andrew's company (he held regular Sunday lunches, which were bacchanalian events that could last until midnight, at his flat in South Kensington); but when I worked for him, he could be trying. Before the first time I met him, for lunch in a Chinese restaurant near Wapping, a colleague who was also coming to lunch said: 'So, this is what will happen. He will be late, probably by about ten or fifteen minutes. He will sit down, find an excuse to be rude to a waiter, and carry on the previous conversation he was having as though we had been part of it. There will be no explanation and no apology for being late. He will hurriedly order some food, although ideally, he prefers someone to order for him; the only problem being that if you order something he doesn't like, you're going to get a bollocking. He'll then tell you what a terrible job you're all doing, and how the magazine would be vastly improved if you did X, Y and Z. Then, after about forty minutes, he'll get up and leave, without so much as a thank you, a goodbye or a well done.'

And that's exactly what happened.

THE SALIENT DIFFERENCE BETWEEN WORKING in independent publishing and national newspapers was, predictably, the reach, being read by millions of people instead of hundreds of thousands. The difference in the nineties was that the journalists like me who had migrated didn't have to adjust their language in order to address the wider demographic. This was a huge change in the culture and meant that when I wrote a cover feature for the magazine, I would write it in exactly the same way as I would have done for *The Face* or *Arena*. Of course, you might occasionally put the word 'architect' or 'designer' in front of someone's name, but basically you were addressing the same people. It's just that with the *Sunday Times* there were just so many more of them. I wrote about pop, fashion, style, cinema, books, clubs, media and the business of culture, and I genuinely felt as though that culture had changed unrecognisably in the ten years I had been a journalist. Where once people like me had felt outsiders, now we felt part of the mainstream. And we liked it. I know I did. I enjoyed being at the paper as I wanted to learn how the whole process worked, but what I didn't need was a bunch of dyed-in-the-wool people telling me I couldn't do things a certain way (principally because they'd always been done a certain way). I argued a lot with subs, who tried to mould my copy into generic *Sunday Times* text. Whenever they did this, I simply rewrote it my way. My favourite retort was, 'So what?' Quite quickly they realised I wasn't going to back down and they left me alone.

On the *Sunday Times*, every day was an adventure. One day I'd be in the Stevenage FC dressing room at half-time during an FA Cup match with Newcastle, the next I'd be editing a James Bond special. One day I'd be interviewing Brett Anderson in rented rooms in Westbourne Grove, the next I'd be arguing with one of our art directors about the best way to lay out an O. J. Simpson piece. No two days were the same, unless you counted the hundreds of days spent in the darkness in Wapping, poring over page proofs and interviewing people over the phone. The best thing was the editorial freedom, and being able to say, 'Stevie Wonder's in town, and I think he'd make a good cover story for the magazine.'

On this occasion, he was, and he did.

Now, you could tell a lot about someone from their press cuttings. You could tell a lot about the journalists who interviewed them, too. If you looked at most interviews with Stevie Wonder, they rarely mentioned his blindness. Perhaps they thought it would cause too much embarrassment, although I thought it was a bit like meeting an alien and not asking where they came from.

Having been blind almost since birth – he was premature and lost his sight after receiving too much oxygen in the incubator as hospital staff fought to save his life – darkness had always been Stevie Wonder's world. He says he was resigned to his condition (a condition which has informed all his work), yet for years rumours persisted about the amount of money he spent trying to regain his sight. In the mid-seventies he even volunteered to be a guinea pig in a series of eye-transplant experiments that had only previously been performed on animals. When I interviewed him, he said that other things were occupying his mind, and his response to questions about his sight echoed this: 'I don't care about it. I'm alive and I'm doing the best that I can in life, given what I have to work with. I'm not going to tell you that I wouldn't care if I was able to see, but I'm not going to spend my life saying how good it would be if I could. I've learned to cope.'

In late December 1994, Wonder arrived at London's Lanesborough hotel, en route from Ghana, where he was looking for a house. I waited three hours to talk to Stevie, not that that seemed unusual: his concept of time was different from other people's; making no particular distinction between night and day, he would sometimes sleep for three days solid. He could stay awake in the studio for even longer, doodling on his custom-made computers and banks of high-tech keyboards. When he was recording his breakthrough album, *Talking Book*, in 1972, in Greenwich Village's legendary Electric Lady Studios, surrounded by his ARP and Moog synthesisers, he often became so immersed in his newfound creativity that he would forget to eat or sleep. He always had a keyboard of some description to hand, and had an extravagant ritual involving his various synthesisers, wherever he went; his assistants had to be sure that he could touch one whenever he felt like it, doodling on the keyboard absentmindedly as others might scribble on a notebook. The singer Syreeta Wright, whom he married in 1971, divorced him eighteen months later, because 'He would wake up and go straight to the keyboard. I knew and understood that his passion was music. That was really his No.1 wife.'

Wonder was led into his suite at the Lanesborough by two large aides who hung around for a while after seating him to make sure their boss was happy. Wherever the star went, he was followed by a cavalcade of minders, assistants, press officers, fixers, friends and helpers. So protective were these people that I imagined this to be the kind of entourage that Elvis surrounded himself with in the seventies. Wonder treated his gofers with care, and they seemed to reciprocate. When we met, there were plenty of pleases-and-thank-yous, and when he asked for some peppermint tea and some 'biskits' in his faux cockney, the assistants laughed benignly.

He said hello politely and extended his hand, asking me various questions without seeming particularly interested in the replies, and then spent some time messing about with one of his aides, guessing coins by the way they fell on the floor ('That's an American coin . . . that's an English coin . . .'). When he was much younger, Wonder used to feel people's faces when he met them, and Motown boss Berry Gordy claimed that when he met young women he would 'let his hands walk'.

Wonder would always say this was purely accidental. (In the eighties the author and comedian Louise Rennison had some success with her stand-up show, *Stevie Wonder Felt My Face.*)

The image you expected was of a large, egg-shaped Black man dressed in loose-fitting, oddly coloured leisure clothing, a man with space-age dark glasses weaving his head from side to side in time to some faraway metronome. His weight had fluctuated over the years, and during the eighties he became so ample that it was necessary to dress him in a variety of ambulatory tents. At the Lanesborough, though, he looked if not exactly svelte, then certainly fairly trim. He was wearing a purple Nehru suit and a pair of sci-fi glasses that certainly lived up to expectations (the only Black celebrity to ever wear more extravagant eyewear was George Clinton). His braids were pulled back to reveal a mass of scar tissue above his right temple – the result of a near-fatal car crash in 1973. Sitting bolt upright in the dining room in his suite he looked like nothing less than a Buddha, impervious to criticism, weather or, come to that, time. He seemed regal – exacerbated by the fact that when you met him you had to do all the running. I had to speak – filling those empty spaces usually taken up with gesture – or else nothing happened. Because of this my words hung heavy in the air: did I say the right thing? Did I mumble?

It is surprising just how much his blindness affects you, surprising how difficult it makes any kind of conversation. The only way I could force the pace or change the topic was by interrupting him, which, I began to think, was a terribly rude thing to do to a blind person. To one of his replies I nodded furiously, then realised what a stupendously stupid thing this was to do.

One wondered what he saw, so to speak. I wondered, perhaps presumptuously, what he imagined I looked like. White, British, skinny hands. Could he tell that I was tall even though I was sitting down? And quite awed by his presence? His demeanour suggested he could see as much as he wanted to, and one got the impression that he didn't want to know any more about me than he could sense already. Having no doubt been interviewed by thousands of hapless hacks, he was probably accustomed to using his blindness not only as a shield but also as a weapon, a particularly intimidating one at that. He had fun with it, too: he habitually talked about 'seeing', and often caught people out by walking into unfamiliar rooms and saying, 'Hey, nice place you have here.'

I loved interviewing people such as Wonder as I liked meeting legends, liked hearing them tell me their versions of stories that had already become legendary, mythical. I enjoyed weaving their life stories into my interviews, attempting to create definitive profiles. This was actually quite a selfish exercise, as I simply wanted to meet them. Often, there might have been better people for the job, but there were occasions where I decided to interview them myself. I didn't think I was an especially good interlocutor as I was too respectful. Whenever I was commissioning other people, I would tend to be extremely specific about what I expected them to come back with; but I was far more benign when I was commissioning myself. I liked to think I made up for my journalistic failings with the way in which I dealt with their legacies; by now I had learned to write to a certain standard where I knew I could give a pretty good account of myself.

I wrote dozens of cover stories for the *Sunday Times Magazine*, as well as many features that nestled incongruously between the ads for opera cruises and Egyptian-style sofas, and I tried to make each better than the one before, whether it was interviewing Jarvis Cocker or Bob Geldof. Of course, the celebrity interview had started to be devalued, diminished by the extraordinary number of people who were now famous. Years ago, in the golden days of long-form journalism – when any new journalist worth his ink would spend the best part of six months with his subject before finally filing his copy – the celebrity interview was 'a very important thing'. But by the mid-nineties, where fame had become so homogenised, was conducting an interview still even a skill?

Time and restrictions were hugely important to the success rate of the celebrity interview, and if you had only been allotted ten minutes or so, then it was often best to go armed simply with twenty quickfire questions that you could turn into a breezy Q & A. Conversely, you might convince your celebrity to spend a few days with you, driving through the Hollywood Hills and hanging out at private views, exclusive concerts or film premieres, and then the interview could evolve into something more unique.

Any decent interview needed a certain amount of compromise; there needed to be a modicum of give and take. Ideally it should have been an 'I win, you win' situation, with both parties coming away feeling as though their lives had been enriched – if only in a small way. Both parties needed to give, while the interviewee needed to be generous with their time and anecdotes.

I interviewed Gwyneth Paltrow on the set of *Shakespeare in Love* for the *Sunday Times Magazine*, and she couldn't have been less interested. She gave nothing but monosyllabic answers and gave a good impression of someone who'd rather be picking skewers out of her eyeballs than talking to me. For me, it was an enervating experience so, having not got what I needed, I proceeded to interview everyone else on the set: the carpenters, the caterers, the sound guys, her chauffeur, the studio concierge, the make-up girls, the hairdressers – anyone I could find who had anything to do with her. I wasn't looking for a particularly negative story but, given Paltrow's unwillingness to talk to me, I had to get a story somehow. The feedback I got from those around her was not exactly positive. I simply asked everyone I met the same short question: 'What's she like?' Nothing else. Nothing supplementary. I just asked the question we all ask when someone we know meets someone notable. What were they like? And their answers – which were about 80 per cent negative – became the story. So, in the end she got what she deserved, which is a shame – for her. I reckon I'm a fairly easy person to charm, and if she had spent half an hour working her magic on me, no doubt I would have come away thinking Gwyneth Paltrow was a born-again Audrey Hepburn. But she didn't, so I didn't. In the *Sunday Times* for months afterwards, she was known as 'the cow'.

*

JOURNALISTS' TECHNIQUES WERE FASCINATING. WHEN A. A. Gill was interviewed by Lynn Barber, he said it was like being interrogated by Columbo. 'Oh, Adrian. Just one thing: you said you were wearing a cummerbund fashioned from yak gut and corduroy on the day in question. Where exactly did you say you bought it?'

For years, I made the cardinal error of trying to impress the people in front of me; I wanted them to like me, wanted them to understand how bright I was, and how well-versed I was in their work. I wanted Paul McCartney to think I was the only person who really understood why he was the most talented Beatle and wanted Keith Richards to think of me as a made man, a groovy young guy who never went to bed and had taken nearly as many drugs as he had. When I met ex-President George Bush in Dubai in 1994, again for the *Sunday Times Magazine*, I tried, in the space of two minutes, to impress him with my view on the conflicts in the Gulf. Once I even tried to contradict Shirley MacLaine's anecdotes about Frank Sinatra.

Fool. I should have just shut up and let them talk. My biggest sin was probably interrupting. You know, just as Siouxsie Sioux was about to tell me who she had been taking crack with last night, I'd butt in with: 'That's great, Siouxsie, but tell me about that bit in "Hong Kong Garden" where . . .' (That's a joke, by the way; I know that Siouxsie Sioux doesn't take crack.)

In general, my problem was I couldn't bear for there to be any gaps in the conversation and, in that respect, I was probably like a lot of journalists. But the trick was always to let the celebrity fill that space because, in reality, they're just as embarrassed by the silence as you. I knew one music journalist who was a master at this: a man who thought nothing of keeping silent for two, three, four minutes after his subject had temporarily stopped talking, thus forcing said rock star to start burbling about nothing in particular. Or, more pertinently, everything in particular.

Another important thing I learned was to never outshine the master. If you were interviewing a comedian, they didn't want you to be funny, they expected you to be the straight man. If you were speaking to a man whose success was predicated on his appearance, then it was important to not turn up looking like a dandy. And if they name dropped, it wasn't advisable to try and match them; much better to just sit back and be impressed.

The *Esquire* and *Independent* editor Rosie Boycott told me once that you could either be a good writer or a good editor, and you could never be both. I have to say that this was borne out by the number of newspaper and magazine editors who never wrote a thing. They might write an editor's letter once a month, or an introductory polemic when a big story was breaking, but basically editors edited, and writers wrote. I never did that, and always wrote as much as possible.

So, I suppose I was always grateful for the opportunity to write and improve as a writer. I also loved meeting people, whether they were politicians or rock stars, movie actors or chefs, fashion designers or artists. I was determined to make celebrity interviews as refreshing as possible, not just by choosing the appropriate celebrities and not just by clever casting with the people chosen to interview them, but also with the angle.

Sometimes, with celebrities, you were told to adhere to ridiculous restrictions, so I would be forced to resort to nonsensical methods. When David Bowie was involved with Tin Machine, he initially refused to do interviews unless the rest of his band were present. This put a lot of people off, but when Tony Parsons interviewed them (at my behest: we were at *Arena* at the time), he turned the situation to his advantage in the most obvious way: he ignored Bowie – for forty-five minutes. He quizzed Bowie's backing band (which is essentially what they were) about stage dynamics, recording techniques and group compositions until Bowie could take it no more. He almost exploded into the conversation, falling over himself to tell Tony the reason for his solo volte-face, and his frustrations with the music industry. By ignoring him, Tony got an extraordinary interview.

Another way to avoid the dark tunnel of product-specific questions was to confront the interviewee with 'the problem'.

'Hi, Mick. Your PR says that I can only ask questions about the record, but you don't mind talking about your sex life, do you? I mean, how does being gay affect your faith?'

'My PR said that? I don't mind at all. I've got some pictures on my phone of me having sex in church, if you'd like to see them.'

Of course, this didn't always work but, as a journalist, you assumed that the PRs' restrictions were rarely imposed by the stars themselves. And even if they were, you could usually cajole your celebrity into talking about the subject – if only in a defensive way.

With most celebrities there would be one question that was for ever off limits: one question that history had taught you to avoid. With Hugh Grant, it might have been his experience with Divine Brown (actually it was definitely his experience with Divine Brown); with Madonna, *Swept Away* (the shocking film directed by her husband Guy Ritchie); and as for Michael Jackson . . . Well, if you were lucky enough to get an interview you could have taken your pick.

But you had to ask it. You just had to. Mark Ellen, the former editor of *Smash Hits*, *Q* and the *Word*, had a failsafe way of asking the 'difficult question'. Throughout the interview he would say things like, 'Look, I know you won't want to talk about the thing, but I'm going to bring it up later,' or 'That's all very well, but I must warn you that we're going to have a little bit of a fight later!' Mark said, 'It softened them up – it let them know you were going to ask them something they didn't especially want to answer. So by the time you got around to it, they were almost relieved.'

When I worked on the *Observer*, we were offered an interview with Eddie Murphy who was enjoying a second flush of fame. The product Eddie was pushing, however, was a fairly useless rap record, and his Hollywood publicist told us that he would only answer questions relating to this particular project. Not only that, but we were only to be given forty minutes and it was to be in Los Angeles – not a cheap place at the best of times. Oh, and the PR had to sit in on the interview. Great! Just about the only thing they didn't demand was copy approval, but it was still a tall order. We ummed and aahed about it, but decided that it was too good an opportunity to miss; we'd have to find someone good enough to exploit the situation. That person, we decided, was Hugh McIlvanney, the greatest sportswriter the world has ever known (Scottish, gruff, then already in his sixties, known to enjoy a drink).

Now, we could have picked someone whose job it was to interview celebrities. Or we could have chosen someone famous themselves (Lenny Henry? Stephen Fry?). We thought about a flirty female who could flutter her eyelashes and cross/recross her legs; we even considered the likes of Martin Amis (who was then writing for us). But we decided we needed someone with some specific attributes: who wasn't going to be intimidated (by anyone), who knew nothing about hip-hop (thus eliminating the need for any protracted discussions about inspirations, motivations, choice of producers, etc.), who was smart enough to sidestep the PR's restrictions, and clever enough to run rings around Eddie himself. And that person was obviously Hugh.

Boy, did we choose the right person. The interview Hugh came back with was remarkable, covering all aspects of the celeb's life: his movies, girlfriends, ambitions, race, politics, sex – the lot. Oh, and there was even stuff about the record (the awful, pitiful record). So how had Hugh done it? The tape of the interview did the rounds in the office for weeks afterwards, and it was almost a masterclass in the art of interviewing difficult, protected and protective celebs. Stupidly, I have since lost the tape, but I still remember Hugh's opening question as though he asked it only yesterday . . .

'So, Eddie. I must say this new record of yours is quite a remarkable thing. I'm not an aficionado of this sort of music at all, but the way in which you paint yourself as the catalyst for this furore around you – the instigator – it strikes me that you are a man totally in charge of your own destiny, if indeed that's what we can call it. How did the making of this record, of all the things you've done, affect the way you see yourself? How does this latest project redefine what you are as a man?'

In fact, the actual question was probably four times as long as that, but the convoluted way in which Hugh approached his subject – and the meandering way in which he asked his question – opened Eddie

Murphy up like an oyster. And, for the next two hours, the comedian talked, and talked, and talked, and talked. Which, after all, was the object of the exercise.

And the record? The pathetic rap record Eddie was so keen to puff? It wasn't a hit.

And sometimes, it was just easy. I interviewed Shirley MacLaine for the *Sunday Times Magazine* at her ranch-style beach house way up in Malibu, the celebrity playground ten miles north of Santa Monica on California's Pacific Coast Highway. Along with Beverly Hills and Bel Air, Malibu was where the real Hollywood money lived, or at least where it came for the weekend. Sleek gunmetal Mercedes coupés, BMW soft-tops, vintage Corvettes, and the occasional personalised Rolls-Royce crowded the dirty beach road where MacLaine had her two-storey apartment. In the rarefied Malibu air, the signs on garages were unequivocal: unauthorised cars would be towed. Immediately. At the owner's expense.

I'd just spent two weeks driving across America, from New York to LA (with Robin Derrick, who was now the creative director of *Vogue*), and had to spend an extra week in the city waiting to interview MacLaine because she was sick. She eventually agreed to see me on her birthday, so on the drive out from the city that day I stopped in Malibu village to buy her some flowers. Assuming the florist was probably as expensive as everything else in the area, I spent about twice as much on a bouquet as I normally would; silly me – when I turned up at her front door, I was carrying a small garden centre in my arms, and probably looked to her like a rather enthusiastic stalker.

She was about sixty, and couldn't care less about being interviewed. She had a film to promote – a rather lame affair starring Nicolas Cage called *Guarding Tess* – and was simply doing the rounds. But she couldn't have been more generous with her time or her anecdotes. She didn't know me from a hole in the Pacific Coast Highway, but she was never going to read the piece anyway; and having been interviewed thousands of times over the years, I'm sure was long past worrying whether or not I was going to be kind or vicious.

Her house was on stilts, with the beautiful (and strictly private) Malibu beach to the front and a miniature Japanese garden, complete with ornamental wooden bridge, to the rear. In true Japanese fashion, it looked more like a hotel suite than a superstar's lair. She had always bragged that she was not interested in material goods, and her home was testimony to this.

There was carved oak furniture everywhere, with an enormous oak coffee table covered in crystals taking up much of the living room. Other tables were covered with African figurines, Chinese pots, Indonesian stone elephants and knick-knacks galore. There were Japanese prints on the wall, big potted palms on bigger rugs, and the obligatory windchimes. Dozens of small, silver-framed photographs showed MacLaine receiving her Oscar in 1984 (she accepted her long-awaited Academy Award, for *Terms of Endearment*, typically: 'I deserve this,' she said, to the hoots of the assembled Hollywood big shots); MacLaine with her parents, husband and daughter; with Warren Beatty; and with her many famous friends, including Jimmy Carter, Liza Minnelli, Jack Nicholson and the Dalai Lama. On the forty-foot veranda overlooking the Pacific there was a doormat. It was very Shirley MacLaine: 'Welcome UFOs and their crews,' it said.

I asked her everything and she told me.

BY 1994, THINGS WERE CHURNING again, both politically and culturally, in the UK and the US, as Britpop started to edge grunge out of the way. Soon, every music paper was hitching itself to the Britpop bandwagon. Its success was also influencing the national press, which meant me.

I met lots of Britpop stars at the time, including Jarvis Cocker. My most memorable interaction with him was at Bonhams in Knightsbridge, where the auction house was holding one of its irregular design sales. Lot 114 was something I had lusted after for years: a complete bound set of *Nova* magazines, from 1965 to 1975, this collection including the dummy edition, as well as – bizarrely – a book of promotional matches. Nova, not only the perfect manifestation of the

Swinging Sixties, but one of the most influential women's magazines of its time, a kaleidoscopic amalgam of provocative fashion, hard-edged journalism and gender politics. The estimated sale price was £500–£800, something of a bargain, so I thought I would be in with a serious chance.

In my eagerness to get a seat, I had dragged my soon-to-be wife to the front row and sat right in front of the auctioneer, so I was completely unable to see anything or anyone around me. I certainly couldn't see anyone else who might be bidding.

As I waited for my lot to come up, I could hear the room slowly filling up, and feel the cold sweat begin to form a shallow pool in the middle of my back. And when we finally got to Lot 114, my heart felt and sounded like Keith Moon's kick drum, only louder. The opening bid was small, in the hundreds, but as it quickly climbed, way up passed one thousand, and then two, there were only two people left bidding – me, stupidly sitting in the front row, and someone right at the back. As it reached £2,400, I shook my head and bowed out. And as I wiped the sweat from my brow, slightly cross I hadn't kept going, my wife leaned over and whispered, 'It's Jarvis Cocker.'

'Him?!' I whispered back. 'What the hell does he want those for? I hope he's going to steal the ideas and use them as well as I was!' In a way he already had. The cover of Pulp's 1995 LP, *Different Class*, was based on an old Nova layout, while the band's designers would continue to plunder the magazine's typography throughout their career. In a way, Cocker had always been very Nova himself: quintessentially arch, decidedly irreverent and studiedly cool. And someone who liked to wear his social conscience on his sleeve. Next to the braiding.

Afterwards, we found ourselves in the same coffee bar. While I queued up for some conciliatory cappuccinos, my wife went up to Cocker and asked him how high he would have gone, though on this occasion Cocker's legendary wit deserted him and he just shrugged and stared at the floor.

A few months after his successful bid, and several weeks after I had stopped putting pins in a small Jarvis-like Action Man doll, he was asked why he bought them. He said he wanted the magazines 'for the look and the graphic style', which he happily admitted to having plundered for the artwork on *Different Class*. When I spoke to him a few years later he said he was taking good care of the magazines, and if he ever tired of them, he'd let me have them. 'But I doubt I will,' he said. Asked in the mid-nineties if he had to go through an ugly bidding war to get the magazines, he said, 'I did actually. My rival was a man I vaguely recognised, and it became a really macho thing in the end. Whoever didn't get the women's magazines was going to leave that room never able to get an erection again.'

LOUNGE MUSIC – THE MUSIC from my childhood that had stayed with me ever since – was gaining some traction, too. This was music that made me feel clean, unsullied, satisfied and complete. It was also the music I inadvertently used to seduce my wife, Sarah. These were the records I played when I dragged her back to my Shepherd's Bush flat, the tapes I played in my BMW as we darted along the A303 on country weekends, the songs I sang to her as we strolled through Notting Hill on Saturday mornings. On our third date, I took her to the Atlantic Bar & Grill, which had just opened off Piccadilly Circus, a venue I had seen for the first time a few weeks previously.

Criticising a friend's entrepreneurial forays is tantamount to criticising their intelligence. It's almost as bad as criticising their partner, or, God forbid, their clothes. So when the future *Great British Menu* judge Oliver Peyton gave me a guided tour of a dilapidated, sunken ballroom in the depths of Piccadilly, telling me he was going to turn it into the biggest bar in London, I bit my lip and nodded enthusiastically. Even with his seat-of-the-pants success – being the first man to import Sapporo beer and Absolut vodka into the UK, running a dozen or so top nightclubs, managing implausibly popular pop groups – there was no way he was going to turn this *Titanic*-style wine lodge, with its brocade furnishings and vaulted ceiling, into a must-visit venue.

What did I know? It soon became the hottest bar in the world. It took me six years to summon up the courage to tell Oliver I didn't think the Atlantic was going to work. We were, quite naturally, in the Spearmint Rhino in Las Vegas. 'You didn't think it would fly?' he asked me, as the libidinous strains of lapdancing disco wafted around our ears. 'Well, neither did I. But I thought, if I'm going to go tits-up, then I may as well do it properly.'

Having been permanently banned from the Groucho Club for an altercation with U2 manager Paul McGuinness, Peyton had nowhere to drink in the evening, and so he did what any self-respecting entrepreneur would do, he opened his own club. He discovered his Valhalla in the basement of the Regent Palace Hotel, just off Piccadilly Circus, an NCP-sized ballroom complete with marble pillars and a super-high ceiling. Then, with money from Goldman Sachs, and a hastily assembled staff all kitted-out in Richard James suits, he opened a completely different type of venue: a club the size of a football pitch with a velvet rope outside. The drinks echoed the size of the venue. Shorts were long. Order a single measure and you'd get a double. Order a double and you'd get a quadruple. The Atlantic was designed in the vaunting spirit of the time, like a postmodern ocean liner. Like the decade it was born in, it wasn't a simulacrum so much as a new version of something old, a genuinely po-mo gin palace.

It was wildly successful, so successful that when I went, I often stopped off in Oliver's office, which was situated just off a landing as you walked down the stairs; often I'd stay in there all night, as most of fashionable London seemed to be in there anyway. Most, but not all. Oliver was somehow back in the Groucho one night with Alexander McQueen and Ruby Wax, and he asked the fashion designer why he never came to the Atlantic. Alex said, 'I can never get in.' So they walk around to the Atlantic, Oliver lifted up the velvet rope, and the security guy said, 'Where do you think you're going?' The staff loved that.

*

ART, AS MARSHALL MCLUHAN FAMOUSLY put it, is anything you can get away with. In the nineties, this was as true of pop as it was of literature, film or fashion, but it had never been so pertinent to the art world as it was then. Not only had quotation marks been used to excuse any artistic diversion into the banal or the kitsch, but because of the media's obsession with Britart, the idea of Damien Hirst making a video with Blur (or Marc Quinn making a video with Jarvis Cocker and Michael Barrymore come to that) was more interesting than the video itself.

Consequently, the time was right for any bright young thing considering a jump into the art pool. You eat cardboard and then videotape yourself defecating? Great! You manufacture quotation marks! Stop it! You and your brother produce pre-pubescent mannequins, with genitalia on their faces? Where do I sign? Well versed in the art of the soundbite, Jake and Dinos Chapman once said the reason they worked as a pair was because together they were only good enough to make one person's art.

'I think one of the reasons we started working together was because we were interested in the possibilities of developing a schizophrenic art practice,' Jake Chapman told me towards the end of 1995. 'When you're working with another person your views have to be that much more defined, much more argued for. It's fascinating because the end result will always be a little alienating. You almost become a spectator.'

Jake (then twenty-nine) and Dinos (twenty-five) became the art world's answer to the Gallagher brothers in 1995 when they exhibited their enormous sex-doll sculpture at the Victoria Miro Gallery, in London's Cork Street. Twenty shop-window mannequins designed as pre-pubescent girls were fused together into a single organism, their noses shaped into erect penises, their mouths and ears carved into voluptuous vaginas. Shocking, beatific and rather beguiling, these gargoyle-like figures looked like the result of a bizarre union between a Robert Crumb cartoon and a Cirque du Soleil dancer.

I wrote about them at the time, and finished my piece saying that whatever the Chapmans made of such comments, one thing was for sure: Marshall McLuhan would have been proud of them. I felt my piece was a perfectly reasonable account of the press reaction to their work, although something I wrote must have upset them. When I went to see their next show a few weeks later – *Chapmanworld* at the ICA, in May 1996 – they had scrawled some graffiti into one of their wallpieces, some of which mentioned me. I was immortalised in a YBA artwork with the following words: 'Dylan Jones is a domesticated twat.'

AT THE TIME, THE PRESS was saying the nineties was just like the sixties, but were the waves of optimism to be believed, or was this just some kind of consumerist mirage, a cheap vaudeville emancipation? Could London really be as exciting as it was in the sixties? Indeed, could London really be as exciting as Paris in the 1890s, when café society was at its peak, when the giddy security of peacetime, a booming economy and streets full of accordions and roses caused sybaritic ripples from Montmartre and Saint-Germain? Could the murky glamour of Martin Amis and Will Self hope to match the seamy romanticism conjured up by Guy de Maupassant, or had cosmopolitanism become as easily manufactured as the theme restaurants that lined Shaftesbury Avenue? Could London match the innocent ribaldry of the Folies-Bergère? Well, maybe, in its own, not-so-innocent way, it could.

Heddon Street, Piccadilly, had never been renowned as one of London's foremost dens of iniquity. In fact, until 1995, this small cul-de-sac that curves off Regent Street was only mildly famous for containing the telephone box that features on the cover of *Ziggy Stardust*. But by the spring a change had come. Not only did Heddon Street feature London's hippest art gallery, it was where Sadie Coles was to open her gallery space in 1997. It was home to Terence Conran's Zinc Bar, along with one of the most talked-about restaurants in London, the love-it-or-hate-it Momo's, the capital's most recent Moroccan bistro of choice. Opened in April by thirty-four-year-old Mourad Mazouz, this was the London branch of his 404 in Paris, for some years lauded as the most distinguished Moroccan restaurant in France. The food at Momo's was fine, though it was the basement that had caused all the excitement, a raffish private members' 'Kernia' bar where famous people occasionally held parties.

Momo's was a Magimix world of bright lights, dim corners, high-pitched sexual tension and fast talk (it was louche and loud), and the first night I visited was no exception. It was 9.30 on a Friday evening and the place was full of fashion designers, PRs, stylists, trust-funders and *hautes bohémiennes*, while pressed against the bar, standing like racehorses, were five women in their late twenties and early thirties, all dolled up to the nines, media women who worked in the fashion business, the music business, in the business business.

They were laughing – of course! – and they were knocking back the Bellinis, but apart from their enormous, expensive rings (all by Solange Azagury-Partridge, the current high priestess of cool), the thing you noticed most was that they were all smoking, one of them even a cigar. Later, there might be the odd spliff, and almost certainly there would be cocaine. 'These days, remembering your drugs is nearly as important as remembering your lipstick and credit cards,' one woman told me.

Luckily, I didn't like cocaine very much. Almost everyone I knew took it, and while I was no stranger to it, and enjoyed the thrill of taking it, I didn't hanker after it. I wasn't crazy about the way it made me feel a) while I was taking it, and b) after I'd finished taking it. What I knew it did was this: it made everyone talk way more than they usually did, and what they said was largely rubbish. On coke, you could fill dead space with any opinion and make it seem inspired. It also makes you drink more. As most people appeared to take coke at some point in the evening, so their night stretched out before them, often on until dawn. So if you took coke you'd find time to drink more, and if you didn't take coke then you'd drink more anyway, as you had to try and keep up with everyone else. If you weren't 'going for it', you had to at least give the impression you were.

I also very quickly lost patience with the cocaine hangover. For those whose drug taking was habitual, the best way to cope with this was to have a little bump at lunchtime; my solution was to stop taking cocaine.

This didn't appear to be an option popular with others. Pearl Lowe, the singer with Britpop band Powder and the girlfriend of Supergrass's Danny Goffey, took so much coke she was nicknamed Dyson. Cocaine wasn't just prevalent in the music industry, though; it seemed to be rife everywhere, particularly in the world of TV comedy. Steve Coogan says the second series of his BBC Alan Partridge show would have been better if he hadn't been taking so much cocaine.

Cocaine was a weird drug as it brought with it a kind of in-built obsolescence, almost as though you were predetermined to forget anything that happened to you while you were on it. This obviously meant that psychologically you were given a free pass every time you took it. Barriers would disappear, inhibitions evaporate, and a vortex of potential bad behaviour opened up before you. Cocaine was a virtual private members' club, which, when combined with an actual private members' club, made it extremely dangerous.

Back in 1994, as Sarah and I made our way along Regent Street, en route to Oliver's new gin palace (my wife wearing an eau-de-nil mini-kaftan and a pair of black Robert Clergerie mules, and me wearing a crinkly anticipatory smile), I swung round a lamp post and burst into song, croaking out the first two verses of Sinatra's 'Learnin' the Blues', about the tables being empty and the dancefloor deserted, etc. My wife said it was this public display of emotion more than anything else that convinced her she should allow herself to be proposed to.

Love is the Drug

Time to Get Married

With Sarah, smiling

I CLOCKED SARAH THE MINUTE I climbed on to the coach. Aurelia Cecil had invited me and another *Sunday Times* journalist, Simon Mills, to spend the day up at Castle Ashby in Northamptonshire, racing cars. In her capacity as the PR for Tag Heuer, she had invited us and dozens of other hacks to spend a day with the former Formula One driver Jonathan Palmer, who now made a living organising corporate race days. Tag were launching a new watch and thought this would be a good way to encourage us to take notice of this fact.

Aurelia had hired a luxury coach to ferry a bunch of us up north, and I saw Sarah immediately. I knew most of the others in the cabin, as the luxury world was a small one, and it was full of people I'd been bumping into for the best part of a decade. As they wearily climbed aboard the coach (it was 6 a.m., a time of the day alien to most people in the luxury world), which was parked outside Aurelia's Kensington offices, I mentally ticked them all off: the Tabathas, Alexandras, Samanthas and Cecilias from *Vogue* and *Elle* and *Vanity Fair* I'd been seeing at cocktail parties for ages. But I hadn't seen this person before. She looked different, too – wild, but not crazy; cool, but not annoyingly so; incredibly sexy and well-groomed, almost as though she'd been styled to appear in a Helmut Newton shoot that very morning; stunning, basically. Not your usual fash-mag readymade.

When we eventually arrived in Northamptonshire, we were given a mock-serious briefing, and then spent the day competitively driving Caterham 7s, 4 x 4s, go-carts, Formula 3000 single-seaters, and souped-up, track-ready VW Corrados. Before dinner that night there was an award ceremony, where we were going to be given little trophies for our endeavours. I found out the racy-looking woman was called Sarah because she collected the award for the Caterham 7 category, which she accepted with the alacrity of someone who appeared to have spent her life receiving prizes. And then immediately after this she was announced as the winner of the go-karting category, and so she got up again, giddy with excitement now, and obviously enjoying herself. She then proceeded to win every other category, five in all, and was immediately the star of the day, of the evening, of the whole event. There was a driver of the day award, and I'm not sure they even needed to announce her name as she came bounding on to the stage to grab it.

Wow. Who the hell was this woman? At dinner, I would find out, because I had been seated next to her. Or at least I thought I would; she seemed far more interested in the CEO of Tag Heuer, who was sitting on her right, and whenever I attempted conversation, she would shut me down with a wave of her hair, almost as Angelica Huston might have done if she had been channelling Miss Piggy. When she eventually tired of the CEO (he was called Neil, and regularly jammed with George Harrison, apparently), she turned to me. Her download was fascinating: she was the fashion director of *Harpers & Queen* but had just got back from four years in South Africa and Zimbabwe, where she had been – sharp intake of breath – a stylist, a video director, a cross-country driver, a hunter's moll and a professional white-water rafter. She was your basic *White Mischief* fantasy. She'd been working for *Vogue*, had gone on a shoot to Cape Town, fallen in love with the place – the landscape, the size, the smell, the freedom – and decided to stay. Having been brought up in the same regimented RAF world I had – we soon discovered our officer fathers were almost the same rank – she had been seduced by the innate wildness of Africa, and had decided to make it her home, exploring the continent with an abandonment she'd never known before. All this came out in a rush as she was pushing her sea bass around her plate, and it was as intoxicating as it was fascinating.

After dinner, having drinks in the bar, we discovered we both owned the same car – a 1988 silver, two-door silver BMW 320i – and so I challenged her to a race around the M25 the following weekend. We both knew it wasn't going to happen, but it was funny, and she appeared to have moved her position from 'uninterested' to 'currently tolerating'. Back at the *Sunday Times* the following day, I wrote her a note: 'Dear Sarah. I capitulate. But would you like to have dinner instead? Dylan x.' The next day, without seeing my letter (it hadn't arrived) she called me in the office to say the same thing. It was kismet.

Our first date was in the Belvedere in Holland Park, where I found out she had initially thought I was gay, that she had never heard of me, and that she was innately suspicious of single men in their thirties. Fair enough. Our slightly testy conversation wasn't helped by the fact Rick Parfitt from Status Quo was sitting on an adjacent table dressed in an electric blue satin suit, the kind of electric blue satin suit that can easily be seen from space. She immediately got it into her head that I had brought her to the Belvedere specifically because I knew he would be here, and that she would be so impressed that she wouldn't be able to resists my charms. She thought this was wildly amusing and proceeded to tell me this in a very loud voice, such a loud voice that Rick Parfitt himself was soon aware of our conversation.

Things moved quickly. We started dating, spending all our time together, and – quite quickly – moved in together. Our friends started to mix, too, with my west London mob bleeding into hers. The Notting Hill of the mid-nineties was like a principality, a world with, at its centre, 192, the Portobello restaurant that became a magnet for west London notables. Sarah and I used it like our own personal canteen, and as well as our close friends, it was regularly full of the likes of Alan Yentob, Malcolm McLaren, Mick Jagger, Jeremy Paxman, Emma Freud, Ozwald Boateng, Mariella Frostrup and Martin Amis, often all on the same table. Notting Hill had its own eco-system, its own way of managing the egos and narcissism of its residents, and we were no different. We felt special living there (even though it is the only place where I have ever had a gun pulled on me – for honking my horn at a stationary car at a green traffic light) but we always knew the postcode was the star, not us.

SOON, WE BOUGHT A TERRACED house in 'West Hampstead' – I love estate agents; it was right next to Kilburn Library – which we renovated and turned into a W11 outpost, where we seemed to have a dinner party every night of the week, usually full of Notting Hill renegades. And if Tag Heuer were responsible for us meeting, then Mulberry were soon responsible for our engagement.

Towards the end of 1996, we had been having a tough time. Sarah wanted us to move forward, and I was dragging my Cuban heels. She wanted kids, I didn't, and that seemed to be that. My own experience of parenthood had been appalling – having spent much of my childhood being punched and slapped in the face, it held very few positives for me – and I didn't feel like replicating the experience. I didn't think about this response with any great sophistication, I just wasn't interested in having children. So, sadly, we were quickly drifting apart. Still sharing the same house, but not the same head space.

One Saturday night, I had a work event I had to go to. None of us relished going out at the weekend, but Mulberry were a big advertiser, and they were hosting some godawful dinner in their store in Bond Street. So, I drove down there – in those days you could drive and park pretty much anywhere in London, even in the West End on a Saturday night – and did my jazz-hands dance while watching a completely unnecessary piano recital by the owner's son. It was one of those never-ending evenings that seemed to stretch out in front of you, no matter how late it got. Halfway through dessert, one of Sarah's colleagues – a lovely fashion heretic called Liz Walker – started listing Sarah's attributes and telling me in no uncertain terms how lucky I was to be seeing her. It was almost as though she had been planted there, Richard Curtis-style, a deliberate walk-on part designed to shift our own personal narrative. It worked. I dropped my spoon, ran out of the shop, and promptly drove back to West Hampstead. I rushed in, desperate to fall on one knee, only to find Sarah fast asleep in front of *Match of the Day*.

The proposal would have to wait.

The next day we were going to lunch at Ascot as a guest of Simon Kelner, who was currently pushing the limits of an industrial-strength entertainment budget at the *Mail on Sunday*. He was entertaining some clients (presumably to help offset the industrial-strength entertainment budget) and had invited a sprinkling of west London faces to spruce up the proceedings. Patrick Marber was at lunch, I remember that, and the fact this was the day after Frankie Dettori 'went through the card', riding all seven winners at the British Festival of Racing (it made him a household name and cost the betting industry an estimated £40 million). As we walked through the paddock after lunch, I proposed. Having received the correct response, we slowly walked back to the enclosure.

'Why have you got that strange look on your face?' asked Kelner as we walked in.

'We've just got engaged,' I said, beaming.

'Really?' he said. 'What did you do that for?'

Kelner, along with his other three *Daily Mail* apparatchiks, would be divorced by the end of the year.

SO, NOW WE NEEDED A wedding, and decided to use the small church in Alvediston, the small village in the Chalke Valley, equidistant from Shaftesbury and Salisbury. We'd been going there for weekends, staying in Samways Farm, and even though we needed special dispensation from the archbishop, this was the place we wanted. Unsurprisingly, I became incredibly prescriptive about the wedding. I thought I was simply being helpful, taking on a lot of the duties that would normally have been farmed out to wedding planners and enthusiastic relatives. But I wanted it to be perfect.

I asked my friend Toby Andersen, who had once formed Funkapolitan with my old college friend Tom Dixon, to DJ, and gave him a list of the records I wanted him to play, and in which order. This contained about two hundred great disco and club tracks from 1973 to 1995, from 'I Believe in Miracles' by the Jackson Sisters through to Skee-Lo's 'I Wish'; I wanted the evening to be the best club night imaginable, full of D Train, Nuance, Space, Donna Summer, Odyssey, the Bee Gees, MFSB, Chic, etc. I wanted a cavalcade of the transgressive and euphoric music we had spent two decades dancing to, from the best gay disco – Coffee's 'Casanova', Lime's 'You Love', 'I Can't Take My Eyes off You' by the Boystown Gang – to club classics like the SOS Band's 'Just Be Good to Me', 'I'll Be Around' by the Detroit Spinners and R. Dean Taylor's 'There's a Ghost in My House'. Toby, the dear love, didn't seem to mind.

I spent weeks honing the speech, but while it went down OK (first line: 'When Sarah told me we were getting married . . .'), and the speech by my best man Robin Derrick contained the perfect amount of skewering, the most effective speech was delivered by Claire Denholm (née Bowen, Sarah's oldest friend), which Tony Parsons said was the best speech he'd ever heard anyone give in public. I think it was appreciated by only about 65 per cent of the guests, seeing that my friends on the tables reserved for 'Fleet Street' had already (and predictably) taken proceedings to another level. One particular hack was responsible for a lot of this behaviour. Later, hearing Toby drop a record he was particularly keen on, he stood up to rush to the dancefloor only to find one of his chair legs caught in his turn-up. After spending a minute trying to extricate himself, he gave up and simply dragged the chair to the dancefloor, where he could be seen for the next five minutes, cavorting with a rented gold-gilt banqueting chair. He then left the dancefloor, and on returning from the loo, announced to what he thought was his own table, but was in fact a table containing most of my family, that this was in fact the first time in several weeks he hadn't peed blood.

It was that kind of wedding.

Of course, this was the mid-nineties, peak Britpop, peak YBA, peak Lad, when London was awash with A-grade cocaine, much of it supplied by a dealer nicknamed the Milkman – because he always delivered. I was adamant I didn't want any class As at our wedding and told a few of my friends who were perhaps a little more enthusiastic in their leisure activities than others. Naturally, they thought I was joking. But I very much wasn't and said I didn't want dozens of people disappearing to the portaloos in order to set themselves up for another twenty minutes on the dancefloor. I was already growing tired of coke culture and didn't want our wedding to be remembered for it. They were disappointed, but reluctantly adhered to what they obviously thought was an extremely strange request.

In the swell and squall of the wedding, which, like all important events, seemed to last both a nanosecond and an eternity, I'd forgotten about this, and was simply enjoying the way in which Sarah and my lives were presently colliding, surrounded by our friends and family, past, present and future. Around nine o'clock, as I was walking back to the farm from the local pub, where I had just deposited my ageing aunt who was staying there, I passed the local phone box, which was surrounded by a dozen of my friends, eagerly listening to one of my ushers. He was on the phone to his sister in London: 'I don't care how you find it, just find it!' I gather an hour or so later, a motorcycle courier arrived with a large briefcase full of supplies. His sister was also soon the lucky recipient of a brand-new Donna Karan dress.

Terry Jones offered to film the wedding, and spent all day interviewing many of the 150 guests. I could see him carefully weaving his way through the tables, grabbing people off the dancefloor, and sidling up to friends and relations as they left the tent. In the end, the tape got lost by the processing lab, although a photographer we knew from New York, Troy Word, had filmed large sections of the meal, including some of the speeches. He was sitting behind the Fleet Street zone, and whenever we played the video afterwards, to our parents, I had to cough at a very particular spot, as one of the overly refreshed hacks shouted an especially profane soubriquet just at the very moment I was cutting the cake.

Friends.

Our wedding day quite rightly remains one of the three most important moments of my life, and it's one I constantly replay in my mind. The moment Sarah walked into the tiny church, looking radiant in her Vivienne Westwood dress, as 150 people gasped in wonder, is something that's always with me.

With Sarah, I started travelling the world. Up until my late twenties, I had never really done holidays, and it was only when I started working for Nick Logan that I began carving time out of the diary. Before then, all I had done was work. I felt so privileged to be gainfully employed, doing something I genuinely loved, that the thought of going on holiday never really occurred to me. I would go on press trips, or travel halfway round the world to interview someone, or host a party in New York, Toronto, Paris, Milan etc., but I'd never decide to just down tools and go to a beach for a few weeks. I hadn't done this as a kid, either; the only holidays we ever had as a family were the annual two weeks in Paignton, on what was still laughingly called the English Riviera. We stayed with my grandparents, and I can't remember ever going outside. We watched television, mostly, or took never-ending car journeys to boring places that took so long to get to, we would immediately start the return journey as soon as we got there. As a family, we didn't do the beach. I could never swim – still can't, even though as an adult I tried and tried and tried – so the adolescent delights of beach holidays, or even dressing for the beach were complete anathema. It's probably why I very rarely wear sunglasses.

But with Sarah, holidays very much became a thing, and the world suddenly opened up. Skye. Essaouira. New York. Tobago. Majorca. Italy. Kenya. All over. And what great fun it was. I had already started spending a lot of time in America, seeking out the places that the previous generation had already fallen in love with . . . Twenty years earlier, as I had been falling for the likes of David Bowie, Bryan Ferry and Elton John, they themselves were falling for America, conflating the realities of the country with the fantasies they'd also had at a similar age. The music they made was initially full of American dreamscapes – the whole idea of Roxy Music was twisted fifties glamour – which quickly transmuted into an Anglo-American hybrid.

It was also incredibly instructional travelling with Sarah, as she packed so well. I would take enough clothes to last a month – any eventuality had to be anticipated, obviously – but she travelled so much for work that she'd learned to pack everything into a carry-on bag. Including me. She also had this annoying habit of wanting to arrive at the airport just as the plane was taking off, which drove me bats. I would very happily arrive a couple of hours beforehand, and spend the time mooching around the shops, or, when I finally got a fancy card, lolling about in the lounge reading newspapers. I always expected any journey to the airport to be interrupted, so I didn't see any harm in arriving early. Sarah had the same attitude towards parking. She would want to drive into the West End in the hope of finding a parking space right outside the restaurant, cinema or theatre, almost as though she had special dispensation from a higher entity. The fact that she was often able to do this infuriated me even more.

GQ: Into the Building and Out of the Traps

Hangover Square

Deep in Vogue House, 2001

'JONESY, APPARENTLY, YOU'RE OFF. IT'S in the papers.'

The chief sub wasn't wrong.

I was working in the newsroom at the *Sunday Times* when I heard I was going to be the new editor of *GQ*. This was March 1999, and James Brown, the ex-*Loaded* editor who had been parachuted into the magazine by Condé Nast chairman Jonathan Newhouse to try and give it some laddish oomph, was out after eighteen months. According to *The Times* I was about to replace him.

This, of course, was news to me. It also wasn't something I thought I'd necessarily be interested in.

I'd been at the *Sunday Times* on and off for six years and had no intention of leaving. I was editor-at-large and was having the time of my life. I had just turned down a big job at the *Independent*, and really didn't think I'd ever leave. My job meant I could work for the main paper, for News Review, for the magazine, and for all the sections – Culture, Style, etc., without anyone breathing down my neck or asking where I was.

My great benefactor was Robin Morgan, a *Sunday Times* veteran who was one of the best newspaper and magazine journalists I'd worked for. When he described a prospective feature, he actually wrote the story as he told it to you. He even wrote the intro. If you were quick enough, you could write down what he was saying, and when you came to write the story, having done all the reporting, you invariably found that the way Robin had written the intro was precisely the way you should do it.

I was free, so why would I want to go back into the brutal regimen of magazines? The piece in *The Times* made my appointment seem like a *fait accompli*, even though I hadn't had any contact with Condé Nast. I'd been sounded out about the job four years earlier, when the magazine's then editor Michael VerMeulen had unceremoniously died (the victim of a tragic and much publicised overdose involving some hookers and several bags of coke in his Islington apartment), but declined the invitation as I was helping Nick Logan – the wizard for whom I had worked at *The Face* and *Arena* – on a new launch.

So why would I be interested now, when my current job afforded me an extraordinary amount of freedom? I'd only just spent three months going through photographer Terry O'Neill's archive for a twelve-part series in the *Sunday Times Magazine*, and had just had three days in Portland, Oregon, where I'd been researching a big feature on Tinker Hatfield and the recent transformations at Nike. I could write reviews and op-eds, jump on a plane to New York or Los Angeles to interview a film star or go to a fashion shoot, or should I choose to, do stints in the newsroom. Life was varied and life was good.

Did I want to edit another men's magazine? I'd already successfully run *Arena* for four years, so did I really want to go back to the world of cufflinks and shoe trees? Also, did I love the idea of being the custodian of a title that was full of flesh? I didn't think I did, but then I started to think that, actually, maybe I could bend this magazine to something I actually *wanted* to do. Selfishly, I thought I might be able to turn *GQ* into a completely modern type of magazine, using its men's magazine casing as a Trojan horse. In the same way that *Vanity Fair* ran its often-fawning cover stories to disguise a thoroughly brilliant package of unparalleled journalism, so I could use pretty girls to do the same for *GQ*.

Then I had a call from Condé Nast encouraging me to throw my hat in the ring for the *GQ* job, and I suddenly felt like a schoolboy who had just been told a girl who sat on the other side of class 'liked' him. In a heartbeat, I realised that not only did I want to do this job, but that I *really* wanted it. I recognised the emotion immediately, as it's something I've been prone to all my life. I'd felt it with jobs, books and, yes, with women too. Of course I wanted to go out with her – what was I thinking! Because basically if I didn't go out with her, someone else would.

So, I went for a drink with Nicholas Coleridge, who was running Condé Nast in Britain. He asked me to come and have a chat at his house in Kensington Park Gardens, in Notting Hill. We sat in the first-floor drawing room, which was painted yellow (all the rooms in houses like this were painted yellow). Nicholas wore a purplish Nehru jacket, which slightly shocked me, as it was the first time I'd seen him in mufti. He drank a beer (something that also surprised me), and I had a glass of white wine.

Afterwards, I wrote a lengthy description of what I would do with the magazine should I be hired. I've still got a copy (I keep everything), and my thoughts were simple and direct: while there was no expectation and certainly no desire for me to do so, what I wanted to do was create the best magazine in Britain. I didn't just want *GQ* to compete with the ever-growing raft of men's magazines – *Esquire*, *Arena*, *Men's Health*, *Maxim*, *FHM*, *Loaded*, etc. – I wanted to produce a magazine to rival Graydon Carter's *Vanity Fair*, or indeed the *Sunday Times Magazine* itself. Perhaps irrationally, possibly arrogantly – in fact, definitely arrogantly – I thought if I was going to go back into magazines then

I needed to do it properly. Comprehensively. Definitively. Wouldn't that be fun, I thought to myself? Wouldn't that be a wheeze? To really go for it, to really put the hours in, to lift up the bonnet, armed with a pantechnicon of Swarfega, and produce something genuinely important, something worth keeping, something benchmark. I knew this would involve making a spectacle of ourselves, and I knew that it would have to ruffle a few feathers in order to properly work. But I didn't care. I had a thick enough hide, I thought.

Don't get me wrong, I wasn't trying to recreate the *Times Literary Supplement* here, and one of the gravest criticisms of *Esquire* was that it was too worthy. We were a men's magazine, after all, and there had to be a certain prescriptive, robust patina to what we did. We were still deeply entrenched in what would become known as the 'lad's mag era', and it would have been commercial suicide to produce anything too genteel. This wasn't going to be a Radio 4 afternoon play. I wanted a magazine with a lot of punch, but with a lot of clout, too. It needed to be a heavyweight title. A heavyweight with a big gold championship belt (and if not gold then at least 10-mm-thick cast metal decorated with white and red gemstones).

Andrew Neil had reinvented the modern-day, post-Harold Evans *Sunday Times* by borrowing from magazine culture, by introducing a multi-sectioned paper that was full of lifestyle, culture and commerce. It worked brilliantly and was copied by everyone else in Fleet Street. I wanted to go the other way: we already had a multi-sectioned luxury magazine and what I was going to do was fill it with the very best writers I could afford from the broadsheets and the tabloids.

I wanted to edit a magazine that was full of metropolitan swagger, that could maybe do for London what *New York* and the *New Yorker* did for Manhattan. We wouldn't have the same budgets as the *New Yorker*, but I could use the same ingenuity we'd used on *i-D*, *The Face* and *Arena*, where we constantly produced world-beating editorial on a shoestring. There was terrific material in the likes of the *Sunday Times*, the *Observer* and the *Independent* so why wasn't it on display in a monthly magazine?

I wanted a lot of politics, and a robust mix of broadsheet and tabloid journalists to write about it. Investigative journalism had all but disappeared from magazines, as it was soon to vanish from a lot of papers. So, I needed some of that, too. I needed proper cultural criticism, and the kind of urban, snarky stuff that New Yorkers did so well, and that the *Independent* had started to do so convincingly. As Tina Brown used to say when she was steering *Vanity Fair*, it was all about the mix. We would do entertainment and celebrity interviews better than anyone else, and we would make the magazine look beautiful.

I didn't understand why Tony Blair hadn't been on the cover of *GQ*, and I didn't understand why the fashion was so pedestrian. The magazine was going to look stylish, and it was going to be bold. It was going to have Simon Kelner taking famous people to lunch, it was going to have Mick Brown and Robert Chalmers writing the kind of pop-cultural, socio-economic broadsides they were so good at, it was going to have Michael Bracewell writing about culture, Stuart Maconie pontificating on music, Danny Kelly writing about whatever he wanted to, and – hey, this might be a good idea! – why don't we ask A. A. Gill to write and direct a porn film? After all, we were living in an incredibly heightened media atmosphere, and magazine publishing in Britain had become extremely high octane. So, wouldn't it be a zeitgeisty thing to get the country's best critic to immerse himself in the seedy world of pornography? *Nova* would have done it back in the sixties, so why couldn't *GQ* do it in the nineties? I was laughing so much at the thought of it – I was already imagining what Adrian would write – that I wanted to get the job simply to see the piece in print.

I rather grandly told Condé Nast I wanted to walk into Number 10 holding a copy of *GQ*; I said I wanted it to be a magazine people felt they had to read, whether they actually wanted to or not. I would imagine my vision for the magazine must have seemed pretentious and tremendously hifalutin, but I meant every word. It was obviously convincing because a few weeks later I was offered the job.

It happened while I was on holiday in Barbados. We were staying at a hotel next to Sandy Lane, which was closed for renovation. Sarah and

I were taking our nine-month-old daughter Edie on an Easter break, enjoying the newfound pleasures of infant jetlag. Rather sweetly, the negotiations took place over fax and phone between myself and Nicholas Coleridge, and rereading the faxes now, I'm surprised I was so bullish. I really wanted this job and yet spent seventy-two hours haggling over the salary. I turned down two offers before settling on a figure that seemed to make sense. Coleridge at one point said, 'I don't even pay [Alex] Shulman that!' I didn't believe him, as I was pretty sure the editor of *Vogue* was going to be more than handsomely rewarded, but by then the deal was done.

I was to start in two weeks, and I was very excited.

WE LIVED IN BAYSWATER, JUST north of Hyde Park (we still do), so I walked to work on my first day, little knowing that this was a journey I'd be doing for over twenty years. My office was on the first floor of Vogue House, in Hanover Square, halfway between Oxford Street and Bond Street, which was also home to *Vogue*, *Tatler*, *Condé Nast Traveller* and other titles, as well as the UK commercial office of *Vanity Fair* (the magazine was editorially identical to the US version, only with British ads; clever idea). Glossy magazines were in their pomp, and the British home of Condé Nast was justly recognised as the citadel of glamorous cool. This was the holy grail of magazine publishing, the red velvet castle, and I had just successfully negotiated its drawbridge. I might soon be falling into the moat, but as I couldn't swim, this was something I tried not to think about.

So many people warned me about joining Condé Nast, saying it was a viper's nest of backstabbing and bitchery, telling me I'd be forced out in months. This couldn't have been further from the truth, as I loved the place immediately. I particularly enjoyed all the (mostly) apocryphal stories about the personnel department's infamous acronyms ('NPLU' for example, Not People Like Us); my favourite was the doctrine that they wouldn't employ girls with fat ankles as fat ankles were common.

I was fairly certain I had fat ankles.

…y parents, Audrey and Michael, in Egypt, late 1940s, with …l the world before them.

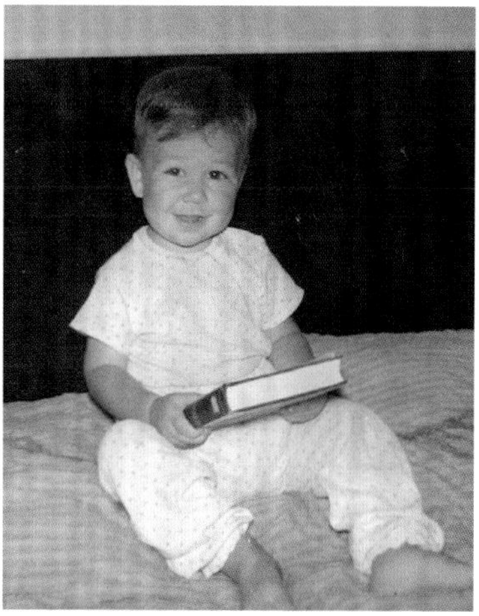

Me, as a small boy.

Daniel Jones: five years younger and the yang to my yin.

Early adopter: *Whizzer and Chips*, *Archie*, *Goal*

1975, aged 15, complete with roll neck, flying jacket and bumfluff, outside The Nag's Head.

1976, aged 16, two days after hearing the first Ramones album. Plimsolls not pictured.

The *NME* in 1972: my teenage bible (both testaments).

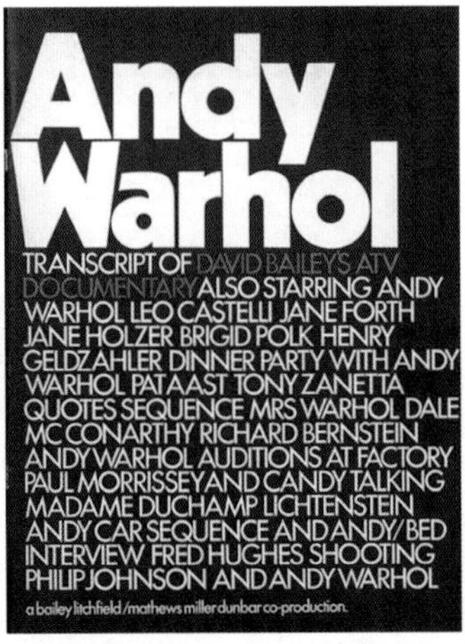

The transcript of David Bailey's film about Andy Warhol.

1975: Bryan Ferry on the first cover of Street Life.

ptember 1977, in the Ralph West Halls of esidence, Albert Bridge Road.

Gabba Gabba Hey! My photograph of Johnny Ramone at Friars, Aylesbury, May 1977.

y photograph of the Clash at the Rock Against Racism rally in Victoria Park, April 1978.

Punk, stolen from Chelsea School of Art, Manresa Road, in August 1977.

1978: Jordan, *Ritz*, and two worlds colliding.

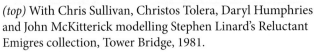

(top) With Chris Sullivan, Christos Tolera, Daryl Humphries and John McKitterick modelling Stephen Linard's Reluctant Emigres collection, Tower Bridge, 1981.

(above left) With Corinne Drewery in St. Martin's, 1979. Photograph by John Ingledew.

(above centre) Boulevard – a world opens up and I dive right in.

(above right) Fiona Dealey and Boy George with Rusty Egan at the Blitz.

(right) In Club For Heroes, 1980.

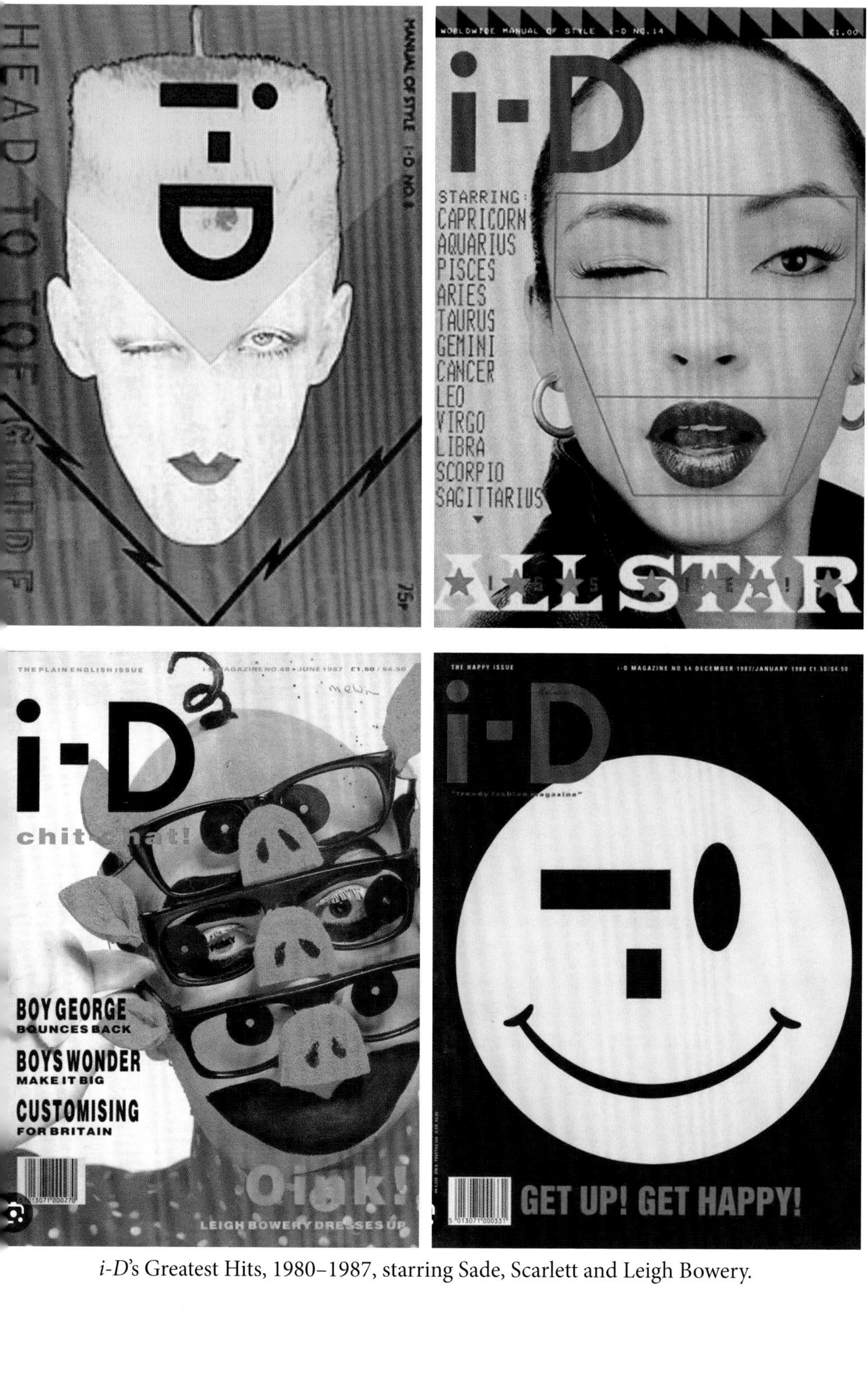

i-D's Greatest Hits, 1980–1987, starring Sade, Scarlett and Leigh Bowery.

"Vaughn Toulouse, Vaughn Toulouse, baby I'm Vaughn Toulouse ..."

With Jonathan Ross at the Trouble Funk gig at the Town and Country Club, 1986.

DJing at a Miners benefit at the Wag Club in 1984, with Harry Enfield, Jerry Dammers, Vaughn Toulouse and Bedders from Madness.

i-D party at Danceteria, 1984, with Rudolf Piper, Leonard Abrams, Nick Trulocke and Alix Sharkey.

Nick Logan's babies: Jerry Dammers, Jean Paul Gaultier, Neneh Cherry, Michael Caine and Arnold Schwarzenegger.

(above) Best men: Robin Derrick and me by Terry O'Neill, in 1993.

(right) Hotness: Sarah Walter.

(left) The Observer: Hunter S. Thompson.

(right) The Observer: Madonna's Sex book.

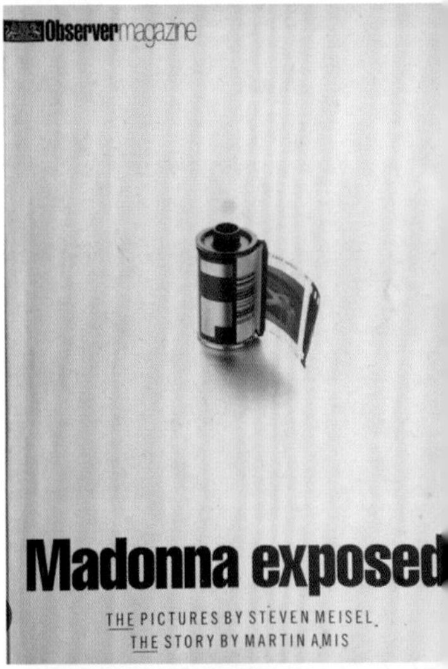

(left) Sunday Times Magazine: Suede.

(right) Sunday Times Magazine: Rachel Welch.

That day, my first, I got a hand-delivered postcard from a friend who already worked in the building, on the upper floors. 'Condé Nast will give you a lot of rope,' he wrote. 'It's up to you if you decide to hang yourself.'

It became the first thing on my new pinboard. And there it stayed until I left, twenty-two years later.

My office had recently been the victim of a visit from a so-called feng shui expert and had so much furniture in it that I could barely negotiate it all. It soon went but, in the meantime, I had to have all my meetings in a large room that looked as though it was an outpost of Furniture Warehouse. Nevertheless, on my first day I fired someone, which was standard business practice, and then very quickly worked my way through the vast list of contributors, most of whom I had no interest in. The new *GQ* was predicated on the very best journalism money could buy, and there were very few people on the masthead I wanted to keep. I had a list of who I wanted to work for the magazine, and so I systematically courted them. I wanted writers gifted in the art of defenestration, who wrote with nuance, who had big voices, ridiculously funny writers such as the lugubrious Robert Chalmers or the sarcastic Adrian Deevoy, and the kind of journalists who were going to elevate the title. I wanted to open up the magazine to those writers who could write at length about the pop-cultural renegades of our time, and of times past. I wanted writers who could tell a story through the prism of access, and who could dance around a subject with deftness and wit. If a writer asked me what I wanted them to write, I'd say, 'Write what you can't write anywhere else.'

I wanted mad stuff, long stuff, big stuff, stuff that was going to stick.

The revolution couldn't be so dramatic that it alienated the reader, but then who were the readers anyway? Editors tended to think their readers were more sophisticated than they were, and publishers always claimed they were, as they knew that's what the advertisers wanted to hear. I thought our readers probably wanted to have fun, enjoy what they were buying, and didn't want to be patronised.

MY FIRST BIG HIRE WAS A. A. Gill, who was still at the *Sunday Times*. I'd always liked Adrian's TV and restaurant columns, but I thought he should be writing features, and he should go out and do some proper reporting. I actually thought he was wasted as a critic because he'd been doing it for so long. So I gave him the opportunity to stretch his legs, so to speak.

When I hired him, I took him for lunch at a smart, futuristic restaurant in Albemarle Street called Coast, owned by our mutual friend, Oliver Peyton. The previous evening, I'd had a completely accidental night out, as another friend, my ex-editor at the *Observer* Simon Kelner, had recently been made editor of the *Independent* and was working his way through media London, having a succession of 'joining' parties, and so I had only got to bed a few hours before meeting Adrian. In fact, this was the only time in my life I have used eyedrops, to try and make me seem a little more human. I sat rather desperately through lunch, showering Adrian with praise, as he peered at me suspiciously, trying to work out what was wrong with me.

Anyway, when I told him how much I was going to pay him – which was an absolute fortune – he stopped peering so intently, and the praise started coming in the other direction. (Writers, I knew, liked three things: a) money: as much as possible; b) company: being in a publication full of other writers they respected; and c) space: having their work displayed over acres of newsprint.)

Everything Adrian would write for us was funny. And trenchant. And poignant. And discursive. And witheringly, brutally honest. Over time we became friends (sort of), and he was someone I always looked forward to seeing, not least because he always had an original take on something, whether it was an election, a plate of pasta or a new bespoke suit ('I see you've got a new Richard James,' he would say. 'It's deliciously awful, isn't it?').

Famously dyslexic, he would dictate his copy by phone, which meant every month one of the features team would be charged with calling him up and typing down his invariably late stream of consciousness. And you could always tell who was enjoying the privilege that month as they would be crying their eyes out with laughter. Either that, or saying something like, 'You can't say that. Adrian, you'll have us in the courts . . .'

He wouldn't tolerate fools, let alone suffer them gladly. If you were out with him, at a party, a dinner or one of the many awards ceremonies where Adrian would be collecting yet another gong for his pieces in our magazine – and in the decade and a half he worked for me, he wrote about everything from golf and fatherhood to sex and Glastonbury (a commission which I'm pretty sure he never forgave me for) – he would usually alight on some poor unsuspecting muggle (or 'civilians', as he liked to call people who didn't share his ridiculously sophisticated worldview), and tease them mercilessly. One of his favourite pastimes was accusing people of wearing something for a bet. He occasionally did this to me, laughing out loud at a tie I had just bought, or questioning the suitability of wearing turn-ups after cocktails (he also had a thing about people wearing the wrong tweed; for him it was as bad as playing with yourself in public). His other favourite pastime was finding new things to tease his best friend Jeremy Clarkson about. Adrian was one of the very few people who could point out Clarkson's most obvious weak spots – the billowing jeans, the bubble-perm, the Hitchcockian beer gut – and get away with it. Principally because they loved each other. Adrian had his own weak spot, too: he couldn't write fiction, but then at least he tried, which is more than most of us have.

Adrian would soon start popping into the office, completely unannounced, usually after lunch, and walk around the newsroom poking his nose in. The staff soon got used to superstar journalists imperiously strolling the aisles and trying to look important, but Adrian was never condescending or trite; he was a journalist through-and-through, and his default position was always one of curiosity: What's this? Why did that happen? Who took these marvellous pictures? Where can I buy these cufflinks? He could see through a piece of writing as though it were an X-ray, and often, after I'd been blathering on about how good so-and-so's most recent piece for us was, Adrian would give me an old-fashioned look and then spend ten minutes telling me precisely why it was anything but. And he was often right. He would give compliments, but they didn't arrive on a regular basis; so when one did arrive, you tended to treasure it. Yes, he could be a snob, but it was a qualitative snobbery that was largely based on whether or not something deserved to be acknowledged as being any good. He hated arrivistes pretending to be posh, as well as posh people pretending to be poor. He loved celebrities, but not as much as celebrities loved him.

MY SECOND MAJOR HIRE WAS Boris Johnson, who I asked to be our motoring correspondent. I took him to Le Caprice for lunch and offered him £1 a word for a monthly 1,000-word column. We sat at the corner table, the one Princess Diana always used to have, and as Boris furiously made his way through the bang-bang chicken, he accepted like a shot.

'What a wizard idea,' he said, looking, rather alarmingly like Doc Brown from the *Back to the Future* films. 'This is going to be a lot of tremendous fun.'

Which it was, until it wasn't.

I hired Boris for two very good and very pertinent reasons: he was not only a very erudite writer but a funny one too. I'd read a piece he had written in the *Daily Telegraph* about driving an Audi for a weekend, and it was so funny that I thought he could give Jeremy Clarkson a run for his money. In a car, that is.

Other writers followed: Michael Bracewell, Andrew Anthony, Jessamy Calkin, Dominic Lawson, Miranda Sawyer, Tom Wolfe (a coup), Peter York, Will Self, Nik Cohn, Philip Norman . . .

And Nick Kent.

AS A DEVOTEE OF THE *NME* in the seventies I had grown up on a diet of Charles Shaar Murray, Paul Morley, Max Bell, Ian MacDonald, Nick

Kent and suchlike, rock scribes who were given the space to delve into their subjects without fear of the sub-editor. If you were a rock writer in the early seventies then sex and drugs came with the territory, as they still do to a certain extent. When Kent kicked into gear – so to speak – rock journalism was going through one of its golden periods. Due largely to *NME* editor Nick Logan, during the seventies the paper became legendary in Britain for its acerbic, cynical and occasionally puerile attitude towards the music industry in general and rock stars (any rock star) in particular.

For me, the *NME* was a gateway drug to everything that came after – *Interview*, *Rolling Stone*, *Ritz*, *Boulevard*, *The Face*, *Vanity Fair*, *i-D*, the *New Yorker* – while its journalists were part of a golden era. Nick Kent was already a friend of mine, and I had commissioned him on *Arena* and the *Sunday Times Magazine*, and I wanted him in *GQ*. In terms of journalism, Nick never had a problem with telling good stories. His problem was only worrying about what to leave out. He was an advocate of the theory that good rock journalism should highlight the power, the glory and the depravity of music, not just the theory. It should concentrate on the flavour of rock, not just the aftertaste. It was all very well getting in a tizzy over the 'validity' of David Bowie's *Station to Station*, or discussing its place in the 'rock canon', but what kind of drugs was the Dame taking when he recorded it? And whose drugs?

It goes without saying that not all rock stars took too kindly to this type of speculation, viewing it as some kind of gross intrusion, incompatible with their own POV. But if journalism doesn't offer to say the unsaid (if not always the unspeakable), then it is little but PR.

Kent was, when all is said and done, the definitive rock 'n' roller. Towards the end of 1986, Nick was dining with his friends David Bowie and Iggy Pop in a little Chinese restaurant in Gerrard Street, in Soho. Confronted with a triumvirate of pop icons, the confused, if starstruck waitress approached the man who most looked like a rock star for his autograph. Bowie and Iggy were shocked. Nick was flattered.

It's not so surprising that rock stars are often disparaging about journalists. After all, having been courted and feted early in their careers, it's natural for them to feel betrayed when these self-same writers start clinically monitoring their descent.

But there are journalists, and then there are journalists called Nick Kent.

Towards the end of the eighties, I started writing a book about the legacy of Jim Morrison and spent over six months travelling to Paris and New York and back, meeting Morrison's common-law wife (who at that time had yet to be interviewed by anyone about the singer) as well as many of his friends, colleagues and associates. I also spent days hanging out at the singer's grave in Père Lachaise, interviewing backpacking Norwegians who'd come to pay homage to him. But one key figure proved elusive: the rather self-aggrandising biographer Danny Sugerman, who co-wrote the notorious Doors tome *No One Here Gets Out Alive* in 1980. Having created his own little industry from posthumous Doors-related material, he didn't appear inclined to help any rival biographers. Understandable, really.

I persisted, as there were certain questions about Morrison that I thought only Sugerman could answer. Having tried unsuccessfully to get through to him, I asked Nick to help. This he did by drafting a letter – actually a fax – to Sugerman, that began: 'Dear Danny, You might remember me. I once OD'd in your bathroom in LA with Iggy Pop in 1974 . . .' Only Nick Kent could have started a letter like that.

Frank Zappa once famously said 'rock journalism is people who can't write, preparing stories based on interviews with people who can't talk, in order to amuse people who can't read'. He wasn't far wrong, though Kent was never just a music journalist. Like Hunter S. Thompson, Nik Cohn and Lester Bangs before him, there existed around Kent an almost mythic glow. Degenerate poseur, celebrity drug addict and genius wordsmith, he was a man who lived rock 'n' roll to the full. ('I could tell you stories about Nick Kent that would uncurl the hair in your Afro,' said Morrissey in 1990.) During the seventies Kent was as famous for his drug intake as he was for his journalism, and from 1974 to 1988 was addicted to heroin, cocaine, methadone and various tranquillisers. 'At the age of 19 I started smoking hashish in earnest,' he said, 'and then moved on to speed and cocaine. Finally, I was offered some heroin, and that was it for me. It was like being in heaven, it was ecstasy. I thought: this is worth getting lost for. But I got hooked and it took me 14 years to kick it. The drug robbed me of my writing talent [not true] and I'm still angry at myself for getting so involved, but it was so seductive. I was on a death trip.'

Towards the end of the eighties Nick moved to Paris, primarily to escape the hundreds of heroin and methadone dealers he knew in London. Before he left, he stayed with me for a while, at my flat in Shepherd's Bush. One day, I found him in my tiny gallery kitchen: 'Dylan, how does this work?' It was a kettle.

THE MAGAZINE'S DESIGN HAD TO change as it was currently too, well, masculine. I wanted *GQ* to look like a magazine from the golden age, a magazine that was as elegant as the coffee tables it was going to end up on.

The elephant in the room, of course, was the fact that the men's magazine market had become so sexualised that it was difficult to wade your way through them all without swimming in acres of female flesh. The market now demanded women on the cover. Even the top-end magazines – *Arena*, *GQ* and *Esquire* – had had to go down this route, but not with any great success, as the gratuitous sexuality seemed at odds with the upmarket premise of the titles. I thought the best way to cope with this situation was through irony, or at least acknowledging the heightened times we lived in.

Some hires didn't really work out. My ex-girlfriend Jessica Berens didn't like the sexuality of the magazine, which was still fundamental to its newsstand success. Ian Hislop politely said he was too busy, and Jeremy Clarkson said he could contribute 'occasionally'. Bryan Appleyard, another *Sunday Times* writer, was there at the beginning, but wasn't especially engaged; I needed writers who were going to buy into the idea of a brash, smart monthly, and what I didn't need was people just doing it for the money.

Assisted by my redoubtable deputy editor Bill Prince – one of the staff members I wanted to keep, and who would stay with me for the duration of my tenure at Condé Nast – I attacked the budget. Everything was going to go into content. I cut back on all unnecessary office fripperies, organised what I thought was an extremely simple system for filling pages with self-generated material, and poured money into the contributors' pot: the money we had was going to be spent on writers and photographers. Having worked in Fleet Street I knew precisely what people were paid, and what the relevant sliding scales were. I started loudly telling everyone how much we were paying, which made the writers I wanted far more receptive when I approached them, as they had already heard how deep our pockets were. I didn't break the budget, and I didn't fiddle the books: I just moved things around so that the money would be seen on every page. Every pound, every penny.

BY 1999, TRYING TO FIND constants in the history of *GQ* wasn't exactly difficult. Style. Technology. Entertainment. Politics. Mental health. Fitness. Finance. Cars. Sport. Food. Even sex. The constituent parts of the magazine had been consistent since the magazine had dropped on to newsstands in December 1988. The pitch was always simple: this is the culture, this is the way it should be done, this is the best.

Of course, even by 1999 the culture had changed beyond recognition: the way it should be done was less about being prescriptive and more about nuance, while the 'best' was no longer determined by strict algorithmic precepts.

By 1999, the late eighties looked like they had stepped out of a movie, although to be fair they looked like they stepped out of a movie back in 1988, too. By the end of that year, the designer decade was already being italicised, already had inverted commas around it, was already a case study in meta. In fact, by the time the bilateral *Wall Street* came out in 1987 – which, in case you've forgotten, pitted a young stockbroker played by an even younger Charlie Sheen against a duplicitous corporate raider called Gordon Gekko played with the broadest of brushstrokes by Michael Douglas (and who uttered the immortal words, 'Greed is good') – the eighties had already been consigned to history.

Nineteen eighty-eight was a tumultuous year, one of the most tumultuous of the decade. It was the year of perestroika, the year of Harry Enfield's Thatcherite cockney plasterer Loadsamoney, the year George Bush ('Bush 41') succeeded Ronald Reagan ('The Gipper'). Nineteen eighty-eight saw Tom Wolfe's *The Bonfire of the Vanities* and Don DeLillo's *Libra* on every man's Tonelli Eden coffee table, saw people queuing up to see *Rain Man* and *Die Hard*, witnessed men careering through the City in their 325i convertibles and their Mercedes W126s listening to Neneh Cherry's 'Buffalo Stance' and previous year's *Introducing the Hardline According to Terence Trent D'Arby*, their customised in-car stereo turned all the way up to eleven and beyond. It was the year of the Lockerbie disaster, the year that Ayrton Senna won his first Formula One world championship, the year that the undisputed world heavyweight champion Mike Tyson knocked out Michael Spinks in just 91 seconds. Spinks never fought again.

Scanning the above litany of late-eighties touchpoints is more than telling. Because not only do some of them seem so distant and so culturally out-of-sync, but what does a twenty-five-year-old now care about Terence Trent D'Arby?

It was the year, lest anyone dare forget, of the yuppie. And it was the year that *GQ* was born, birthed into the world of opportunity, of new money, of shiny new frontiers. The magazine launched with the December 1988 issue, just two short years after the City's 'Big Bang' – London's sudden deregulation of the financial markets – a magazine born into a world where the celebration of success was no longer frowned upon. A world where aspiration was apparently an aspiration in itself. The eighties was one of the most divisive decades of the twentieth century, but when the going got tough, the tough found there were good times to be had if you just looked hard enough. Or worked hard enough. Or worked hard enough at looking hard enough.

Some, of course, were suspicious of this new world, as design started to turn up in plays and films of a satirical or left-leaning kind as a metaphor for dishonesty or overt manipulation.

The eighties was the decade that put the arch into postmodern architecture, the decade of the oversized car phone, the overpriced mountain bike, the over-marketed compact disc, the over-stuffed Filofax, the power dressing for men (when David Bowie said that padded shoulders would become the flares of the eighties, there were few of us who doubted him).

GQ was launched to reflect the aspirations of a generation who assumed a designer lifestyle was their birthright, a lifestyle that – for a while – was defined by the matt-black dream home: by matt-black hi-fis on matt-black tech-towers in matt-black open kitchens. 'Designer' became the prefix *du jour* – designer jeans, designer drugs, designer nightclubs (the Haçienda in Manchester, Otto Zutz in Barcelona!), designer cars, designer lettuce. Design was everything, and everything was design.

The *GQ* generation had ambition and self-fulfilment hardwired into it from the get-go: and its readers seemed to like it that way. They embraced the exercise book as the body beautiful became a male ideal, and they all started to become educated consumers; in fact, consuming more like women (the most sophisticated consumers of all). Some tried to label us New Men, which is fascinating in light of what's happened since the #MeToo and #timesup movements kicked into gear, as the core components of the New Man look increasingly like a perfect role model. He rose to prominence during a decade where reinvention was almost a necessity rather than a pipedream, an exotic creature who apparently was as happy washing up as he was changing a nappy. According to the *Oxford English Dictionary*, the New Man was someone 'who rejects sexist attitudes and the traditional male role, esp. in the context of domestic responsibilities and childcare, and who is (or is held to be) caring, sensitive, and non-aggressive'. But even this description now seems incredibly outdated, as one of the DNA strands of the New Man was based on the fact that he didn't mind being emasculated, which was hardly female empowerment. Were New Men really feminist-influenced sexual revolutionaries? Regardless, at the time, *GQ* was the manifestation of what we secretly hoped was true: we can have it all.

THE FIRST ISSUE FAMOUSLY HAD Michael Heseltine on the cover ('On the road back to power with Britain's beautiful bad boy' the cover lines ran, without so much as a hint of irony), while the first few issues included contributions from Peter York, David Bailey, Martin Amis, Terence Stamp, Richard Rayner, Nicky Haslam and Nick Foulkes, names that would crop up again and again over the years.

In a sense, those early issues were comically macho – to wit: 'Fast Girls, Fast Cars – What's so sexy about speed? Richard Rayner risks his standard equipment to ride the coital collision course'. Of course he does! Images were by Bob Carlos Clarke, then one of the kings of erotic photography. Elsewhere there was Julian Barnes on mistresses ('they never get pregnant, they are good at sex, and they always have perfectly ironed blouses'), Martin Amis on cool (as he certainly was, back then at least) and an apparently mandatory article about polo shirts (although no mention of popped collars). In issue three there was the magazine's first (but by no means last) profile of David Bailey, this one by Terence Stamp ('That's some whistle you got there, Bailey'). And just to prove that journalistic clichés have to start somewhere, *GQ* was the first British magazine to publish Hemingway's account of the Pamplona bull run (although sadly it would not be the last).

From the first issue onwards, the magazine was intended as an invitation to the best party in town, a hard card of luxurious enticements. Success with style – that was the ethos around which *GQ* was created, a provocative mix of the very best writing, strong visuals and an unrivalled sense of style. Taste and achievement, intelligence with irreverence, the ultimate urban man's tip-sheet. Top-end fun, in other words.

Looking back now at those early issues, one can detect a certain brittle bravado, as though the magazine didn't really believe it was entitled to such things – but *GQ* soon hit its stride, becoming the unironic print embodiment of the Gillette ad: The Best a Man Can Get. (Of course, its success also resulted in a generation of men for whom the height of sophistication was learning how to pronounce Gstaad correctly. Some became so good at this that they made sure to include it in every conversation they ever had, which obviously made them somewhat negligent in the entertainment department.)

To look at the dozens of men's magazines that launched in the nineties (seven or eight years after *GQ*), you could have been forgiven for thinking that the Alpha Male had – perhaps unwittingly, perhaps wittingly – had some sort of frontal lobotomy. Apparently, you couldn't be a man unless everything you consumed, everything you appreciated, everything you read, watched and listened to came complete with its own inverted commas. Big yellow foam inverted commas that proved you didn't take things too seriously.

GQ, meanwhile, was pretty steadfast, largely keeping its head above the murky waters of this new publishing boom, and continued to produce the same top-end journalism and slick fashion pages it had been producing since its launch in 1988. *GQ* was born on the back of a massive consumer boom, and reflected all the traditional, route-one virtues of manhood. *GQ* was born during a period when men had started to consume in ways they never had before, embracing designer lifestyles that had hitherto been denied them. Whether the *GQ* reader was an architect or a banker, whether he had spent his formative years reading *The Face* and *Arena* or the *Guardian* or the *Financial Times*, in 1988 he found a place to rest his head – or rather a place to rest his Montblanc fountain pen, the keys to his Porsche 911 or the Soul II Soul CD (that place probably being a Matthew Hilton 'Flipper' glass coffee table, complete with steel shark fins masquerading as legs).

WHEN I JOINED *GQ*, I wanted to inject some proper journalism into the magazine. Condé Nast's men's bible had been a kind of arbiter of style for over a decade, but I thought we could expand the horizons of the magazine's written components. The magazine was notable for many things, but award-winning journalism wasn't one of them; it had published some terrific pieces by some terrific writers but, in the mix, they seemed almost incidental. So that was what we were going to do – make it the best-read title in town. Boom!

There were writers I wanted to keep, including Irvine Welsh, Jason Barlow, Robert Elms, the brilliant Paul Henderson and, of course, Tony Parsons, who I had commissioned at every place I had ever worked, and who was already one of my best friends. Anyone who knows anything about the throughline of British journalism will know that Parsons started his career at the *NME* in 1977, escaping the gin factory to become one of Nick Logan's infamous hip young gunslingers. The paper knew that it needed some young blood to write about the burgeoning punk scene, and having interviewed dozens of potential young hacks, hired Julie Burchill and Tony. The *NME* was where he made his name, interviewing everyone from the Sex Pistols to Iggy Pop, from the Buzzcocks to Johnny Thunders. Tony became synonymous with punk, although ironically his career has lasted a lot longer than most of the people he interviewed back then. That career took on another dimension in 1999 when Tony wrote *Man and Boy*, a phenomenon that was published in over forty countries – a remarkable achievement for someone who used to interview Sid Vicious in the toilets of the Marquee.

Ever since I first started working with Tony, back in the mid-eighties, he could be relied upon to make mischief. His job was to mix the tabloid with the broadsheet, offering opinions that most people, indeed, most columnists, would shy away from. I don't think Tony has ever shied away from anything. Or anyone. He wrote many memorable features for me when I was editing *Arena*, perhaps most notably 'The Tattooed Jungle', a piece detailing the decline of the working class, which turned into something of a cottage industry, spawning many magazine and newspaper articles, as well as a TV series presented by Tony. Some of Tony's best work back then were his invoices, and our managing editor was for ever coming into my office and asking if

Tony had hit the repeat key on the zero. And I always told her that the repeat key on the zero is why most people get into journalism in the first place.

Like all good columnists, Tony's world is a black and white world, one unencumbered by indecision, confusion or compromise. I was reminded of this once back in the autumn of 1992. Julie Burchill, who was once married to Tony, was about to publish her second novel, the follow-up to *Ambition*, a rather less ambitious book called *No Exit.* I'd just joined the *Observer*, and we had been offered an interview with Julie to publicise the book. The same day I had lunch with Tony in the Groucho Club, to discuss some of the features I was going to try and get him to write over the next few months. We had a perfectly convivial meal, as usual, but it was only on my way back to the office in the car that the metaphorical lightbulb suddenly burst into action. Why not ask Tony to interview Julie? What a brilliant idea! Yes, like everyone else, I knew that they had famously fallen out, and that there was a terrible war of attrition between them, but wouldn't this be a great way for them to make peace with each other? So as soon as I got back to the office, I rang Tony and left a message on his machine, explaining what a good idea I thought it would be if he interviewed his ex-wife.

A couple of days later I received one of Tony's traditional handwritten postcards, of which I probably have several hundred at home, with a message that reinforced Tony's ability to distil emotion into just a few words: 'Dear Dylan. Thank you for lunch, it was lovely as always. And I would love to interview Julie . . . only I make it a policy not to interview fat, untalented cunts.'

Even I blanched at that.

WITH THE WRITERS MOSTLY ON board, I started flatplanning a template for the magazine, creating a kind of jigsaw, a magazine that was going to be completely different and completely the same each month. The trick was to give the readers exactly what they wanted while continually surprising them. And it gave me so much joy, as I had this *GQ* noise in my head, a constant whirr that accessorised everything else I did. I was literally living and breathing the magazine.

Cover meetings in Vogue House, I very soon learned, were short and perfunctory. A small group of us would gather in Nicholas Coleridge's wood-panelled office, where we would pore over prospective covers, expensively mounted on vinyl and card, and then placed delicately on his long Dutch sofa. There would be me, Peter Stuart, our ebullient and hilarious publisher, our art director and a couple of people from the circulation department.

(Peter would work like stink until 12.30 p.m., when he would down tools and walk to Le Caprice. Which is the last anyone would see of him until the next day at 8.30 a.m. On my first week at *GQ*, I walked into his office to excitedly tell him I'd organised a meeting with a big client for 4 p.m. the following Tuesday. He looked at me and, deadpan, parried with, 'Why would I want a meeting in the middle of lunch?' He was extremely dry. When he was making small talk in a meeting, if anyone ever asked how many people worked at *GQ*, he would say, 'Oh, about half.')

The execs were always full of praise for whatever you showed them, almost as if you had performed some kind of magic. We would spend two, five, sometimes twenty minutes looking at the covers, deciding which one would work best, which one would sell the most. Often the choice would be a *fait accompli*, as I had already promised the cover to a particular celebrity, so I couldn't go back on my word, not unless the photographs were absolute howlers. The good thing about Coleridge was his complete disinterest in meetings, along with his ability to make quick decisions, which I liked; I couldn't stand people who couldn't make up their mind or prevaricated over what I thought were incredibly simple decisions. As a manager I always made quick decisions; sometimes they even proved to be the right ones. If Nicholas said, 'I don't love it,' it meant he absolutely hated it and that the offending image needed to be ceremoniously burned on a bonfire in the middle of Hanover Square. Mainly, he would listen to reason, and would indulge you if you were particularly passionate about something. The other thing I often had in my back pocket would be the fact that no one apart from myself and the designer knew who the cover star was anyway.

Every day I would be at my desk at eight-thirty, unless I had a breakfast meeting, which would invariably take place at Claridge's or, soon, the Wolseley. The rest of the team would dribble in between nine and nine-thirty. There were a few who thought they were still living in the James Brown era and might not appear until after ten. I soon stopped this. Offices were for working, not shirking, and if you didn't want to work then you shouldn't come to work. These people were encouraged to leave. There were a couple of tricky staff members who I knew wouldn't last, but initially I kept them on as I needed to know where the bodies were buried. As soon as I knew how everything worked, the difficult ones were put through the process and asked to leave. If I've learned anything, it's that your initial misgivings about someone will always be borne out. They won't improve, they won't bend to your will, so you should just get rid of them. And I have never been proved wrong.

LOOKING BACK AT MY FIRST issue today, it doesn't look that much different from the ones that preceded it, which had been made by what was left of the previous team, under my guidance. Of course, I thought I had reinvented the wheel, but the August 1999 issue was proof positive that the new wheel looked almost the same as the old one, only with much better writing. There was a nice piece on Johnny Gold and the history of the legendary London club Tramp by Nick Foulkes that I quite liked, and a long feature on Simon Kelner's arrival at the *Independent* (*Private Eye* had a field day with that one), a funny romp about Israeli special forces jumping on the management training bandwagon, and Boris Johnson's first motoring column, which was everything I wanted it to be; but all in all there were too many polo shirts and mediocre fashion stories.

Things would get better.

Issue two felt more like it, with an Ian Schrager exclusive, a trawl through the death of the It Girl, Cosmo Landesman's media column (what a disappointment he eventually turned out to be), a luscious Paolo Roversi shoot with Nino Cerruti featuring Christian Bale, Alec Baldwin, Harrison Ford and Peter Beard, and Robert Chalmers's grade-A, five-star piece on the time the *Observer* invited Hunter S. Thompson, the king of gonzo journalism, to London from his formidable bolthole in Aspen, Colorado, to attend the Braemar Games in Scotland. There, so they thought, Hunter would be able to write about the royal family and the British royal press pack with his usual, er . . . colourful irreverence. Hunter S. Thompson, the author of *Fear and Loathing in Las Vegas* and hundreds of ribald journalistic exploits, here, on British soil, with his customary cigarette holder, hip flask and jaundiced view of the world, with Chalmers along to ride shotgun. The crumbling House of Windsor! The rabid paparazzi! And the savage Hunter S! What could possibly go wrong?

I asked Chalmers to write this story as I was part of the *Observer* team at the time, and the true story had never been told. We were confident that we could control America's most unwieldy and drug-addled reporter. But we were wrong.

When Hunter emerged from customs at Gatwick airport, his breath suggested he hadn't stinted on the in-flight service, while his first communication was to lament the fact that he had not brought more drugs with him. 'It is the curse of cowardice,' he said, 'cowardice, terror and guilt.'

It immediately became apparent that he was magnetic to an almost intolerable degree.

He was taken straight away to the Fox and Anchor, a pub in Smithfield meat market whose opening hours were designed for porters, and where the good doctor proceeded to order two large Bloody Marys, a pint of bitter, two pints of orange, a coffee, a triple Scotch and a vodka and tonic. Oh, and a full English breakfast. 'For the sake of your sanity,' his assistant advised the waitress, 'bring every condiment in the house.' Half an hour later, Hunter started snorting cocaine on the pub table, and, in Chalmers's words, began talking as though he were William Burroughs reading *Finnegans Wake*.

He was then delivered to the London Metropole, a gargantuan hotel on the Edgware Road, where Hunter was to stay before flying up to Scotland. There, he abused the staff, enjoyed the elasticity of his room service facility, and refused to answer the phone. He had, however, been using the device himself. The following day, having apparently consumed all of the pharmaceutical elixirs in his suitcases, and having ordered three large Bloody Marys for breakfast, he made three calls, to British Airways, United Airlines and TWA. The hotel receptionist said it wasn't 'the behaviour of man contemplating domestic travel'.

In the end, he never left his hotel room.

On the fifth day of his trip, before he was meant to fly back to Aspen, we hosted a party for him at the Metropole. We had invited the great and the good – P. J. O'Rourke was there, eager to reconnect with his old buddy – and had laid on an evening of fine wines, food and festivities. But he never appeared. Unable to face his temporary benefactors, he had fled back to Gatwick, and Aspen, leaving us with a huge bill, a disappointed crowd and a rather dispirited team. Amphetamine psychosis had got the better of him. We did what we could to rescue the evening, and ended up in the Victoria Casino, a few hundred yards away.

I left that night having won £400.

'Some people will tell you that London is a nice town,' Hunter wrote to us on his return. 'But not me. I will tell you that London is the worst town in the world. For a lot of reasons, but fuck them. Just take my word for it. London is the worst town in the world. You're welcome.'

Chalmers's piece went on for days, twisting and turning like the world's longest shaggy-dog story, highlighting Thompson's freakish complexities and hilarious dependencies with a mordant wit and adjectival brutality. And I loved it.

More was to come.

David Bailey, Boris Johnson and A. A. Gill

Here Come the Big Boys

Best buds: Jeremy Clarkson and A. A. Gill, *GQ* party, Mayfair, 2004

THERE SOON APPEARED TO BE something of a problem with Boris, as the managing editor started to get rather a lot of parking tickets. And when I say a lot, I mean A LOT; in Boris's own words, they started accumulating 'like drifting snow on the windshield'. Every month they'd arrive – often even earlier than Boris's invoices – and every month we'd pay them. They were collateral damage, I thought, like a speeding fine, a traffic altercation or a dink in the hubcap. Nothing to get too worked up about.

But then the accounts department started to complain. And I was beginning to understand that when the Condé Nast accounts department started to complain, then you really needed to start to take notice. So, I called Boris to a meeting (he arrived at Claridge's on his bike, flustered), and told him he had to start taking a bit more care when he drove our cars for review, and in future would he mind parking them a little more, well, legally?

Boris did his Boris thing and said, with bardic theatricality, 'Sorry boss, bad Boris,' and then promptly asked for a pay rise. 'Is mister big boss annoyed with Boris? Hmm, yes, well, the thing is, you see, I often forget where I've left them. And the Johnnies from *GQ* who deliver them are very kind and everything, but I don't always listen when they're talking. In fact, I rarely do. Honestly, do you?'

'You've got to buck up, or else the company are going to ask me to get rid of you,' I said, lying through my teeth. Condé Nast weren't going to ask me to fire him, they just thought he was ridiculous.

'OK, my liege, I shall rein myself in, toe the line, and all the other etceteras,' he said, while saluting like Benny Hill. 'It shall stop!'

But of course, it didn't stop, and the parking tickets kept arriving. Every month. He collected dozens of parking tickets and fines by casually double parking the cars outside the likes of New Scotland Yard, Vogue House and the Royal Festival Hall, and more than once an underling had to be dispatched to rescue the car from the pound.

Boris would tend to miss the session at which he would be shown by the delivery driver how to use the vehicle. Ann Sindall, his adorable assistant, said, 'The thing is he's so busy sometimes I'll have [*Spectator* writer] Mary Wakefield outside the office learning how to use the car. He'll ring me and ask, "How do I use the door?"' Wakefield later confirmed he would ring her too: 'He called me all through Saturday to get me to talk him through it, because he hadn't concentrated and couldn't work out how to open the door from the inside. He must have been stuck inside it. You had to turn a little dial to open the door.'

The people in the accounts department got so cross they said they were no longer going to pay his parking fines. Which meant I then had to get the features team to pay them and then claim them back on expenses. Which, perhaps unsurprisingly, for a while at least, worked like a dream.

At the time, Boris was the editor of the *Spectator*, and the car column was something he fitted into his busy life along with his pieces for the *Telegraph* and his occasional appearances on television. Jeremy Clarkson told me Boris had been asked to appear on *Top Gear* once, on the 'Star in a Reasonably Priced Car' slot. They spent forty minutes or so rehearsing, and then there was a twenty-minute break while the team got ready to film the segment. Clarkson said Boris frantically started asking around to borrow a laptop, and, when he finally found one, set to work writing his next column for the *Telegraph*, which was due about an hour before he started the rehearsal. Clarkson said Boris had no more than twelve minutes to write his piece; and yet when he read it the following day it was such a carefully argued column that it looked as though he had spent a week on it. That's how good a writer Boris was, able to turn things round almost at whim. Which made me rather suspicious of his car reviews.

Interestingly, especially considering the cursory way he treated his loans, Boris never got any speeding tickets. And I've got a pretty good idea why. When the cars were delivered to his house in Islington, the car company always made a note of the mileage, something that is standard practice. The mileage would also be noted when they came to pick them up again. And on more than one occasion – OK, on many, many, many occasions – the mileage was precisely the same.

The situation reminded me of a cartoon I once saw in *Private Eye*. Two literary types are at a book launch, both holding overflowing glasses of wine.

'Have you read the book?' asks literary type A.

'Of course I have,' replied his friend. 'Although not personally.'

My most memorable phone call with Boris involved a tank I was trying to get him to test drive. It could only be driven on the South Downs, but after two or three days of trying to get Boris down there, he called me in a rather agitated fashion and said, without a hint of irony, 'Sorry old boy, but I'm a bit pushed for time this week, I don't suppose you could deliver the tank to the *Spectator* could you?'

It is one of my minor professional regrets that unfortunately we were unable to do so. The then Conservative MP for Henley careering down Piccadilly driving a Soviet armoured vehicle was something that would have livened up his motoring pages no end.

Boris was always late. It was somehow hardwired into him. He had absolutely no respect for anyone else's timetable but his own. I'm still amazed he managed to appear at Prime Minister's Questions on time – at least he had some respect for the sanctity of government. But obviously not for anyone else.

I liked to go to the *Spectator*'s Parliamentarian of the Year awards as it was not only fascinating to see politicians out of their natural habitat, but it was also tremendous fun watching them slice bits off each other, as the speeches were always coruscating. One year, I was seated between Boris and the Labour MP Harriet Harman, which was certainly between a rock and hard place (especially as she more or less refused to speak to me). He was the guest speaker but arrived late and had come completely unprepared, and so spent twenty minutes furiously scribbling on a piece of paper. I took great joy in trying to interrupt him, and he took an equal joy in telling me to fuck off – 'It's not as easy as it fucking looks, you know.'

BORIS ENJOYED BEING PHOTOGRAPHED. FOR him it was a way to indulge his comedic side without having to talk. In that respect, he would have made a good silent comic, a kind of modern-day Oliver Hardy. We took endless pictures of him at *GQ*, as we always needed to shoot him with the cars he was ostensibly driving. He was good at having his picture taken, too. When Boris became the mayor of London, I asked if he'd be photographed by David Bailey for a series we were running on powerful men (Martin Sorrell, Richard Caring, Matthew Freud, Ed Victor, etc.). After the traditional haggling (once they reach a certain level of fame or notoriety, no one ever agrees to an appointment unless you offer them at least three alternatives), he eventually turned up at Bailey's studio, bouncing up and down like a shameless puppy.

I loved Bailey, but he was a cantankerous sod. He would never say yes when he could find a reason to say no, and he appeared to have a perpetual grudge against the world and most people in it. He found people challenging, and while I didn't subscribe to his worldview, I'm glad someone like him had it. He told me once he thought common sense was a misnomer as so few people had it.

'Uncommon sense, more like,' he said, then laughed like a deranged, asthmatic hyena.

Bailey was a terrible bully, and we would regularly fall out, but I genuinely loved him. I considered him a mentor of sorts, regardless of how he behaved (often appallingly). I would take any opportunity to visit him in his Bloomsbury studio, just to hang out and hear his stories, to hear him tell me how rude he'd just been to someone important. He would hold your hand or your arm in the most affectionate way. He would even do this in restaurants, which made us look like lovers, but then he did this with a lot of people. He wasn't in the least bit feminised and yet he had no qualms about being overtly tender. It was almost a way to unnerve you. He certainly did this with people who came up to his studio to be shot. He would sit with them for a while – sometimes over an hour – just to suss them out and feel their vibe, often grabbing them by the arm, building a connection. Then, when he had decided how he was going to shoot them, he would almost shove them in front of the camera.

He was a brute, but he had the kindest heart.

'How's your wife?' he'd asked, after he and I had some almighty row about something. It was his way of moving on.

Our biggest row happened when he called me up at work and demanded I increase his page rate, or he wouldn't deliver his latest set of pictures. I said I was perfectly prepared to up his page rate but I didn't like being held to ransom and he had no right to withhold his pictures.

'You stupid fucking cunt,' said Bailey. 'You're just a fucking editor, you don't fucking do anything. You're just like all those other cunts at Condé Nast. Lazy, posh, stupid fucking cunts. If you want these fucking pictures then come and get them, you cunt.'

As he was just about to call me the C-word again, I put the phone down.

No one put the phone down on Bailey.

The managing editor, who had heard all this (everyone who lived in the same postcode had heard it), came into my office and asked me what we were going to do with the sixteen-page gap in the magazine where Bailey's photographs were meant to be.

'Wait,' I said. 'Just wait.'

Three minutes later, Bailey was on the phone asking us what form we wanted the pictures in. I had won. Like many bullies, he buckled when challenged.

When pressed, Bailey would talk about photography as an art. He was more than happy to talk about the ridiculous nature of celebrities, more than happy to gossip about the uselessness of magazine editors, but he was happiest when talking about his passion, his work.

'People often say I was lucky because I came along at the right time, but then everyone does,' he told me. 'Terence Donovan did, Brian Duffy did. Everybody in history comes along at the right time or else you would never have heard of them. But the reason I've lasted as a photographer isn't just because I came along at the right time, it's because I care passionately about what I do. I always have done. I was always on time, never late. All I cared about was making images.'

He would talk endlessly about taking portraits, about how difficult David Bowie was ('He could never decide who he wanted to be'), how easy Johnny Depp was ('When he turned up at the studio I said he looked so appalling I'd have to shoot him in a skip – which he loved'), how he told Nick Clegg how stupid he was for telling *GQ* how many women he'd slept with ('Why on earth did he do that? I mean, do I really want to know what an underachiever he is?'), and how much he liked Margaret Thatcher ('I called her "Toots" and she loved it'). He said one of the most dignified responses to a request from him to photograph them came from Orson Welles. He sent Bailey a very nice letter back saying, 'Thank you very much for your kind offer, but I don't want to be remembered for the way I look now.'

The rest of my team hated working with him as he had no interest in treating them with even a modicum of respect. This was a particular problem for our art director, who had no relationship with him at all. Which, considering I'd signed Bailey to a contract that necessitated him shooting for every issue, meant I was the conduit for every negotiation. Not that I minded, as it gave me another opportunity to spend time in his company, which I treasured.

But you had to give as good as you got. I first met him when he photographed me for an ad campaign for Gieves & Hawkes, the Savile Row tailors, and halfway through the shoot he said, *sotto voce*, to his assistant, 'He looks like a long streak of piss.'

I shot back with, 'The term is long streak of paralysed piss, actually,' which defused the unpleasant atmosphere he was so obviously trying to create. After that, we were fine. Largely.

I loved him. Warts and all.

BAILEY WAS RARELY SHY ABOUT coming forward, and when Boris walked into his studio, after I'd shaken the mayor's hand, came steaming up and said, 'You're the only politician I've ever voted for. Firstly, because you're the only one who appears to have read a book, and secondly because the others are all wankers.' Boris was uncharacteristically speechless after this outburst, but soon acclimatised, becoming his old naturally unguarded self, mooching about the studio looking at the framed prints of John Lennon and Paul McCartney, the Krays and Kate Moss.

Bailey had never met the mayor before, but before Boris could even begin to try and charm him, the legendary photographer got him in a headlock and told him he wished he'd bothered to get dressed properly that morning (Boris was certainly dishevelled). He then told Boris that it had only taken him twenty-four hours to become a hate figure in the capital. 'I was in the back of a cab going through Trafalgar Square the day after you won the election, and the roadworks were so bad, the driver got so frustrated he turned round at one point and said, "Bloody Boris!'" Boris responded by doing his best impression of the Michael Heseltine *Spitting Image* puppet, the one with the dribble and the flak jacket.

The talk turned to the war in Afghanistan, and specifically the drug problem there. The two of them spent so much time talking about the war that Boris almost didn't have enough time to have his portrait taken. But then Bailey started swearing at him and Boris suddenly found another twenty minutes in his schedule.

They weren't so much Alphas as little boys with quick repartee. When Bailey told Boris he'd made the journey to Downing Street to photograph Gordon Brown for *GQ* a few weeks earlier, Boris asked why he'd been forced to come to Bailey's studio instead. 'When you become PM I'll come to you,' said Bailey. 'Until then, you come to me.'

THE MAGAZINE WAS CHANGING. IN six months we had profiled Porfirio Rubirosa, the most famous playboy in the Western world; spent seven thousand words (and twelve pages of Peter Lindbergh photographs) with Keith Richards; published an extraordinary Philip Norman piece about the infamous restaurateur Peter Langan; photographed Puff Daddy in the Hamptons; featured Rob Ryan on Leonardo DiCaprio, Will Self on the Mile High Club, Christopher Hitchens on Bill Clinton, and published exclusive short stories by Nick Hornby and Alex Garland. We'd had Nick Kent on Tommy Lee, and Paolo Roversi on Kate Moss. We even had a Sopranos fashion shoot that took six months to organise, featuring James Gandolfini, Edie Falco and David Chase, and Juergen Teller had shot Paul McCartney. Oh, and we found a long-lost Beatles album. Oh, oh!

And we gave dozens of pages to Terry O'Neill's marvellous pictures of Michael Caine. The Cockney Knight was a *GQ* constant. In 1988, Caine (which, as any self-respecting cinephile knew, should always be pronounced 'My cocaine') had just starred in *Dirty Rotten Scoundrels*, the Frank Oz film co-starring Steve Martin that reinterpreted the Marlon Brando/David Niven farce *Bedtime Story*, and was thought to be yet another career high for Caine. By the time I stepped down in 2021 – and having starred in another sixty films since then (including *The Cider House Rules*, *Little Voice* and *The Dark Knight*) – Caine was still giving gold in movies such as 2018's *King of Thieves*, the British crime film based on the Hatton Garden safe-deposit burglary of 2015.

The Cockney Cary Grant had been in some of the world's greatest films, and – contributing hugely to his appeal – some of the worst (he once rather brilliantly went from *Hannah and Her Sisters* straight on to *Jaws: The Revenge*). He wrote the best-ever book about the practicalities of acting, *Acting in Film*, which famously instructs you how to stand up on screen (slowly), as well as containing some legendary quotes: 'First of all, I choose the great roles, and if none of these come, I choose the mediocre ones, and if they don't come, I choose the ones that pay the rent.' He also wrote one of the greatest books about Hollywood, *What's It All About?* (which has to be one of the three best autobiographical titles ever, along with Auberon Waugh's *Will This Do?* and Bob Geldof's *Is That It?*). And he was never not funny: He said as a boy in south London, he feared being romantically successful. 'If you kissed a girl three times, four brothers came round and made you marry her,' Caine said. 'It was like living in Sicily – without the spaghetti and the sunshine.'

I hosted a celebrity dinner for Caine after a private screening of his vigilante movie *Harry Brown* when it came out in 2009, and as they sipped vintage Dom Pérignon the assembled guests quizzed him on various stars he'd worked with. Towards the end of the evening, when some guests had had a few more glasses than others, someone asked our star whether a certain leading man he had worked with was gay. Let's call him Tom. Caine stopped talking for a moment, took another sip of his vintage fizz, and then used a phrase his dresser Roy – with whom he had first worked on *The Italian Job*, over fifty years ago – had apparently been employing for years.

'Well, I wouldn't say Tom's gay. But I think if they were busy, he'd probably help out.'

HAVING BRAGGED ABOUT WHAT A great idea it was, I thought I'd better make the A. A. Gill porn film a reality. To that end, shortly after I took on the editorship in 1999, I got in touch with Vivid, one of the largest distributors of adult films in Hollywood, and I convinced them this would be a good idea, to take one of the most celebrated journalists in Britain and get him to write and direct his own onanistic paean. And so Adrian spent about three months writing this film. Unsurprisingly, seeing that he was still the *Sunday Times*'s restaurant critic, it was all about food, and was full of scenes of people having sex on, in and with various types of food. Cake, ice cream, marrows, a veritable smorgasbord of orgiastic delights. I sent the script to Vivid ('This is much better than the stuff we normally get'), and then I bundled Adrian and his girlfriend Nicola over to California to spend a week directing the film. Which he did, and then promptly came home again.

Two months later I got a call from the CEO of the porn film producers Metro, a very charming and excited woman, who was eager to tell me about Gill's film. She said regardless of the intricacies of the plot, having been edited to a regulation Metro blueprint, Adrian's porn film was now exactly the same as every other porn film the company had ever made. And although Adrian probably wouldn't think so, this was a huge compliment. The film itself was called *Hot House Tales*, it was set in a cheap boarding house, and the all-star cast included the world's biggest porn star at the time, Houston, and industry legend Ron Jeremy. It was filmed, like most porn, in Van Nuys, California.

Gill's article was called 'Double D meets Double A', and it wasn't just funny. It was a fascinating fumble beneath the bedsheets of a silicone-enhanced industry that in reality was as dull as it was prescriptive. Adrian's piece was one of the most illuminating features I'd ever read about the genre; there was a small vignette in the piece where the gaffers, grips, runners, sparks and the 'lube boy' all turned from the action on set to the action on the monitor. As Gill said, five feet away from them two live girls were having sex, but they preferred to watch it on screen. Because pornography is something that happens on a screen. 'This is its familiar, omnipotent voyeurism; its erotic charge comes from being disengaged.'

By making his film, Adrian came away convinced these were not exploited people. 'The set is matriarchal with the women choosing what they'd like to do and with whom,' he said. 'Only the film crew are cynical about the act – but then, all film crews are cynical. The stars are surprisingly innocent. I mean that in a fundamental not a physical sense. They are incredibly kind to each other.'

IN JULY 2000, WE PUBLISHED a deliberately sensationalist cover, featuring Kylie Minogue lifting up her tennis skirt in an homage to the infamous Athena seventies poster. The pictures, taken on Long Island by Terry Richardson on a particularly blustery day, featured Kylie deliberately in a state of undress, and when they were released to the press, the press went mad. The photographs weren't just incendiary, but there was also the question of whether or not Kylie had known her knickers were going to be airbrushed before publication. The saga dragged on for days, and having spoken at length to her publicist, we made sure there were a series of deliberately contradictory statements by both parties in order to keep the story going. Remarkably, the story lasted a week, and our sales went through the roof. We had learned the not-so-subtle art of media manipulation was ours for the taking.

GQ was starting to attract a lot of media attention. Most issues were generating at least half-a-dozen stories in the press each month, with some, like the Kylie Minogue story, fully permeating the papers. Kylie would go on to grace our cover a further six times. We were still making the occasional mistake – we thought cleverly photographing soap stars was a legitimate meta exercise, whereas most people just thought we'd photographed a soap star – but they were fewer and fewer.

Then, in September, we had our first global exclusive, a political bomb that almost blew up the Tories. We had been offered an interview with the Conservative Party leader William Hague by his press secretary Amanda Platell. I can't remember what the peg was meant to be, as political interviews were always offered in order to support a completely uninteresting policy announcement. I'd commissioned Dan Macmillan to take the pictures, as he was still pursuing a career in photography, and asked Nicholas Coleridge to interview him. Coleridge had spent the weekend in Hague's company a few months earlier, also with Bob Geldof I seem to remember. I knew Nicholas would deliver a breezy and occasionally spiky piece, as when he wrote he had a unique ability (sadly lost to management) to smile whenever he was sticking in the metaphorical knife. And the piece he handed in was just as I thought it would be, apart from the fact it had a solid gold nugget in it, about a third of the way through.

In among a lot of breast-beating guff about how dreadful the Labour Party were, Hague let on that, as a young man, he regularly drank fourteen pints of beer a day. Hague was born and raised in South Yorkshire, in a suburb of Rotherham where his family owned a lemonade factory, Hague's Soft Drinks.

'Working at the lemonade factory was my holiday job from when I was 15 to 21,' Hague told Coleridge. 'I was the driver's mate, delivering the bottles and beer around South Yorkshire. Anyone who thinks I used to spend my holidays reading political tracts should have come with me for a week. There were crates of soft drinks – "pop" we used to call it – and barrels of wholesale John Smith's bitter, and we delivered them mainly around the working men's clubs of Barnsley and Rotherham. We used to have a pint at each stop – well, the driver's mate did, not the driver thankfully – and we used to have about ten stops a day.'

'You drank ten pints a day when you were a teenager?' asked an incredulous Coleridge.

'Oh yes.'

'That's impressive.'

'You worked so hard you didn't feel you'd drunk ten points by four o'clock, you used to sweat so much. But then you had to lift all the empties off the lorry. It's probably horrifying but we used to do that, then go home for tea and then go out in the evening to the pub.'

'So, you were drinking 14 pints a day?'

'I think when you're a teenager you can do that, especially if you're working hard in the heat – this was always in the summer, and it was hard manual work – you get through a lot of liquid.'

The rest of the article was lost in a blaze of headlines and cartoons, which led the news agenda for at least a month. It didn't do Hague's standing any good, as he was treated like a bit of a fool for a while after that, but I'm not sure he was being deliberately provocative. He had probably exaggerated the amount he drank, but, being a politician, couldn't possibly contradict himself. The story was massive, although it didn't help sell many copies of *GQ*. After about five minutes the story was owned by every news organisation in the country, as well as many abroad, so we didn't actually benefit that much.

It did, however, firmly put us on the map.

OUR NEW MAGAZINE WAS STARTING to work. It had to. Ultimately, we had to produce a commercial hit, and it needed to look and feel like a men's magazine. The project needed to be a success or else there was no point doing it. I was confident, though, that the market could cope with a brash, quirky, bold, hi–lo magazine. I knew what we needed to be confrontational; I needed the media to take notice of us, and readers to take notice of us – not just our readers, but other people's, too. In order to do this, we would have to put our heads above the parapet, but I didn't care. It was simple: in order to make news we had to become news.

These were just ideas, of course, things I wanted to happen. Making them happen would come later.

About three months into the job, Jonathan Newhouse, my boss and chairman of Condé Nast, took me for lunch at the Ivy (he always paid in cash, with folded notes inside a steel money clip, just like a mafioso, and he always left a big tip). At lunch he paid me some compliments, said he was enjoying the magazine and then asked me what my strategy was for success. So I told him, at length, unfolding my 'big ideas' as though I was playing Patience. He looked at me, in the way that Si Newhouse, his uncle, would whenever I met him, and said, with a knowing grin, 'Well, it's great if it works.'

I got the message. I'd better make it work.

We were already starting to become a target for various London libel lawyers, and while I wanted to continue sailing close to the wind, I figured I'd better hire in a more experienced crew. This resulted in me amping-up the subs department, and getting pieces read by our own libel lawyers at earlier and earlier stages. Often, I would tell the commissioning editors not to show me any stories until they had been read by the lawyers. We were already becoming quite adept at turning round weak covers, or badly executed fashion stories – the solution was always to be bold and striking – but we needed to be better at the magazine furniture (the captions, pull-quotes and headlines); I often used to tell young writers who were joining the title that it was more difficult writing an award-winning 300-word piece than a 6,000-word feature. And I almost meant it. (I also encouraged them to imagine people reading what they had written months afterwards. I used to say that, before someone had seen or heard something, they probably wanted to read the shortest review, while afterwards they probably wanted to read the longest – there was always an appetite for beautifully written reviews.)

I remember walking back to the office from the Ivy that day, and doing what I always did in newsagents (and in those days there were at least two on each street): I would go into each and every one with the same purpose, to see how the magazine was racked on the shelves, and then move them around so they were in a more prominent position. Sure, it was petty, but marketing was marketing, and every little helped. (I also didn't believe fellow editors when they denied doing the same thing.)

I wasn't oblivious to Condé Nast politics, either, and I knew I was being watched. A couple of people in the fashion department were feeding information back to management. I think the company had been so burned by the James Brown period and had been so surprised that his antics had such commercial ramifications, they were monitoring their new investment. One of those keeping an eye on me was John Morgan, a strange Walter Mitty-type character who lived in rooms in the Albany, the chi-chi apartment block just behind Savile Row. He allowed rich widows to take him to the opera and tea at Claridge's, and lived wildly beyond his means – his wardrobe was full of dozens of bespoke suits. He was a style writer by day, and a walker by night. He was gay, but cautious, and we all speculated about his performative skills. I tolerated him, but didn't trust him; he would endlessly walk by my office in order to see who was in it, who I was entertaining, who I was taking a meeting with. I hadn't been there long before he threw himself out of a window in his third-floor flat, leaping to his death. He was essentially living a lie, the poor man, and after a while that lie simply caught up with him. It was terribly sad, but then so was he.

New York: These Vagabond Shoes

The Bronx is Up and the Battery's Down

Suited and booted with Tommy Hilfiger,
Central Park South, 2008

IN 2001, I WAS IN the basement of Waterstones in Piccadilly when the second plane flew into the Twin Towers. I was doing my weekly trawl of international magazines, hoovering up esoteric titles in the newsagents, and wondering why the television was so loud. Why were they screening a disaster movie so early in the mor . . . oh. Shit. What? No . . . It can't be. Couldn't be. When it dawned on me what was happening, I rushed back to Vogue House to find the entire team – all fifty of them – squashed into my office watching the events unfold on my TV. I spent the day calling friends and colleagues who lived in New York, trying to offer pastoral care as much as anything. Like any disaster, the salient emotion was one of confusion. People were rushing uptown away from the fires, and others were rushing downtown, offering to help, reporting for media outlets, or just to stare. No one knew what was coming next. Would there be more attacks? Would the towers fall? How far would the fires spread? There was so much misinformation – driven, in myriad ways by the media – that literally no one knew what was going on.

I didn't go to New York for several months, but by then Ground Zero had become a tourist attraction; not just that, but the biggest in town. No one liked admitting it, but it was true. Somehow the site of this enormous tragedy had been turned into a garish spectacle. People were still going to pay their respects, although many more appeared to be going just so they could say they'd seen it.

Like me.

I queued up, lemming-like, with all the other out-of-towners at the South Street Seaport for my ticket, and then walked towards Ground Zero accompanied by Frank Sinatra blasting out 'Heavenly Dreams' and the aroma of sugar-coated almonds. For months after September 11 the smell of burnt electrical wires and chemical ash was all over Manhattan (as well as Brooklyn, where the wind mostly took it), although by the time I arrived, that had all gone. There was nothing. New York has always been a city of symbolism and ironies but by the new year you couldn't escape them.

I queued again when I reached the actual site, moving glacially alongside makeshift trestle tables policed by street vendors hawking the most unsavoury tat. I could have bought a hat with 'Ground Zero 9/11' stitched into it, or a Twin Towers tie showing the *Mayflower* fuelled by Stars and Stripes sails, both for just $5 each. The most shocking thing was a man with a laptop showing the CD-ROMs he was selling; what was on them? Oh, only United Airlines Flight 175 crashing into the South Tower.

'You can't beat it,' he said, as I quizzed him. 'Take a little piece of history home with you.'

When I reached the viewing platform, the fifteen-storey high rubble was gone, and the area looked not so much like a demolition site as a construction site – it was the charred buildings surrounding the massive hole that gave you some idea of what it must have been like after the fires had stopped. The Millennium Hotel was all boarded up, while the Woolworth Building was still covered in protective netting; this landmark skyscraper was pummelled by falling debris from the South Tower and set ablaze. Elsewhere, both St Paul's Chapel and Trinity Church stood proud and defiant in yet another vignette of unavoidable symbolism.

Many writers tried to turn the events of September 11 into a metaphor, as a way of finally laying the twentieth century to rest. Cultural analysts had actually been trying to do this for years, as had novelists, particularly where New York was concerned. When *Time* magazine reviewed Tom Wolfe's *The Bonfire of the Vanities* back in 1987, they said it exposed how 'a culture geared to profit from the immediate gratification of egos and nerve endings is not a culture at all, but an addiction'. Which was why we all liked New York, I suppose. I was certainly addicted to the place for a while, although 9/11 changed it for ever. Suddenly the city had a vulnerability.

Although the city was awash with people wearing 'I Love New York More Than Ever' T-shirts, you couldn't disguise the fact NYC was quiet. Nobody wanted to shop, the restaurants were less than full and rush hour felt like rush hour in San Francisco or Seattle. There was a different vibe on the street, and it was palpable.

'We used to laugh at bridge-and-tunnel people,' said someone I knew who worked for Calvin Klein, as he smoked his way through a hurried Marlboro Light in the modern downtown trat Barolo. 'And now we want them back. We need them back.'

Restaurant culture had changed, too, as the new smoking ban meant it was now illegal in any place that had more than thirty-five seats. Unsurprisingly, perhaps, very few people seemed to have taken notice of this, and most of the restaurants I visited on this trip not only allowed surreptitious puffing, but they also supplied ashtrays.

Sex appeared to be much in evidence. Former mayor Rudy Giuliani may have moved all the sex away from Times Square, but it seemed to have found its way to other equally visible parts of the city. As I walked past a downtown sex shop called Toys in Babeland (the sign said they gave seminars on female ejaculation, the G-Spot and everything tantric), I overheard one side of what could only have been a New York conversation.

'OK, this is a good dildo: it comes with a thirty-day warranty, but you won't need it. Not if you use it properly.'

The store was on Rivington Street, on the 'funky' Lower East Side, or LES as it had recently become known, joining SoHo, NoHo, Tribeca and WoBo. 'Funky' was the word New Yorkers used for anything remotely authentic, working-class or ethnic. The Lower East Side had been trendy back in the eighties, when it was overrun with artists, new romantics and style journalists. But by 2002 it was home to a retail revolution as prohibitive rates pushed anything idiosyncratic even further to the margins.

I'D BEEN VISITING THE SKYSCRAPER national park that was New York since the eighties, and the pace of the place had always been bewildering. That was one of the exciting things about it. Having spent so much time in the city over the previous twenty years, the visceral nature of the island had worn off a little, but when I visited in 2002 it felt like a completely different city entirely. There was always a frisson of excitement whenever you stepped onto the sidewalk in New York, and after the September 11 attacks that appeared to have evaporated.

No one will ever forget their first trip to New York – mine was in 1984 when three of us from *i-D* magazine had been flown over by the legendary New York nightclub duo Haoui Montaug and Ruth Polsky to co-host a party at the legendary downtown club Danceteria (one of the three most important clubs in the city; Area and Limelight were the others) – and while I was as excited by its vibrancy as any other newbie, there was always something parochial about the city, I felt.

The three of us – Alix Sharkey, Caryn Franklin and me – had started to travel the world, bringing London DJs, dancers, photographers, groups and 'scenesters' to everywhere from Paris, Milan, Berlin, Toronto and Sydney to Brighton, Manchester, Liverpool,

Birmingham, Bristol and Glasgow. In our heads this was our own bpm-driven version of Andy Warhol's Exploding Plastic Inevitable, a way for us to publicise our magazine in the time-honoured Factory tradition. And now we were in New York, invited by Haoui and Ruth and accompanied by the DJ Jay Strongman, the photographer Cindy Palmano, *The Face*'s Neville Brody, and club runners Nick Trulocke and Cristian Cotterill. We smugly felt a bit like visiting royalty, as we were swept up by the town's irrepressible demi-monde, in the shape of the club scene's Dianne Brill and Rudolf Piper, designer Stephen Sprouse and, tangentially, Warhol himself.

'Uptown is for people who have already done something,' he said once. 'Downtown is where they're doing something new.'

By 1984, Warhol lived uptown, but he still loved going downtown, and that year when I visited the city, he was all over it. The New York I saw that year was a city that appeared to have been co-opted by Warhol. He seemed to be everywhere – having dinner in Odeon (apparently with Jean-Michel Basquiat, but we couldn't see), sitting in a booth with Sting and Billy Idol in Limelight, arriving amid a flutter of paparazzi cameras at Area, on the balcony at the Ritz for Frankie Goes to Hollywood's New York debut (against the odds, they were good) and, obviously, at Danceteria. Andy was like Zelig, popping up like a clockwork cuckoo. (The only thing more ubiquitous than Warhol was the dancefloor smash 'Loveride' by Nuance.)

Disappointingly, the only place I didn't see him was at the Chelsea Hotel – which, thankfully, was reassuringly tacky, its hallowed corridors reeking of past indiscretions. When we eventually met him, we were also slightly disappointed by Andy's lack of curiosity (were we really that boring?), asking only if everyone in London was now shopping at Crolla and wearing patent leather shoes.

Warhol was a tourist attraction in his own theme park, an attraction of his own making. He seemed to bestow a benign kind of patronage everywhere he went, like a village priest. He was the alternative mayor of the city, an honorary position he'd earned by dint of just turning up. If anyone deserved a social long-service medal, it was Andy. Each time I saw him he was wearing the same uniform – black jeans, black turtleneck, black trainers and a black backpack; he looked like a large black match, a magnified stick insect wearing a white candyfloss hat. I later found out that Warhol had mostly stopped doing clubs by this time, but this must have been a particular week – like fashion week, maybe – bookended by enough parties and concerts to keep him interested. What did we know? It was his Disneyland, not ours.

NEW YORK WAS AMAZING, BUT it wasn't London. Over the years, the encroaching gentrification would make it a lot less culturally exciting, and the culture was what made the city breathe. Sure, the city was loud and fast and intoxicating and electric, but I never felt it had the cultural dynamism of London. Sometimes it felt terribly old-fashioned. The latent insecurity of many of the people who lived there was something I found oddly quaint.

I had quite a lot of friends in New York, and they all seemed so anxious. Yes, I knew the city was driven by power and status, but it all seemed a bit Trumpian to me. Colleagues would ask if you had been to a particular restaurant, and when I said I hadn't, they reacted as though I had admitted walking into the Condé Nast building wearing last season's Calvin Klein. They would get quietly hysterical about particular tables and couldn't believe I hadn't been savvy enough to purloin one. Of course, if you ever went to these places – which admittedly I sometimes did (I wasn't going to be left out) – you'd find a noisy room full of people rubbernecking their fellow guests in case someone more important had just walked in. This was the New York restaurant experience of the eighties, and it was almost a sport. It was certainly a spectator sport. I secretly loved it, but probably not in the way my friends expected.

New Yorkers were always obsessed with the tipping point and would rather feign madness or congenital stupidity than admit to eating at last week's hotspot. For a while, guerrilla restaurants didn't even bother putting signs up outside; they'd be gone in a month, so what was the point? Pop-up restaurants didn't have names, just addresses and cross streets (and unlisted reservation numbers that generally belonged to the GM's assistant's cell phone, who never seemed to answer it).

Manhattanites took their restaurants very seriously. In some places the waiters discussed the menu with you as if they were sharing wisdom picked up in the Himalayas. Every time a new eatery opened in Harlem the press went berserk – 'One of the most downtrodden and dangerous areas in New York City, Harlem is in the throes of a serious rejuvenation!' – and even antiquarian neighbourhood places could command half a page in a Sunday paper – 'The Taco Joint That Loves Ernest Borgnine!'

Per Se was opened by Thomas Keller (who also owned the French Laundry in California) in the Time Warner building and was once one of the hardest restaurants to get into in Manhattan, and feted by food tourists all over the world. I was due to visit not long after it opened in 2004, having made a reservation a month before. Then, on the night in question, I ended up cancelling as Sarah wanted room service instead. When I asked the concierge of my hotel to call and cancel, you would have thought I'd just asked him to give me a colonic.

'Are you serious? You're crazy! Do you know what you're doing? It takes months to get a reservation. You'll never get a table again. I've never heard of such a thing!'

I started to stay uptown when I visited, as did many other Brits, as the clientele at new downtown hotels seemed to get younger and younger. Old money was becoming more reliable than the new. Even fashionistas were tiring of SoHo, principally because it now looked like an urban regeneration theme park, one that's now been copied from Chicago to San Francisco and back again. Years ago, back in the eighties and nineties, I would always try to stay at whatever trendy hotel had just opened downtown, but I finally decided that loud music, imperious service and slow food (the old kind) might have had their day. It gradually hit me that I (the guest) was always the least important component of the business transaction, and that I had to be subservient to the emotional complexities of the front-desk staff's upward inflections ('I'll be right with you, sir? As soon as I'm finished talking to my agent? Sir, did you want to make a reservation for dinner? We can fit you in at 10.45?') and the intolerance of the interior designer. When I stayed at the Royalton for the first time, in 1988, the Tinguely-like taps on the bath – stainless steel, circular, so enormous it looked as though it had been airlifted clean out of the Playboy mansion – were so complicated that I didn't wash myself properly for two whole days; I was shown around by Steve Rubell, and it was surreal being shown how to use a bathtub by the man who used to lift the velvet rope at Studio 54.

IN MY TIME AT *GQ*, I went to New York about fifty times, and no trip was ever complete without a visit to the Strand bookstore on 12th Street, which in my view is the second-best secondhand bookshop in the US (the best being Powell's in Portland) and was an autodidact's dream. So attached to it did I become that I got protective about it in the way that New York cab drivers got protective about skyscrapers and public buildings; I noticed every nuance of change, and while I hated change, learned to accept it if not exactly embrace it.

When Nora Ephron moved to the Upper West Side, she said that after a few weeks she couldn't imagine living anywhere else. She began, in her own words, 'to make a religion of my neighbourhood' and became an evangelist for the area, obsessing about every retail detail. I fell in love with the Upper East Side; it was the most gentrified part of the city, and at its very heart – around the Mark and Carlyle hotels – it felt like an oddly sanitised film set. You felt cocooned, too, which is what I think Ephron was alluding to. In your own neighbourhood you felt so cut off from every other part of New York that you could just as easily be living in the middle of Oklahoma.

But the great thing was, you weren't.

As ever, New Yorkers will always be defined by their resilience and their sense of humour. Which, while not exactly torn from the gallows, could only ever come from one place. Throughout my time at *GQ*, I had three *New Yorker* cartoons stuck on my office pinboard, cartoons that summed up the three fundamental characteristics of your average New Yorker: the work ethic, the self-centredness, and the ability to be brutally honest when the occasion demands.

The first features two guys in a bar (*New Yorker* cartoons always feature guys in bars); one says to the other: 'Basically I like to keep the coffee buzz going until the martini buzz kicks in.'

The second shows a man behind his desk trying to find a lunch slot for the person on the other end of the phone: 'No, Thursday's out. How about never – is never good for you?' he says, hopefully.

The third shows a couple walking along a windswept Hamptons beach, with the woman saying to her friend: 'I do think your problems are serious, Richard. They're just not very interesting.'

Even though I always told interns that they could never use a taxi driver anecdote in a travel story, I couldn't resist repeating what a Lithuanian had said when he delivered me to JFK: 'New York gives you a chance. It doesn't give you more than that, but it gives you a chance.'

I ALWAYS LIKED GOING FOR three or four days, as it always felt like the city should be an episodic experience. Everyone always wanted quintessential New York experiences, which I guess is why we kept coming back. Obviously, many of these experiences were ad hoc. In 2010, I was in New York for a meeting with Tommy Hilfiger when Tracey Emin asked if I wanted to have dinner that night with John Richardson, the grand vizier of art history and biographer of Picasso. Sitting around his circular dining table smoking extraordinarily strong grass with a gaggle of his friends was intoxicating enough (he had a deep, mellifluous voice, and was a terrific gossip; *W* once described him as 'the man all New York wants to sit beside at dinner'), but his apartment was something else again. The 5,400-square-foot former dance studio loft occupied the full seventh floor of 73 Fifth Avenue in the Flatiron District (otherwise known as the Kensington) and was designed with architect Ernesto Buch to create an enfilade of rooms connected via mahogany doorways crowned with neoclassical pediments, which looked unerringly English. Filled with works by Picasso, Kathy Ruttenberg, Sir Joshua Reynolds, Salvator Rosa and Lucian Freud, with piles of magazines and antiquarian books, Chinese vases, statuary casts and small tables laden with framed photographs, tiny sculptures, a whale's penis (obviously) and a stuffed turtle wearing a red ribbon around its wrinkled neck, it looked like an English country house that had been turned into a museum. There was an enormous ethereal landscape by Lucien Lévy-Dhurmer and a large portrait of Richardson by Warhol, an eighteenth-century four-poster bed and one of the bathrooms was decked out entirely in blue and white Moroccan tiles. The inimitable blend of the ancient, old and new was positively baronial. Like his friend Nicky Haslam, Richardson was salty. He was born in suburban London, in a house outfitted by his elderly father, a Victorian quartermaster general who, apparently, 'had no taste whatsoever'.

NEW YORK WAS EPISODIC, AND random. Two months before I met Richardson, I had been in New York for the second annual Norman Mailer Center and Writers Colony Benefit Gala at Cipriani 42nd Street. I was there as part of a team to present the winner of British *GQ*'s inaugural Student Writing Award (which had been judged by Sir Peter Stothard, Lily Allen, Tony Parsons and Ed Victor). Tina Brown, Jann Wenner and the super-cool Gay Talese were all in evidence, along with Taki, Michael Wolff, the irrepressible Larry Schiller and Mailer's beautiful widow Norris. When I asked Tom Wolfe how his new novel was coming on (*Back to Blood* was at least three years overdue), he said, 'If it's not finished next year, I'm going to be spurting blood instead of ink.'

One of the winners at the awards gala was Ruth Gruber, aged ninety-nine, who won the distinguished journalism award. Reporter, photographer, author of twenty books, she was the first foreign correspondent to interview prisoners in the Soviet Gulag. After the dinner, the *Vanity Fair* writer Patricia Bosworth went over to congratulate Gruber, who she had known since she was a little girl. 'Ruth,' she said, 'what does it feel like to be ninety-nine years old?' Gruber smiled and in her soft little voice said, 'Oh, Patti, being ninety-nine feels just like being ninety-eight.'

As part of the prize, our winner spent a month in the Norman Mailer Writers Colony in Provincetown, Massachusetts, the place Mailer called home. I spent a night in Mailer's house, sleeping in his bed and reading a first edition of *Tough Guys Don't Dance* (which is set in the fishing port). That night I'd spent an hour upstairs, rooting around his studio (which had been left exactly as Mailer left it before he died in 2007). The room at the very top of the stairs was the house's holy grail, Mailer's studio, the place where the heavyweight champion of the word wrote his books, where he crafted many of the convoluted, Thesaurus-combed pieces that made him famous, where he spent his days trying to conjure up a book that would generate as much acclaim as *The Naked and the Dead* or *Ancient Evenings*. Here you'd find old manuscripts, the daybed where he would take naps, unopened packs of highlighter pens, his rocking chair, the plastic clothes hangers on which he'd hang his blazers, and a multi-gym he used only once, but was too heavy to dismantle. The detritus in his studio showed his propensity for exhaustive research, and the room was still littered with books he was using for his uncompleted Third Reich tome. I also found a huge magnifying glass; research papers would be photocopied twice the size so he could read them, while his handwritten pages would be faxed to his secretary in New York to type up. As you walked up the stairs to his studio the first thing you saw was a Bellevue sign prominently placed in a bookcase, as Mailer wanted to be reminded every day of the awful thing he did to his second wife in 1960, when he stabbed her with a penknife, nearly killing her.

The Colony afforded me another quintessential New York experience, in another almost unimaginable location. Two days before the Cipriani dinner, Norris had invited me to lunch at the Brooklyn Heights apartment she once shared with Norman. This is where they hosted parties attended by John Lennon, Bob Dylan and Woody Allen in the home Mailer designed to resemble a ship. The landmarked four-storey, walk-up brownstone, built in 1840, overlooked Brooklyn Bridge Park, the Statue of Liberty and the East River and had one of the best views on south Manhattan. You could look out from the terrace and imagine yourself travelling all the way to California, flying over New York with the wind in your face, feeling like a king. Which is no doubt how Mailer felt whenever he opened his sliding doors. It was outfitted with gangplanks, hammocks and a jungle gym, and there were artefacts from the Pulitzer Prize-winning writer's life all over the place: a button for Mailer's quixotic 1969 campaign for New York City mayor that says 'I would sleep better if Norman Mailer were mayor'; a Wurlitzer jukebox; a photograph of Mailer boxing with José Torres, the light heavyweight champion who taught Mailer how to box on the condition that Mailer taught him how to write.

Mailer used to cook his own breakfast – hash browns, eggs and pears, a dish he learned as an army cook in the Second World War – but in the small kitchenette Norris made me an elaborate chef salad, all the while talking about her life with Mailer, and her life in Manhattan. She was sixty-one, still beautiful, still pointy, with a lovely infectious laugh, and yet there was an innate sadness about her. She had been battling cancer for over a decade and had endured six major operations. A month later she would be dead.

I CHAIRED THE AWARDS GALA the following year and arranged for Keith Richards to come and accept an award for his autobiography, *Life*. When he stepped up onto the stage at the Mandarin Oriental to collect his award from a bumptious Bill Clinton, he appeared to be almost speechless. Words eventually came, though, if a little tentatively.

'I'm not usually fazed by stuff,' said Keith, almost humbly, glancing at the ex-president, 'but I'm fazed by this.'

In the room, it was difficult to tell who had the most star power; the great and the good uncharacteristically took out their mobiles to take snaps of Clinton, while Keef charmed everyone with his completely unintentional impression of Paul Whitehouse's Rowley Birkin.

I interviewed Keith twice during this period. The first time we photographed him on the rooftops of midtown Manhattan, with the Human Riff showing off his Gianfranco Ferré overcoat and black Gucci jeans against the Gotham skyline. When he looked at the pictures taken by Peter Lindbergh, his jaw ever so slightly dropped. The legend set down his rather large tumbler of vodka and fizzy orange and looked in my direction, if not squarely in the eye. Because of the hastily arranged drapes covering the windows in the hotel it was difficult to make out his mood, but his mouth said it all. 'You know what, man?' he said, playing with his pirate rings as he absentmindedly sprinkled the pristine hotel carpet with cigarette ash. 'You've made me look like Keith Richards. And believe me, that's not as easy as you might think.'

Every flat surface in his hotel room appeared to have been covered with a scarf of some description. I met him at dusk, and he looked like something out of a gothic horror movie, a man who lived according to his own particular timetable within his own parameters. Fifty years of fame had allowed him to indulge himself to the extent that he operated on Keith time and on Keith time only. His simian good looks and delicate little body should have been diminished by his habits, but they had actually, largely, been strangely enhanced – even if he did still have the nonchalance of the dead. He was still sipping vodka and was apparently still smoking grass (he was carrying some extra-large Rizlas 'more in expectation than anything'), yet was sprightly on his feet.

And he still looked great in a Versace coat.

If Mick Jagger still seemed like an overwound toy, Richards was still the quintessential urban cowboy; his gait that of a bowlegged junkie looking for his horse (or his guitar, which he never used to sleep without). He was approaching sixty yet his skin was clear and the lines he carried on his face were, in his own, rather elasticised words, 'built from laughter'.

He was more than intrigued by his own image, happy in the knowledge that no one else had ever looked quite like him. When he was young, he wanted to look like Elvis and Little Richard, then Buddy Holly and then finally, for ever, himself. 'I don't really study my legacy,' he said in his increasingly macabre-looking hotel room. 'It's got to the point where it's like a shadow that you drag around behind you. Now and again I just pull the Keith Richards look and scare the living daylights out of somebody just because they're in my way; it's just a little something you have in your locker. It's a look and a quick move.'

A lot of New York cab drivers change shifts around 4 p.m., so getting a cab in the middle of the afternoon can be testing, to say the very least, especially if you're downtown. As I tried to hail a cab after leaving my interview with Keith, on my way uptown, an empty bus stopped, I haggled with the driver, and he took me all the way to the Carlyle for $20. When I told him what type of business I was in, he seemed nonplussed: 'Journalism? No, I don't know . . . You sure you got the fare?'

FOR A WHILE WE DISCUSSED the possibility of Keith writing for *GQ*, but the logistics eventually proved impossible. Sometimes I was totally prescriptive in terms of what I wanted people to do, and at other times I just acted as an enabler of serendipity. My opinion was usually, 'Why not?' If I met someone and liked them, I'd want them on board, even though I didn't really know where they might fit in. I did this with Tracey Emin, Simon Schama, Hugo Rifkind, Guto Harri, even Robbie Williams. At one point I even hired Giles Coren, but only to stop him writing mean things about me in the *Evening Standard*.

We would discuss covers relentlessly. Was there a perfect cover? It was a Sisyphean question we took extremely seriously. Sometimes a meeting about possible covers could last all morning, often all day, and we wouldn't stop until we'd alighted on something truly fresh, something original that would take some persuasion to pull off. I'd sit in our brilliant new creative director Paul Solomons's office and we'd spitball ideas until we fell on something we liked. I always used to say it was my job to come up with the bad ideas, although in reality they came from anywhere – from Paul Solomons, myself, one of the features team or someone who just happened to be walking by. I was still a big fan of the 'Let's just do it upside down and in green' idea, by which I meant let's do something completely at odds with what anyone might expect us to do. For a while, this involved asking famous women to take their clothes off in interesting and complex ways, but we soon tired of that, and deliberately tried to make the covers more iconic and more like news magazines. I knew precisely what I wanted to do with David Beckham, however, when we colluded on a cover story to coincide with the 2002 World Cup in Japan and South Korea.

We had started to become very good at stunts, whether it was asking an unlikely person to disrobe (the disgraced Tory MPs Neil and Christine Hamilton appeared to be willing to do anything for the sake of publicity), or having hi–lo concepts that involved the great and the good (getting Tracey Emin to dress up as the Stig, from *Top Gear* – 'The things you do for love,' she said later). Beckham had become media catnip, and it seemed whatever he did made the papers, whether it was wearing a sarong to a party or having his hair cut. He was becoming a gold-standard phenomenon, at the risk almost of upstaging his Spice Girl wife, Victoria.

So for our cover, we had two ideas.

The first was to dress Beckham up as David Bowie *circa* 1975, the *Young Americans* Bowie, complete with felt fedora and baggy pants (in the end Beckham chose a Panama). For the second set-up I wanted him almost naked, covered in baby oil, in a gym, in a deliberately homoerotic vignette.

And Beckham was up for both.

We organised to shoot the covers and do the interview in a studio in Manchester, as he was still playing for Man United. I travelled up to see the shoot, having already commissioned the campy, hi-gloss David LaChapelle to photograph him and David Furnish to interview him. Victoria was already there when I arrived, as was everyone else, including GQ's longstanding fashion editor, Jo Levin. Jo and I occasionally clashed, and she could be terribly belligerent when she chose to be, but she was also incredibly dynamic and occasionally brilliant.

If I asked her to do something, and she could see the possibilities, she threw herself into the idea, whether it was ingratiating herself with a celebrity or pursuing a photographer. The word dogged could have been invented for her, and her dedication was impressive. By the time I arrived at the studio she was conducting the shoot as if it were an orchestra. At the time, this was the most expensive cover shoot in the magazine's history – £80,000 – and it involved flying LaChapelle and his six-man entourage from LA. There were twenty professionals primed to cater to Beckham's every whim, including a make-up artist, set builder, hairdresser, security, drivers, caterers, even a DJ – and me, worrying about how much it was all costing.

The thing that surprised me was how self-possessed Beckham was, and how eager he was to push the envelope; for instance, whenever Jo suggested something for him to wear, he'd flick along the rail and plump for something even more outré. 'What about this?' he'd say, pulling out a leopardskin shawl. As he tried on the clothes, he slowly moved his body in time to the blaring music, nodding his head enthusiastically to Usher and Zero 7. I think he already knew what effect he had on people, on the media, and how he could use this to amplify his image in a way that no British sportsman had done before. We would end up working with him for over twenty years (we gave him at least a dozen covers), and he always knew how he wanted to look. In Manchester, when he walked into the part of the studio that LaChapelle's team had designed to look like a kind of kaleidoscopic gym, and saw the bottles of baby oil, the denim cut-offs and the dumbbells, Beckham frowned and said, 'OK, I can see where this is going.'

And he could. Half an hour later, naked from the waist up, his torso covered in baby oil, his fingernails painted jet black and wearing a pair of Yves Saint Laurent Rive Gauche baggy pants, he didn't look like your average British footballer. He knew what jewellery he wanted to wear, what scarves he should be shot in and where to draw the line between glam and camp. 'He's just like a rock star,' said Jo, as Beckham lay back on the studio floor with his hands down his trousers. 'Only a rock star could do this.'

Sometimes sportsmen confounded you, sometimes they just disappointed you, and then you realised the media perception of them was completely accurate, even possibly underplayed. Back in the mid-nineties when Paul Ince was still playing at Manchester United, when everyone in the United squad was being encouraged by the media into thinking they were proto-Galácticos, I saw him at a party at Giorgio Armani's house in Milan. Having already chatted to another England player, the delightful David James, I went over to Ince, introduced myself and said I was a big fan. Ince, who at this stage in his career was still referred to as 'the Guvnor' by the Old Trafford faithful, looked up at me as though I'd just accused him of stealing my car, curled his lip and said, 'Yeah? Me too,' before pushing past me to the bar.

Paul Ince would never appear in *GQ*.

The Men of the Year Awards

The Greatest Show on Earth

The only game in town, Tate Modern, 2017

AS SOON AS I STARTED at *GQ*, there was something called the Men of the Year Awards that kept being mentioned by Peter Stuart, our delightfully old-school publisher. It wasn't talked about with fondness, though, rather in the way that someone might talk about a wayward uncle who was about to pay a visit. The Men of the Year Awards was an idea that had been stolen from the Americans by Peter; it seemed, however, that the US company didn't think much of it, and had seriously downgraded it, while Peter thought it could be a good way to market the magazine in the UK. The idea was to celebrate various men who had been exemplary in their particular fields during the previous year – sportsmen, comedians, designers, actors, etc. It wasn't an especially sophisticated idea, and apparently the first one (organised the year before I arrived) had been held in a hotel suite in central London, and had been a bit of a damp squib (no one famous had turned up).

But the sponsorship for this year's event had been sold, and so the bad smell refused to go away.

I liked the proposition, though, and thought it could be a good way to emphasise to our readers, our advertisers and the media our new areas of interest. We could celebrate a wider range of culturally important people, we could create a spectacle, and we could have some fun along the way. As well as producing what I wanted to be the best magazine in the country, I was also trying to build our very own ecosystem around the brand, trying to give it its very own halo. The magazine didn't just need to have a big idea, it needed to shout about it too.

Of course, there were some who thought we created the Men of the Year Awards simply in order to *have* a party, although these tended to be the kind of people who had never been invited, and never would be. After a couple of years, the awards dinner certainly managed to create its own celebrity microclimate – a place where you might find Amy Schumer swapping punchlines with David Walliams, or Pharrell Williams comparing backhands with Andy Murray. After one year where we unsuccessfully hosted the event in a nightclub, in 2000 we decided to go for it and host a sit-down awards show. I was adamant that the people giving the awards should be at least as famous as the people receiving them, and often more famous (one year we asked Martin Scorsese to present an award to Giorgio Armani, for instance; somewhere, perhaps in some strange, shadowy, parallel universe, his speech is drawing slowly to a close), while it was crucially important that our guests should be flattered by who they had been seated beside.

This meant I was fastidious – obsessive, almost – about the seating plans, which would be fiddled with for ten days using coloured Post-it notes stuck on to large tables in the company boardroom (which was tripled locked each night, in case any wandering tabloid hack attempted to find out who this year's winners were). I made sure that politicians sat next to rock stars, who sat next to journalists, who sat next to luxury-goods behemoths, who sat next to models who perched perilously on their chairs next to boxers, etc.

Everyone and their mother (and a lot of guests would invite their parents) needed to feel flattered.

And while we obviously knew that the collective power of the extraordinary people in the room (try Eddie Redmayne, Emma Watson, Benedict Cumberbatch, Naomi Campbell, John Legend, Sacha Baron Cohen, Daniel Kaluuya, Elisabeth Moss, Sir Patrick Stewart and Led Zeppelin – who reformed in 2007 just to attend the awards – for size) added to the lustre of the celebration as well as the very idea of the thing itself, I liked to think that the awards remained a reflection of achievement. They were a way to acknowledge success in everything from literature to sport and from comedy to architecture and back again, applauding supermodels, design icons, photographers, film directors, chefs, entrepreneurs and Olympians (standing ovations being wholeheartedly encouraged).

The seating plan was choreographed so that, regardless of where you sat, as a guest, as well as sitting next to someone famous, notable or interesting, there would be a triple A-lister – maybe two, maybe three, maybe more – in your sightline. I wanted everyone to enjoy the evening, and I wanted everyone to be comfortable. Over the years, I co-hosted many dinners with Nick Jones from Soho House – for ten years we produced the Land Rover-sponsored marquee dinner at the Hay-on-Wye literary festival, as well as the dinner following the Royal Academy Summer Exhibition private view – and we would always differ over the appropriateness of *placement.* Nick hated placement as he wanted people to be able to plonk themselves down anywhere, thus creating a genuine mix. I hated this idea, as I thought it simply made people insecure, and worried about where they were going to sit and who they were going to end up with. And I think I was right. If you were a famous person you would sit with all your famous friends, and if you were a shy person you would sit on the periphery somewhere. And if you were late, you'd probably find there wasn't anywhere to sit at all.

So, I was obsessive about seating plans, making sure that a table of twelve contained at least three extremely famous people, plus a chef, someone from the luxury goods industry, a journalist, a model, a staff member and an artist – say. Plus, I would liberally sprinkle the tables with interesting society figures and friends who I knew would be flattered and flattering. Guests would find themselves sitting next to Pelé or Steve Coogan, George Clooney or Tony Blair, Heidi Klum or Kim Kardashian, and they would feel happy about life.

I wanted everyone to have a good time.

Of course, sometimes celebrities wouldn't like where they had been seated, and would either make a fuss or simply swap the placement cards without telling anyone. Which resulted in chaos and raised voices. A fight nearly broke out one year when Noel Gallagher and his wife moved the cards of John Bishop and his wife as they wanted to sit closer to the stage, which Bishop didn't appreciate when he arrived five minutes later. Artist Wolfgang Tillmans also created a fuss one year when he discovered that the sponsor of his award was a gallery of which he didn't approve. He was about to walk out until Tracey Emin told him not to be so silly.

Sometimes, the problems were insurmountable.

David Furnish came up to me one year and said, 'There's a problem with Piers Morgan.'

'What's that?' I said, suddenly concerned.

'He's here.'

IT WAS A TOUGH ROOM for a host as there were always so many comedians in the room, which meant that some people were wary of accepting the gig. This may have been one of the reasons why James Corden and Graham Norton were unsure about doing it. On a typical night, we might have Rob Brydon, Steve Coogan, David Walliams, Ricky Gervais, Jonathan Ross, Rowan Atkinson, Rory Bremner and Billy Connolly in the room. Who on earth would want to try and make that lot laugh?

We always tried to hire the most appropriate hosts, and these included Samuel L. Jackson, Jonathan Ross, Elton John, Lily Allen, Stanley Tucci and Michael Sheen. Most worked fine. We would organise for the scriptwriter to work closely with the talent, in order to create something that would work in the room. The only time it didn't work was when I asked David Walliams to host, and he said he would like to co-host with Jimmy Carr. This made me nervous. Carr had hosted the awards before, and it hadn't been a roaring success. Sure, he had been funny, but his schtick was too aggressive for the crowd; I never saw the point of inviting people halfway round the world and then insulting them in public. That year, I was staying at Paul McGuinness and Kathy Gilfillan's house in Ireland the week before the awards and spent much of the weekend on the phone arguing with Carr, encouraging him to downplay the aggression in his speech. In the end, he got his way, and he died. I knew the vibe of the room and he thought he could alter it. He couldn't.

WE ALWAYS WENT OUT OF our way to celebrate icons, those who had climbed the mountain time and again, and whose interstellar status could sometimes be taken for granted – Ray Davies, Tom Wolfe, Iggy Pop, Burt Bacharach, Salman Rushdie and Sir Bobby Charlton, for instance – and those who actually helped shape the lives of those in our constituency.

Occasionally, such icons would make themselves available only at the very last minute. Tony Bennett agreed to come with only four weeks to the show. I had been trying to get him to come for years, so I was thrilled. The lateness of the booking meant we needed the interview and pictures for the magazine to happen immediately, so I flew to New York, interviewed Bennett, transcribed the tape and wrote a five thousand-word profile on my BlackBerry on the flight back, filing the piece as the plane touched down at Terminal 5, all within forty-eight hours. Maybe I did learn something from Boris.

THE MEN OF THE YEAR Awards traditionally happened every September, towards the start of the month when everyone was just back from holiday. It was always the first event of the new season, so everyone had a suntan and was eager to gossip and show off, having just spent six weeks in the Med or the Caribbean. As it was at the very beginning of the awards season, many Hollywood A-listers used the event as a way of kickstarting their Oscar campaigns.

I always thought of it as armour night, a group of seemingly disparate people convening in an empty museum or intimate aircraft hangar, eager to quickly revalidate themselves using everything available to them: protecting their status with a funny story involving a boldface name who had spent some time on their yacht; a new job; the same job; a new girlfriend (usually younger, although occasionally, and intriguingly, older); some new fancy duds. Most people came back from holiday with a bronzed face and an additional layer of fame that it would take half-a-dozen drinks to soften.

One thing that regularly annoyed me was certain guests' deliberate and premeditated indifference to the event itself. One year at Tate Modern, I sat Top Shop king Philip Green (known as PG to anyone who did actually know him) on one of the best six tables (there were only ever six, although I obviously lied about this habitually), and put him between Chancellor George Osborne, Liz Hurley, Jonathan Newhouse (my ultimate boss), Keith Richards and Tom Ford. It was like one of those joke Radio 4 shows where you pick your fantasy dinner party. But Philip sat through the entire ceremony stony-faced, refusing to engage with his fellow diners, seemingly unable to applaud any of the winners, and generally looking like a cross between Mr Glum and Mr Angry. I suspected that one of the reasons he was looking so uneasy was because he was unable ostentatiously to order some better wine for himself like he would at a restaurant. But the main reason, it turned out, was simply because there was no way for him to take credit for the evening.

A few days later, there was a drinks reception at Downing Street to celebrate the opening of London Fashion Week. PG (Tracey Emin once told me his middle name was Ian) came up to me and told me that he'd willingly help with next year's awards. 'I think there's a couple of things we could do differently,' he growled. I leaned right into his face and said that not only did I not need his help, but that if he wasn't prepared to act a bit more enthusiastically, I would simply give his invitation to someone else.

I liked Philip. He could be excruciatingly rude to people – he tried it with me once, until I shouted back and told him to stop being so ridiculous – but I took his bad-tempered nature in my stride and just thought he was being petulant in order to show people how powerful he was. Of course, the way he acted was completely unnecessary, but his inability to understand this almost neutered my dislike at his attempts at being beastly. For a good number of years, he had a fabulous director of communications called Tania Foster-Brown, a no-nonsense blonde who handled Philip as he needed to be handled, with weary resignment.

I once had an appointment with Philip in his office (I was no doubt asking him to sponsor something – he could be extremely generous), and was waiting in Tania's own office as he finished a call. We could hear him shouting in the background, and when he finally stopped, her internal phone rang.

'Yes, Philip,' Tania answered, in her best cut-glass accent. 'Of course, Philip, I'm sure that must be most egregious.'

There was silence as PG continued his aimless tirade on the phone. This went on for a minute or so, and then when he had stopped talking, Tania, in a voice that sounded as though she was asking for new balls during a Wimbledon final, said, 'And which particular fucking cunt are we talking about, Philip?'

PHILIP GREEN WAS ONE OF a handful of guests who could be difficult at the awards, but Michelle Russell, who ran the show (impeccably), and our celebrity booker, the completely unflappable James Williams, always acted with judiciousness and calm. Nothing was above or beyond them. Sometimes winners arrived early, presenters arrived late, and occasionally people didn't arrive at all. Michelle and James coped with it all, treating every problem, every micro-aggression, as though it were completely natural. They had a default backstop rationale based on common sense: while something could be monumentally inconvenient, no one was going to die. I did occasionally feel embarrassed that they had to put up with such poor celebrity behaviour – tardiness, rudeness and a general sense of entitlement. And the things they said! One year, a hugely successful female singer of Eastern European origin arrived with only minutes to spare before she was due on stage. As she was backstage, climbing into her evening dress, she said, to no one in particular, 'I'm so sorry, I reek of cock.'

The rest of the team were also phenomenal, ranging from *GQ*'s creative director Paul Solomons, who designed all the publicity materials and commissioned the films, photographic sessions and digital content, to deputy editor Bill Prince, who always provided wise counsel. Perhaps Jonathan Heaf and managing director George Chesterton had the hardest job, which was to tell me no. Heaf would tell me we couldn't possibly give an award to such-and-such just because they were a friend of mine; and Chesterton would tell me we couldn't afford to do something I desperately wanted to. This inevitably resulted in many stand-up rows.

We all had personal connections, and the ability to deliver the occasional boldface name, but it was Stuart McGurk's responsibility to marshal everyone's contacts and make sure that on the first Tuesday of September every year, twenty of the most famous people in the world walked on to the purpose-built stage at the Royal Opera House or Tate Modern.

OUR FIRST MEN OF THE Year sit-down event was fairly entry level – we attracted Chris Tarrant, Jamie Oliver and about thirty other stars. But we also managed to secure a genuine legend, Paul McCartney. He seemed to enjoy himself – he sent a note the following day, thanking us for the award as well as the vegetarian food we'd served at dinner – and it was this as much as anything else that gave us the confidence to do it again the following year, and make it bigger and better.

Which we continued to do every year, for twenty years. And what started as a marketing event became, quite quickly, not just one of the biggest awards shows in the industry, but the biggest multi-genre awards show in the country. Everyone came: from Jay-Z and Beyoncé to David Beckham and Harry Styles to Prince Charles and several prime ministers – Tony Blair, David Cameron, Boris Johnson – and more knights of the realm than you could shake a polished steel sword at: Michael Caine, Richard Branson, Ian McKellen, Elton John, etc.

Having worked in the industry all my life, I knew how challenging celebrities could be, but then I also knew that they only became challenging when they were uncertain of what lay around the corner. Famous people don't like any surprises, and neither do the people working for them. So, my strategy was always the same: make sure they're comfortable; make sure that everything happens exactly the way it was meant to. Soon they started to trust us, and with trust comes everything else.

So everyone came. If, in the early days, it was tough to convince people to come, after a while, we waited for people to call us. We purposefully also had an incredibly small team; I didn't farm work out to an agency, as most awards shows do (you'd be horrified) but kept it tight. Michelle, our events supremo, soon became the most-feared woman in Condé Nast. You crossed her at your peril, and few did. As we got closer to showtime, there were dozens of Condé Nasties who would try to slime over Michelle, implying that they might want a ticket. She never buckled, even when *Vogue* were on the phone. 'Create your own damn awards show,' she said to one annoyingly persistent caller.

Predictably, some people who came behaved like entitled fools, although these tended to be those who had been famous for only five minutes or so.

One year, we were celebrating a respectably successful British actor, Paul, who came with his annoyingly entitled American wife. They were being put up (by us, obviously, and at great expense) in the St Martin's Lane Hotel, which was about a 400-metre drive from the Royal Opera House, where the event was being held. Naturally, we had arranged for a car to ferry them to and from the event, although word soon came through from a particularly shrill PR that Paul's wife had demanded a car with bulletproof glass.

So what did we do? We sent a car with 'bulletproof glass', although seeing that no one made an attempt on her life that night, no one would have been any the wiser if we hadn't. And guess what: we didn't.

A few years later, we flew a former Bond girl all the way from Jamaica to present an award to our Actor of the Year. We flew her first class (everyone was always flown first), and she was put up in a suite at Claridge's for four nights. We also arranged for her to have various beauty treatments and a private shopping experience at a department store. So far, so unexceptional.

Then, around four o'clock on the day of the dinner, one of our team got a call from her publicist, telling us that her employer didn't feel very well and wasn't sure if she could make the awards that night (in exactly two hours' time). We were then informed that she would start to feel a lot better if we gave her £5,000 in cash within the next hour. So we had a quick conflab, and decided to try and get the money. Now, I had a policy of never paying anyone – not even those footballers who were still represented by dodgy agents – so this was an unprecedented decision. I figured, however, that having gone to the great expense and trouble of flying her all the way here, then an extra £5,000 wasn't going to break the bank.

Jamie Bill, then our publishing director, found the money, and I then instructed a workie (a work-experience employee) to walk it over to Claridge's – all of 400 yards. Before he left my office I said, 'Make sure you wrap it in a brown paper envelope. It won't mean anything to her, but it will mean a lot to me.'

A few hours later she glided on to the stage at Tate Modern as though none of this had ever taken place.

THE AWARDS GENERATED A RIDICULOUS amount of publicity (expertly organised by our redoubtable Publicity Director, Nicky Eaton), so we could be guaranteed that any altercation would end up on every newspaper front cover and every celebrity website the next day. There was the year I ejected the idiotic Russell Brand for insulting our sponsors, Hugo Boss (he was later found hypocritically to be a fan of the label), the year Kate Moss allegedly stormed out after a spat with Jimmy Nesbitt, and the year in which Elton John and Lily Allen were meant to have had a huge row when they were co-hosting the event (completely untrue). (Rule: never ask two people to co-host an event, as invariably they each think the other one is doing the work.) With Brand, I wasn't going to cause a scene during the awards (he had already done that himself), but as soon as they were over, I walked up to him and asked him to leave. He gave me a mouthful of abuse but by then the security guards were hovering and he soon left. Earlier in the evening, Rod Stewart had berated Brand from the stage, accusing him of ungallant behaviour towards Stewart's daughter. After this, Brand was banned from all Condé Nast magazines and events, which, when his Hollywood career refused to take off, must have been difficult for him.

I even banned Tracey Emin from the awards once. And she is a friend of mine. We were presenting the Clash with a lifetime achievement award and the guest presenter had failed to turn up. Iggy Pop was meant to present the award, and we were going to fly him in by private jet from Italy, but he had fallen off the stage at a festival earlier in the day. At the last minute, I asked Tracey if she would present it instead, although to be fair she wasn't exactly in the right condition to do so. The result was a shambles, although it was my fault for asking her in the first place. It was the most drunken, the most profane, and possibly the longest speech anyone in the room had ever heard. In fact, in some parts of the world I think it's still going on . . . Nicholas Coleridge, my boss, was sitting on a table with the MDs of Cartier, Louis Vuitton and Chanel, and said the experience was, and I quote, 'like watching pornography with your grandparents'.

There was always a fracas or two, some of which had been internally engineered, like sitting warring supermodels, or two politicians who were not-so secretly going for the same job, next to each other. We knew we could generate at least half-a-dozen stories in Londoner's Diary in the *Evening Standard*, and there started to be so many misdemeanours that both the *Mirror* and the *Sun* started to run double-page spreads on the awards for three to four days afterwards. We should have charged: we delivered so much content, year after year after year, all free of charge. We should have been compensated.

We even managed to get coverage about our goodie bags: we had bags for the guests, for the presenters and for the winners. The winners' bags were worth over £50,000, and people clamoured for them. They were good because we made them good. My ask was simple: make them better than the goodie bags you get at the Brits or the BAFTAs. They were. We won. So there, yah-boo sucks.

We invited Sacha Baron Cohen to accept the Editor's Special Award in 2018, an invitation that was not best received by our sponsor, Hugo Boss. The German lifestyle brand had been enthusiastic and incredibly supportive partners for some years, but they were always concerned about the possibility of something untoward happening at the awards and were therefore wary of outspoken comedians such as Sacha. They hated controversy while I loved it, courted it and, although this sounds like an editorial and logistical nightmare, it actually created its own, very workable and incredibly successful dynamic. Ever since the Russell Brand debacle, though, we had been extremely mindful about inviting people who could potentially embarrass us all. Out of courtesy, we had started to show Boss our list of potential winners to give them the opportunity to raise a red flag, but we always managed to persuade them that what we wanted to do would work well, and we weren't deliberately kicking up dust just for the sake of it.

Sacha was a relatively late addition to the roster, and when Boss found out, they freaked; we could almost hear the screams emanating from their headquarters in Metzingen: 'Nein danke, nein danke! Bist du bose?'

They immediately asked us to disinvite him, we refused, and so began a tortuous back and forth that lasted an entire week. In the end, we got our way, but not before some compromises had been agreed. On the night of the awards, Sacha and his wife Isla Fisher were to be secretly given their own security detail who would monitor them throughout the evening, shadowing them from the moment they stepped out of their car until they left the Tate Modern. There was a concern that Sacha might change into a costume before he was due onstage, so we even had him followed when he went to the lavatory. There was also a completely irrational fear that Isla might have stuffed a costume into her handbag, and so there were secret cameras monitoring her too.

Only four of us knew this was happening, which was embarrassing for me as I was sitting between Sacha and Isla. Of course, nothing happened, apart from Sacha making an impassioned acceptance speech about freedom of speech. He didn't know Big Brother was watching.

BECAUSE WE ATTRACTED SO MANY celebrities, we soon became the most syndicated magazine in the company (selling content on to French *Vogue*, Taiwanese *Vanity Fair*, Russian *GQ*, etc.), which predictably annoyed the Americans. They wanted to treat us as poor relations, but because we punched so much above our weight, and because we brought in so much money, they couldn't.

As the Men of the Year reached its pomp, there would sometimes be at least two hundred genuinely A-list celebs in the room, and so consequently they sometimes had to be kept apart. David Cameron won Politician of the Year once (OK, we weren't infallible), and as there was a highly politicised pop group who were winning their own awards that night, we made sure their award came just before Cameron's, so they were in the publicity den speaking to the press while the PM was on stage.

The Men of the Year Awards was the only place where I've seen David Bowie really lose his temper. I had spent a good year trying to convince him to come all the way from New York to accept an award, which had involved me flying to see him in Switzerland, Manhattan and Los Angeles. He hated awards shows (he didn't like the way you only got one if you turned up; this didn't apply to us, as we regularly had people accepting by video), and he went out of his way to try and rebuff me. But, eventually, I got my way, and he duly turned up at the Natural History Museum to collect it. He was let into the backstage area by his long-standing publicist, the ever-forgiving Alan Edwards, and looked elegant and cool in his specially tailored Hedi Slimane suit. Stella McCartney was giving the introductory remarks, as she was going to present him with the award. But the acoustics in the museum were so bad – we would eventually move the event back to the Royal Opera House – that Bowie couldn't understand a word she said. As this was obviously making him uneasy, he suddenly exploded and demanded to know why he couldn't hear what she was saying. Anyway, he made his way to the stage, and behaved with all the panache we came to expect from the man, although he was rather chilly with me for a while after the show.

He gave his publicist merry hell, though. Alan Edwards had, as usual, given him a detailed brief of what he ought to do while he was here, in order to generate as much publicity as possible. He had suggested he be photographed with Holly Valance, who was one of our winners and who was then a ridiculously successful soap star. Bowie refused. Thought she was a bit naff. Didn't think she was important enough. I've still got all the photographs from that evening filed away in the hundreds of shoeboxes I keep in my London study, and they're largely full of men. Stella McCartney is in a few of the pictures, but basically, it's Bowie, Paul Smith, me (gurning so much I look like a competition winner), Travis (all of them) and Jonathan Ross. And the following day, unsurprisingly, the tabloids weren't that interested. We were a bunch of smug white men of a certain age. This was the period when Bowie was still a bit of a mystery in terms of his convening power, and so the papers were rather circumspect about including him in their coverage. Alan Edwards nearly lost his job, even though the fault lay with Bowie, and is still rather surprised he didn't.

'He was furious for days,' Alan told me. 'I kept telling him the PR was coming and of course it never did. He knew it wasn't coming, and so did I.' So be it: Alan would live to fight another day. Easily the best independent music PR of his era, barely a day went by when we didn't speak to each other.

ONE OF THE THINGS I learned quite quickly about dealing with celebrities is that their expectations didn't often tally with those of their assistants. As long as they were feeling comfortable, then the famous were usually perfectly reasonable. The people who worked for them, however, had to constantly validate their jobs. Every day. And the easiest way for them to do that was to invent problems simply in order to solve them.

One rather brilliant example of this happened in 2010, when we were celebrating an internationally recognised sportsman. Actually, not a sportsman, more of a legend. A genuine legend. Pelé. He had been working for a watch company in Geneva (talking, showing media his wrist), and we'd had him flown over in a private jet to attend the awards. As soon as the plane landed, in Northolt, one of my team got an overexcited call from one of Pelé's assistants. She was screaming at the top of her voice, although her complaint was easily understood. Why was the airfield so far from London, and was there anything we could do about it?

To his credit, James Williams parried back immediately with, 'Of course; where would you like it moved to?'

We tended to use private jets a lot, although one dour Mancunian pop star still owes me £30,000 for refusing to get on the plane I sent all the way to Madrid to pick him up for the awards. I wouldn't say his name was Steven, although it obviously is. (This was the same dour Mancunian indie darling who, while being photographed by us in his bungalow at the Beverly Hills Hotel, asked his assistant to call his other assistant in London, instructing them to call us with the news that he didn't want to continue with the shoot. Honestly, some people.)

We invited Harvey Weinstein one year and asked his office to supply a short showreel of his greatest hits. The film was delivered on time, but it was three minutes too long. I called him up and said we were going to have to cut it, and he kicked off, moving quite quickly from affable-friend-of-the-media to generic do-you-have-any-fucking-idea-who-you-are-dealing-with-here? After half-a-dozen calls in which we made no progress at all, I acquiesced, telling him I wasn't going to edit the film, and that I was thrilled he was attending. I then cut three minutes out of the showreel, assuming that in the heat of the moment he wouldn't notice. He didn't, and at Matthew Freud's after-party he came up to me and thanked me for backing down.

Many notables were more than happy to turn up and involve themselves in exchange for the tsunami of press attention that would immediately come their way; others, like U2, needed to be courted. I'd known their manager Paul McGuinness for quite some time, but I didn't immediately pitch the awards as I wasn't sure it was the right time for either of us. The band needed to know that our interest was genuine, and that it wasn't a completely transactional exercise; and I needed to make sure the award was a bona-fide medal of recognition. We wanted to celebrate an extraordinary body of work, not just be a part of a marketing campaign to shore up an album.

Bono, the Edge, Adam Clayton and Larry Mullen Jr had collectively been criticised almost from U2's inception for the way in which they espoused their principles, but I was a true believer. I loved U2. I liked them as people (although I had never really got to know Larry), I liked their music, and I respected the way they had attempted to diversify while always trying to stay true to themselves.

We asked Salman Rushdie to present their award when we eventually invited them, and in among the mentions of philanthropy, morality and musicality, he told the story of how, after U2 had used his words for the lyrics of 'The Ground Beneath Her Feet', he was inundated with requests for his services: 'Alex James [of Blur, who was in the audience that night, as he was most years] and I had a meeting which he prepared for by as I recall drinking a bottle of absinthe, and during the meeting he said he'd had this great idea, a "fucking great idea". He said, "You write the music, and I'll write the words." And when I said I don't write music or play a musical instrument, he said, "I'll teach you to play the guitar in half an hour, there's nothing to it. You write the music, I'll write the words. Fucking fantastic." That song did not happen.'

SOMETIMES, THE ACCEPTANCE SPEECHES WERE so good we printed them in full in the issue following the awards. Unless Samuel L. Jackson was hosting and had threatened the recipients, the speeches could go on for twenty minutes, which nobody minded as long as they were funny. When the Arctic Monkeys received an award in 2013, Alex Turner began with, 'I think sometimes my face falls in such a way it conceals any excitement, but this does mean something to us . . .'

'Oh my God, you guys,' said Amy Schumer when she accepted the Woman of the Year award in 2016. '*GQ* Men of the Year. Finally, we are celebrating men. Thank you for calling me a woman . . . In the future I know things aren't going to go as well for me. I won't be at places like this, and I'll be forgotten, and I'll show up at the door and I'll be like, "But what about me, Dylan?" . . . I want you guys to know that a lot of the things you hear up here tonight will be lies, and people will try and say the right things so you'll like them, or they can get more work, and I want you to go home knowing that this is the truth: Patrick Stewart has come all over my tits, more times than even he remembers [looks at Patrick Stewart, who is in on the joke] . . . Guys don't know this but you kind of have to make a shelf with your hands so the come doesn't fall. It's the saddest shelf in the world.'

Half an hour later, when Billy Connolly was accepting a Lifetime Achievement Award, he said, 'I hate to disappoint you, Amy Schumer, but I can come on my own tits.'

*

PERHAPS OUR BIGGEST CELEBRITY COUP came in 2007, at the Royal Opera House in Covent Garden. We were celebrating the designer David Collins, and we asked Madonna to present the award. After some very brief wrangling (we found this surprising), she agreed, and so we set about making her appearance as painless as possible (for all of us).

It was protocol that every major star be given a minder, and on this occasion our features editor, Alex Bilmes (who would go on to successfully edit *Esquire*), volunteered to look after her. We gave her the option of arriving after the red carpet photo call, and slipping in the back way, via the kitchen which is exactly what she decided to do. 'All I had to do was get her and her entourage from the stage door to the dressing room, and five minutes later from the dressing room to the stage, and then off and back out,' said Bilmes. 'Half an hour door to door, tops.'

But it didn't work out that way. The awards were running late (they always did), Madonna arrived early, and so suddenly there was a major international mega-celebrity crisis careering over the mountain. Or at least into the Royal Opera House.

'As soon as I opened the car door and introduced myself she seemed to decide to have a bit of fun, not exactly at my expense but certainly in my vicinity,' said Bilmes. 'It wasn't cruel or bullying. It wasn't flirtatious, either. It was just a kind of arch, almost camp role-play. Her: "What do you do?" Me: "I'm the features editor." Her (as if honoured to be in the presence of such an important figure): "Oh, you're the FEATURES editor." Me (weakly): "Yes." Her: "And are you a NICE features editor?"'

When they got to the dressing room everyone realised there was no phone signal, so they immediately left, and it was just Bilmes and Madonna in the room. He poured them both a glass of champagne. What he noticed: she was extraordinarily still, composed, neat, compact. She didn't move unless necessary, and then she moved swiftly and with purpose. She appeared completely calm and perhaps wryly amused by the situation. Trapped, albeit very briefly, in a room with a bumbling journalist. According to Bilmes, it was striking how easy she was to talk to, despite the weirdness of the situation. They talked about what they'd been up to in the summer: she'd been horse riding at her place in the country. Bilmes bored her (and then the rest of the world) with a story about his ill-fated driving holiday in France. She told him an indiscreet anecdote, with much eye-rolling, about lunch with Sting and Trudie (the details of which Bilmes has seemingly forgotten). She asked him his star sign.

From Bilmes's point of view, they were getting along famously, like old pals. Then, apropos of nothing, she just said, sweetly but firmly, 'I'm ready now.'

'I scuttled outside to check and was told it would be another five to ten minutes. I went back in and lied. "Two minutes," I said.

'"I'm ready now," she said. "Let's go." No anger, no concern, just matter of fact: this is what's going to happen.'

So Bilmes led her out and down the stairs to the side of the stage where they stood and waited. I remember looking at her at the time, from my table: she was so unbothered by all the fuss around her that she could have been reading a magazine, waiting for her hair to dry. She even looked benignly at Elton John, who was hosting the awards (brilliantly) that year. They had recently had the mother of all public fallings out, and having not been told he was going to be there (she hadn't asked), there was always the possibility she could have flounced. But she just looked on passively (or maybe implacably), waiting to do her thing.

When she'd done the presenting and the hugging and the photos and the blah-blah-blah, Bilmes walked her back to the car. Before she got in, she turned and shook his hand, very businesslike. She smiled, leaned forward and spoke into his ear: 'Next time I'll keep you waiting.'

She was teasing, of course, and the next day her publicists rang to ask when next year's awards were. That was always the point: I wanted everyone to have a good time. When the boldface names were sitting in the back of their chauffeured Mercedes, on the way to Matthew Freud's after-party, I wanted them to turn to their husband, girlfriend, hairdresser, manager, mistress, and say, 'You know what, I'm glad we did that.'

The comment I treasured most about the Men of the Year Awards came from Michael Lewis, whom we invited one year to accept an award in honour of his bestselling books, which include *Moneyball* and *The Big Short*. As he left that night, sandwiched between Angelina Jolie and Justin Timberlake, he turned to me and said, 'Thank you for the most incredible night of my life. I've been to the Oscars. This is better than the Oscars.'

In its pomp, it was.

To Live and Nearly Die in LA

Despatches from the Polo Lounge

If these walls could talk. Luckily, they did . . .

WHENEVER I WALKED INTO A hotel in Los Angeles – upscale or downmarket – it was always easy to assume that race determined the natural order; greeted by whites, served by Eastern Europeans, wiped clean by Hispanics. But outside the climate-controlled tourist traps, I was always aware of a city devoted to social mobility. LA was built on the principles of reinvention, and although it always excelled at creating sun-drenched ghettos, it still hosted North America's greatest lifestyle parade: car culture, food culture, body culture and relentless retail therapy.

It was always fun to visit. The weather, the architecture, the food, the sense of deliberate abandonment.

Californians had never exactly lacked the means of self-expression, even those at the thin end of the food chain, and in Los Angeles, everyone was encouraged to use the city as some sort of lifestyle canvas. As ever, the best soundbites were always found on T-shirts. One of the funniest slogans I ever saw was worn by a young jogger on the boardwalk in Santa Monica: 'Define "girlfriend"?' his shirt announced.

I always loved California as it was the place where world cuisine collided in the most appropriate way. You had Pan-Asian cafés, state-of-the-art destinations like the French Laundry, Hollywood-particular Jewish delicacies and some of the best Italian restaurants this side of Rome. In Los Angeles you had the sickly sweet smell of cinnamon pumped out into department-store malls, forcing you to sit right down and immediately order a coffee and a bagel. On one hand, this was the culinary equivalent of the city's pick 'n' mix architecture, and on the other simply a manifestation of LA's mania for the new.

But this obsession with feeding the beast could usually be guaranteed to bring out the worst in the city. As the noughties handed over to the tens, I was still confronted by too many 'servers' intent on telling me the name of the farm where my zucchini came from (taking provenance oh-so-seriously), and too many waiters who took a little too much pleasure asking, 'Are you familiar with how our menu works?' Also, there were still too many vodka sommeliers (brand-calling was almost as fashionable as the razor clam), still too many menus that were bigger than the table you were eating at.

Another trick employed by serving staff was ownership of the food, something I noticed in shoe shops too: 'I don't have any of the ranch pork and heirloom squash, but I do have a half-timbered black walking boot in a nine and a half. I can seriously recommend it. They come as a pair.'

However, I loved that Angelinos had made body maintenance an art form, whether by exercise, surgery or diet (and, increasingly, all three). Back in the eighties, one LA resident told me people should drink eight large glasses of water, eight ounces each, every day. Soon, '8 x 8' became a Californian mantra, adopted by nutritionists from Napa to San Diego. I had similar advice at a wedding in Sussex in 2004, where I was told the best way to cope with an unappealing seating plan was to drink six glasses of champagne before six o'clock.

On any business trip I would drive down Sunset Boulevard, park outside Tower Records, and after dropping a hundred dollars on imported Steely Dan CDs, would wander over to Book Soup, where I could easily waste a couple of hours determinedly looking for the esoteric and the autobiographical. (I would sometimes visit the Hustler store, too, although I promise you it was only because of the free parking.) I would also find time to visit a Hollywood icon, whether it was the Amoeba record store, MacArthur Park, the Capitol Records Building or somewhere like the Stahl House – the famous Case Study House #22 designed by Pierre Koenig and built in West Hollywood in 1958. With its simple steel frames, floor-to-ceiling glass walls and angular layout, the Stahl was the quintessential bachelor dream home, the sort of place difficult fashion photographers or retroactive movie producers might have chosen to live. With its unbelievably beautiful view over the city – it might just have been the most exalted in the state – its boutique swimming pool and Japanese design sensibility, it looked like a West Coast Blue Note album cover come to life. Cool, for want of a better word. Movie-star architecture, for want of three more. When I dropped by, the staff were preparing to be visited by two hundred Belgian architects. The Stahl was rather small, and most of the iconic photography was quite deceptive, having been achieved using wide-angle lenses, making the L-shaped construction appear as though it was jutting considerably over the rock's edge, and deliberately ignoring the fact that one side of the building practically abutted the mountain road. But no matter, in my eyes at least, number 22 was still something of a magic number.

THE TRIPS I MADE WITH *GQ* were initially to see agents, and they were always eventful. On the few occasions I did a proper agenting trip – I would soon pass on the reins to Alex Bilmes, Jonathan Heaf and Stuart McGurk, as they were much better at schmoozing the publicists and agents than I was – even I was surprised by the transactional nature of the meetings, almost as though all human emotion had been sucked out of a conversation before it began. The deals were always mathematical, logistical and prescriptive – when something was going to happen, where, how, what the topics of conversation were likely to be. We never listened to the conversational guidance (I don't think journalists ever do), and even when we were knocking it out of the park every month and generating headlines all over the world for our cover stories, the publicists and agents still persisted in guiding us through the process; in order to validate their retainers, they had to be able to tell their clients that they were fully in charge of the situation. This was fine for me, and I made sure to create a culture of collaboration in the *GQ* office. LA agents and publicists were not to be treated like the enemy; after all, they had jobs to do too. If you spoke to any features editor or commissioning editor on a national newspaper supplement, or maybe a monthly lifestyle title, they'd all tell you that the people they disliked most were Hollywood agents and publicists.

They would say that they get curt, one-word answers to carefully composed, page-long emails detailing the extraordinary benefits of getting coverage in their publication. They would explain that agents never responded to telephone calls and that, if they were lucky enough to get through to one of their assistants (plural), they would be put on hold for what felt like hours. They would say that when they did eventually get to speak to someone with power (and, for the record, in Hollywood, nobody with the word 'associate' in their job title appeared to have any power), they would be rude, dismissive and quite possibly abusive. Then they'd say that, if they were lucky enough to secure the agent's client for their publication, the agent or publicist would always find something wrong with the article, focusing on the one adjective to which their mollycoddled actor had taken exception. Inevitably, there would have to be a protracted argument about which photographers you were allowed to use, as the one you suggested wouldn't be good enough, while the one they wanted would be hideously expensive and otherwise engaged on the dates their client was available.

Seriously, if you spoke to these editors, it was as though their lives weren't worth living, as though their every waking hour was spent arguing with hordes of disinterested industry bods on the West Coast who didn't give a damn about them or their publications. These journalists could bore for Britain about Hollywood agents and publicists. But I never took what they said seriously.

GQ had an extraordinarily good relationship with Hollywood agents, a relationship that had been refined over the years by constant trips to Los Angeles, and by dozens (probably hundreds) of breakfasts, lunches, dinners and cocktail parties. We put the hours in, and we played nice. Of course, we were in the lucky position of having a brand that most agents and publicists wanted their clients to be associated with – being on the cover of British *GQ* was generally regarded as a 'good thing'.

We got exclusives – any story that wasn't an exclusive was essentially worthless – and we got proper quality time with the talent. If you were only going to get a twenty-minute interview and a forty-minute photo session, then you may as well have passed. A collaboration only really worked when both parties were completely happy with the outcome. But we never took our position for granted, and we always treated everyone in the industry with respect. Because of that, we tended to get respect in return. And if we didn't? Well, then we dealt with it.

Whenever anyone joined our features team (and as our online offering grew, we were adding people all the time), I always told them to ignore all the negative white noise surrounding the so-called demons that were Hollywood agents and publicists. I simply told them this: if you sent a long, three-page email and you got a one-word response in reply, so what? Be happy and build your response from there. If the publicist kept knocking back photographers until the photographic editor was pulling their hair out, then keep going – find a photographer who works for both the magazine and the client. Compromise. Deal with it.

People did business in different ways, and one of the jobs in the industry was to find out how people liked doing business and then fit in accordingly. Yes, agents and publicists could be difficult to work with, but then so could journalists. And like any relationship – professional or personal – you had to operate on an 'I win, you win' basis, or else you were going to get lost extremely quickly.

I always told my team to be honest and straightforward, and then, if it all went wrong, to deal with the problem in a way that didn't destroy important relationships. My motto? 'Big smile, short memory.'

AROUND THIS TIME, I WENT to a dinner in London hosted by an Italian fashion designer, Angelo Galasso. He'd just done a deal with Al Pacino, who was sitting at the other end of the table, telling stories to a bunch of his travelling companions. I didn't talk much to him during the meal, but I did sit next to his personal publicist, Pat Kingsley, a woman who, in her prime, was the most feared person in Hollywood. She'd been so formidable that the big, burly men who ran Hollywood studios would literally start shaking when they heard she was on the phone.

Weirdly, I had already been talking to her for about ten minutes before I could be certain she was the person I thought she was – she was talking about her family rather than any of her former clients, and she was incredibly good company. When pressed, she was really good on Hollywood gossip – not maliciously, but in an incredibly precise, perceptive way, which I suppose made complete sense. When I asked her what her biggest problems had been when dealing with the press, she took a sip of water, smiled, and said, 'It was always the same thing and always will be – managing the expectations of the media. And let me tell you – my clients always won.'

She laughed, but then she looked ruefully across the table at her charge. 'If he's happy, I'm happy, and we're all happy. I always liked working with people who made me happy.'

I ALWAYS USED THESE LA trips to meet writers, stylists and photographers, having dinner in Cecconi's, Spago, the original Soho

House on Sunset Boulevard or the Polo Lounge in the Beverly Hills Hotel, with the likes of Chris Ayres, Richard Bacon, Gavin Bond, Kim Bowen (yes, her again, now married with children), David Furnish or one of our Hollywood specialists. On one trip, Bill Prince, Alex Bilmes and I were schmoozing Sanjiv Bhattacharya, a *GQ* writer who had recently relocated to the city. We were taking him to drinks on the rooftop bar of the Standard Downtown, a hotel that had just opened in the financial district. After ninety minutes or so, we got back into my car to drive back to Beverly Hills for dinner at the Four Seasons. Alex was the designated driver, enjoying the handling of our Bentley Arnage turbo, which had been gifted to us for the week. As Alex increased his speed, every traffic light on Wilshire Boulevard was turning green; we had hit the sweet spot, as every junction opened up for us as though we were suddenly hurtling through space.

Consequently, Alex's speed kept increasing, until we were driving at 130 mph. As I was in the passenger seat, I was more mindful of this than Bill or Sanjiv; I was also becoming uncertain about Alex's ability to drive, as he appeared to have drunk just as many negronis as the rest of us. My concerns were validated when we hit a small, raised bridge in the road, which sent our car spinning up into the air, swerving over the central reservation, where it spun in a 360-degree flip, before landing back on the tarmac, pointing in the same direction, but now obviously stationary. For the four of us it was as though time had stopped; we all looked at each other and couldn't quite believe we were still alive.

'I pulled over to the side of the road to give my co-pilot and me adequate time to burst into tears and send silent prayers of thanks to our ethnic-specific Gods,' said Bilmes, when he wrote about it later.

When I think about what happened it is always in slow motion, as though we were being directed by Martin Brest in a sequel to the *Beverly Hills Cop* movies, being chased by Yaphet Kotto or Steven Berkoff. We vowed never to mention the escapade to anyone, which we didn't, until about five years later, when we thought time and distance had probably defused any spousal disapprobation.

My personal assistant at the time was a lovely woman called Anthea, whose father was Paul Anka, the hugely successful teen idol of the post-Elvis era who went on to write the English lyrics to 'My Way'. She said on this trip that we should look him up, as he'd love to meet us, and whether or not this was true, I leapt at the opportunity. I'd been a huge Frank Sinatra fan for years and was keen to ask Paul what he had been like. There was only one problem, however, as Anthea had briefed us to not at any point mention Frank Sinatra or 'My Way'. She was vaguely aware that there had been some sort of bust-up between them and that we shouldn't tempt fate by reminding him of this (on stage Sinatra would occasionally joke about the 'little Arab' only writing a song for him every ten years).

We booked Paul's favourite table at the Ivy in Los Angeles, dressed-up in our finest Savile Row threads, and turned up a respectable twenty minutes early ('Sir, you might be more comfortable in this seat, as Mr Anka likes to sit there,' our server pointed out before my Richard James trousers had brushed the banquette). We all had jetlag, and after a while started wondering whether this was going to be much fun after all. If he was such a hard ass about where he sat in his 'favourite' restaurant, then maybe he was going to be a drag.

Twenty minutes later, bang on time, in walked Paul Anka, looking like he'd just stepped offstage at the Sands. He had tinted glasses, wore a great midnight blue suit, and had a tan that would have shamed George Michael, George Hamilton or indeed any other tandooried George. He looked terrific, which is what he said to us as he shook our hands and promptly sat down. 'You boys look terrific – so *GQ*!'

We dutifully asked him how his Vegas residency was going, how his publishing was doing, and what life was like on the road ('Great,' 'Great,' and 'Great'). At no point did we mention Big Frank, the 'song', or indeed anything of the sort. I think Alex at one point half-mentioned the fact that the Rat Pack were becoming quite popular again in London, although I'm not sure our guest heard (seeing that Alex's observations were curtailed somewhat sharply by both Bill and me kicking him in the shins under the table).

But after only about ten minutes or so Anka floored us all by asking, completely unprompted, 'So, are you boys Sinatra fans?'

We looked at each other, unsure which direction to go in, and so we hedged our bets for a while, until we were interrupted.

'Come on, you gotta be Sinatra fans!' said our guest.

And then it all came out, and you have never seen three grown men try and ingratiate themselves so much.

'Yes, Paul, I've got every original Capitol album before he left to set up Reprise.'

'Yes, Paul, I actually saw him on his last trip to London.'

'Yes, Paul, I especially like the bossa nova albums he made in the sixties,' etc.

We were nauseating, but I think Paul was pleased. We'd loosened up, stopped acting like British stuffed shirts, and carried on blowing smoke up his ass ('So Paul, what was he really like?' 'Was he a shit in the studio?' 'Were there, you know, always women around?'). I'm sure he could tell that we really were massive Sinatra fans because after a while he began telling us about . . . the 'song'. Sinatra had called him up and asked him to work on it, and Paul told us how he'd sweated for days to get the lyrics right, how Sinatra had asked him to tweak it, and, finally, how Sinatra had invited him to the session.

We were ploughing our way through the Pinot Grigio and Barolo by this time, and we were all getting worked up, as was Paul, in the retelling of the story. Finally, he turned to me – maybe realising that, out of the three of us, I was the saddest, most obsessive Sinatraphile at the table – and said, safe in the knowledge that he had the answer on hand, 'Guess how many takes it took Sinatra to nail it?'

I think the responses were in the low numbers. But none of the guesses was right.

'You know how many takes it took Sinatra to nail "My Way"?' asked the man who wrote it. 'One, just one damn take. Now that man was a professional. That man was the man.'

We ended up in the small hours in a cigar club somewhere in deepest Hollywood, where we all sat around smoking Silk Cuts and

Cohibas. As the three of us got up to leave Paul to his cigar (our jetlag had finally got the better of us), he asked if I'd like to hear Frank's first take of 'My Way'. As rhetorical questions go, this was one of the best I'd ever had, and obviously I said yes. 'I'd love that, Paul, that would be great.'

'Well, I'll send it then,' he said, as a curl of blue smoke coiled its circuitous way from his mouth up to the ceiling.

Thirty seconds later, in the lift going down to the car park, Bill turned and said, 'That, I guarantee, is not going to happen.'

But it did. Ten days later a package arrived by FedEx from LA, inside which was a freshly cut CD in a blank jewel case, and a little note from Paul. 'Enjoy', it said, in case I had entertained the thought of doing otherwise.

And when I played it – on my Mac, about five seconds later – that's exactly what I did. The CD contained Frank Sinatra's very first take of 'My Way', the one you hear on the record; although unlike the record, all you can hear is Frank. You can vaguely make out the backing track seeping from Sinatra's headphones, but for the purposes of argument it is only Frank's vocals you can hear. The first time I played it, it was like some sort of quasi-religious experience, like listening to Paul McCartney first play 'Let It Be' for the rest of the Beatles (*Anthology III*), or watching the Clash perform 'Complete Control' in front of a captive audience (Victoria Park, east London, 1978). Considering how good studio jiggery-pokery is these days, it would be easy to assume that Paul had simply edited out the instruments, leaving Frank to sing to his heart's content, but this was an actual take – the first take, for fuck's sake! – of Frank Sinatra singing not only one of his trademark songs, but one of the defining popular songs of the twentieth century – live, by himself, unaccompanied!

The song took me right back to my childhood, listening to my mother sing along with Frank, and I immediately wanted to play it for her.

Paul's CD has since become one of my most treasured possessions, which is ironic seeing that 'My Way' was never one of my favourite

Sinatra songs. For me, 'My Way' was always a prime example of Pub Frank, one of those obvious karaoke Sinatra songs such as 'Strangers in the Night' or 'Chicago' that over-refreshed Sinatra fans think they can get away with come closing time, one of the broader, more populist tracks from the Reprise years rather than the classic Capitol years. But without the strings, the embellishment, the heavy-handed production, 'My Way' becomes a plaintive letter from the checkout lounge, a poetic summation of a life lived large.

THE POLO LOUNGE ALWAYS FELT like the quintessential LA bar. It always felt like the golden age in there, one of the last surviving links to a time when movies really mattered, an oasis decorated with Brazilian pepper trees, roses and magenta bougainvillea, surrounding booths in which Hollywood met itself for iced water and McCarthy Salads (beets, chicken, eggs, tomatoes, cheese, bacon and avocado). I would reserve a table for 6 p.m., only to find myself surrounded by a phalanx of identikit couples: old men oozing entitlement and money, and young girls hoping their rendezvous wasn't what they thought it was (and it always was).

Los Angeles had always been a town that liked to play fast and loose with its history, and yet the Polo Lounge probably had the greatest IP of any Hollywood watering hole. While the Garden of Allah, the Ambassador Hotel and the Tropicana Motel have all fallen victim to the wrecking ball, the Polo Lounge was testament to the notion that location was as important as architecture, and that heritage will always trump novelty.

Every time I visited the city, the sixties were still very much alive and kicking. If you knew where to look, that is. Laurel Canyon was often written about as the place that gave the world Crosby, Stills and Nash – which was obviously why a lot of people hated it – the place that inspired Joni Mitchell's *Ladies of the Canyon*, Danny Sugerman's *Wonderland Avenue* and the neighbourhood of benign bad behaviour. Everyone from Clara Bow and Christina Applegate to Frank Zappa and

Marilyn Manson had lived there, and it retained a genuine local feel – an almost implausible ambition in LA. The area had also had its fair share of dark moments, not least the Wonderland cocaine murders in 1981, when four gangsters were bludgeoned to death, and which were meant to have involved the infamous porn star John Holmes.

Despite being the subject of standard-issue gentrification, the Canyon had kept the funky, rainbow-coloured charm of the Love Generation, something that was most apparent when visiting the Canyon Country Store, the neighbourhood social hub. Wedged along the twisting Laurel Canyon Boulevard in the Santa Monica Mountains, this was the place mentioned in Jim Morrison's 'Love Street', the wooden-floored grocery shop/deli/liquor store/café that was still the place to go for Canyon dwellers with the munchies, or for those looking for an espresso having spent all night partying in the Valley. Here you could find Dandy Don's ice-cream, Dave's Kombucha (fermented tea), bespoke sandwiches, hearts of palm salads, and the almost-but-not-quite-legendary decaf almond milk latte. The Country Store was also the site of the annual Photo Day each October, where the residents of the Canyon all came together to have a group picture taken. The tradition dated back to the late eighties, a celebration of the sort of community spirit you tended not to find elsewhere in LA.

Over the hill, the temporal nature of Hollywood was always in full effect. Here, in the village of bougainvillea and watery melodies, time stood still. And if you wanted to wear your bell-bottoms and feathers, you'd always be encouraged to don't think twice, it's all right.

Me, I would always make a pilgrimage, driving up from my hotel for a coffee and an email pause between meetings.

FAMOUS PEOPLE WERE EVERYWHERE IN Beverly Hills. In a single afternoon I saw Arnold Schwarzenegger at the lights in a Hummer, Zac Efron shopping on Rodeo Drive, and Monica Bellucci in the lobby of the Four Seasons, speaking so loudly on her phone I thought she might be involved in air traffic control. Quincy Jones lived twenty minutes away from the Four Seasons, up in the Bel Air foothills, in a 20,000-square foot mansion he bought from Julio Iglesias. This was real luxury, a proper Hollywood mansion with extraordinary views that stretched all the way to Long Beach. The house was full of the trinkets of success. This was a house of spoils, a house of acknowledgement, the recognition of a creative life lived to the full. The walls of his screening room were covered in framed movie posters of many of the films he'd scored, while the rest of this wing, the music wing, was full of gold discs, Emmys, Grammys, framed album covers, silver table frames containing photographs of Quincy with just about every triple-A famous person in the world, with art lying on the floor waiting to be hung or mounted. I had to be careful how I trod in case I knocked over an Oscar or ASCAP gong.

The main living section of this wing was an enormous circular room surrounded by a tropical garden containing over a hundred speakers powered by his three Crestron sound systems, which pumped out jazz and classical music all day. At the back of the house, in the middle of the driveway, a leafless tree was covered in Chinese lanterns.

It was a long way from where he'd started in life.

Quincy Jones's most vivid memory of his mother is perhaps not one that many of us have when thinking about our parents. I'd say it was so rare that its lingering existence – burned into Jones's hard drive, no matter how hard he has tried to bury it – would have driven most people to the brink. Of addiction, of aggression, of suicide, of madness. It was madness where it all started.

When he was ten years old, Quincy and his younger brother Lloyd were taken by his father to see his mother in an asylum, where she had been since she was incarcerated two years previously. One morning, they left their home on the south side of Chicago and drove out to the country. Once inside the hospital, Quincy immediately smelled something putrid, 'like sheets soiled with urine and sweat'. There were people lying all over the floors, writhing, screaming, curled up into balls. The patients were muttering to themselves, pointing at each other and laughing inanely, making funny, but not-so-funny noises.

And then, standing quietly against one of the hospital's interior walls, Quincy saw his mother, Sarah. After acknowledging their presence with a small nod, she began ranting, about Jesus, the Pope, about the boxer Joe Louis. Her voice got louder, until she was almost hysterical, waving her arms around in the air.

And then it happened. She stopped throwing herself around, and squatted down on her haunches, before putting her hands behind her knees. Then she defecated into one palm, drew her other hand out from beneath her, and pushed a finger into her own faeces. Then, using her finger as a fork, she lifted it to her open mouth.

Memories.

When I transcribed the tape of our interview, I noticed he had barely paused for breath, moving from problems in Darfur, his humanitarian escapades with Bono, Barack Obama's budget problems, Joe Pesci's ability to sing jazz, gangsters old and new, black and white. It was almost a stream of consciousness that took him around the world and in and out of the years, moving from Brazil to Paris with ease, via philanthropy and family tragedies, a pinball monologue masquerading as a conversation. Quincy was one of those people who tended to answer a dozen questions at once, probably because a) he'd been interviewed so many times that he had a spiel that he used on journalists and people he hadn't met before, and/or b) it was a defence mechanism.

Obviously, in many people's eyes, Quincy's career had been defined by his work with Michael Jackson. When Jackson decided to make his first proper solo album, there was one man whose advice he sought first. He had worked with Quincy on the film *The Wiz* and had started to put his trust in him. They first met on the set on the day Jackson had to rehearse a scene in which he read a Socrates quote. When the crew started stifling their laughs when he spoke – he pronounced it 'Soh-crates', to rhyme with 'low rates' – he knew he'd screwed up. It was Quincy who whispered the correct pronunciation in his ear. And when Jackson asked Jones to recommend someone to produce his record, the producer naturally suggested himself.

Although they fell out, Quincy never stopped being in awe of Jackson's talent, his myopic dedication to his craft. Initially, he couldn't believe Jackson's professionalism, his devotion to study (he would watch tapes of gazelles and cheetahs and panthers to imitate their natural grace). Jones talked about Jackson's dedication at length: 'At his place in Hayvenhurst, he used to have a mouthy parrot with a lot of attitude as well as a boa constrictor named Muscles. One day Muscles was missing. They looked all over the property, inside and out, and after two days they finally found him dangling from the parrot's cage, with the parrot's beak sticking out of his mouth. He'd swallowed that sucker whole and couldn't back his head out of the bars because he hadn't digested the bird yet. In a way, that's a metaphor for Michael's life after *Thriller*, because at a certain point, he couldn't get back out of the cage. It all became overwhelming for him.'

Up in his Bel Air mansion, surrounded by the dozens of gold and silver discs celebrating Jackson and Jones's success, I asked him how he felt now that his protégé's indiscretions had been made public. 'You know, I always deal in forgiveness, and I'd forgiven Michael a long time before he died. We did some amazing work together, produced some remarkable, special records, and you can never forget that. You shouldn't. I forgive people because I expect people to do the same with me. If you don't forgive then it's a poison, and it eats you up.'

Once, when Naomi Campbell was in my office in London trying to get hold of Prince for an interview she was trying to do for *GQ*, her route one option was to call Quincy on his mobile – 'Q will know how to get hold of him!' It was the wrong time of day (Quincy was probably asleep), but the message she left was indicative of the relationship she shared with him, and probably indicative of the relationship he had with hundreds of others. 'Hi Q, it's Naomi. How are you, Daddy? I need your help so please call me back. Love you, miss you.' Quincy was not just the conduit, he was the switchboard, the hub and the nub, the control tower. And you were in a holding pattern until it was time for Quincy to bring you in.

*

AS IF HE WERE IN Stella Street, Burt Bacharach lived down the road, about twenty minutes away. I'd seen him in various hotels in LA, and seen him in concert many times, but I'd never been to his house before. The day we met, he was pattering around the den in his vast Pacific Palisades dream home, dressed in a quite extraordinary monogrammed burgundy tracksuit. Burt Bacharach looked like a man with a pretty busy day ahead of him. He was finishing a tuna sandwich and kept looking intently at his phone. It was 2006 and he was seventy-seven years young, but still moved with the agility of a man thirty years his junior. He was hunched, his skin was thin and his voice was quiet, yet he spoke with an assuredness that sometimes seemed to take even him by surprise.

Bacharach had never really been known for his outspokenness, and his interviews were usually as commonplace as his music had been preternatural. But when we met, as he prepared himself to enter his ninth decade, he was about to embrace the spirit of Bob Dylan and release his first overtly political record, *At This Time*. Recorded with hip-hop super-producer Dr Dre and featuring drum loops a-go-go, his album contained elaborate, seven-minute mini-operas, abrasive orchestrations and fairly forthright political sideswipes.

'I hate what's going on in America,' he said, with barely concealed contempt, 'and I want to say something about it.'

One song, 'Go Ask Shakespeare', featured Rufus Wainwright. Another, the unapologetic 'Who Are These People?' was sung by Elvis Costello. When I interviewed Bacharach the summer before, for another *GQ* project, he was still at the demo stage of this song and had asked me who I thought should sing on it. Having at first suggested Nick Cave, I told Bacharach he should ask Costello to do it, seeing that they had worked together on the *Painted from Memory* album. Which is obviously what he had done.

The composer of 'Walk On By', 'I'll Never Fall in Love Again', 'What the World Needs Now Is Love', 'I Say a Little Prayer', 'Raindrops Keep Falling on My Head' and hundreds more loungecore classics lived just a few miles from the Pacific Coast Highway, an evocative stretch of tarmac that once lent its name to one of Bacharach's great instrumentals, and one of those parts of California that so inspired the extravagantly landscaped architecture of his songs. This was the coastline that bore the brunt of the Santa Ana winds, the coastline that inspired so many baby-boomer songwriters, the beach that broke and then ruined the Beach Boys.

His den was exactly as one would have wanted it: sitting on a ground-floor corner overlooking the hissing of summer lawns, he tinkled at his piano, the charts of a yet-to-be-finished song scrawled over the property section of the *Los Angeles Times*. A small cassette player on which he still recorded all his demos sat on top of the piano, as he closed his eyes and played. A framed cover of *Newsweek* from 1970 picturing Bacharach with the cover line 'The Music Man' hung behind him, as did a poster for the B-movie classic *The Blob*, for which, inexplicably, Bacharach wrote the score, as well as dozens of photographs of him with the likes of Stevie Wonder, Elvis Presley, Dionne Warwick, Elizabeth Taylor and his former writing partner, Hal David. There were also pictures of him with his beloved racehorses (he had bred for years) and glass awards for winning just about everything.

He had just come back from playing at the opening of Steve Wynn's eponymous Las Vegas hotel in front of Rupert Murdoch, Steven Spielberg, Barry Diller and the first President Bush. He was meeting me this lunchtime to celebrate being handed *GQ*'s Inspiration Award, the special gong we reserved for those luminaries who truly deserved the title 'Legend', and which we regularly handed out at the Men of the Year Awards. He had been something of a hero of mine since I was a boy, and I allowed myself to wallow in the moment a little.

As I got up to leave, to drive my loaned racing green Bentley Flying Spur back to the Bel Air Hotel, Bacharach saw me notice a small photograph of him taken with Cherie Blair and Lauren Bush.

'Oh,' he said, embarrassed. 'I've been meaning to get rid of that.'

*

IT'S SAID THAT WHILE EMBARRASSMENT lasts a moment, regret lasts a lifetime, although as LA is only ever interested in the moment, regret is only ever existential. Unlike my deputy Bill Prince, who had to be physically removed from Burt Bacharach's limo outside the Bel Air Hotel one evening after mistaking it for his own, my embarrassment happened at the Mondrian Hotel on Sunset. I was in town along with some colleagues from the British Fashion Council (no names, no numbers) for a big industry event in Rodeo Drive. The night before, we had all been invited to a fancy cocktail party at the Mondrian to honour one of the West Coast's most flamboyant but less significant designers. And as we were in the city, we thought we'd turn up and be good soldiers. Our mistake was going to the Malibu Beach House for a late lunch, where we were joining some friends who worked for a big Hollywood studio.

As cannabis had just been legalised for recreational use, one of our guests brought along some gummies, and – enlivened by a glass and a half of not completely unpleasant Sauvignon Blanc – we all decided to take one. Of course, the sensible thing to have done would have been to have waited for them to kick in, and then while away the afternoon before our event back in the city. But no, so excited were we by the thought of acting like teenagers, that we compounded the crime by deciding – after what would have been no longer than fifteen minutes – that they weren't working and that we should obviously take some more. Which we did, and which caused all of us to immediately giggle at the naughtiness of it all.

Big mistake. Ten minutes later we were all convulsed with laughter as the drugs seriously kicked in, and we started having trouble talking coherently. We certainly couldn't order our food without collapsing with uncontrollable snorting. This continued for the rest of the afternoon until one of us remembered that we were due in Hollywood in less than an hour. We dutifully paid our bill, scrambled into our cars and drove – with a ridiculous amount of care and attention – down the Pacific Coast Highway and then turned left along Sunset. We arrived, handed our cars over to the valets in an orderly fashion, and then trooped off to the event. I was brimming with confidence and looking forward to an evening of high-jinks masquerading as industry networking, when the velvet-rope security guy placed his hand on my chest.

'I'm sorry, sir, there's a dress code and I'm afraid I can't let you in.'

'Really? But we're invited! We've come all the way from London for this party,' I said, probably a little too casually.

'I'm sorry, sir, but it's hotel policy,' he countered, and not unreasonably.

Having, like a travelling salesman, dutifully put my tuxedo, shirt, tie and dress shoes in the back of my Bentley, I had completely forgotten to change, and was still sporting my T-shirt, camouflage cargo shorts and far-from-box-fresh Birkenstocks.

I looked myself up and down, and said, with as much dignity as I could muster, 'Actually, I don't blame you.'

Peter Mandelson, Celebrity? David Cameron, Leader?

Downing Street or Bust

Peter Mandelson, Mick Jagger and Sabrina Guinness, in mufti

I HAVE SEEN POLITICIANS DO many things. I have seen them attempt to dance (Gordon Brown, in Washington, at his brother-in-law's wedding; not so well). I have seen them attempt to tell jokes (William Hague, doing his after-dinner routine; very funny). And, on one occasion, I even saw one play air guitar – although to be honest with you, it was actually a politician's wife (her husband was too busy having his chest hair shaved in full view of thirty, frankly astonished, members of a magazine team).

This in itself was odd, as air guitar had usually been the domain of the adolescent boy, or at least any man who was an adolescent boy at heart. I had been as guilty as anyone else, and although I hadn't done it since my twenties, during my youth I was up there with the very best, noodling for Britain, the Commonwealth and the Empire. The first record I can remember pretending to play the guitar to was the Beatles' 'Revolution' (I was eight, and already apparently hardwired into the spirit of counter-cultural agitprop), and started to seriously get into it around the time of David Bowie's Ziggy Stardust records, pretending to bend a pool cue in the style of Mick Ronson (not that I ever managed to find a six-stringed pool cue). I can think of very few things from my adolescence that gave me as much fun as bouncing around the bedroom playing air guitar to 'The Jean Genie', 'Five Years' or 'Starman'.

I never used the family cricket bat – heaven forbid – although there were various secondhand badminton and tennis rackets that came in very useful when trying to get to grips with the intricacies of the convoluted guitar solos in Steely Dan's 'Reelin' in the Years', the Allman Brothers' 'Jessica' or 'Bell Bottom Blues' by Derek and the Dominoes. In truth, I was rather better at the 'air snare' and would happily while away the hours drumming along to the fills in the Who's 'Baba O'Riley'. And let me tell you this came in very handy when it was determined by the gods that I was going to be a drummer rather than a guitarist.

But I hadn't indulged in either for years, which is why I was rather shocked when Christine Hamilton jumped up on a table during the *GQ* Christmas lunch in the Vogue House boardroom to expertly strum along to Rod Stewart's 'Maggie May'. If it had been Tony Blair, I would have been less surprised – when he was in Ugly Rumours he was a dab hand at the Stratocaster swipe – but he hadn't accepted our invitation that year (I think he was with Cliff Richard or Silvio Berlusconi, maybe both). Our celebrity politicos that year were the disgraced Tory MP Neil Hamilton and his bubbly wife Christine – principally because we'd just photographed them naked for the magazine, posing as Adam and Eve (a joy to organise, let me tell you, although not necessarily to behold), and I thought it would be a wheeze to ask them along.

I couldn't have wished for more enthusiastic sports, and while Neil stripped down to his boxers in order for one of our assistants to shave his chest hair (having failed to get him to shave his head), Christine, perhaps emboldened by five or six glasses of vintage champagne, leapt on to the boardroom table and played some of the most desirous air guitar I'd ever seen, belting out Townshend-esque windmill chords to Rod Stewart's greatest hits without a care.

When I woke the next day, I couldn't quite believe it, but I suppose that's the point of office parties. You never knew what was going to happen, and considering what could and what did, it was probably best that way.

ONE OF THE MOST IMPORTANT things I learned in my early days at *GQ* was the fact that everyone, and I mean everyone, had an ego. In 2004, I spent around six months courting Peter Mandelson, as I wanted him to be our political correspondent. Since Tony Blair's famous election win in 1997, Mandelson had become relatively famous as the architect of New Labour, the great media manipulator, and the man ideologically and personally closest to Blair. Yet, he was also the 'Minister Without Portfolio' who had failed to get onto the National Executive Council of the Labour Party, a man with serious social ambitions external to government. In Labour's first term, he lasted just five months at the helm of the old Department of Trade and Industry, resigning in December 1998 following the disclosure that he accepted a £373,000 loan from then paymaster general, Geoffrey Robinson, to buy a house in Notting Hill. He came back as Northern Ireland secretary in 1999 but quit in 2001 after being accused (inaccurately, we would later discover) of helping one of the Hinduja brothers get a British passport in return for a £1 million donation to the Millennium Dome. And so he was free to work.

After many emails and meetings (he seemed to like visiting the office and meeting the staff), I finally convinced Mandelson to join our gang, and his columns started extremely well. The first was about how there would never be peace in Northern Ireland, a story that made the *Today* programme, *News at Ten* and the front page of the *Telegraph*. It was even discussed at Prime Minister's Questions in the

House of Commons. Things couldn't have started better, and they went very well for a while. But then the standard began to drop, and I felt he – or whoever was writing them (I could never tell if he wrote them himself; I thought not) – was just knocking them off. So I took him out for lunch to talk about it. We sat in the Ivy (him in his Richard James suit, me in mine), with his bodyguards at an adjacent table, and we talked through what I figured were the various topics he should write about. He appeared distracted, and kept knocking back my suggestions, so eventually I said he should write about the press. The media was one of the areas he was not remotely circumspect about, and he tended not to pull his punches. I said that he'd been treated incredibly harshly by the press, and it had obviously got to him.

'But imagine how much worse it would be if you were a celebrity,' I said as I cut up my liver.

And suddenly Mandelson grabbed my arm, and said, in a rather loud voice, 'But I am a celebrity.' There was not a scintilla of irony, not a hint of self-awareness, just a tiny Mandelson whine. 'That's the thing that people don't realise. I am a celebrity.'

Mandelson could be magnetic when he chose to be. He would walk very slowly and carefully, especially when he was entering a room or a restaurant, and would almost encourage people to surround him. In the set of photographs taken of him at a *GQ* party in Isola, Oliver Peyton's short-lived postmodern trattoria in Knightsbridge, he is surrounded by the likes of Gordon Ramsay and A. A. Gill. And he is not just holding court – judging by the expressions of those around him, he's delivering good manna from heaven. He liked people admiring him, enjoyed people staring. In this he reminded me a bit of David Bowie's attempts to act 'famous' when he started to be managed by Tony Defries in the early seventies, and who I interviewed for my book *David Bowie: A Life*, after Bowie died. Defries told Bowie that one of the first things he needed to do, immediately, was to stop opening and closing doors himself. 'Never touch a door handle,' he advised, suggesting he should always let someone else do it for him. (One of the other things he told him to do was stop carrying money.)

Mandelson was good at drawing attention to himself; at a party in a ski lodge in Davos one year, during the World Economic Forum, around midnight, Peter (wearing a very fetching ski jumper) reached up with both hands to grab an exposed beam and started doing pull-ups (he was pretty good); this had the desired effect, and the entire room – which included Rupert Murdoch, Naomi Campbell, George Osborne, Gordon Brown, Rebekah Brooks and Matthew Freud – stopped to watch him, like moths around a flame. He always reminded me a little of Shere Khan as played by George Sanders in the original Disney version of *The Jungle Book*.

Mandy was always very keen to be invited to our parties, and in the email correspondence between us, when I reread it all, a lot of the messages were about party and dinner arrangements. When were they? Could we make sure he was invited? When he chose to be, he could be extremely funny, too (he always managed to make Elton John laugh, weirdly).

He called me up once, pretending to be in a panic, and said, 'You're not a sex magazine, are you?'

'Only if you want us to be,' I said.

'Not yet, I don't think,' he replied.

Anyway, Mandelson took my point about his columns, and he buckled down to work. I started to enjoy his writing a lot more, but he didn't necessarily improve as a person, and after a while became a bit testy. After we eventually parted, he published his autobiography, *The Third Man*. All I needed to know about him was contained in one of the photographs in one of the many eight-page plate sections in his book: he was lying prone on a chaise lounge in someone's stately home ('Relaxing'), with Sabrina Guinness and Mick Jagger artfully arranged in the background. There he was, Peter Mandelson, finally, a celebrity.

ONE DAY IN JUNE 2007, I found myself sitting with David Cameron on the back seat of his chauffeured Prius as it made its way through the suburban streets of west London. There was a by-election coming up, and Cameron was campaigning on behalf of the local candidate, popping into local greengrocers, dry cleaners and newsagents, spreading the new Tory love. Having been the Conservative leader for only two years, he was doing his best to convince anyone who would listen that his new breed of 'compassionate' conservatism was the only one on the table, and that all previous iterations of Tory ideology should be banished. And so far, he appeared to be doing a pretty good job. His personal ratings were high, and the media was taking notice.

Around 11.30, just after Cameron swiftly consumed a cappuccino, his mobile rang. Still in opposition, these were the days when his phone might only ring once an hour, the days when he might call one of his assistants to ask if there had been any calls, only to be told there hadn't. This morning, the person on the other end was Boris Johnson, calling at Cameron's behest to discuss the Tory mayoral candidacy for London. Cameron needed someone to stand against the incumbent, Ken Livingstone, who in many people's eyes was still the obvious favourite. Boris had been in the frame for some time, at least internally, but recently he had appeared to be wavering.

Having successfully bagged a safe seat in Henley, the MP wasn't sure he wanted to give it up for what many were still calling 'local government'. He also wanted Cameron to beg him to do it. Cameron, who kept telling the press that running for office was 'definitely Boris's idea', was keen to persuade him to commit. Whenever anyone asked, Boris would say, 'I'm definitely not a candidate,' or 'It would be a fantastic job, but I enjoy what I'm doing.'

'Hello, Boris,' said Cameron cheerfully, probably for my benefit as much as Boris's. 'So, you're not going to let us down, are you? We really need you to run against Ken, and we all think you'd do a wonderful job. Your party needs you, Boris. Will you say yes?'

Boris then responded, in the only way he could, fulsomely, at length, with many circuitous conversational diversions, talking so loudly I could hear him say he didn't want the job.

Cameron butted in with a rather curt, 'But yes, but that's exactly the point. We need you to sort it out. We need you in London, and we need you to run for mayor. You are literally the only man for the job. Boris, I'm begging you. If you don't run for mayor, then we are going to lose London.'

Boris then swore, told Cameron he'd call him back, and the line then went dead. Whether Johnson just wanted his boss to beg him to take the job (likely), or whether he was genuinely conflicted (unlikely), Boris soon threw his cycling helmet into the ring, and eventually swept to power a year later. He would go on – against the initial odds – to trounce Ken Livingstone in the London mayoral election, while Labour would lose an astonishing 331 council seats in other local elections – the party's worst performance at the polls for forty years – perhaps indicating that the country was finally ready for a change in administration. And just a few weeks before the anniversary of his first year in office, Gordon Brown had taken another massive hammering in the polls. A YouGov poll showed that Labour had slumped to its lowest levels of support since records began back in the thirties, putting the Tories on 49 per cent with Labour trailing on 23 per cent. As a Westminster insider said to me, 'There's a feeling in the House now that he ought to just close the door of Number 10 and put the keys through the letterbox. There is nothing that Gordon can do to make people like him. It almost feels as though he is an ex-prime minister.'

IN JUNE 2007, I STARTED a book project with Cameron, and I found him to be compassionate, committed and wily. My wife wasn't sure about him, and she tends to be a good judge of character, but I was prepared to give him the benefit of the doubt. My idea was to have a really long conversation with Cameron – which I did, starting during the disastrous Ealing by-election in 2007, and finishing with the rather more successful Crewe and Nantwich by-election the following May. My year with Cameron would also have a powerful narrative arc, because when we started the project, he couldn't have been in a worse position. Vilified by the press, the opinion polls and public alike, Cameron had to watch as Gordon Brown experienced a protracted coronation.

I spent hours talking to him about his profoundly disabled son Ivan, and how his view of the NHS has been shaped in part by Ivan's reliance on it. The first time I visited their home in North Kensington I saw Ivan's influence everywhere: the specially installed lift, his toys, the medicine being prepared in the kitchen. The Cameron household was Ivan's own little church, and everything the family did at home revolved around him. It broke my heart, but then I got the feeling that David and his wife Samantha's hearts had been broken a thousand times over.

Samantha, though working for Bond Street luxury stationer, Smythson, tended to wear high-street brands head-to-toe, and was surprisingly grounded. Unlike Cherie Blair, who came to be seen as something of a liability while she was in office, Samantha was regarded as a glamorous asset, both inside and outside the party. (Cherie, I could never get on with, as I found her too shrill. I had written something about her in one of my columns, and I'd heard that she wasn't best pleased by it. A few weeks later I was in the Calvin Klein store in New York, where, on the top floor, I spied her. So I did what any self-respecting coward would do: I hid behind one of the shop's conveniently placed pillars. As she moved around the floor, I jumped from pillar to pillar. This went on for about ten minutes before I darted down the stairs and out the shop.) My wife liked Samantha too. I didn't necessarily disagree, but I thought her husband was smart, I enjoyed his company, and – far more importantly – I was convinced he was going to be the next prime minister.

If he didn't eat himself to death.

Cameron reminded me of the gigantic Italian fashion designer Gianfranco Ferré, who would spend his day grazing. No biscotti, panettone or panforte di Siena was safe in Ferré's Milanese studio, as it would be swooped upon and hoovered up in an instant. Ferré was a big man and I often wondered if Cameron would follow suit; Gabby

Bertin, his press secretary, was constantly on 'bun duty' and would grab any stray cake that found its way into her boss's paw.

When he eventually became prime minister, Cameron found himself eating more pie, of the humble variety, when he had to publicly apologise to his new deputy, Nick Clegg. In my book, I had asked him what his favourite political joke was, and without hesitation he had said, 'Clegg. Nick Clegg.'

I started the project not really knowing where it would take either of us, not really knowing if I was shadowing a chancer, a maverick or a visionary. David Cameron was certainly not without faults, although it soon became obvious that he had a very clear idea of what he could do for Britain, and how he could start to produce change. Not everyone warmed to him – and there was still an element of inverted snobbery running through the country that hadn't been eradicated by a decade of New Labour – but more importantly, people were now saying that whatever their reservations, they were prepared to give him a chance. He was helped in his quest enormously by Andy Coulson; in fact I would say it was Andy who made him electable.

CAMERON WOULD, OF COURSE, BE remembered for what he failed to deliver on 23 June 2016. There were so many reasons why a large proportion of the British public felt so angry towards David Cameron. One of the most galling, obviously, was his seemingly premeditated decision to step down when the European Union referendum vote went against him in the summer of 2016. This, for many, was a shining example of what was always considered to be his rather relaxed attitude towards governing, or in other words a complete dereliction of duty. In an act of supreme petulance perhaps worthy of José Mourinho, Cameron decided to walk off the pitch, seemingly never to return, having thrown his tracksuit, his tactic sheets and his team sheets behind him. That was another problem, at least in the eyes of those who criticised his bungled attempts to convince the British public to vote Remain: he repeatedly mistook tactics for strategy, offering a Brexit vote that was almost infantile in its simplicity and naivety.

As Richard Dawkins said so eloquently in his Brexit video commissioned by BBC's *Newsnight*, constitutional amendments are, or should be, hard to achieve – in the US, it takes a two-thirds majority in both houses of Congress. 'It's easy to see why the bar is set so high.' he said. 'Unlike ordinary law-making, constitutional changes are for keeps. Voters are fickle. Opinions change. We have no right to condemn future generations to abide, irrevocably, by the transient whims of the present.' Some felt that Dawkins was too strident and patronising in his broadside, but for Remainers, he managed to encapsulate their anger. 'If ever a decision needed a two-thirds majority it was Brexit.' The beef of his argument echoed what many said about the inexpert way in which Cameron presented his big idea to the public: not offering a two-thirds majority cut-off, not suggesting a second vote after a cooling-off period, and not producing a granular cross-party examination of the pros and cons. Those speaking in Cameron's defence said that the 'European question' was never going to go away, and that it just happened to fall on his watch, which was such a trite excuse for a vote that was only organised to appease those voters who were drifting to the right, and more precisely, to UKIP.

Cameron's Etonian arrogance was the same one that made him think he could be prime minister in the first place. It was this complacency, the famous 'chillax' orthodoxy that had tainted him since he was elected. When, back in the days he was still sitting in the back of a dodgy Prius, he was asked why he wanted to become prime minister, his answer was simple, emphatic and very DC: 'Because I think I'd be good at it.' And until 23 June 2016, he was.

He called it wrong. I was at the Hay Festival at the end of May that year and went to a dinner with one of the most public Remainers, Roland Rudd. That night I heard a phrase repeated twice that was unfortunately one of the reasons the country eventually voted Out: 'The problems with these Brexiteers is that they're just not educated.'

*

GQ WAS THE FIRST MAJOR publication in the country – actually anywhere – to put him on the cover and were one of the first media outlets to pronounce publicly that we thought he was going to be prime minister. Like everyone else, I had no idea his legacy would be Brexit. He would be brought back into government, as foreign secretary, by Rishi Sunak, in 2023 when I was editing the *Evening Standard*, and it seemed that Cameron had suddenly found a platform for redemption. Not for the country, perhaps, but maybe for him.

Nevertheless, our cover had sold well.

It's easy to forget how important the newsstand was at the time. We would spend hours each week trying to find ways to incentivise subscriptions, but it was always an uphill struggle as you had to invest so much to try and either get people to continue their subscriptions or, far more difficult, conjure up a new subscriber out of thin air – often by offering them a ridiculously cheap deal along with a pantechnicon of mediocre beauty products. I tried to encourage the subscription department to think laterally but, in the end, it was a numbers game; they understood that if you threw enough muck against the wall then a certain amount of it was going to stick, so that's the way they were going to do it.

Each month we would have a circulation meeting with our distributor, COMAG, in the boardroom at Vogue House. We would spend so much time analysing the minutiae of covers, and every element would be subject to the same level of scrutiny – the suitability and scarcity of the cover star, the quality of the photograph, the size and colour of the logo (coral was big for a while, really big), the cover lines ('Why are they so small?'), the weather (if it was sunny, no one bought magazines), the competition, cover price, what was on TV, the likelihood of big sporting events diverting people's attention away from the newsagents (the World Cup, Wimbledon), the increasing importance of mobile phones, everything. These meetings were steered by Lynn Doughty, who I knew from my days with Nick Logan, and she was refreshingly withering when the occasion demanded it. Asked why the recent issue of a rival title hadn't performed as well at newsstands as we had all expected, she'd offer a view based on common sense (which wasn't always as common as you might have thought). 'It was boring,' she might say, or, 'No one wants to sleep with George Clooney any more. Apparently.'

Often, I would be baffled by what actually did sell, but in the end the customer was always right. And if they didn't want a Clive Owen cover then they didn't want one and there was nothing I could do about it. Apart from wishing we hadn't printed 250,000 of them.

There was a lot of nonsense talked about covers. People would get obsessed about numbers ('Does it have to be forty-nine great things to do this summer? Could it be fifty instead?'); or try and tell you that black and white covers didn't sell as well as colour ones (not true). For years, I had to fight to get men on the cover, until I proved that they worked. Well, the right men, of course. I wasn't about to put Peter Mandelson on the cover.

Joking aside, I knew that politicians would work as cover stars, as long as I chose the right ones. I never managed to put Tony Blair on the cover, but I think we were just slightly too late. (Like many in the country, before he became embroiled in the Iraq War, I had a lot of time for Blair, and thought he was just what the Labour Party, and the country, needed.) We would go on to have Cameron, Boris, Sadiq Khan, Obama, Biden, even Jeremy Corbyn and Chuka Umunna (I know, what was I thinking?). If you caught them at the right time, they were just as legitimate as movie stars, sportsmen, football managers, artists, musicians, TV actors, models or racing drivers.

The reaction you wanted with a cover was always, 'No . . . yes.' If the crowd of people at a cover meeting or distribution meeting were initially shocked at your cover choice, then you knew you'd won. In 2018, when I put Skepta and Naomi Campbell on the cover, naked, locked in a passionate embrace, I dared people to take issue with it.

Luckily, they didn't.

Covers were all about intuition, common sense and execution. Everything else was just luck.

Our creative director Paul Solomons was key to the look of *GQ*, both inside and out. Paul was complicated. On first reading he looked like a jock or a rugby player (he was Welsh) – big, good looking and deliberately unpretentious. But he had such an amazingly clinical design sensibility. I probably spent more time with Paul than any other member of staff during my time at Condé Nast. He knew about design, knew what was good and bad, understood the difference between really good and sensational, and had the ability to show me, and everyone else, what he meant. He understood all the mechanics of producing a magazine, in the same way he would soon master the vocabulary of film and digital media. He was a wizard.

He was adept at turning the unlikely into cover stars. He did it with James Corden, with Simon Pegg, even with Ed Sheeran. I would also spend hours with him trying to rescue a feature, and he would indulge me even when he knew I was making the wrong decision (which I did frequently). But then he'd spend three hours redesigning it and would email it to me later that night, just as I was sitting down to watch *Breaking Bad*. Along with Robin Derrick, he was the best creative director in the company, and his most important editorial skill was his ability to make a story look commercial as well as consequential. Anyone could lay out a fourteen-page fashion story by Nick Knight or Steven Meisel, anyone could treat an Annie Leibovitz portrait with reverence, but it took genuine talent to fashion something special out of thin gruel. He was relentless, and I would spend inordinate amounts of time encouraging him to take more holiday, to not work weekends and to delegate more. But Paul wanted to do everything himself, as he knew he was the best. He was.

Sometimes every day was filled with meetings, but they all had a purpose. Short meetings were best, with a small group of people and a definite aim. I hated spitballing meetings, as I thought they rarely achieved anything. If we weren't approaching a conclusion, I would sometimes throw a spanner in the works, just to wind up the team. When they challenged me, I always said it was my job to come up with the bad ideas. I liked fairly early meetings, too. Three times a week I would leave the house at six-thirty, walk to the gym in the basement of Home House in Portman Square, and after brutalising myself for an hour, walk to work. So I'd be at my desk between eight and nine, ready to spend an hour with the papers.

We had our disappointments – I couldn't convince Tina Brown to pose naked for us, I didn't manage to get Boris to test drive a tank, and for some reason Andrew Neil had no qualms about rejecting our offer for him to be our new sex correspondent. But I hired some great new writers, journalists who enjoyed – nay, felt compelled – to go out into the field, often to conflicted lands; people such as Sam Knight, Sean Langan and Anthony Loyd.

BY 2004, THE MEN'S MAGAZINE market had been in rude health for well over a decade, although I had inadvertently been responsible for giving oxygen to its baseline reader. Thirteen years earlier, in March 1991, I was sitting in my ground-floor office – well, an oblong glass bunker, actually – in the Old Laundry, a converted workhouse in Marylebone, just a short walk from Oxford Street. The Old Laundry was the HQ of *The Face* and *Arena* when I was ensconced as a contributing editor of the former and the editor of the latter. It was a blazingly hot day, and I was sitting behind my desk in shirtsleeves, drinking a take-away cappuccino and reading a copy of the *Independent*, yet the man approaching me was wearing his usual overcoat. The contributors who worked for *The Face* and *Arena* were an idiosyncratic bunch, at least sartorially.

Sean O'Hagan, while not being one of our major contributors, was known around the office for his miserable manner, his fondness for Stalinist indie bands and the fact he never appeared to take his overcoat off, even when it was sweltering. He had come to see me this morning to pitch an idea, one centred on a new type of man he had stumbled upon, one who had apparently outgrown the idea of the New Man and had morphed into something called the New Lad. I told him the idea didn't sound very plausible, and that I thought he was simply making it up. 'Dismissive' is how I would describe my reaction, but then I was wrong, just as I had been wrong when I questioned why Tony Parsons wanted to write 'The Tattooed Jungle' – his polemic about the working class that eventually turned into a cottage industry.

I told O'Hagan if he really thought his thesis stood up, then he should go back to his one-bedroomed basement in Stockwell and write it. Which is exactly what he did, and the piece was so convincing, and so well argued, that we published it a few weeks later ('Here Comes the New Lad').

So, it was me who was partly responsible for inflicting the New Lad on the world. The publication in *Arena* of O'Hagan's piece set in motion a series of events that resulted in the publication of a lot of clever, funny, ribald but ultimately tawdry magazines that appeared to want to celebrate little but the rather more reductive and imbecilic elements of masculinity, namely the Old Lad. As O'Hagan explained it, the New Lad was 'a rather schizoid, post-feminist fellow with an in-built psychic regulator that enables him to alter his consciousness according to the company he keeps. Basically, the New Lad aspires to New Man status when he's with women but reverts to Old Lad type when he's out with the boys. Clever, eh?'

O'Hagan's essay identified men's sympathetic responses to feminism, yet their inability to embrace it wholeheartedly. As Tony Parsons would later write, in one of the many responses to O'Hagan's piece,

> Any modern man who read Sean O'Hagan's essay had no difficulty at all in saying – God, that's me. Sensitive, enlightened, caring – but only up a point, and the point was where you had to surrender your manly soul. Every man who read O'Hagan's treatise on the New Lad had known nothing but girls and women who had been shaped by decades of feminism – and so we had been touched by it too. And we were even broadly sympathetic to its aims, as long as we could still go to the football on a Saturday afternoon, and as long as all the stuff we really liked wasn't suddenly seen as symbolic of an oppressive, patriarchal society.

O'Hagan's piece coincided with the publication of Nick Hornby's *Fever Pitch*, a book that not only elevated football to a cultural position it hadn't really held since the glory days of 1966, when England won the World Cup, but also explored men's obsessional tendencies in a way that had barely been done before, creating a publishing genre that was swollen by Hornby's next book, *High Fidelity*, which explored the male obsession with cataloguing music.

The problem was that the men in O'Hagan's piece had actually read *The Female Eunuch*, as had Hornby; but by the time the New Lad had been interpreted by the publishing industry, Hornby's new consumer appeared to be interested in old-fashioned yobbism. Seemingly overnight, the generation of men who were coming of age in the heady days of Britpop and Britart were co-opted by a media intent on treating them like oafs, while celebrating all the things from which magazines such as *The Face* and *Arena* had tried so hard to distance themselves.

The first modern British magazine designed to appeal to men – *Arena*, launched at the end of 1986, soon followed by both *GQ* and *Esquire* – were titles full of top-end journalism and slick fashion pages, born on the back of a massive consumer boom. *Loaded* ushered in another kind of man completely. Launched in 1994 by an ex-*NME* journalist, James Brown's magazine was an instant hit, a genuinely inspired magazine that was anti-style, anti-metropolitan and unashamedly antediluvian. *Loaded* was a magazine for all the men – and there were rather a lot of them – who had no interest in the fancy world depicted by the likes of *Esquire* and *Arena*, had no interest in unnecessarily trendy fashions or chairs that were difficult to sit on. The *Loaded* reader didn't understand why the other men's magazines didn't do more sport, didn't understand why they couldn't laugh a little more at their obvious failings. The *Loaded* reader didn't mind admitting he couldn't afford a Porsche. Which is one of the reasons it was so successful.

I was working for the *Sunday Times* when *Loaded* launched, and I looked forward to each issue with great anticipation. It was brash, audacious, funny and completely unlike the men's magazine world I had recently left. Bits of it were puerile – actually, parts of it were extremely puerile, and there was a lot of stuff in there that didn't warrant a second glance – but it had an attitude and a spirit that was all its own. The *Loaded* parties were often better than the magazine, too – long, ribald affairs full of the most unlikely people.

Loaded was a genuine phenomenon, and it was only natural the market would respond; soon there would be many more mainstream titles jostling for space on newsagents' shelves. I would regularly go into the WHSmith at Holborn Circus at lunchtime, and each time I would see a crowd of largely twentysomething men, six or seven deep, poring over men's magazines, working out which one they were going to buy. They would patiently stand behind each other, reading *Loaded*, *GQ*, *FHM*, *Esquire*, *Arena*, *Maxim* and all the other entrants into the men's magazine market, laughing, soaking up their lunchbreak and then taking one lucky winner back to their desk. Not only did I find the sector compelling from a personal perspective, but having been asked to be the launch editor of *Maxim*, and having turned it down, I found the development of these magazines completely fascinating. For a while, there was a sense that culture at large was becoming louder than it had ever been, almost as though everything had to have some sort of profane prefix. Records, books, magazines, films and every kind of art were all fucking loud and fucking big and fucking outrageous and fucking funny and fucking sexy and fucking noisy and fucking cool and fucking out of it and fucking fucked. The nineties were turning into one big exclamation mark, or as it was called in the printing world, a dog's cock. A fucking big dog's cock.

The thing is, as a lot of these magazines had simply turned into pornography, the magazines at the top end of the market – *GQ*, *Esquire* and *Arena* – were desperately trying to form a breakaway group, and the very last thing we wanted to be associated with was *FHM*, *Maxim* or what *Loaded* had turned itself into. We wanted to eradicate the bottom of the market, little knowing that it would soon eradicate itself.

THE YEAR 2004 FOR ME ended on a disquieting note. Three days before Christmas, I left my office for the holiday break. I took a car home, laden with various hampers from clients and some of the gifts I'd received that I hadn't passed on to the team. I got the car to stop off at Harvey Nichols because I needed to buy some last-minute presents, and by the time I got back in the car I'd been sent a message from the *News of the World*, encouraging me to call back. I didn't, but as I arrived home, they called again, with disturbing news. Apparently, they had proof that I had been having an affair with Kimberley Fortier, and did I want to make a comment?

I was so shocked that I think they found my denial implausible. I would have called Andy Coulson, who was editing the paper then, but he was in Barbados, so I had to spend ten minutes remonstrating with one of his deputies.

The thing is, Kimberley had been all over the papers for weeks. She was the publisher of the *Spectator* (Boris Johnson was the editor), and married to Stephen Quinn, who was the publishing director of *Vogue*, so consequently someone I knew very well. Kimberley had been having a three-year affair with the blind Labour MP David Blunkett, and when the newspapers found out, she started to be the subject of a lot more scrutiny. Earlier in December, Blunkett was forced to resign as home secretary amidst allegations that he helped fast-track the renewal of a work permit for Fortier's nanny.

At the time, other members of the *Spectator*'s staff had admitted dalliances with fellow toilers in its townhouse offices in Doughty Street, London, resulting in a new Fleet Street nickname, the *Sextator*. Boris Johnson was forced to resign from the Tory front bench when his affair with the columnist Petronella Wyatt became public knowledge. And Rod Liddle was subject to a bruising media row with his wife when his affair with Alicia Munckton, the magazine's receptionist, was leaked earlier in the year. Then it emerged that the *Guardian* journalist Simon Hoggart (who also found time to regularly write for the *Spectator*) had been the third man sleeping with Kimberley, although their relationship had apparently started before she married Stephen Quinn.

In this light, it perhaps wasn't so surprising that the tabloids had started cold calling her friends and acquaintances in the hope of catching a fourth volunteer. I batted back the *News of the World*'s accusations, knowing full well I was innocent. I assumed they had simply taken photographs of us having lunch at the corner table in Le Caprice (Princess Diana's old table again), the one nearest the window. But then, of course, as the phone-hacking narrative gathered momentum, I figured there might have been other issues at play.

That night, after telling the *News of the World* to think very carefully about what they were considering printing the following Sunday, I called Simon Kelner, who was still editing the *Independent*.

'It's disconcerting, isn't it,' he said. 'When you're called by a tabloid, you immediately feel guilty even if you're innocent.'

Inventing Piers Morgan

The GQ Interview

Man cradles baby, baby becomes President, 2008

IF YOU WANT TO BLAME anyone for Piers Morgan being on television, then blame me. I hired him in 2004 after he'd been fired as editor of the *Daily Mirror* for refusing to apologise for authorising the paper's publication of fake photographs of British soldiers 'torturing' an Iraqi prisoner. Morgan refused to take responsibility for the mistake, despite a report from the British government saying the photos had been forged and taken in northwest England, saying, 'If nobody knows the provenance of these photographs, why should we apologize?'

I hired him for one particular reason. I wanted him to interrogate the notable and the powerful, at which he turned out to be brilliant. Piers was unrelenting in his questioning and would always press his subjects to answer his questions (and they were always difficult questions), where other journalists would simply give up. Big Q & A interviews, warts and all, highbrow, lowbrow, nobrow.

I wanted the slot to be deliberately gladiatorial.

(Confrontational interviews always appealed to me when I read them, as I felt as though I was learning something. Even when I was young, I could tell which interviews had genuine worth, as the best ones often made the subjects uncomfortable. In hindsight, I wasn't overburdened with empathy, and I didn't really care what people thought while they were being skewered. I just found it interesting. This lack of empathy was something that I took for granted. When I was young, whenever there was a natural or man-made disaster, I would secretly think that the net result was positive. Why? Because there would be fewer people in the world.)

I offered him the job as I was walking to work one morning, striding across Hyde Park. We did the deal in about 200 yards. I ended up paying him far more than I wanted to, but he turned out to be worth every penny. When I got to the office and told the team what I'd done, they thought I'd gone mad. Alex and Jonathan in the features department both said nobody would ever agree to be interviewed by Piers, as he was so confrontational; they went so far as to say he was toxic. I loudly disagreed and vowed to make it a success. Which it immediately was. In fact, it worked in exactly the opposite way, as Piers was already something of a celebrity and people wanted to find out what he was like.

The magazine needed a regular dyspeptic interview slot in which we could take people to task, a self-contained feature that would have a tone and a personality almost outside of *GQ*. Thus making it 'The Piers Morgan Interview' gave us a little distance from it. So, when friends and enemies came up to me and said they couldn't believe what Naomi Campbell, Boris Johnson, Sharon Osbourne or Donald Trump had said in *GQ*, I wouldn't have to shoulder the blame.

'Oh, that's just Piers,' I would say, and shrug.

He never appeared to mind.

He started getting up people's noses, which was the point of him. As a journalist, he had innate reporting skills as well as being able immediately to see the way into a story. Same with personalities. He wasn't overly obsessed with nuance, but this was a professional reflex, not a personal one. When the lofty media commentators came down hard on Piers, they often made the mistake of assuming that what he did was all he could do, whereas that was far from true. He first identified what it was about a person that made them interesting (he wasn't always right: I offered him Iggy Pop once, and he was completely dismissive, as he couldn't see what the point would be), and then he'd weave his way into the conversational narrative to make the experience properly combative, and a treat for the reader. He knew precisely what buttons to press, understanding exactly what he wanted to get, and he pretty much always delivered. After spending a couple of hours with Nick Clegg, Simon Cowell or Arnold Schwarzenegger he would call me, excitedly, letting me know what had just happened, and what indiscretions had been laid at his feet.

If he had a flaw, I don't think he was great with women. I could always sense that, perhaps out of an odd kind of chivalry, he didn't go for the jugular like he did with men.

And he always got his man.

ONE MORNING I WAS WALKING through the features department, and I saw a press release on Stuart McGurk's desk. Stuart was a remarkably perceptive and dogged reporter with a keen journalistic instinct, as well as being a magnificent writer. But we had turned him into a brilliant commissioning editor, too. Under the tutelage of Jonathan Heaf, he had become a cerebral bloodhound who took as much joy commissioning other people as he did commissioning himself. But he'd missed this one. The press release was a puff for a new children's book written by Alan Rusbridger, the gnomic and self-regarding editor of the *Guardian*, and someone who had continually rebuffed Piers's requests to interview him. I tapped it and said, 'Could be good for Piers.'

'Rusbridger will never do it,' said Stuart.

'Ask,' I said. 'What have we got to lose? The publishers will have set up a day of interviews and he probably won't even look at the itinerary. He's a busy guy.'

This proved to be the case, as the publishers came back and said he'd love to be interviewed by *GQ* about his children's book (we didn't tell them we were sending Morgan). The PR obviously had no understanding of what this could mean in the bigger media world.

The result, predictably, was glorious. I would have loved to have seen Rusbridger's face when Piers walked into the room, as he would have immediately realised the cosy fireside chat he had been expecting was instead going to be rather more bellicose. After only a minute in his company, Piers was quizzing him about his salary, suggesting he was being fundamentally hypocritical by earning so much when his paper was struggling financially.

A lot of people suddenly put in this situation would have walked out of the interview, leaving Piers with little but a snarky anecdote. But Rusbridger sat there for another ninety minutes, and unnecessarily subjected himself to an expert filleting. I put this down to ego and machismo. If you were a politician then you would have had to sit there and suck it up, but anyone else – actor, sportsperson, musician, TV presenter, newspaper editor – could have just upped sticks and vamooshed. The interview wasn't being filmed – we would only start filming these interviews when I replaced Piers with Alastair Campbell, because by then our website needed the material – so he could have thrown a hissy fit, blamed his PR and left. But the likes of Rusbridger and Boris Johnson simply thought they could get the better of Piers, and so they stayed, glued to the spot in the vain hope of coming out on top.

They never did.

These men always lost the fight, crawling back to their corner of the ring – broken, battered and defeated. And the battles were often bloody. One of the worst was when the deputy prime minister Nick Clegg told Piers just how many women he had slept with. This information didn't exactly endear him to the electorate (this was

2008, and Clegg revealed he had slept with 'no more than 30' women in a toe-curlingly frank interview).

Piers's interview choices could sometimes be idiosyncratic, and counterintuitive. Which is how we filled the rest of the magazine, too. The trick was to always trust our instincts, to go with what we felt rather than what we thought other people might expect us to do. This was not an original thought, but it was an important one. As Henry Ford once said, 'If I'd have asked the public what they wanted, they would have said faster horses.'

It was, in the end, sport, and Morgan and Rusbridger knew each other socially. 'Despite his perpetual rank hypocrisy, I am very fond of Rusbridger and his paper,' said Piers. 'The *Guardian* plays an important role in our society and acts as an effective foil to right-wing papers such as the *Daily Mail*.'

After skewering someone in *GQ*, Piers would always go up to them afterwards if he saw them in a restaurant, or on a plane. 'Hi mate, all forgiven?' In that sense he was difficult to dislike.

Not everyone liked him, mind. In 2005, I went to Downing Street to interview Tony Blair in front of a select group of journalists on behalf of the British Society of Magazine Editors. There were some questions from the floor – human rights in China, European alliances, the prospect of Gordon Brown being run over by a bus – and when I brought the meeting to an end by asking if he had read the passages about him in Piers Morgan's diaries, Blair looked at me as though I might possibly be mad. I've got a photograph of the moment and does look quite cross.

'No,' Blair said, emphatically. 'I have somehow not found the time to read the references to me in Piers Morgan's diaries and I sincerely hope I never do. I am rather busy, you know.'

Which I took to mean that he had not only read them, he'd re-read them and digested enough to know he didn't want to read them again.

David Remnick, who was in the room writing a piece about Blair for the *New Yorker*, couldn't wipe the smile off his face.

*

MORGAN'S COLUMN STARTED TO BE a place where some celebrities would find a kind of media redemption. They knew he would start by eviscerating them. But he would slowly reach an arm around their shoulders, somehow making them bigger in the process. So, Piers could be kind as well as heartless. What he wanted was stories – lines – which is what I wanted too. And each month he delivered. Each month his interviews would generate headlines nationally, internationally and locally, all three markets that were of vital importance to us as a brand.

Piers was one of those journalists who could tap you on the arm and ask, 'You did, didn't you? Come on, you can tell me.' And he got away with it – people did tell him. He even managed to get George Galloway to admit he thought it was morally justifiable to assassinate Tony Blair.

When Boris Johnson was the mayor of London, Piers asked him if he was a celebrity (a question he liked to fling at all politicians). His answer was this: 'I think Disraeli was once asked why people went to the House of Commons, and he said, "We do it for fame." And it was Achilles who said the same thing – that fame or the desire to be known is not in itself necessarily disreputable. Achilles said he was doing it all for the glory of immortality.'

Piers was, predictably, his own worst enemy. At the after-party at Matthew Freud's Primrose Hill house following one of our Men of the Year Awards, Piers was standing with Justin Timberlake, Samuel L. Jackson and Pharrell Williams, eating Soho House dirty burgers and discussing gun control (Timberlake and Jackson both come from Tennessee and grew up around guns). It was quite an intense, animated conversation, and then in walked Jeremy Clarkson. He went up to the group and said, 'Who's making all this bloody noise?'

Morgan recalled: 'And I say, "Jeremy!" and he says, "Oh, I might have bloody guessed." Anyway, I shook his hand and it's all very civilised. And as I shake his hand, he sees these luminaries who clearly have no idea who he is, and just give him the eye. You know, "Mate, it's time to move on."'

Piers pointedly refused to introduce Clarkson.

Perhaps unsurprisingly, Clarkson is one of the many people to have turned Piers down; they famously had a fight at the Press Awards in 2004 after Clarkson ran something probing about Morgan's personal life at the *Mirror*. In fact, when we asked Clarkson if he'd like to be interviewed by Morgan, his exact words were, 'You must be fucking joking.'

Occasionally, Piers would be so brutal with someone that it would create so much attention it would be impossible to find anyone important enough for him to interview. There was always a queue of politicians who were up for a fight, and yet if they weren't a secretary of state, or had a cabinet position or actually led a party, there wasn't often much point. One month, when the well was well and truly dry, I even suggested Piers interview himself. I wasn't in the least bit surprised when he leapt at the idea.

Interviewing celebrities was something of an art, and there were many I kept well away from Piers. With a lot of celebrities, especially those in the entertainment industry, you needed to tread extremely carefully. He was much better with politicians.

BY THE TIME I HIRED Piers, *GQ* was officially hot, and it appeared that people were taking notice of everything we did, which obviously meant we had to make sure everything we did was worth taking notice of. Not everything worked in the way I wanted it to, including the sex columns. I was tiring of them – the magazine had always had sex columns – and I felt the readers were too. But Nicholas Coleridge liked them (I think he felt all men's magazines had to have sex columns), and so they stayed. I never asked men to write about sex, as I didn't think they could tell the truth (I asked Piers to write one once and it was a disaster, and never published). Women were funnier about sex, and usually far more honest. But that wasn't the problem; I could tell the mood music was changing. The tawdrier end of the men's magazine had started to dip, and so they had all started hitting the sex button pretty hard. As desperation bedded in, to a man they all thought that the way to survive was by becoming 'sexier'; but as 'sexier' was what the internet was starting to do with unsurprising success, so these magazines started to all look alike. And as soon as the market embraced weeklies such as *Nuts* and *Zoo*, I figured it was over.

I also increasingly ignored the perceived wisdom that it was commercial suicide to put men on the cover, and as our upmarket competition was still sticking with women (usually in black bikinis, mugging for the camera), so we started focusing almost exclusively on men. Sales weren't affected and advertisers loved it. So we started making even more money for the company. Around this time, someone on one of the upper floors said, 'You know there are only two magazines in Vogue House, don't you?' I didn't interrupt as I had no idea what he was going to say. '*Vogue* and *GQ* are the only two that people take notice of.' I thought this was unnecessarily catty, but knowing how things worked, I would imagine similar things were being said to other editors, using different magazines as the punchline.

Every now and then I would be offered jobs or encouraged to think about what I might want to do next by people who weren't employed by Condé Nast. There was *Wallpaper*, *Esquire*, *Arena* (again) and various approaches from the *Telegraph* and the *Evening Standard*. But I had no intention of going as I was enjoying myself so much, enjoying the freedom, and I loved working for Condé Nast. As the company started to realise it had a hot brand on its books, steered by a team that weren't in any way going to embarrass them, they vanished, and to a large extent we became autonomous. We were making a lot of money for the company, we never *ever* went over budget, and we started winning awards. They trusted us, and we repaid that trust. I almost couldn't believe there was a publishing company that cared so much about editorial, and was prepared to fund it properly, a company that was indulgent without being profligate. It also felt like we were running in the very top lane, the fast lane. I was experienced enough to know that things wouldn't stay like that for ever (they didn't; not only does everything always end, but it often ends badly), and so I was determined to enjoy it while it was good.

These were the good old days.

A call came from New York, though, which had potential. Would I like to have lunch with Jann Wenner in a few weeks' time? Would I like to discuss some developments at his company? Well, I thought to myself, I probably would. So, in a couple of weeks' time – I was in the city meeting writers anyway – I went to see Wenner, whom I'd admired from afar for years. He was a true publishing titan, a genuine maverick and a brilliant journalist. *Rolling Stone*, which he co-founded in 1967, may have faltered in the noughties, as it appeared to be going through some kind of personality crisis, but from its inception to the nineties it had been a powerhouse.

Wenner was sensationally charming, and lovingly explained how his organisation worked, and the latitude he gave his editors. He gave me what I detected was a finely rehearsed tour of the '*Rolling Stone* Wall', an insanely long, curved room divider wallpapered with every cover of the magazine. As a cultural sweep of America in the intervening years, it was colossally impressive; I had read so many of these issues, and indeed had hundreds of copies at home in my library. But *Rolling Stone* would have to wait as the carrot he was dangling was *Men's Journal*, a significantly less impressive title, one that looked unloved and unfocused. To my mind, it had always looked like a title that didn't really know what it was; I used to call it '*Men's Health* with cigars'. I had also heard that Wenner could be a hard taskmaster – people said he could be difficult and interfering – and having had enough experience of being professionally interfered with, I passed. And didn't have a single moment of regret.

FELIX DENNIS AND I ALSO had various conversations over the years, but I think we both knew there was no way I was ever going to edit *Maxim*, even in the US. Also, he used to delight in telling me that editors ought to be recycled regularly in case they got stale, so I was never intrigued enough to want to work for him. He was wonderful company, though. I first met him at a dinner at the founder of *Time Out*

Tony Elliott's house, in St John's Wood, where he used the occasion to launch into a monologue about how easy it was to start a magazine in the US. All you needed was a vast amount of money and the fortitude to endure the notion that most of the magazines you'd be printing would end up as landfill in Arizona. It was all about getting people to buy subscriptions, even if they didn't want them, or even get them. For Felix, publishing wasn't an art, it was a science, and was based purely on subscription. He used to tell me that it was cheaper to buy an existing magazine rather than launch a new one.

'If you want to launch a food magazine it's cheaper to buy a car magazine in the hope that your subscription retentions will be 5 per cent, which they probably will be.' Felix could even make the minutiae of magazine publishing fascinating. Sort of.

By the time I visited Mustique, Felix had largely stopped going, primarily due to ill health. He used to regularly fly party girls to his house on the tiny Caribbean island. They came on Concorde to Barbados, and then they'd get a hopper over to Mustique. His optimum number was always four and they were all told to bring 'toys' (dildos, etc.), and would cavort about on his enormous bed while he sat in his chair drinking cheap Sauvignon Blanc and hoovering up vast amounts of cocaine. I fell in love with Mustique and was soon taken into the circle of trust regarding the misdemeanours of some of the homeowners, particularly regarding Felix's hookers.

Dennis was larger than life, although perhaps not as large as his own. In the nineties, his *Maxim* brand was one of the biggest in the publishing industry and he would regularly commute to its New York HQ from his house on the island. My friend Greg Williams started working for *Maxim* in the late nineties and had only been there a few days when, one lunchtime, he heard a huge commotion in the reception. He then saw Dennis storm into the boardroom, swearing profusely, and immediately light up a huge cigar. Thinking this was an ideal opportunity for him to ingratiate himself, my friend walked in and asked if he was all right.

'Am I all right?' repeated Felix. 'No, I am not fucking all right, seeing that you fucking asked.'

'Oh, I'm very sorry about that, Mr Dennis,' said my friend. 'Why is that, sir?'

'Why is that?' mimicked Dennis, who was by now screaming at the top of his voice. 'Because my fucking doctor has just told me I have to give up fucking crack. That's why!'

He wasn't joking.

Dennis is much missed on the island, as he had the ability regularly to shatter Mustique's air of calm. He had bought his house from David Bowie, who in turn had been inspired to build on the island in 1989 by Mick Jagger, who had owned properties there since the seventies. This was during a time when the island was experiencing its second flash of fame. Spend any time on Mustique and you'll start to meet Bowie's ghost, whether it's in Basil's Bar, the waterfront dive bar where everyone on the island still congregates after dark (Bowie was a regular and would occasionally get up to sing with whatever house band happened to be playing there; he would also refer to one of the house cocktails as a 'Penis Colada') or at the Cotton House Hotel, where every Tuesday there is still a weekly meet-and-greet, at which you get to see who is staying on the island ('It's dog and lamppost time,' says my friend Mark Cecil, the unofficial mayor of Mustique), or, indeed, on one of the many beaches. When Bowie was on the island, he tended to be extremely sociable and even before he started coming with Iman would spend his evenings carousing with the likes of Jagger and Bryan Ferry. He sang in the choir in the local Bamboo Church every Christmas and even ventured out onto the ocean (he didn't learn to swim until 1980 and was never very confident in the water).

Bowie was a big entertainer at his home, but he started to tire of the island once he'd met Iman. A few people on the island said one of the reasons she wanted to leave Mustique was because all the 'help' were black and it made her feel uncomfortable.

In 1994, Bowie sold his house to Dennis, who immediately started reconfiguring the property, while commissioning a huge sculpture of two mating tortoises that can still be seen from the road today. The house came with most of its contents, at least most of the furniture. Apparently, there was a painting Iman wanted to keep, which had been included in the sale. David Cherry, who used to work for Dennis, says that when Bowie asked Dennis if he could have the painting back, Dennis said, 'Sure, if you buy the whole house with it.' He asked Cherry to make a CD-rom game, called *Mandalay Mystery*, which was an interactive tour of the house that revealed the painting to be at the bottom of Dennis's infinity pool. The house's garden designer, Made Wijaya, said the house was destroyed when Dennis bought it. 'He was a bit famous for his Philistine behaviour.' He said the house was 'a blaze of Victorian exotica. It really was very special. Then Felix came along, ripped it out and installed an air-conditioned games parlour. He got some shop dresser from Harrods to do the interiors and then went over to Bali and bought all this mindless crap. It was depressing.'

Dennis was to Mustique what Peter Langan was to his eponymous London restaurant in the eighties. His legacy is those fornicating tortoises, an arresting sight that still brings a touch of frat-house authenticity to the otherwise luxe tranquillity of the island. He would have loved Piers, and Piers would have loved Felix.

EVENTUALLY PIERS HAD TO MOVE to New York, to work for CNN as Larry King's replacement, as he'd not just run out of people to interview in the UK, he'd run out of prime ministers to annoy.

Just before Piers moved to America, I was at a dinner with David Cameron and asked him if he would agree to be interviewed for *GQ*. We had been the first magazine to put Cameron on its cover, and I thought it would be a fitting farewell for Piers, and perhaps his greatest scalp.

Cameron leaned into me and said, 'There are two things a Conservative politician should never do: firstly, he should never have anything to do with the European Union, and secondly, he should never agree to be interviewed by Piers Morgan for *GQ*.'

Piers blamed every one of his public firings on me. He called me his curse. In 2003, he was given *GQ*'s Newspaper Editor of the Year award for the *Mirror*'s coverage of and campaign against the Iraq War. Six months later he was fired. He later won *GQ*'s TV Personality of the Year award in 2013 for his work on CNN, speaking out about gun culture. Seven months later his show was axed. Then, in 2020, I offered him the award again for holding government ministers to account during the COVID-19 pandemic on *Good Morning Britain*. At this, Piers told me he was extremely wary of accepting again, but he relented when I persuaded that lightning never strikes three times. Six months later, he was forced to resign following controversial comments about Meghan Markle. I sometimes fall asleep imagining what other awards I could give to Piers.

Bowie, Elton and Bryan Ferry

What You Like is in the Limo

That David Bowie joke in full, with Nicholas Coleridge and Alex Shulman, Wembley, 2003

IN LONDON, EVERY NIGHT THERE was something to do. There would be multiple book launches, shop openings, film screenings, cocktail parties, dinners, opening nights, previews, private views, talks, gigs and extravagant fashion events that would start with a fashion show, then a dinner and then probably a party afterwards. In the early years of my editorship, I tried to do as much as possible, which meant I could be out at least four nights a week at multiple events, doing my best jazz hands. The trick was to stay sober and cover as many events as possible, a kind of Exocet strategy, breezing through rooms as quickly as you could. I would usually take a car, and never wear a coat so I didn't have to waste time in the cloakroom. In and out, that was the policy. I enjoyed it all, but I didn't want to end up having endless pointless dinners. There were so many people to see, so many relationships to build. I encouraged the team to do the same, and as everyone had their own patch – food, auto, luxury, film, fashion, politics, etc. – I didn't like hearing that a member of the team hadn't gone to something important. We needed to be out, and we needed to be seen. A lot of what we did was transactional, but I also enjoyed that side of the business. I wanted to build genuine partnerships with people with whom I liked spending time. And if you had the right mindset, it was easy to do. I enjoyed meeting notable people, but I didn't rush around town trying to collect celebrities. I made friends with the people I liked, and if some of them happened to be famous, then so be it.

There were other evenings that now feel as if they appeared like mist: a dinner in the private room at Annabel's with Larry Gagosian, Tracey Emin (after a while, we became legally obliged to invite Tracey to everything we did), Nick Rhodes, Naomi Campbell and Zaha Hadid; after-hours drinking with Bono in a club that neither of us could find in daylight; and 1,001 nights in the Groucho, in Dean Street. (When one of the cubicles in the downstairs gents was closed for repairs, a sign on the door read: 'Out of order – ceiling collapsing. Soon, an enterprising hand replaced 'ceiling' with 'nose'.) These were the kind of nights you only remembered from the pictures you saw afterwards.

You could, if you wanted to, move through the tributaries of London's social scene as though it was an actual job. It was all to do with stamina and expediency. I liked doing some of this, but I didn't confuse it with friendship. I just thought it was fascinating.

One night I went to dinner at a media bigwig's enormous flat in Mayfair, just behind the Curzon. When you were invited to dinner by her you never knew if you were going to be eating with two people, twenty people or two hundred. This night there were only a few of us: Roger Alton, the editor of the *Observer*, George Michael, Andrew Lloyd Webber, Janet Street-Porter, Jemima Khan, Peter Mandelson and Nigel Farage. It was like a pop-up book of bold-face London. As the evening progressed, and the conversations got louder, our hostess physically

The many worlds of *GQ*: Kylie, Beckham, Obama & Prince William.

The Men Of The Year Awards, featuring Tom Ford, Samuel L. Jackson, Michael Douglas, Justin Timberlake, Tracey Emin, David Bowie, Stella McCartney, Paul Smith, Fran Healey, Jimmy Page, Elton John, James Corden and Harry Styles.

olange, Charlie and Mel at our wedding, June 997.

Vould you rob or nick a Rob and Nick? Pen-Y-ryn, 2021.

Vith Harvey Goldsmith and Gary Kemp at the unch of my David Bowie book.

With Jay Z in London, 2007.

In 2014, Samuel L. Jackson, Sofia Davies and I organised a charity karaoke evening at Abbey Road Studios. Sam and I sang Sam and Dave's "Hold On I'm Coming"; Sam was Sam and I was Dave, obviously.

Larry Schiller, Tom Wolfe and myself at the Norman Mailer Gala in New York in 2010.

With Oliver Peyton, Bono, the Edge and Larry Mullen in Berlin, in 2015.

That's how we rolled: Prince, Bilmes, Heaf, Las Vegas, 2010.

With David Bailey in Kabul before our flight t
Camp Bastion, in Helmand Province, in 2010.

The family Jones, Hyde Park, 2001.

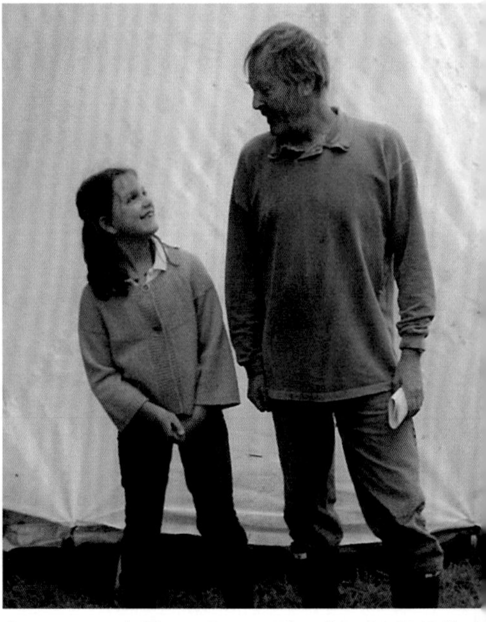

Georgia with Terry Jones, Llandrindod Wells, 2006.

Vith Edie in Los Angeles, May 2022.

Vith Spas Roussev at Capitol Records in Los ngeles, in 2013, with Frank Sinatra's Capitol ıicrophone.

Vith Bryan Adams and Charlotte Tilbury at .s house in Mustique, summer 2018.

Piggies! Vlad at a porcine assembly at Bittescombe Manor, 2023.

Mark and Katie Cecil, Priors Marston, July 2020. Mark's rocket just out of shot.

Bursting out of lockdown in 2021 at the Berkeley Hotel with John Reid and Alan Edwards.

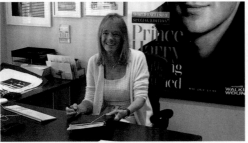

Ruth Rogers in my office in Vogue House, 2017, just before making our lunch.

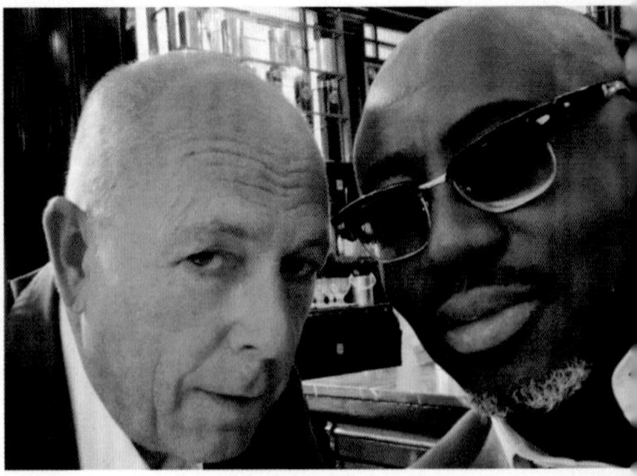

With Edward Enninful in The Wolseley, 2024.

Diliana Roussev in her garden in Mustique, 2018.

Gillie and Jake, Zanzibar, 2013

Jac, Jane, Debra and David, Hampstead, 2021.

The devils.

(above) With Claire and Al in Annecy, 2023.

(right) The Queen

Vith William Hague in Westminster, 2000, fter he admitted to drinking 14 pints of beer a ay as a teenager.

With Peter Mandelson at my 40th birthday party at Oliver Peyton's Isola in 2000.

nterviewing Tony Blair at Downing Street in 005, having just asked him if he'd found the me to read Piers Morgan's diaries.

With David Cameron and George Osborne in London in 2008.

n New York with Caroline Rush, Anna Vintour and Boris Johnson.

(above) Alastair Campbell playing the bagpipes at the dinner to celebrate my 20th anniversary at *GQ*.

(left) With Keir Starmer in the grounds of the Imperial War Museum, 2023.

Interviewing Tom Jones after the death of his wife at the Hay Festival, 2016.

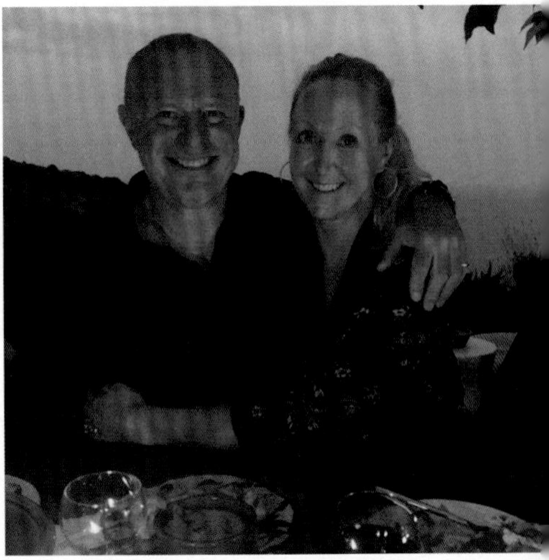

Sam and RCB on the fig terrace.

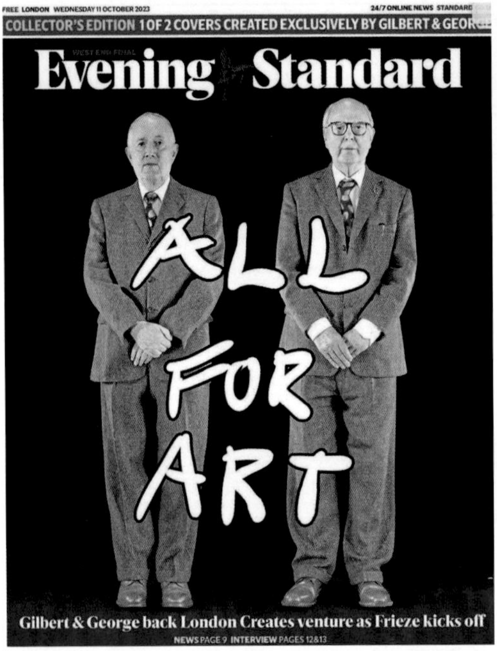
FREE LONDON WEDNESDAY 11 OCTOBER 2023 24/7 ONLINE NEWS STANDARD

COLLECTOR'S EDITION 1 OF 2 COVERS CREATED EXCLUSIVELY BY GILBERT & GEOR

WEST END FINAL

Evening Standard

ALL FOR ART

Gilbert & George back London Creates venture as Frieze kicks off

NEWS PAGE 9 INTERVIEW PAGES 12&13

The legends of the walking weekend: Stuart, James, Piers, Tim, Rusty, Trevor, Al et al, 2021.

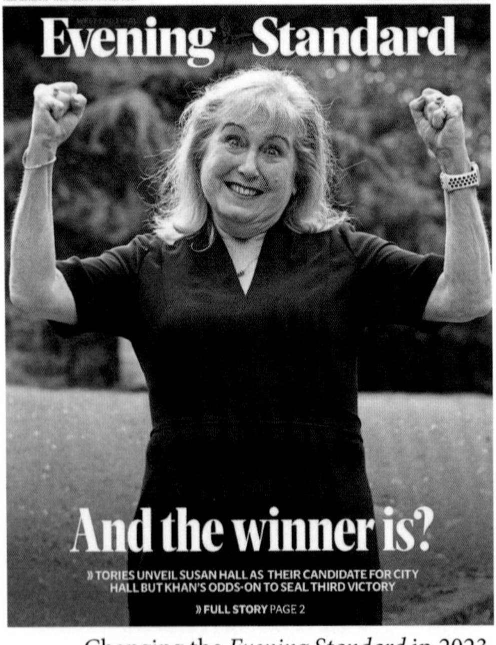
REE LONDON WEDNESDAY 19 JULY 2023 24/7 ONLINE NEWS STANDARD.CO

Evening Standard

And the winner is?

» TORIES UNVEIL SUSAN HALL AS THEIR CANDIDATE FOR CITY HALL BUT KHAN'S ODDS-ON TO SEAL THIRD VICTORY

» FULL STORY PAGE 2

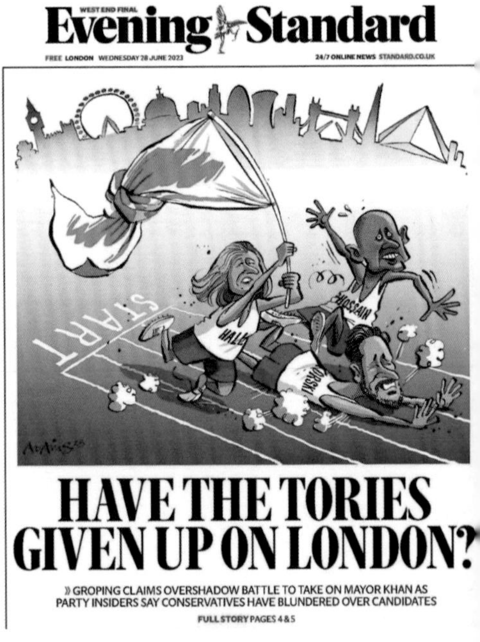
WEST END FINAL

Evening Standard

FREE LONDON WEDNESDAY 28 JUNE 2023 24/7 ONLINE NEWS STANDARD.CO.UK

START

HALL

HOSSAIN

HAVE THE TORIES GIVEN UP ON LONDON?

» GROPING CLAIMS OVERSHADOW BATTLE TO TAKE ON MAYOR KHAN AS PARTY INSIDERS SAY CONSERVATIVES HAVE BLUNDERED OVER CANDIDATES

FULL STORY PAGES 4&5

Changing the *Evening Standard* in 2023.

and emotionally withdrew, like a female Gatsby, enjoying the sport before her – a transactional dinner party where people would be perfectly nice to each other in person and then slag each other off in tomorrow's papers (this is certainly what I remember happening between Jemima and Farage).

If I had wanted to, I could have done this every night of the week. But I didn't.

SAYING WE WERE OBSESSED WITH making the magazine a work of art each month somehow denigrates anyone else involved in the same business. No one was deliberately attempting to make their product somehow less good than it could have been, but nevertheless we were completely obsessive about doing the very best we could. For a while, we became so focused that we almost forgot about the consumer and became obsessed with how our peer group would feel about what we had done. This manifested itself in an irrational kind of pride that was more narcissistic than it was anything else.

For a few years, we, perhaps unadvisedly, held an annual conference, where we would take over a country house hotel and spend two to three days spitballing, paintballing, horse riding, clay-pigeon shooting and having fun. We would invite a national newspaper editor or Hollywood executive to come and talk. The conferences were boisterous, often extremely drunken, and were a chance for the half of the team who didn't get the gravy to let off steam. They did, inevitably, encourage some bad behaviour, not least the destruction of an antique glass chandelier, irreparable damage to several nineteenth-century oils and, once, a bar bill that ran to five figures (how we paid that one, I have no idea). They became rather legendary, so much so that some of the younger members of the team began to feel empowered by their seventy-two hours at large.

One year, a relatively new staff member took it upon himself to tell me how he really felt about me. In Vogue House, he would skulk around the office and tended to internalise things to such an extent that he looked perpetually wounded. I didn't understand him, and he knew it.

On the second night, when he had obviously drunk his body weight in cheap champagne, he sidled up to me around midnight and said, in the boldest voice he could muster, 'I like working at *GQ*, but I think you're a little bit of a cunt.'

'Oh, I wouldn't worry about that,' I said. 'I think you're a little bit fired.'

I got rid of him the following day.

At these conferences we sometimes held a fancy-dress party. One year, this took place on Thanksgiving, so it was decided we should all dress up as famous Americans. Everyone put a heroic amount of effort into it, spending weeks getting their outfits together, and on the night we were treated to Stevie Wonder, Barbie, Tippi Hedren in Hitchcock's *The Birds*, Marge and Bart Simpson, Charlie's Angels, John McEnroe, Slash from Guns N' Roses, Marilyn Manson and thirty other wonderful recreations.

There was only ever going to be one winner, though. As we assembled in the banqueting hall of our country house hotel, slapping each other on the back or tentatively asking, 'Er, I don't get it. Who are you?', a porter arrived from the lobby pushing a trolley. On it was our deputy art director, strapped to a piece of board, head shaved, dressed in blue overalls and a purpose-built (well, bought on the internet) brown mask. He received a standing ovation, some fava beans, and a nice Chianti.

If I needed any further evidence that, as far as possible, and as far as I am concerned, fancy dress should be avoided, I was offered some a few weeks later by someone at a party celebrating a mutual friend's fortieth birthday. As this bizarrely dressed chap tried to move round us in the crowd – wearing a multicoloured high-necked shirt, a velvet suit of indeterminate colour, and the sort of patent leather shoes that could be used to bounce sunlight into outer space – my wife asked him who he'd come as.

'Oh, do you like it? I've come as Dylan Jones.'

*

QUITE QUICKLY, WE STARTED RAMPING up our own events. There was already a series of scheduled events with luxury brand advertisers, but I initiated regular dinners for talent, PRs, contributors and brands with whom we wanted to work. I let the team know I expected us to be the first media partner to be approached in relation to any imminent, important London launch. If a new hotel or a swanky restaurant opened, the team knew I'd be unhappy if we weren't the first people to have a party there. Very soon we were the most connected magazine in the business. This didn't happen by accident, and I'm sure a lot of our rivals couldn't have cared less about the social side of things, but I was intent on creating our own ecosystem, one that grew and grew. After a while, we started to host dinners and parties abroad, too, in fashion capitals – Milan, Paris, New York – and in entertainment capitals such as Los Angeles and Cannes. It was important for us to connect regularly with these worlds as it was good for business.

Which is where Elton John and David Furnish came into play. I was having lunch in the Wolseley with David one day, as he was writing features for us (in 2004, he interviewed Ozzy Osbourne and counted 259 fucks in the transcription), when he suggested he and Elton could host a party for us the next time we were in LA seeing agents. And so that's what we did. All we needed to do was find a sponsor – easy – and we were away.

Elton and David's generosity was overwhelming, and we eventually ended up co-hosting dinners together in LA for ten years, in the Beverly Hills Hotel, the Chateau Marmont, Cecconi's, Soho House in West Hollywood and a variety of other cool spots. These parties were unbelievably helpful, and enormous fun to boot. At one, in 2010 at Soho House, we were also celebrating Elton's triumphant concert with Leon Russell at the Hollywood Palladium (a venue that managed to look both futuristic and nostalgic at the same time). And party we did, with *Mad Men*'s Jon Hamm, Benecio Del Toro, Stephen Fry and Hugh Laurie, Brett Easton Ellis, Green Day, Sharon Osbourne and legendary producer T-Bone Burnett, the man who twiddled the knobs on Elton and Leon's album, *The Union*, to namedrop a few. I loved Hollywood parties like these, as you never really knew who was going to turn up, and it seemed rather surreal to be standing, twenty-odd floors above LA, looking out all over the twinkling city lights, in a room with the enigmatic and actually rather annoying fashion designer Hedi Slimane in one corner, and Ant and Dec in another.

Hamm was not only the hottest guy on television at the time, he was the man everyone stared at when he entered a room. We had our photograph taken together (I know, lucky him) and, as the flash went off, I whispered in his ear, 'By the time we publish this in *GQ*, your hair is going to be on my head.'

After another party, Elton decided he wanted to take a few of us to dinner, to a new steak place, the Cut, in Beverly Hills. As we finished our starters, and apropos of nothing, Elton started telling me about his sex life when he was younger. My eyes were on stalks as he described all this in intricate detail. He wasn't being indiscreet, just open.

I had interviewed Elton many times, but when I looked back at all my old interviews with him, I was struck by how much I focused on the luxuriant trappings of fame – the clothes, the houses, the art gallery, the excess. It was easy to get sidetracked by the things surrounding Elton, and always important to remember he was – first and foremost – a songwriter and piano player. You only had to see him perform to understand this. The acclaim and the attention and the fawning he expected – as one of the most famous men in the world it would be surprising if he didn't – but the real thrill he got on stage wasn't from recognition, it was from his own performance, and from watching his fingers run up and down the keyboard, making people smile and cry and dance in the process. Elton was never happier than when performing, losing himself in the moment. And the use of 'Tiny Dancer' (possibly Elton's very best song) in Cameron Crowe's *Almost Famous* in 2000 had introduced him to a whole new audience, once perhaps ignorant of his massive troubadour status in the early seventies.

Like David Bowie, Elton on occasion could be extraordinarily funny. We were doing some quickfire Q & As for a feature on him in the magazine around the time of our first dinner (which we threw for him in London, in the private room of the Cipriani), and when I asked him what the most disgusting thing was he'd ever put in his mouth, quick as a flash he shot back with, 'A clitoris.'

At that dinner (at which Jay Joplin had insisted on bringing a portable TV so we could all watch England play a World Cup game), Ozzy Osbourne asked Elton about the recent death of a particularly venal tabloid columnist.

'What did she die of?' asked Ozzy.

'Cuntishness,' said Elton.

BOWIE HAD A KEEN SENSE of humour, he loved a dirty joke, and he always tried to demonstrate this when appropriate. Why else would he have appeared in *Extras*, Ricky Gervais's glorious BBC sitcom in 2006, in which Bowie created a coruscating song that belittles Gervais's loser character Andy Millman as he looks on? In this three-minute performance, Bowie proved what an instinctive comic actor he was, and makes you wish he'd pursued more parts like this, rather than some of the dramatic roles he secured. (In 2016, Judd Apatow tweeted, 'Bowie on *Extras* was as good as comedy gets.') Bowie had emailed Gervais after meeting him in London. 'I don't know how he got my email address,' Gervais said. 'He's like the FBI. But he said: "So I watched *The Office*. I laughed. What do I do now?"'

Indeed, why would he have appeared, brilliantly, in a cameo in *Zoolander* if he didn't hanker to play against type and wasn't afraid to look foolish? He also loved SpongeBob, so much so he voiced a role in a 2007 movie spinoff, *SpongeBob's Atlantis SquarePantis.*

His own humour was, like Elton's, quite base, which is why he enjoyed a lot of television comedians from the seventies and eighties (he loved Peter Cook, Spike Milligan and Eric Idle) and also why he liked slapstick. 'There's still a lot of Buster Keaton in everything I do,' he once said. When Bowie found out one of his pet photographers, Steve Schapiro, had worked with the Hollywood star in his later years, he instantly took him under his wing and they became friends. Bowie even paid homage to the actor in the video for his 1993 song, 'Miracle Goodnight'. 'He also loved Tony Hancock and the Ealing comedies,' said *Absolute Beginners* director Julien Temple. 'He could watch Tony Hancock's *The Rebel* on a weekly basis, and he would laugh and laugh and laugh.'

Bowie was a genuinely funny man. Furiously bright, and able to decipher a situation immediately, he would use comedy to defuse a difficult issue or neuter a problematic journalist. Whenever I interviewed him, I could tell when he was nervous about a question by the way in which he smiled and tried to turn his answer into a joke. Like all celebrities he occasionally displayed his thin skin, but invariably he would employ humour to deflect and disguise his true feelings.

He used it in his acting, too. Bowie wasn't the best actor, but he was self-aware enough to know this. In an interview with the *NME* in 1980, he said, about the appalling *Just a Gigolo* in which he had starred with Marlene Dietrich, 'Listen, you were disappointed, and you weren't even in it. Imagine how we felt . . . It was my 32 Elvis Presley movies rolled into one.'

On chat shows he could be a riot and would regularly trade messages with Jonathan Ross after he had appeared on his show. This isn't so surprising. Before Bowie became successful with his Ziggy Stardust creation in 1972, he had spent almost a decade trying other ways into the entertainment industry. He had been in an R & B band, he had been in a folk duo, he'd tried mainstream pop and had even attempted a career as a children's entertainer. He'd done mime, jazz, and even gone down the comedy route for a while, masquerading as a poor man's Anthony Newley. Bowie didn't appear fully formed at the start of the seventies, and already had ten years of experience behind him, experiences which all fed into his new, sexy space-age guise. No, there wasn't a lot of comedy in Ziggy Stardust, but then the character didn't call for it. There wasn't a lot of call for anything remotely comedic in the Thin White Duke years either, but seeing that Bowie was then attempting to be the world's best cocaine addict, this is hardly surprising. But when he loosened up later in his career, you could see that comedy was always lurking just below the surface.

One afternoon, when I was still working at the *Sunday Times*, the phone rang and I immediately picked it up instead of letting it go to voicemail, as we tended to in a busy office. I was expecting a call from a PR about a story I was trying to set up. But it wasn't a PR on the end of the line, it was David Bowie.

'Bloody hell, you don't sound very much like my mother,' he said. 'Are you putting on a voice? Ha, ha!'

I had interviewed Bowie the week before for a project he was involved with at the Imperial War Museum, and he obviously still had my number in his book, on the same page as his mother's (we were both Joneses). Charmingly, he stayed on the line for nearly fifteen minutes, gossiping, laughing, and was evidently gassed there had been a mix-up. He wasn't embarrassed, wasn't chilly, but was genuinely funny, suggesting other people he might have called by mistake. Was he being ingratiating? I don't think so; he could have simply offered a quick 'Sorry, Dylan!' and put the phone down. But he was a funny man, and he was enjoying a funny situation.

Who knows, it could have been the germ for a little film, or a sitcom, or something with a proper punchline.

David Bowie: wasted comic.

I WAS IN AWE OF Bowie and saw him play so many times around then. One of the best was a barnstorming gig at what I would always call the Hammersmith Odeon, the site of Ziggy Stardust's final performance. As the show was ending, Alan Edwards tapped Oliver Peyton and me on the shoulder to see if we wanted to go backstage. Of course we did.

We traipsed through the rabbit warren at the back of the Odeon and joined the queue to see Bowie, ready to genuflect with the great man. Usually, you would be in and out quite quickly in this sort of situation, as there was always a long list of people who wanted to meet him backstage. We'd chatted to him a few years earlier backstage at Wembley Arena – I was with Nicholas Coleridge, Robin Derrick and Alexandra Shulman – and even though he spent quite a long time with us (I think he got a genuine kick out of being surrounded by the Condé Nast heavy mob), he was soon off, chatting to Brian May and Eno. But tonight, the queue just wasn't moving. Earlier, we had seen the novelist Jake Arnott ahead of us, and I knew Bowie loved his work, but he had already left, so we had no idea who was occupying so much of Bowie's time. We eventually got to speak to Bowie, and while he was extremely happy to hear our flattery, I could tell he was preoccupied. After we had bid him farewell, I asked Alan who had kept Bowie occupied for so long. Alan nodded to a man over by the bar. 'There he is,' he said. 'That's the reason David was so preoccupied tonight. I thought I had met every Bowie nut in the world, but he knows more about David than I do. In fact, I think he knows more about David than David. It was extraordinary, and I think David was a little overwhelmed.'

As we looked over to the bar, Oliver and I were jointly flabbergasted that the world's biggest Bowie expert turned out to be the Liberal Democrat leader, Charles Kennedy.

To us muggles, 'work' always seemed the most important part of an artist's life. To them, it was often simply a piece of the jigsaw of their life, fitting in alongside family, sex, investments, holidays and seeing friends. When Bowie moved to Switzerland at the end of the seventies, he took up skiing, and along with fellow tax exiles like Roger Moore and Tina Turner, spent an inordinate amount of time in Gstaad. He and Turner were close and skied together frequently (before her legs became so famous her insurance company refused to cover her unless she stopped). In early 1984, as Bowie was contemplating the follow-up to *Let's Dance*, he invited Iggy Pop to stay with him in Gstaad, which, seeing that he had never skied, to Pop was something of a novelty. After a few days, Turner asked if they'd like to go heliskiing, the very apex of off-piste adventure. Pop leapt at the opportunity, without the slightest idea of what it meant. At the last minute, Bowie couldn't go, and so Turner took Iggy up by himself.

'How did it go?' Bowie said to Tina when they met for dinner that night.

'It was a great day, although your friend didn't seem to know what to do,' replied Turner, with a worried look on her face.

'Iggy? Didn't you help him?' asked Bowie.

'I didn't get a chance,' said Tina. 'As I was about to explain it all to him, he had already jumped out of the helicopter.'

This was the first and last time Iggy Pop ever went skiing.

I would try and see him every time he swept through London, whether he was touring or not. Once, as we were having tea in the Halkin Hotel behind Buckingham Palace, we spent a good hour discussing exactly why Robbie Williams was famous. This would have been in about 2002, when Bowie was thinking of releasing an album called *Toy*, which was going to be made up of covers of some of the songs he'd released in the sixties. He seemed to be somewhat bewildered by Robbie's success, as to him he appeared to be little more than an exotically homespun old-school song-and-dance man. Bowie had spent most of his career following his instinct and hoping it would collide with public taste, and so when he was presented with a phenomenon that he didn't understand (like Robbie Williams), he wanted to get to the bottom of it. Bowie was mock-incensed that Robbie had co-opted so much of the John Barry Bond theme 'You Only Live Twice' for his song 'Millennium' and wondered how on earth he had got away with it.

The following year I went to Oyster Bay on Long Island to interview John Barry himself, and he was equally perplexed.

WHAT WE WERE DOING WITH *GQ* was building a brand, something I'm not sure the company ever completely understood. To them, we were already a brand, a magazine, but everyone at the coalface knew that magazines were, by dint of digital delivery systems, soon to be destined for oblivion. So, we pushed hard into our website and our social feeds, creating a company-busting affiliate scheme. We pushed hard into events, creating the Men of the Year Awards, our Best Dressed List, Car Awards, Food and Drink Awards, our Grooming Awards, The Power List and *GQ* Heroes, our version of Google Camp or TED. And they all made a ton of money. I forged links with literary festivals, first Cheltenham, then, properly, Hay. We collaborated with brands in the film industry, hosting parties in Cannes and Los Angeles, and fostered relationships with the likes of Warner and Universal to underscore our ability globally to support emerging artists as well as industry legends.

Regardless of who we were working with, we wanted to be the first port of call. And all these projects were editorially initiated, editorially driven. We would bring the commercial team on board when necessary – always working with Michelle Russell – and they never let us down. We were committed to being the most commercially minded brand in the building, which is why we all worked so well together. Nick Sargent, our publisher, would pop into my office and ask if we were doing anything at the Toronto Film Festival as there might be a commercial angle, and twenty minutes later we would be the hosts for the opening party.

It wasn't all beer and skittles, though. The day started at 6 a.m. on my BlackBerry and wouldn't end until midnight, often in the Groucho or Le Caprice. I was away maybe twenty weekends a year. People may think the life of a magazine editor is an easy one, and it is, if you want it to be. I had a great time – a ridiculously great time – but I poured so much into every day because I wanted us to be the very best. And in order to do that you actually had to work hard. I couldn't have done any of this without the support of my wife, and I know that sometimes she found it difficult, particularly in the early days, but I think she understood there was a purpose to all this.

I wanted the team to be out every night, to be seen every night, to be photographed every night. But they needed to be at their desks by nine the next day. I used to tell them, 'Don't go out if you can't come in.'

We started having so much success with our covers that I suggested to the circulation department that we start shrink-wrapping the issues, so that people couldn't open them in the newsagents. This seemed to confuse them, as they thought the 'architecture of tease' (my copyright) would discourage sales. It didn't.

PRIVATE JETS DIDN'T EXACTLY BECOME habitual, but they were part of the high-octane nature of the magazine, and we certainly started using them with more regularity. We used a ten-seater NetJets Falcon to take Bryan Ferry to Sofia, accompanied by myself, my very good and very well-connected Bulgarian friend Spas Roussev (who had once been sounded out about becoming the country's prime minister), and a small coterie of *GQ* apparatchiks, including the best-dressed man in Shepherd's Bush, Nick Foulkes. I sat next to Ferry on the way out, and he genuinely seemed fascinated by what happened in Vogue House. He loved the idea that each magazine had its own floor – 'It's like a department store of style,' he said – and wanted to know what various editors were like.

'Alexandra Shulman, is she terrifying?' he asked.

'Alex, she's a beast,' I replied, waiting for him to smile.

'My goodness, is she?' said Ferry.

And so on.

Some of my friends were big in Japan, some of them were big in America, and some of the larger ones were big all over the world. But for a short period in 2006, I was big in Bulgaria, big enough to warrant a mention on the early evening news (bumping Prince Charles's birthday celebrations into second place, I kid you not).

A few years previously I had written a moderately successful and rather arch etiquette book – *Mr Jones' Rules for the Modern Man* – which kicked up some dust, but which didn't exactly cause Jeremy Clarkson to look over his shoulder, sales-wise. In the emerging markets, though, it had gone gangbusters, and there were editions in Russia, China, Poland, Hungary, Korea and Romania as well as Greece and the United States. It was Bulgaria, however, where I was 'really' big, and this had caused me some reflection.

We were being flown to Sofia for the opening of Spas's new hotel, where Ferry was due to play his flatpack Roxy Music show, whizzing his way through 'Virginia Plain', 'Love is the Drug' and 'These Foolish Things'; I was also there to do some promotion for the book. Tickets for the hotel opening were changing hands for €250 on the secondary ('black') market, and for a while I seriously thought about selling my own. There was a TV crew on board the plane, who interviewed Bryan and myself for the following morning's Bulgarian equivalent of the BBC's *Breakfast*, and who kept asking pointed questions about Gordon Brown's ability to manage the economy. ('He can't,' I said, to their obvious delight.)

But why was Bulgaria clasping me to its bosom? Sofia was rapidly becoming an Eastern European city to watch, what with its casinos and nightclubs and regional outposts of Vitra, Vertuu and B+B Italia. There were cafés and restaurants that looked as though they could have been in Milan, and boutique hotels straight out of Covent Garden. Trade was frenetic, and Bulgarians had embraced the West with gusto – had been, in truth, even before the communist dissolution in 1989. And now even the luxury-goods companies were moving in, emboldened by men such as Spas. He had successfully opened restaurants and clubs at the top end of the market, had created a stylish magazine of his own, and had just secured the rights to launch *GQ* in Bulgaria too.

The day before the party, I appeared on another breakfast TV chat show (*Good Morning Bulgaria*, on the BTV channel, owned by Rupert Murdoch), a bewildering experience for me that must have been even worse for the audience, as squeezed between the two hosts and me was an interpreter, turning my bon mots into Balkan. My appearance seemed to do the trick, though, as five minutes after the broadcast a junior minister from the Sofia outpost of NATO called up for tickets to the launch. Or maybe they were simply fans: for the last two weeks the book had been serialised on Bulgarian radio, meaning that the local denizens had been treated to my advice on how to build an equity portfolio and how to behave at a lap-dancing club. That afternoon I did a further six interviews for TV, radio, the weekly magazine *Capital* and the national daily, *Dnevnik*. I was big in Bulgaria.

Some in the UK were not so keen.

AT *GQ*, WE GOT TO sample everything, so much so that we inevitably became rather blasé. If you were running the marketing department of a new private airline, a seven-star hotel, top-end resort, designer restaurant, bar or nightclub, *GQ* was one of your first ports of call. Our competition was *Esquire* and *Wallpaper*, but as we sold more than both combined, we usually had first dibs. In traditional media, we also vied with the *FT*, *The Times*, the *Sunday Times* and the *Evening Standard* for stories and advertising, although we had the advantage of an enormous bombproof database. In terms of luxury lifestyle, and targeting upscale male readers, we were the sweet spot.

There was a lot of interest in the magazine, and the press regularly turned up on the first floor of Vogue House to profile me or one of the publishing directors, usually accompanied by a photograph of one of us perched on the edge of our desk. International press was almost the most fawning, the trade press was usually scrupulously straightforward (if your sales were up, you were perceived to be doing a good job, end of), while the only British paper that was regularly negative was the *Guardian*. They carried a feature on me, and the strapline began, 'Love him or loathe him, you can't deny . . .' I thought, *Really?* Did they revile success so much? The article seemed to imply that we at *GQ* should all be a little less ambitious, as should the people who read it.

Sometimes the abuse was funny – 'He's a snobby, gobby, nasty, balding faceache . . . and he's got the cheek to call us thick and ugly', ran the headline in a local Tyneside paper after I appeared on a reality TV show up there – but only one was truly offensive. It appeared, predictably, in the *Guardian*, in a piece written by Brian Schofield, someone I once fired. He called me 'evil', and compared me to, of all things, a Nazi. 'He doesn't just look like Goebbels, he channels him,' wrote Schofield, obviously very pleased with himself. When I complained to his line manager, Steve Busfield, saying this might be actionable, Busfield merely acknowledged that I had been called a Nazi, rather than apologising. Schofield then wrote a piece the following day refusing to apologise for comparing me to Hitler's propaganda minister. Perhaps unsurprisingly, I was slightly bewildered by this.

SURPRISINGLY, CONSIDERING ITS APPARENT CONTEMPT for me, for a while I had a media column in the *Guardian*, in which I would pontificate on the vagaries of the industry, being rather too prescient about some titles' imminent demise. I also wrote a column in the *Independent* (politics, lifestyle, culture), and another for the *Mail on Sunday*, which was slightly more strident, and a lot more ribald. For this, I created a character called Vlad, which was entirely based on my great friend Richard. Because he was so funny, and because I knew him so well, I started to exaggerate his personality, turning him into a crazed, espresso-fuelled banker (he was a partner at Goldman, after all). I also wrote about his various attempts to kill me – on skis, in cars, on boats, on shooting weekends and, of course, in bars. Come to think of it, in hindsight, none of this was remotely exaggerated. Everything was content – the lap-dancing club on the Champs-Élysée, the tasting menus in El Bulli, the espresso martinis in Shanghai Tang, and yet another attempt to kill me – this time with altitude sickness – in Bhutan.

Life was busy. The October issue of *GQ* was always our biggest, and consequently always the most important editorially. It was always thick with drama, and it was often a drama getting the proofs to me. The issue was produced during July and August, and because it was necessary for me to see every page, the page proofs would be couriered to me wherever I was on holiday. We would normally be staying with Richard/Vlad and his wife Sam, so every few days during August, a harassed local rep from FedEx or DHL would deliver gigantic cardboard boxes to villas in Portugal, Ibiza, France or Formentera. Later, of course, everything would be sent digitally, but in the early days I would be poring over proofs with a Mont Blanc biro in one hand and a large glass of iced rosé in the other, wondering whether or not our Justin Timberlake picture captions were good enough, and almost certainly deciding they weren't. Being temporarily removed from the editorial process also made me more dispassionate about the content, which I think helped me make better decisions. I'm sure the staff took great exception to me being away and still in charge, but that's how I operated. There wasn't a single day when I wasn't working, whether I was in the office or not, but I did manage to do many bizarre bits of PR, some more successful than others.

I travelled to Dublin one night to appear on *The Panel*, a chat show hosted by Dara Ó Briain, and on this occasion featuring the football manager Ron Atkinson, the comedian Pauline McLynn (famous for playing Mrs Doyle in the Channel 4 sitcom *Father Ted*) and me (not famous for playing anyone in any Channel 4 sitcom ever). I can safely say this was probably my very worst TV appearance, as I was completely ill-equipped to be on it. This was a comedy show, so you were either hired because you were a professional comedian, a celebrity who was used to the back-and-forth of live TV or someone who might rise to the occasion. My performance was a disaster, but it was rescued by the after-party, which was basically a pub crawl that ended with me and Ron Atkinson dancing to Madonna in a gay disco by the Liffey. Ron's attire was supplemented by a small, Italian-style manbag no bigger than a large purse; that night Ron and I were the talk of the town.

THE WRITER DAVE RIMMER WORKED at *Smash Hits* in the early eighties, and the things he found to be valuable while there pretty much echoed what I felt about the *GQ* sensibility: the value of mischief, the beauty of concision, the importance of having fun with your work, and how to use that in giving personality to a publication, the necessity of never underestimating your audience.

I always thought that magazine editors should be benign dictators, although I gave my team a lot of freedom. I told them what I wanted,

I told them how I expected them to achieve it, and then I let them get on with it. If they didn't deliver, that was a problem; but I didn't go looking for issues to solve. Unlike a lot of editors, I read every word in every issue at least three times, and remained ferociously obsessive about 'display furniture'.

I banned references to and photographs of children, and had a list of words that shouldn't be used: *advert* was one – it was either ad or advertisement – along with *eponymous*, *totally*, *bijou*, *supremo*, *mega*, *journey*, *padding*, *like*, *mate*, *'fashion stakes'*, *superlative*, *cause célèbre*, *toilet* and dozens of others. *Fashionable*, *stylish*, *trendy* and *cool* were acceptable as long as they were contextualised (usually ironically). Swearing was unnecessary unless it was absolutely necessary, especially the 'C' word. There was never, ever to be a profanity in display copy.

I didn't want to see copy until it had been properly edited by one of the features team, and sometimes a feature needed three or four sweeps before it was ready to be sent to the sub-editors. Every piece of copy was legalled immediately; I'm not convinced *GQ* even used libel lawyers before I arrived. And when I filed my own copy, I didn't like it if someone cut it; I would stroll into the subs department and say, ever-so-quietly, 'Did you think I wrote the 150 words you cut for the benefit of my health?' When the subs blamed the art department (which they tended to), I told them to redesign it. I was obviously happy when they improved my copy (which they invariably did), but I could never understand why they would cut copy 'because it didn't fit'. If the copy was good enough, you made it fit. I was fairly intolerant with designers; the team I inherited had been used to getting their own way and I had to put a stop to it. In the end, I didn't need to, as Paul Solomons did it for me.

I COULD COMMISSION ANYTHING I wanted to, so I did. I found out one night at dinner that a friend of mine was hiring men for sex. My friend was single, but wanted occasional sex, and she had found that the best thing to do was go down the transactional route. She told me she did a hell of a lot of research before choosing a man to sleep with. OK, before choosing a man to fuck. She would select half-a-dozen twentysomethings from various reputable high-end websites, and then she would arrange to meet them for a coffee, to see if she liked them enough to spend three sweaty hours with them. Having chosen someone (maybe; if she didn't like any of them, she'd start the process again), she would ask them to get tested for all sexually transmitted diseases, including AIDS. She would then meet them again to discuss the precise parameters of what she wanted to do with them: what she wanted, and what she very much didn't want. Of course, this process wasn't cheap, but then neither was my friend.

She explained this in such a sophisticated, matter-of-fact way that I asked her if she would write about it for me. Luckily, she loved the idea. She used a pseudonym to protect her identity, and I agreed to pay all the costs. I can't remember what her invoice looked like, but I didn't have the patience to navigate an invoice headed 'sexual services' through the Condé Nast accountancy tributaries, especially one headed 'male sexual services' – quite possibly I added some 'travel' costs to her already exorbitant fee. But I suppose if you squint you could say that Condé Nast owner Si Newhouse once paid for a friend of mine to get royally and righteously fucked.

DEALING WITH MANAGEMENT WAS RELATIVELY straightforward, principally because Condé Nast had a vertical reporting structure without any of the lasagne-style middle-managers you had in most publishing houses. All editors, publishing directors and department heads reported to Nicholas Coleridge, and he reported to Jonathan Newhouse, our chairman, and that was that. There were probably around seventy people who worked on *GQ* eventually, and whenever I had a problem with someone from the editorial team, I would say this, quietly but firmly: 'When Nicholas or Jonathan say "Jump," I say, "How high?" And that's exactly what I expect from you. If you want to stay, then you adhere to that. And if you don't, well, we know what happens then.' Usually, by the time you were having this conversation you knew if you wanted that person to stay, but occasionally you'd be dealing with someone who had a mercurial or quixotic disposition, and the 'talk' could have gone either way.

Nicholas and Jonathan cared about three things: profits, reputation, and the behaviour and welfare of the people who worked for Condé Nast. And as I knew that managing people was always the most trying part of any enterprise, I always tried to put myself in their shoes. Consequently, I never went to either of them with a problem unless I had a readymade solution. I did the same thing with my team, and whenever someone came to me with a grievance, I would ask them what their proposed solution was. Surprisingly, disappointingly, a lot of people didn't know what to say then, only that their lives would be improved if I fired the person immediately above them on the masthead (which almost never happened). Of course, by the end of my tenure at Condé Nast, the whole nature of HR had changed completely, whereby the exit process could take months. I remained a big fan of the 'take this cheque and leave immediately' approach. It saved a lot of grief in the long run.

AS OUR COVER STARS STARTED to become more international, so it became even more important what they were wearing on those covers; or rather 'who' they were wearing. Fashion PRs would focus intently on getting their clients' clothes on the cover, using their advertising spend as leverage. The Italians even came up with a cleverly calibrated system that literally showed how many editorial pages they thought they deserved compared to the amount of money they were spending on advertising. Many editors thought this was somehow a corruption of their editorial integrity, whereas I thought it was a completely understandable way of doing business. I always put myself in the position of the client; if I was Giorgio Armani, say, and I was spending hundreds of thousands of pounds, actually millions of pounds, on ads supporting Condé Nast, I would expect a generous amount of editorial payback. And if I didn't get it, I would feel completely justified in moving my ads to a rival title or publishing house. Consequently, there were continuous meetings about how we were going to keep advertisers happy without looking as though we were compromising our standards. I always found this a relatively easy thing to do; seriously, don't sweat the small stuff. Increasingly, big movie stars were generating their own commercial relationships, so we knew that if we shot them, they would demand to wear, say, Dolce & Gabbana, Tom Ford or Dior.

Often, we were fighting to secure fashion exclusives for our covers, too, and if Kim Jones, Tommy Hilfiger or (the awful) Hedi Slimane had produced something genuinely inspirational, then we would try and make sure we featured it first. Sometimes the designers or their PRs would opt for one of the smaller, younger and ostensibly cooler titles, and I never particularly minded about this. Those magazines weren't competing with us. Everything was always about optics, anyway; designers always wanted to use the latest models, even though they all had twenty-eight-inch waists and would have represented men who were too young and poor to buy the clothes; and designers often wanted to use the latest fashionable photographers, who usually wanted to work for the smaller magazines. It was a circus, a court, and we all knew it. After a while, *GQ* became so big, such a juggernaut, that we became an orthodoxy, and we stopped worrying about it.

Some of the most gratifying responses to the magazine came from women. I was continually being told they enjoyed the features in *GQ* more than women's magazines, and this was deliberate. Our commercial team sold *GQ* as the most successful upscale men's magazine, and this was true, but I went out of my way to make the magazine more appealing to women. This was a strategy we pursued in tandem with slowly taking the flesh out of the magazine. It would have been commercial suicide to eradicate it completely, but I knew it would eventually have to go, and go it did.

We were running so fast that there often wasn't time for any kind of genuine self-reflection. Occasionally – very occasionally – if I was in the back of a car, on a plane or sitting in a bar on a beach, I would attempt to take myself back to that nervous teenage boy who had barely escaped a childhood of abuse, who wasn't sure where he'd come from, let alone where he was going. I would try to recreate how I had felt at the time and to imagine what that boy would have thought of the life I was now living. Of course, I couldn't – we were two very different people. I found it impossible to imagine being so belittled. Having spent ten years being told I was worthless, I couldn't conjure up that sense of abandonment or fear. And even though I understood intellectually we were the same person, I had come too far. It was as if, in rushing away from my past, I had become a different person altogether. In these fleeting moments, when I tried to scroll back, I just as quickly rushed back to the present. I knew where my past was – I just didn't want to revisit it.

Fashion: Turn to the Left, Dress to the Right

Ozzy Osbourne v. Tom Ford

Launching fashion week with Prince Charles,
Harold Tillman and Caroline Rush, St. James's, 2012

THE FIRST TIME I FLEW into Milan, way back in 1987, I thought Giorgio Armani somehow owned the city; there was a huge Emporio Armani neon sign across one of the hangars at Linate airport, and it looked like a piece of municipal branding, albeit a piece of municipal branding conjured up by Fellini. Frederico's 1960 masterpiece *La Dolce Vita* begins with one of the film's most striking sequences, two helicopters flying over Rome, passing over ancient ruins and heading towards St Peter's. The first helicopter, flying over a broken Roman viaduct and a gaggle of sunbathing bikini-clad women, has a large statue of Christ suspended from its fuselage, its hands outstretched in benediction. The passengers of the second helicopter are paparazzi, who are covering this story as a prank for their tabloid papers. The religious symbolism was crass, but effective.

Armani's gigantic neon suggested he might have some serious religious connections.

I would decamp to Milan twice a year, along with all the other fashion capitals – Florence, Paris and New York as well as London – for the international fashion weeks, a Bacchanalian extravaganza that could sometimes last up to a month. Most of the journalists, photographers, fashion editors and stylists who were part of the charabanc were there for a mixture of editorial and social reasons, seeing what the designers had been up to, breaking bread or drinking cocktails with their peers and ingratiating themselves with PRs. Each season I took a team of eight, although I principally went for business meetings, to make sure our advertisers were happy with the coverage we were giving them and making sure they were being properly serviced by my fashion editors; if they were happy, the advertising would follow.

The men's shows were always a lot less hysterical than the women's shows, although they still attracted their fair share of highly strung flibbertigibbets whose lives appeared to be defined by their front-row status and by what gifts had been delivered to their hotel rooms by the big fashion houses. For years, one despised, diminutive fashion director who worked for one of the British women's magazines (let's call her Lucinda) demanded her team bring all their gifts to her suite, so she could decide which ones she wanted to keep. These gifts were, I have to admit, often overwhelmingly generous: flowers, champagne, clothes (always in the right size), shoes (ditto), sunglasses, jewellery, laptops, iPads, phones, cameras, cakes, vases, hampers full of exotic foodstuff, candles the size of small standard lamps, cushions the size of beanbags, coffee-table books the size of coffee tables, etc. You could go out in the morning and by the time you returned to your room after dinner you'd open the door to find enough extravagant freebies to fill the Conran Shop.

I went through a succession of fashion directors, all of whom were more than adept at navigating the treacherous tributaries of their industry (my favourites were Catherine Hayward, Luke Day and Teo van den Broeke). They were all well-versed in the backstage compliment, delivered with panache and as much sincerity as they could muster after each runway show. Sincerity is a currency often abused in the fashion industry and my team were the very best at forging lasting relationships. As was I, and I developed genuine relationships with many designers, execs and PRs, which turned into real friendships.

In other ways, fashion week was simply transactional, a lying context. There was one designer in Milan whose power and advertising spend seriously outweighed his talent, although we were all experts at fanning his ego and blowing wind up his skirt. We would regularly traipse backstage after one of his dreary shows and, literally lost for words, say, 'You've done it again!' or, my favourite, 'Only you could have designed that.'

When I went to work in television after I left *GQ*, I soon learned they have their own equivalent, and after a screening of an especially tedious/grotesque/appalling film, you bound up to the director/producer/leading actor, point, and say, in the warmest voice you can manage, 'You!' How anyone ever gets away with this is a mystery to me, and yet people appear to do it all the time.

A lot of international fashion PRs I only saw twice a year, at the shows in January and June. Our interactions were remarkably similar, each and every time. My team and I would arrive at a venue and the PR would greet us as though we were long-lost members of her family (they were almost always women), feigning mock delight, hugging us all and giving us their very biggest smiles. Of course, all this was done with their eyes flicking over our shoulders, just in case someone more important came in. They would then ask a series of questions so quickly it was impossible to ever answer, and, knowing my responses weren't really needed (or wanted, actually), I didn't bother. These included 'How are you?', 'How was your holiday?', 'Where are you staying?', 'When did you arrive?', 'When are you leaving?' (for Paris, New York or London) and 'Do you have time for lunch?' This last question was always the most perfunctory and the most hastily delivered, lest I actually responded affirmatively, which would have caused an unwanted logistical reorganisation. It was naturally assumed that I didn't have time for lunch, and if there was a supplementary exchange this would involve setting something up for next time, in six months' time, when we both would have obviously forgotten all about it.

There was one PR, a sweet man who worked for one of the American brands showing in Milan, who was the best exponent of the eye flick. He wouldn't even look at us as we walked in and would keep his eyes firmly focused on the door, almost as though he knew someone more important was going to walk in just as he started speaking. Because of this he didn't bother with any of the niceties and opted instead for one generic question.

'How is everything?' he would say, almost as though this obviated the need for any further exchanges.

We all found this hilarious, and after a few seasons we started imagining what would happen if we actually responded.

'How is everything? Well, I haven't been well, actually, as I had some tests and they came back positive. So I couldn't go on holiday and at home the kids are crying all the time. Which made Christmas a nightmare. Business isn't so great, and half the team are worried they're going to be fired. Plus, the room service in our hotel is awful and we were wondering if we could all come and stay with you?'

We knew that even if we did respond, nothing would have registered, and he would have still kept his eye on the door in case the buyer from Bloomingdale's walked in.

Fashion editors could get incredibly entitled, thinking their position, their taste and their power as a conduit made them invincible. They were soon disavowed of this when social media arrived, although whenever I had any trouble with any of mine, I'd simply put them down the masthead; I had one editor who often refused to shoot an advertiser's clothes because she didn't like them, and whenever this happened, I just asked her assistant to shoot them instead. An early fashion editor of mine was particularly self-serving and cared more about her work than she did about the magazine. She famously didn't read it, although she professed to. One morning I handed her an advance copy of the new issue and asked her to find Robin Morgan's (excellent) sports column, and she had no idea where it was. This reminded me of a lunch I once had with Sir Bernard Ingham, Margaret Thatcher's famous press secretary. She only ever read what he put in front of her, something which actually shocked him. 'One day I passed her a copy of the *Daily Express* and asked her to find the leader. She had no idea what I was talking about.' She would have made a great fashion editor of *GQ*.

Every season, without fail, a PR would decide it would be a good idea to host a dinner during fashion week for their designer with the British press; or worse, *without* the designer. Which meant you were supposed to have supper with a bunch of people you spent the rest of the year avoiding. Sure, I had lots of friends in the industry, and enjoyed finding myself sitting next to the likes of Katie Grand, Alex Bilmes, Peter Howarth or Tom Stubbs, or one of the many other people I liked, but invariably the inefficiencies of the PR meant you'd be sitting between two people you couldn't care less about, a Savile Row fop or a style-magazine 'maven'. After a while, I simply stopped going to these things and took the designer or the PR out to dinner myself.

MY FAVOURITE FASHION CITY WAS Florence; in June, when it was boiling, busy and quintessentially European, and in January, when it was cold, austere and empty. For advertisers, it was vital that we went, so we did, singing and dancing for our supper, and those all-important ad pages. After spending a couple of hours in Pitti Uomo, the trade fair in the Fortezza da Basso, we were on our own, free to disappear into the countryside, have long lunches in the vast number of extraordinarily well-appointed restaurants, or roam the labyrinthine backstreets searching for rare books, wine or secondhand furniture. Importantly, you needed to make sure you weren't too available. If you were seen at every show, every presentation, every dinner, you became part of the herd. Much better to pop up now and again, giving the impression you were insanely busy when in reality you had probably spent the afternoon in via dei Serragli or the Uffizi.

When I returned to the office, battle-weary from too much flannel, and too many plastic-coated hybrid sports shoes, I was always asked the same question: 'What were the shows like?' to which I always gave the same answer: 'Well, thankfully trousers still have a leg at each corner.'

Some designers, I loved. Tommy Hilfiger became a good friend, as did Paul Smith, and most of the young British designers were always good company. I always managed to have fun with Tom Ford and enjoyed the company of Ralph and David Lauren. Domenico Dolce and Stefano Gabbana were always terrific to work with, as were their support staff, in particular Simona Baroni. Most of the PRs were smart, approachable, funny people (Daniel Marks, Paula Fitzherbert, Sophie Homes, Tanya Rose, Marsha Monro, Gillian McVey, Nancy Oakley, Lara Mingay, Julian Vogel, Tanya Hughes, James Massey, Jenny Halpern etc.), and there were few better ways to spend an afternoon than talking to the likes of Jonathan Akeroyd when he was looking after Versace, or Marco Bizzarri when he was in charge of Bottega Veneta. I tended to have better relationships with those designers who operated as businesspeople rather than auteurs (such as Alexander McQueen, Stella McCartney, Christopher Bailey and Kim Jones, and I also liked spending time with the Savile Row tailors, people like Richard James, Ozwald Boateng and Richard Anderson. In fact, I don't think I knew a Savile Row tailor or CEO I didn't like).

The fashion world, like no other, is defined by smoke and mirrors. If you go to a concert, part of the experience is the relationship between the performer and the audience, one that ebbs and flows according to the scale of appreciation. At a fashion show, the relationship is one of blind adulation. You sit, you clap and you whoop, regardless of how you feel about it. That's just the way it is. Occasionally, though, the mirror cracks.

For a while, my good friend Mark Ellen was looking after *Arena*, which had recently been bought by the publishing behemoth, EMAP. Mark was a brilliant, inspirational editor, and had a storied career steering *Smash Hits*, *Q*, *Mojo* and more. He had been drafted into *Arena* as it had been struggling and was now having a crash course in 'fashion' – meeting clients, schmoozing designers and lending editorial support where necessary. He was doing the shows, being escorted around by the fashion editors he inherited. I spent quite a lot of time with him that season, and he put on a brave face as he navigated the unfolding world of an industry I think he found somewhat ridiculous. But his patience evaporated at one show in Milan, when he burst out laughing as soon as the models started walking down the runway. Mark started pointing at the models, openly guffawing at what they were wearing. It was professional suicide, but it was a joy to watch. The emperor had been disrobed. As the rest of the front row sat there, in their preposterous dark glasses, tightly holding on to the handbags on their laps, or furiously scribbling away in their notebooks, Mark was slapping his thighs as though he was watching a vintage Tony Hancock sketch. The subtext was brilliant: we don't want any advertising, ever.

GOSSIP SWIRLED AROUND THE SHOWS like smoke. This one was always hungover, or perpetually on barbiturates; this one was sleeping with that one; this one (the one with the wig and twinset and pearls) kept a hipflask in her handbag; this one never wore any underwear. It was a court, the object being to keep your precious seat on the front row. When designers started seeding Instagram influencers on to the front row, the fash-mag harridans were all up in arms, angrily complaining that these newbies weren't proper journalists. All they were doing was protecting their seats. There was one fashion editor who worked for me who was particularly haughty. One season, while we were waiting for the Tom Ford show to start in Milan, she noticed that a large section on the opposite side of the catwalk was full of what she assumed were people from China (who as consumers were obviously becoming more and more important).

'Who are all those ghastly people?' she whispered, rhetorically.

'Maybe you should find out,' I replied, a little less rhetorically.

By dint of their very nature – the glamour, the excess, the personalities involved – fashion shows always generated a lot of stories. Once, during fashion week in Paris, a hoity-toity fashion editor arrived at a runway show in the Louvre just as it was about to start. Seeing that the editor's seat had already been taken, a greeter seated her in a phenomenally famous pop star's place in the front row. The star hadn't shown, and frankly there was nothing more embarrassing than an empty front-row seat. And so the editor sat down, waiting for the lights to dim and the models to come rushing up on to the stage. Suddenly, as if from nowhere, as the room plunged into darkness, what looked like an ageing gymnast in a shawl came pushing along the aisle and stopped in front of the editor.

'That's my seat,' she said, in a barely audible growl.

'No, it's not,' snapped the hoity-toity editor, theatrically turning away from her.

'Yes, it is,' said the shawl.

'No, it isn't,' repeated the hack. 'And who are you anyway?'

'I'm Madonna,' said Madonna, 'and that's my seat.'

One French editor, a newbie, wallowed in his newfound freedom. Encouraged by working for a publishing company that didn't understand the way in which the industry worked (as long as the ads kept arriving, they didn't really care what he did with his time), and emboldened by a company credit card, he would arrive a day early in Milan – staying at the Palace, the Principe, the Grand or the Armani – and immediately load up with rent boys, cocaine and champagne. You might occasionally see him at an afternoon show – in summer, he would always wear shorts, a bandana and a thin layer of sweat – and gaze off into the distance. If you had the misfortune to sit anywhere near him, he smelled like a fetid laundry basket.

For a while, Tom Ford always had the best parties, deeply sensual affairs with great DJs, free bars offering from vintage Krug and Don Julio tequila, along with the most exotic food to be found in Milan or Paris. Fashion weeks were decadence personified, and the men's shows even more so. Women's fashion weeks were always more anal affairs, as so many of the people involved were scared of losing their positions. Designers, models, photographers, fashion editors, publishers, make-up artists, hairdressers and stylists were all fuelled by insecurity, and they let it rule both their professional and personal lives. Fashion week was a revolving circus of microaggressions, and someone could go in and out of favour in the time it took to order a cocktail. At men's shows, people were more collegiate, there was a little less grandstanding, and – certainly in my case – there was a sense that we were all convening in order to do business, rather than just to have a week-long bitch-fest.

WHILE I LOVED THE INDUSTRY, and many of the people in it, I was always circumspect about certain aspects of it. Like film, theatre, music and publishing, many of the people involved in fashion were prone to indulgence. Self-importance were two words that could have been invented for it. My friends – my real friends – felt the same. Once, during fashion week in Paris, I spent the night in Le Bain Douche, the famous nightclub, with Robin Derrick, when he was the creative director of British *Vogue*. We got back to his apartment around four and had an early start the next day. Robin overslept and turned up at the Issey Miyake show wearing last night's clothes, an ensemble that included white/silver jeans, bright-red mountain boots and a gargantuan orange flying jacket that looked as though it had been designed by Christo. In fact, Robin looked a little like an Italian *paninaro* who was about to tackle the north side of the Eiger. Given his position, Robin's seat was in the front row, where he plonked himself down, sweating overpriced vodka out of every pore. Two minutes later, American *Vogue*'s André Leon Talley (who, it has to be said, was no stranger to bizarre outfits himself) sat down next to Robin, looked him up and down and said, quizzically, 'Do you work in the fashion industry?'

Most other people in the industry would have been mortified at this beautifully delivered putdown. Robin couldn't have been happier and repeated the story for weeks afterwards.

Talley, who I always found rather preposterous, embarrassed himself a few months later by being the only guest to be thrown out of David Bowie and Iman's wedding ceremony in Florence (by Bowie himself), for attempting to take photographs, having been expressly asked not to.

SAVILE ROW WAS A BEACON of tradition, and a place with which I fell in love. I especially fell in love with Richard James, or at least his clothes. Our relationship started, naturally enough, with a wedding (although not our own, obviously). It was 1997 and I was about to get married and, having had suits made for me since the eighties, it seemed to make sense to commission the very best wedding outfit I could. I had started having suits made for me because I couldn't find anything to fit me. In the early eighties, unless you were built like an American footballer and had incredibly broad shoulders, suits didn't really work. Especially if you were as tall and as skinny as I was. Even though all suits in the early eighties had humungous shoulder pads secreted about their person, on me they simply looked like someone had wrapped a beanpole in a bedsheet. So, I decided to get some suits that made me look like a human, rather than a cartoon.

I started in 1984 with a lovely old tailor called Jack Geach in Harrow, who used to make suits for teddy boys, and who was rather surprised by some of the things I asked him to make, such as herringbone drape jackets, for instance, with bright-red peg pants. Then a year or so later I moved a little closer to London, alighting on a man in Kentish Town, an ex-boxer called Chris Ruocco who was introduced to me by ex-Blitz Kid Chris Sullivan. He used to make suits for the likes of Spandau Ballet, George Michael and many others who spent their lives on *Top of the Pops*. George used to get one of his assistants to ring up a store in South Molton Street called Bazaar and ask for a dozen suits to be sent round to his house in order for him notionally to choose something to buy. Then he'd choose one, ask for a massive discount, and send the others round to Kentish Town to be copied.

Then, after a few years, I moved again – getting closer to Savile Row all the time – this time to Timothy Everest, the sagacious tailor based in Spitalfields. This was the early nineties, and I was now working in newspapers, and so needed some rather more formal suits, outfits that weren't going to scare the horses or the sub-editors. He made me half-a-dozen navy-blue pinstripe suits that I wore until they fell apart, and I loved every one of them. After New Labour came to power in 1997, I was asked to recommend a tailor to Gordon Brown. As soon as Tony Blair found out where he was getting his suits from, he started going there too.

By 1997, however, and with my wedding coming up, I decided I needed to move to Savile Row, to Mayfair, to the very epicentre of bespoke tailoring. I wasn't especially interested in going old school, as I didn't want any arguments. Today, the legacy tailors in the Row are far more accommodating but, in those days, they tended to do things rather more traditionally, and I was adamant that I wanted something with a twist. I didn't want to be steered in a particular direction, as I had very clear ideas of what I wanted. And what I wanted was something modern.

Richard James and his business partner Sean Dixon had already been in the Row for five years, yet they were still being treated like interlopers by many of the old-timers on the street. Because James and Dixon designed suits made out of denim, out of camo, out of Astroturf, pretty much out of anything they liked, the Row tailors tended to sneer and were openly disparaging about them. Shame on them. They did the same thing with Ozwald Boateng, another Savile Row maverick.

James and Dixon couldn't have cared less, however, and had already built up a healthy fan base, a clientele who understood that in order to be well dressed one didn't have to adhere to old-fashioned ideals. One didn't have to lope around in a three-piece pinstripe with scuffed Oxfords and an old school tie covered in dark brown soup from one of the fustier clubs in St James's.

My suit, in hindsight, was actually rather traditional, being a two-piece bright-blue mohair creation with slanted pockets and a purple lining. It wasn't exactly a loud bright blue, but perhaps not the kind of blue one might have worn at the time in a boardroom. I've still got it today – it's nestling in the back of my wardrobe like a ceremonial trophy – and although I've had the waist altered a few times, it appears to have shrunk as there is no way I can fit into it any more.

Over time, I probably commissioned at least twenty Richard James suits, and although I have occasionally veered up and down the Row to sample the delights of their competitors – some of whom are exceptionally good – I always came back to Richard James, as that was where I felt most at home (and where I got the biggest discount). They became a bit like family, and whenever I was asked who my suit was from, usually by a Japanese reporter during fashion week (for some reason they always wanted to know, even though I only wore navy-blue suits), unless it was patently obvious it was designed by someone else, I tended to say 'Richard James' almost by default. It was just easier. Flying the flag and all that.

For years, Savile Row appeared to be impervious to change, uninterested in the swirl of sartorial egalitarianism that was engulfing the rest of the city. Sure, the occasional rock star might fall out of his Bentley before ordering a dozen bespoke suits from the likes of Tommy Nutter, or Anderson & Sheppard, but largely the Row was an oasis of obsolescence. This was strange, as the rest of Mayfair was certainly modernising. Mayfair had often been the home of dandies and show-offs, especially during the sixties, when nascent pop stars roamed the neighbourhood in search of entertainment and expensive trousers. The postcode seemed to encourage a kind of sartorial extremism, almost as though it were some sort of fashion theme park. Over in Soho, on the other side of Regent Street, the Carnabetian Army (in Ray Davies's famous words) may have been marching in time to the metronomic reveille of seasonal trends, but in and around Berkeley Square, the fops, coxcombs and recently emancipated young musicians from the suburbs were wandering around in bright feather boas, snakeskin boots, Regency suits, kipper ties, extravagant scarves, fur coats and feathered hats.

But not Savile Row tailors, which for years appeared deliberately to shun the sartorial whirlwind around them. Until Richard James and Ozwald Boateng moved in, that is, and helped set about a revolution.

REIMAGING THE POSSIBILITIES OF THE human body was a constant in the world of fashion, conjuring strangely gorgeous garments and avant-garde provocations while marshalling the collective expertise of all those who had been here before. Context had always been key, as had the overly verbose mission statements placed on the seats before the show. Music was crucial; even better if it had been specially commissioned. Increasingly, fashion designers started to use rock stars in their shows – to model (Comme des Garçons were especially good at finding contrary models such as John Cale or Nick Cave), perform (watching the Killers play before a Cavalli show, for instance), or maybe just to sit in the front row and genuflect. They didn't magically appear, these people; they were paid to be there, and the bigger the designer, the more celebrities they could afford.

In 2003, the Prince's Trust came up with a way to fuse these two worlds together, creating Fashion Rocks, a bumper fashion show matching pop stars with fashion designers, all in the name of charity. The first Fashion Rocks took place at the Royal Albert Hall, an event involving twelve of the world's top designers, along with the likes of Robbie Williams, Beyoncé, Bryan Ferry, Duran Duran and Jane's Addiction. It was so successful, raising more than £1 million, that the organisers decided to put on another one, and were then invited to do so in Monaco in 2005. They then asked me to chair the event (pro bono) and ensure it happened. Was I mad? I soon began to think that I was.

Around the boardroom table the day of our first meeting were representatives from the Prince's Trust, Clear Channel (who were producing the show), Initial (who were doing the TV show), Jane Boardman's Talk PR and about a dozen other people I'd never met before. I was overawed by the talent in front of me, but also rather apprehensive at the thought of spending fifteen months trying to put the event on in the land of sun-kissed excess, fast cars, over-accessorised women, burnt sienna men and clandestine glamour. Could we really get a dozen grade-A fashion designers, a celebrity host and twelve top entertainers all in the same place at the same time? I wasn't Bob Geldof, and I knew it.

Over the coming months, I was to have over a hundred meetings like this, but the first was the worst. As I voiced my concerns, Graham, a Clear Channel stalwart who had worked on dozens of events like this, told me not to worry. 'I know it sounds like a nightmare, but trust me, it'll be fine in the end. They'll all come together at the last minute; I promise.' Now, I liked Graham, but did I believe him? I wasn't sure. In fact, I didn't. I was considering the logistics of organising a dozen fashion shows, each of which required fifteen models with their own hairdressers and make-up artists, their own peccadillos and rivalries. And securing a dozen rock stars to perform, trying to figure out where to park two-dozen yachts in Monaco harbour (all in prime position, obviously), as well as organising two thousand rooms in the right hotels (not that there were any bad hotels in Monaco), hundreds of helicopter transfers, and where to seat two thousand people, with every one of them feeling happy about where they were sitting. Oh, and getting Alain Ducasse, our chosen caterer, to feed them all after the show. How on earth was it all going to happen?

As the meeting ground to a halt, I heard from the back of the room another line that would stay with me over the next fifteen months. 'If you're not interested in Lionel Richie, I've got a number for Gwyneth Paltrow's personal trainer. Does anyone want it?'

Hold on a minute, I thought to myself, *who says I'm not interested in Lionel Richie?*

We started with the fashion designers, since, without clothes on the catwalk, we were nothing, and it was the designers who had made the first show so extravagant. And I had to be uncharacteristically diplomatic. We knew the designers we wanted, and we went and got them – Giorgio Armani, Alexander McQueen, Burberry, Calvin Klein,

Dolce & Gabbana, Prada, Roberto Cavalli, Tommy Hilfiger, Versace (one of my favourite Donatella memories is the look on her face when she discovered that, having asked her minions to invite all four members of Blur to attend her fashion show, she was subsequently introduced to the members of Blue), Viktor & Rolf and Vivienne Westwood – but when we were approached by designers we didn't want, it became more difficult. There were at least six for whom we simply didn't have room. (We were approached by one British designer who wanted in, and as it was too late to secure her an artist, we said we'd only give her a slot if she secured her own. This resulted in a week of intense worrying, with the committee hoping that she wasn't going to have any luck. Thankfully, she didn't.)

The process quickly gathered its own momentum. Crucially, Prince Charles (or 'HRH', as we were all encouraged to refer to him, almost on a daily basis) was incredibly helpful, as were the legions of people from the Prince's Trust. And when Prince Albert of Monaco agreed to be the guest of honour, we found him to be equally accommodating.

As the meetings gathered pace, so things began falling into place – the creative director, the stage producers, the stylists, make-up artists, etc. We had to organise flights and began offering every agent in town the use of a private jet. I was not certain we should be promising this, as I was fairly sure we didn't have access to one, but it seemed to do the trick. I'd learned this from Hollywood publicists, promising the world and worrying about it later.

Jerry Hall soon agreed to host the event, while every record-company chief and pop-industry mogul began making themselves known to us. Did we want X? Were we interested in Y? Would Z be able to do anything? Having never chaired anything like this before, I was bowled over by the level of benevolence and general good will towards the Prince's Trust. People gave time, money, expertise and, most importantly, phone numbers.

Mostly. The equally surprising thing about being involved in such a huge charity project was just how dismissive people could be, treating it like any other party, any other fashion event. Could they get free tickets? Would someone fly them to Monaco for the weekend? Could they sit next to Elizabeth Hurley or Victoria Beckham? Could they get their photo taken with Prince Albert? I lost count of the number of people who expressed an interest in coming until I told them that it was going to cost them at least £1,000, just for a ticket.

One of the most disappointing moments involved a celebrated photographer who had agreed to introduce one of the fashion designers. After he had kindly consented to do it, we organised to fly him in (first class) and put him up in a suite in one of the swankiest hotels. We then started telling everyone he was involved. Two months later, when he got a big advertising job that conflicted with the event, he suddenly became unavailable. A great shame, but I never forgot it, and made a point of telling everyone on the project that he had let us down. He was to experience a rather dramatic fall from grace a number of years later when he was accused of serially abusing young male models.

AS THE MONTHS DRAGGED ON, I began to sleep less and less, waking up at four o'clock in the morning to scribble some mad idea on a piece of paper, or to remind myself to call someone back. I began losing weight, drinking too much coffee, and – something I also never do – having a glass of wine with lunch. During two family holidays to Spain and Portugal, I was never without my BlackBerry, and once, during an especially boozy dinner at a beach bar in Cascais, I had an email exchange with Jay-Z's agent that lasted ninety minutes, at which point my wife demanded I give her Prince Charles's private number (like I would have it) so she could call him up and berate him for ruining our family holiday.

A particular low point was a committee meeting at which we were discussing what prizes we had been offered for the auction after the show. These included the use of luxury yachts, portraits taken by various boldface fashion photographers, a dozen five-star safari holidays and dinner with one of the guest presenters, but we were still at least a dozen prizes away from a memorable evening. As I worked my way around the table, a little voice said: 'Well, we have been offered a lorryload of organic carrots by a farmer in Wiltshire.' I must admit, I felt like giving up.

Then, just as things were beginning to gel and we were about to announce our first big acts, Bob Geldof announced Live 8 for July 2005, just a couple of months before our Monaco event, and every act went quiet. For two months, nobody wanted to know about anything but Live 8, so all our finely calibrated negotiations had to be put on hold. This was my darkest time, when I was seriously worried the whole thing was going to collapse. Not only had I and dozens of other people worked for over a year on this event, but the Trust desperately needed to recoup the money it had already spent. If it turned to dust, the charity would lose a fortune. Far from being worried about what people thought about the event not happening, my main concern – everyone's main concern – was losing the cash.

But just as one celebrity had managed to put the event on hold, so it was another who helped to kickstart it again. A few weeks after Live 8, I was at a party at Elton John's house in the south of France (where, incidentally, I spent most of the night dancing to Ibiza house tunes with Des O'Connor and Paul McKenna), and I bumped into Lucian Grainge, the head of Universal Records and one of the most powerful men in the music industry. Suddenly, Bon Jovi were involved, then Jamie Cullum, and then they all came, just as Graham said they would. In the next few weeks, the team – many of whom were working eighteen hours a day – secured Mariah Carey, Bryan Ferry, David Bowie, Skin, Earth, Wind & Fire, Blondie, Róisín Murphy, Kasabian, Craig David, the Kills, Amerie and Ray Davies, and everyone very quickly felt a hell of a lot happier.

THE WEEKEND ITSELF IN OCTOBER 2005 was a cornucopia of overabundance, overindulgence and glitz, with parties on boats and in nightclubs, and a truly memorable reception in the Grimaldi

Palace. It was almost as if for seventy-two hours Monaco allowed itself to be turned into a gargantuan ice sculpture, standing proud as this mammoth, candlelit extravaganza unfolded beneath it, the centre of which was a fashion show that demanded peony fireworks, horsetail shells, Klieg lights and every neon stovepipe in Monte Carlo. We raised over £1.5 million for the Prince's Trust and contributed to an IP that meant the Fashion Rocks brand was eventually sold for £6.5 million.

It was also a weekend of contradictions, absurdities and, in hindsight, not a little sadness. The most ridiculous moment occurred during the finale, when Mariah Carey was meant to arrive on stage via a hydraulic lift underneath it. But as she rose, and as the crowd started hollering when they realised who it was, the lift stalled and Mariah was stuck there, with half her body above the stage, and the rest of it submerged. It was a moment that could have been scripted for a fashion *Spinal Tap*. In the end, she had to return to the bowels of the auditorium, while the hydraulics were overhauled, and then she did it all again.

There were some extraordinary people in Monaco for Fashion Rocks, including Isabella Blow, the muse of hat designer Philip Treacy, the great benefactor of Alexander McQueen, and the woman who discovered the models Sophie Dahl and Stella Tennant. As she walked into the Grimaldi Palace, she was wearing what could only be described as a Brobdingnagian fascinator that looked as though it had been fashioned by H. R. Giger, the *Alien* designer. Clearly confused by her entrance, Ozzy Osbourne, in the loudest stage whisper I'd ever heard, said, 'Jesus Christ, she's got bird flu.' Less than two years later, Blow was dead by her own hand, having drunk a bottle of the weedkiller Paraquat. At the inquest, Lavinia Verney said that after she discovered her sister had ingested the poison, Blow told her, 'I'm worried I haven't taken enough.' Three years later, McQueen hanged himself in his Mayfair apartment four days after the death of his mother. In December 2020, having struggled with mental health for years, Tennant also committed suicide, in Duns, on the Scottish Borders. She was just fifty.

*

MONACO WAS ONE THING, BUT I would try and put London on the map of men's fashion shows when, encouraged by Caroline Rush, the CEO of the British Fashion Council (BFC), in 2012 I launched men's fashion week as chair of London Collections: Men (LCM), again pro bono, and while continuing to edit *GQ*. Typically, the idea of a fashion week dedicated especially to men started almost as an afterthought, a desire to compete on the global stage with the likes of Paris, Milan and New York, the other major cities that had held similar weeks for ages. For what seemed like years, the menswear element of London Fashion Week was always tacked on to the end of the women's shows. But there had increasingly been so much interest from designers wanting to show, and so much interest from the press and consumers alike, that the BFC decided to create their own men's fashion week – London Collections: Men – and to move it to a more relevant time in the calendar. After all, by the time of the men's day at the end of London Fashion Week, all the important press and buyers had disappeared to Milan in order to see the Gucci show, and – far more importantly – the day was in completely the wrong part of the season (by the time all the department store buyers arrived, they had already spent their budget).

Which is why we moved it so that our men's fashion week preceded Florence, Milan, Paris and New York. Having been asked to run it, I spent six months espousing the idea, trying to encourage those British designers who had previously decided to move abroad – Burberry, Alexander McQueen, Vivienne Westwood, etc. – to move back and show in London.

We knew that in order to encourage all the hundreds of press and buyers to put another three days in their diary and come to London, we had to make the experience fun. We wanted them to wake up in Milan (the fashion week that immediately followed ours) with the mother of collective hangovers; we wanted them all to tell anyone who would listen: 'You know what? I went to London, and even though I can't find my shoes, I had a *seriously* great time.'

Our pitch was simple: come and show your clothes in the coolest capital in the world, come and show your wares in the city with the best restaurants, the best museums, the best art galleries, public spaces, parks, hotels and cocktail bars.

Come to where the action is.

Sure, you could have chosen to show your clothes in Milan. But then you'd be showing your clothes in the ugliest city in northern Europe that wasn't in Germany. Sure, you could have shown your clothes in Paris. But then you'd be showing your clothes in the most bourgeois city in Europe. Alternatively, you could choose to show in New York. But then you'd only be showing in the most neurotic city in the world.

Seriously, why would you want to be anywhere other than London? London was the home of the hobnail kiss, the dyslexic tattoo and the double-barrelled pinstripe. If you wanted your world to be edged with studs, you came to London. If you wanted sparkle, you came here.

Caroline and I were also aware of needing to celebrate our city. London was less a metropolis and more of a lifestyle choice, a place from which to launch yourself into the world, and a place to land having investigated everywhere else (and obviously found them wanting). The latest iteration of Swinging London was a wonder, with a multitude of reinvigorated urban villages, new art galleries and more A-star restaurants per square mile than any other city in the world. So, LCM became as much of an advertisement for London as it was for our burgeoning (as well as established) menswear talent.

WE ASKED PRINCE CHARLES TO officially launch LCM for us, and convinced Elton John and David Furnish to throw open their home for a dinner and a showcase by the hot new Irish R & B band, the Strypes. We asked magazines and newspapers to get involved and have parties (the project wasn't going to work unless it was inclusive and everyone felt as though they could take ownership of it), and we asked celebrities to become ambassadors, encouraging them to spread the message on television and radio.

The ambassadors included the hip-hop star Tinie Tempah, broadcaster Nick Grimshaw, model David Gandy and TV behemoth Dermot

O'Leary – and they were soon joined by others including David Beckham and David Furnish himself. We celebrated LCM each season with a dinner, usually gifted to us either by a new restaurant or one that wanted a little bit of stardust. We usually had such a good guest list – from Tom Ford to Kate Moss to Harry Styles – that there was fierce competition to host them. One season, we were encouraged back to Hakkasan, where we entertained 120 people from 8 p.m. until the bar closed at midnight, when we were all expected to push off into the night. I never liked to hang around and was just about to make a move for my car when Caroline Rush – who was never backward about going forward when celebrations were in order – said that a member of Tom Ford's team had started ordering tequila shots. As the gifted tab had just been closed, these were all on us. I still have the bill at home: a piece of paper that is half a metre long, totalling £1,200. There were only thirty or so people left, but in forty-five minutes we had managed to consume over 250 shots. Oh, and one glass of red wine for Dermot.

After a few seasons, the mayor's office began to see the commercial possibilities of LCM, especially in terms of attracting visitors to London. Boris Johnson stepped up to the plate, as did the mayor's head of cultural policy, Justine Simons, encouraging us to work with UKTI, Visit Britain, the Museum of London, the Victoria and Albert Museum and even the great campaign to build various cultural and retail programmes. Commercially London was already seeing the benefit of LCM, with increased revenue for hotels, restaurants, taxis and the services of hairdressers, models, make-up artists, etc. The total global media value generated by LCM in its second season exceeded £40,000,000, which is no small beer, even for a week that was largely driven by champagne.

We also had a few surprises. One of the things we had not anticipated was the overseas interest in heritage, which is something we tended to ignore in this country. The press and buyers from Asia and the Americas were especially keen to attend our Savile Row shows, and loved being able to visit St James's Palace, Jermyn Street, Spencer House, St Paul's, Lord's Cricket Ground and all the other cathedrals of tradition where we held events. Because of this, we asked David Cameron to get more involved, hosting press events and receptions at Downing Street, especially for the foreign press.

PREDICTABLY, THE OTHER FASHION CAPITALS were not exactly thrilled by what we were attempting to do. Some of the senior figures at our rival organisations went public with their disdain for the idea, some made a great point of ignoring us, while others lobbied hard behind our backs, trying to convince their designers to stay put. One of the great by-products of setting up a men's fashion week in London, however, was the fact we attracted international fashion designers from everywhere – New York, Paris and Milan, of course, but also Copenhagen, China and Hong Kong – and radical newcomers as well as the big names.

London Collections: Men came about because we felt menswear was suddenly becoming more interesting than womenswear. There were now more commercially minded, critically acclaimed young menswear designers than ever before, people such as Agi & Sam, Christopher Raeburn, Jonathan Saunders and Lou Dalton – highbrow, conceptual, deconstructionist, unobservant of trends, and often thoughtful renunciations of the usual markers of luxury. Unlike the menswear designers who I grew up with in the eighties, and who filled the pages of style magazines such as *i-D*, *The Face* and *Blitz*, this new generation understood that in order to compete on a global stage, you needed a properly commercial business, not just a bunch of press cuttings from trendy Japanese magazines.

DURING THE TWO ANNUAL MEN'S shows in London, I would spend four days from 7 a.m. to 2 a.m. cocooned in a liveried Mercedes with Jane Boardman, the CEO of Talk PR who was my minder during fashion week throughout my ten-year tenure at the BFC. Even though I was the chair, it was Jane who made everything happen, Jane who got me from A to B, Jane who successfully bickered over directions with our trusty driver Wayne (rather helpfully, Wayne appeared to know every policeman in London; 'Look the other way,' he said one day, as he hurtled the wrong way down Piccadilly, late for a show. 'If we get stopped, just leave it to me'). Jane knew my blood sugar level dropped alarmingly if I didn't eat regularly, so she and Wayne made sure the car was stuffed with a huge array of increasingly esoteric junk food: cheese strings, cheese straws, crisps, Discos, cheap chocolates, jelly babies, and – essential – Mini Cheddars. No chauffeured S-Class was ever complete without an armrest full of Mini Cheddars. We behaved like overgrown children in the car (reverting to 'adult' mode whenever anyone else got in), and Jane made the whole week a joy.

My blood sugar issue hadn't really made itself apparent until Milan fashion week a few years earlier. If I hadn't eaten by around 2 p.m., I found myself getting grouchy, and starting to snap. My mind would start to wander. I'd be sitting in the front row of a fashion show of an important advertiser, waiting for it to start, and all I could think about was food. Midday appointments were tricky, too.

'Shall we go to the Belstaff presentation?' one of my team would ask, not unreasonably.

'Will there be food?' I'd reply.

'We're not sure,' would come the response, immediately spreading the blame.

'I'm not feeling it,' I'd say. 'Can't we just go for lunch?'

Some people were desperate for a glass of rosé by lunchtime, whereas all I wanted was a cheese sandwich.

LONDON, OF COURSE, HAD BEEN a centre of subcultural excellence since the early sixties, when the likes of David Bailey, Michael Caine and Mary Quant redefined the city as a quasi-classless template for the future. Since then, every decade, usually around the midpoint, our urban lotus land rose up again: punk, club culture, Britpop, you name it, London had been the centre of it. And menswear had always been at the heart of this cultural rebellion. Not only did we have the greatest tailors in the world in Savile Row, not only did we always have the best youth culture and street style in the world (we invented everything from the teddy boy to the punk), but we also had some of the world's most high-profile fashion designers in Paul Smith, Kim Jones, Christopher Bailey and Alexander McQueen.

We excelled at both tradition and rebellion, and we'd always done it better than anyone else.

At its best, fashion had always been about play-acting, an elaborate form of disguise or fancy dress. Fashion still had the ability to shock us in ways to which we thought we'd become immune, and over the years it encouraged us to look like gypsies, tramps and thieves, as well as hoodlums, members of the Baader–Meinhof Gang or undernourished Nepalese peasants. London also didn't need lecturing about cultural appropriation, race, gender or any trans issues. The fashion industry here was unquestionably the most diverse, the queerest, the most semiotically curious and the most intellectually aggressive in the world.

To the world at large, London really became the centre of street style during the Swinging Sixties. Looking back now, it almost seems as though everything happened at once. In a decade dominated by youth, London suddenly burst into bloom. It was swinging, and it was the scene. The Union Jack suddenly became as ubiquitous as the black cab or the red Routemaster, and all became icons of the city. Carnaby Street's turnover was over £5 million in 1966 alone. Quite simply, London was where it was at. In the space of a few months the skies over the city had become kaleidoscopic, full of multi-coloured swirls and curls, and curlicues of every imaginable shape and size. It was as though colour had replaced coin as a symbol of wealth and success, as though pigment was the cure for all known evils. There appeared to be no affliction not tempered by the application of some glitter mascara or the donning of some extravagant garb. Colour became almost confrontational. Fuelled by growing prosperity, social mobility, post-war optimism and wave after wave of youthful enterprise, the city captured the imagination of the world media. Here was the centre of the sexual revolution – the pill had been introduced in 1961 – the musical revolution, the sartorial revolution. London was a veritable cauldron of benign revolt.

And so it was in 2012, when Olympic-fuelled London was on the march again.

Ah, these foolish things.

Tracey Emin Goes Rogue in the South of France

Have Tent, Will Travel

Birthday party, St. Tropez, 2015

THE PLAN WAS A RELATIVELY simple one. Having missed her birthday party on the Côte d'Azur earlier in the month, I was going to fly with Tracey Emin down to her remote farmhouse in the south of France, stay a few days – perhaps sampling a little Ricard along the way – and interview her in the process. Having been friends for over ten years, both of us found it strange that I'd never formally interviewed her, even though she had been *GQ*'s 'feng shui editor' for over a decade (a title bestowed on Tracey as an homage to Ralph Steadman's longstanding gig as the non-gardening 'gardening editor' of *Rolling Stone*), had written a monthly poem for us for the last four years, came to all our parties and had appeared in the magazine on countless occasions.

Like I said, simple. Although as I had already learned to my cost, things with Tracey were rarely simple. Fun, yes, simple, no.

Firstly, we couldn't agree where to meet in Terminal 5. Then, having spent the flight gossiping about the bad behaviour at the Serpentine party (which we agreed was probably the best one ever, if a little noisy in parts – they appeared to have banished much of the nouveau riche element, although considering their patronage kept the place afloat, we wondered how), we successfully negotiated the vagaries of the car-hire offerings at Nice airport (we settled on a convertible black Renault Mégane, largely because they didn't have a gunmetal grey Porsche 911) . . . and then proceeded to spend two-and-a-half hours on a journey that should normally take ninety minutes. Tops.

All because Tracey couldn't remember where she lived. Well, she may have known where it was, but she was having difficulty finding it. Her and me both.

Admittedly, we had an old Nouvelle Vague CD and a fairly staggering sunset to distract us, but a two-and-a-half-hour car journey is still a two-and-a-half-hour car journey (and there is only so much Nouvelle Vague a poor boy can take).

After a few false dawns, and a real sunset, we eventually found her village, but then we – well, I actually – decided we should go and have something to eat before driving all the way up to her house. This had nothing to do with the fact that the last time Tracey had cooked for me and my wife at her French house we ended up eating a roast chicken at half past midnight.

Then, around nine o'clock, as we were walking along St-Clair beach in Le Lavandou, we bumped into serendipity, in the shape of Jerry Hall (you learn to expect serendipity if you spend a lot of time with Tracey). Jerry had a house nearby and, after dinner at a local restaurant (deep-fried courgettes, followed by the dorade, if I remember correctly, which I do), we went back there for a few hours, principally to discuss the pros and cons of the serendipity, before leaving.

Which is when the evening began turning surreal. Tracey's house was only twenty-five minutes from Jerry Hall's, but we were still looking for it two hours later. We drove north, south, east and west, and most points in between. And then we drove them all over again. Just in case. Whenever I asked where I should go next, Tracey would simply point to a roundabout exit and say, 'There.' To her credit, she did this with such conviction that, every time, it took me more than twenty minutes before I realised she had absolutely no idea where she was going. None at all. We went round one particular roundabout six times and the final time we did this even Tracey was beginning to think we might end up sleeping in the car. Lionel Richie's 'All Night Long' wasn't on the radio, but it may just as well have been.

The denouement to this particularly protracted part of the evening was me dramatically stopping the car on some dusty hillside, leaping out in true John Cleese style and screaming at Tracey, 'You have absolutely no idea where you live, do you?' with as much dignity as I could summon (not much, by this stage in the evening, I have to say). 'And not only do you not know, but you don't even seem to care. THIS IS RIDICULOUS! AND YOU ARE DRIVING ME INSANE! AND THAT WASN'T MEANT TO BE A JOKE!'

It was only when Tracey offered to drive that I came to my senses, calmed down, crawled back into my bucket seat and continued my search. Not only was Tracey not really in any condition to drive, but the only reason she was never the 'star in a reasonably priced car' on *Top Gear* is because she can't drive stick shift ('I asked Jeremy to change the rules for me, but he wouldn't,' she told me later). And a Provençal hillside in the middle of the night didn't really seem like the place to learn.

Miraculously – and I can only put this down to some sort of misguided divine intervention – we found Tracey's village and eventually even found our way home. Obviously, we celebrated this, frankly, unlikely achievement by toasting ourselves with a small glass of Ricard, although by this time of the evening – and by then it wasn't technically evening any more – I wasn't convinced there was much to celebrate.

Tracey's south of France idyll sat high above the beach in a remote spot just half an hour, but half a lifetime, from St-Tropez. It couldn't have been more different from the Côte d'Azur's foremost playboy hotspot, as up here – closer to the clouds than the sand – serenity ruled.

Well, it would have done if Tracey hadn't talked quite so much. 'Here, I'm a different person, I'm free, I'm liberated, I feel peace, I feel good. St-Tropez is only half an hour away, but I never go there, in fact I hardly go out at all when I'm here. In London I can go out all the time, but here I try to stay in and work. And it suits me fine. In London I'm only fifteen minutes away from Mayfair, fifteen minutes from Soho, fifteen minutes from anywhere. But here, I'm fifteen minutes away from a mountain.'

I'D ALWAYS FOUND TRACEY FASCINATING, and I was a huge admirer of her work. I loved the fact she was so anti-establishment, and yet had managed to create a brand that was bombproof. As soon as I started at *GQ*, I wanted to meet her, and asked Alex Bilmes, our features editor, to set something up. We met in Liverpool Street station – I'm not sure why, maybe it had echoes of *Brief Encounter* or some long-forgotten wartime movie – and I liked her immediately. Funny, whip-smart, sarcastic, and with an acute understanding of what she was and where she was going. Tracey was properly unique, someone you could trust, and I could tell we were going to be friends for ever.

She started working for me, I wanted her at all our events, and I made her an honorary member of the team. She wrote poems for us, reviewed hotels and, of course, enjoyed her editorial nod to Ralph Steadman as our feng shui editor – even though she knew as much about harnessing energy forces and establishing harmony between an individual and their environment as Steadman did about the Hibiscus. She could occasionally be a handful – she drank, but later discovered her body had an inability adequately to process it – but I tolerated the occasional misdemeanour because she was my friend. She was real, properly real, and I liked real people. We were building a community and I wanted to fill it with people I liked and admired, and people I trusted. Friends, in other words.

In 2017 I would invite Tracey to come to the Hay Festival, the world-renowned literary festival near the Brecon Beacons in Wales. I had been involved with the festival for over a decade, as a vice president, as a trustee and as chairman of its charitable foundation. I also did my fair share of interviews – everyone from Jimmy Page, Mark Hix and Bruce Robinson to John Bishop, Michael Wolff and Viv Albertine. Tracey sold out the festival's largest tent in under an hour, an example of her enormous popularity. That day in May it reminded me that whatever the press said about her, she was a genuine national treasure. Even in Wales.

If I've ever taken anything for granted, it's instinct, and making the right decisions about people, jobs, ideas, approaches. I haven't always been right, but I've been right enough. Because I was the co-custodian of a global brand, I was always more circumspect about potential business partnerships, because in business you could never be wrong. Editorially I was prepared to take more risks, as if something didn't turn out the way we thought it might, I could kill it and move on. I hated killing stories, not least because of the cost, although sometimes it was inevitable. There might be a fashion story that didn't work, an interview that didn't deliver, or maybe a sixteen-page project we all loved ended up running on a column at the front of the magazine. But instinct protected me and protected the brand.

So, Tracey started writing for the magazine, and we began commissioning other artists, illustrators and art photographers to do our fashion stories, rather than rely on the same kind of imagery every other magazine was generating. We commissioned Alan Aldridge, the famous Beatles illustrator, asking if he could draw the autumn collections for us, and we did something similar with Guy Peellaert, the genius behind *Rock Dreams* and the *Diamond Dogs* cover. I interviewed Aldridge not long after on stage at Central St Martin's Cochrane Theatre, as part of an extended series of interviews with various notable designers. He was engagingly indiscreet. Having told us all about working with Lord Snowdon ('I was working alone in his house once and the phone rang. "Hello," I said, "can I help?",

"Yes, is Margaret there?" "No, love, she's out. Who wants to know?" "Her sister . . .' "), his frustrations with the Beatles ('At Apple it was very difficult to get paid') and the saga of the cover and aborted film of Elton John's *Captain Fantastic and the Brown Dirt Cowboy* (with Hollywood showing its homophobic side), he told us about creating the sleeve for Cream's final album, *Goodbye*, in 1969.

Aldridge had always been something of an enigma, and even when he was riding high as the rock 'n' roll graphic designer du jour in the sixties, always tended to let his work do the talking. But in the noughties, he began to talk himself, and with great self-deprecation.

Cream had already broken up when they came to release *Goodbye*, and literally couldn't stand the sight of each other. So for the cover, he had to tell Eric Clapton, Jack Bruce and Ginger Baker that they would be photographed separately and the pictures glued together afterwards. When they arrived at the studio, they discovered that Aldridge was pulling a fast one, and that the only way the picture would work was if they were in the same frame together. Cue the sound of toys, drumsticks, Fenders and plectrums being thrown out of prams, and three of the world's biggest rock stars screaming like children. Frustrated beyond belief, Aldridge went outside for a cigarette, only to see the dancer and choreographer Lionel Blair about to board a bus. As a last resort, the designer coerced Blair into coming into the studio to try to convince the band to sit for the session. Remarkably, Blair did just that, and soon had the band running around, posing and laughing as though they were in the first flush of youth.

I also asked Sam Taylor-Wood to photograph a fashion story we were attempting to shoot using clothing by Richard James, the Savile Row tailor. The idea we alighted on – which came from our fashion director Jo Levin – was to shoot a series of famous actors crying. Someone at a dinner party had said that in times of stress, women cry and men get angry, so we decided to subvert the idea. *Crying Men* showed an extraordinary array of Hollywood stars 'stripped of their defences'. Taylor-Wood photographed her subjects in a most vulnerable state, an unguarded emotional display that not only usually has no witnesses, but also one that at the time was not usually considered appropriate. She would later exhibit the pictures and turn them into a book, but the idea was kickstarted by Levin – Daniel Craig, Ryan Gosling, Paul Newman, Robin Williams, Brad Pitt, Dustin Hoffman and more all bawling their eyes out. Clint Eastwood wouldn't, Sean Penn couldn't, and for some reason Tom Cruise wasn't even asked. The *Guardian*, who were starting to seriously take exception to much of what we did, didn't like the pictures at all: 'As far as Taylor-Wood's glycerine-streaked mummers are concerned, aside from the one or two performers (Gabriel Byrne, Daniel Craig) who seem to be able to emote at will, these images aren't so different from any glossy spread in *Vanity Fair* or *Vogue* . . . The only question they might raise is the little matter of whether men also fake it.'

It was, they opined, enough to make you weep.

Ouch.

HAVING WORSHIPPED PETER BLAKE AS a teenager, it was always going to be a pleasure to work with him. I'd interviewed him a few times for *The Face* and *Arena*, and had commissioned illustrations from him at the *Observer*; in 1995, I'd curated a book on music journalism, *Meaty, Beaty, Big & Bouncy*, and I'd asked Peter to do the cover. We made sure he felt like one of the *GQ* family, and we invited him to all our events, celebrated him, and asked him to contribute to the magazine. I'd visited him in his home in Chiswick, which was a treat in itself, although this paled in comparison to an invitation from my friend Nicky Carter to visit Peter in his studio in Hammersmith. I'd always assumed Paul Smith had the most eclectic and cluttered office in London, and I was wrong, as Peter's wasn't so much an Aladdin's Cave as a jungle of dreams, a kinetic pop-history Tinguely sculpture, with a cultural sweep stretching from the clunky art-school building blocks of post-war pop art right up to the frenzied digital world of 3D printing and the archival metaverse. It was the most glorious scrapyard, and proof that Peter's genius was no less storied in the noughties than it had been in the late fifties. 'Peter understands that collage places one time on top of another,' said David Hockney, and he was right. He redefined collage as a collision of media, genre, time and space. Peter's gift had always been to recontextualise images and symbols as he was painting them, a gift (or perhaps a sensibility) that was far more American than it was British – even though everyone always said the opposite was true. As he said himself, there were two groups of pop artists in the fifties. In America, there was Robert Rauschenberg and Jasper Johns, who were precursors of pop art, and in the UK we had the Independent Group, with Richard Hamilton and Eduardo Paolozzi. And then there was Blake, who wasn't really a member of either. And yet as the inventor of a particular strain of pop art he possessed an irony that every other artist had trouble approximating. His studio of curiosities was a jigsaw of styles, a portal into a magical world full of paintings, sculptures, curios, old posters, rubber clowns, headdresses, plastic bags, huge wooden letters, toy cars, postcards and art deco cigarette boxes. It was the harvest of a proud kitsch-adoring collector, a collection in which Elvis memorabilia was afforded the same respect as a musket ball fired during the 1643 siege of Arundel Castle. It contained one of the very finest collections of ephemera, with sections devoted to wrestling, Victoriana and the alphabet.

Peter understood the hi–lo mix, understood the quiet desperation of the English lower middle classes, and the alluring fantasy of a fictitious world across the water. For him, Pax Americana had been an opportunity to explore frictionless cultures, and to plunder the vast amount of imagery that was pouring out of Hollywood or Denmark Street, Greenwich Village or the Cavern, Carnaby Street or Fleet Street, wherever. In doing so he became the king of collage, a man who was part Max Ernst, part Kurt Schwitters and part Elvis Presley. In a double denim suit, of course. This is why Peter understood magazines so well, and why he enjoyed working with them so much; he understood that crucial mix of the ephemeral and the eternal.

In 1962, Blake featured in Ken Russell's celebrated BBC television film *Pop Goes the Easel.* This documentary, plus a feature about him in the recently launched *Sunday Times Magazine*, turned Blake into something of a celebrity and one of the first representatives of a new phenomenon: Swinging London. In 1967, in collaboration with his then wife Jann Haworth, he created the cover of the Beatles' album, *Sgt. Pepper's Lonely Hearts Club Band*, still the most identifiable image of that place and time.

I did a lot of work with Paul McCartney, and if I'm honest could have easily done something every year with him. I was always more of a Paul man than a John man, as I was continually overawed by his ability to conjure melodies seemingly at will. I was also impressed that he went out of his way to emphasise the normalcy of what he did, even though it was so extraordinary. He was always all smiles. I didn't often show off to my parents about what I'd been up to, but I knew my mother would get a kick out of the fact I'd met him. After he came to his first Men of the Year Awards, I called her up the following day.

When I told her, she covered the receiver (I don't know why) and said, 'Mike. Mike! He's only gone and met Paul McCartney.'

I WAS OBSESSED WITH SWINGING London, and it became something of a lingua franca for *GQ*, both as a subject and as a metaphor. We knew that there were many further iterations – punk, the style explosion of the mid-eighties, Britpop, etc. – and we rather hoped we were contributing to our own somewhat fractured version. We even commissioned Nik Cohn to write a piece about the myth of Swinging London. Cohn was one of the pre-eminent chroniclers of the period, and one of its harshest critics. 'Swinging London was tiny – 500 people and three nightclubs,' he said. The day *Time* published its famous 'London' issue in April 1966 – when the magazine officially anointed London as 'The Swinging City', turning it at once into a Mecca for American tourists as well as an international symbol of cultural upheaval – he had a ploughman's lunch and a pint in an Irish pub in Shepherd's Bush. According to Cohn, it was a 'khazi', which was why he liked it: stale bread, sweaty cheese, sour beer. It was the other side of London, the London not populated by the fabulous 500. He once got into an argument with a regular who owned a hideous white mongrel and who worshipped Bobby Moore. When Cohn suggested that Pelé was perhaps a better footballer, the man gave his dog a sly nudge with his boot and 'the mutt upped and pissed down my trouser leg'.

Cohn first heard about the *Time* issue from a mod acquaintance called Colin whom he had befriended for the purposes of his work. Colin was a purist mod from the Goldhawk Road who dealt speed to pay for his clothes habit (he bought a tailormade suit every week and would change his shirt sometimes three times a day). Colin hated the way in which mod culture had been commercialised and, in his view, civilisation had peaked in 1964, just before the media had started to report the mod–rocker battles. And in Colin's eyes, the *Time* story was Swinging London's death knell. 'This is the end, the fucking end,' he said.

Cohn agreed with him and said that not only did London not 'swing', it hardly oscillated. Cohn had arrived from Newcastle in 1963, aged seventeen, and was determined to make a name for himself. With the arrogance of youth, he set upon the city with a vengeance, forging a career for himself as a journalist 'in the know', even though he'd only been in town for five minutes.

'My timing was perfect,' he said. 'Nineteen-sixty-three was the year the Beatles released "She Loves You"; suddenly, the mood was vivid with new possibilities. The post-war austerity was finally over. Even more important, national service had been lifted. Upstarts like myself, with bad posture and worse attitudes, no longer stood to be shipped to Cyprus or Malaya and hammered into shape. For the first time since the Twenties, the young were in charge of their own fates.'

Almost immediately, though, Cohn started making his name by disparaging the dizzying velocity of the time, while the *Time* story convinced him that 'this dog had had its day'.

Cohn's point was that London was exciting primarily because it was exclusive in pockets, and that those in the know started getting irritated as the scene began being mediated. As the 500 stretched to 1,000, and then 5,000, the originators, the flag-wavers, those who had first crossed from east to west, well, they suddenly felt superfluous. Perhaps not the ones who had become rich and famous, but if you were one of the magic 500 for whom fame had not rung, you felt rather left behind.

In the early sixties, the East End was as different from the West End as England was from France. Although there was a slow migration of talent from east to west – David Bailey, Terence Stamp, Terence Donovan et al. – in those early days rarely the twain would meet. If you were from the East End, you were more likely to visit Kent than Oxford Street.

'Back then the East End all looked the same, right from Bow and East Ham through to Hackney and Dagenham and Barking and beyond, just rows and rows of little 1880 houses,' said Bailey. 'People were so poor you'd see market stalls covered in second-hand false teeth. It was quiet there, too, and cars were still something of a novelty, even in the early sixties: as kids we'd follow George the milkman as his horse plodded along the road.'

The only people with cars that Bailey knew were the gangs, such as the Krays, and they all had pre-war cars, like old V8 Fords. Too often, the area felt like one big ghost town, deserted in the evening, empty on Sundays.

'If you came from the East End and you wanted out, there were only three things you could become – a boxer, a car thief or maybe a musician,' said Bailey. 'But just because you're born in a stable doesn't mean you have to grow up to be a horse. I didn't. Back then the East End was a bit like Cuba, because you could only get out if you boxed, stole or sang.' Among many other hand-to-mouth jobs, Bailey even worked as a bad-debt collector for a well-known boxing referee called Mickey Fox. 'Mickey was an incredibly tough man, and I was his sidekick. He used to put milk bottles on top of the doors, so you'd find out if the guy who owed money had been back or not. And if they were smashed, he knew to hang around.'

'The "Swinging Sixties" did not swing in Lambeth,' wrote John Major ruefully in his memoirs, and there were many who agreed with him. One of the tartest descriptions of Swinging London was provided by a reader's letter that *Time* published two weeks after its 'Swinging City' piece: 'Thousands of young people with the same haircut, the same facial expressions, rush out every Saturday to buy what everyone else is wearing so they can look different.'

Two months after the *Time* article, the cover of *Queen* magazine featured a pun that would later be used by the artist Richard Hamilton as the title of one of his images of the Rolling Stones: 'Swingeing London'. Inside the issue, the article summed up the increasingly cynical feeling: 'London? No, not more about London!'

I WAS FASCINATED BY THE way pop culture had developed, both in the UK and the US, and was obsessed with the minutiae and architecture of famous events, and the intricacies of power that surrounded them. And although I used people like Alan Aldridge, Guy Peellaert and Cohn, there was perhaps a sense that I was trying to rehabilitate them, which I admit I was, in a way.

Cohn, like many journalists at the time, had made a name for himself by turning sacred cows into hamburgers, demolishing the myths of the great and the good. This soon became a traditional and acceptable form of comment, the radical reappraisal of something we previously held dear. My friend Mark Ellen always said this originated from the arts desk of the *Guardian*. He said, and I paraphrase, that the editorial policy of the *Guardian* was simple: 'You know that thing you love? Well, it's shit.'

Soon, this negative volte-face would be hijacked by equally contrary journalists who did precisely the opposite; instead of coming to bury artists we liked – Hockney, the Beatles, Dickens – they came to celebrate the previously disparaged. For example: if, in 1985, you were one of the many millions who hated anything released by the Norwegian band A-ha, by the mid-noughties you would be reading a fanatical reconsideration of their oeuvre, probably in the arts pages of the *Guardian*. I like to think I started this back in the eighties, when

I would regularly and purposefully celebrate people I knew other journalists absolutely hated. And I did this not to be contrary, but simply because I liked whatever it was that they did not.

Like Daryl Hall and John Oates. Hall and Oates were never cool. Not ever. Not at the start of their career (when David Bowie was cool), not at the height of their success (when Madonna was about as cool as cool can be), nor indeed in the mid-noughties (when a lot of people were considered cool, including a lot of people who shouldn't have been cool at all).

The problem was a simple one. Even though they made – and occasionally continued to make – some of the best blue-eyed soul ever recorded, they had an image problem, with Daryl Hall looking like a market-town hairdresser, and John Oates looking like Super Mario's smaller, uglier brother.

They were a duo, but although it was more than plain what Hall did (sing, a lot, very well), it was never apparent what his partner did. In that respect, they were like an American Wham! Not only that, but whereas some people were born with a sense of how to clothe themselves, and others acquired it, John Oates always looked as if his clothes had been thrust upon him. And whenever he wore something expensive it looked stolen. In essence, Hall was the tall, blond, good-looking one who sang all the songs, while Oates was rather short, had a small unnecessary moustache, and hair like badly turned broccoli. Hall looked like the one who had all the fun, whereas Oates had the melancholy appearance of a man who had spent too much time searching for the leak in life's gaspipe, with a lighted candle.

More importantly, though, they were still around. In the music business, a partnership is considered a success if it outlasts milk, but theirs had already turned out to be one of the most enduring partnerships in the business. Hall and Oates already had a permanent home in the global jukebox hall of fame, and you could have filled an iPod Nano with their greatest hits: 'She's Gone', 'Sara Smile', 'I Can't Go for That', 'Every Time You Go Away' . . . songs that had become as ubiquitous on the radio as Motown standards or *X Factor* cover versions. They were the most successful duo in the history of pop. Not that you were allowed to admit it. When I first worked at *The Face* in the mid-eighties, one junior editor almost went into shock when I recommended one of their records. In her eyes the only thing worse than admitting to liking a Hall and Oates record would have been to actually *be* Hall and Oates. But their records sounded great, especially in the nightclubs of Manhattan. On my first trip to New York, in 1984, Danceteria, Area, Limelight and all the other downtown hotspots reverberated to the thumping sounds of Afrika Bambaataa, Nuance, the SOS Band. . . and Hall and Oates's 'Out of Touch', one of the great forgotten dance anthems of the decade.

I first saw them perform in the same year, in a place called Cedar Rapids in the wilds of Nowhere – which, if you closely studied a map of Iowa, was in the upper reaches of the state, right near the border. They were playing a sports arena, to around five thousand screaming hermaphrodites – at least that's how I remember them. These people were all aged between eighteen and twenty-five, and all had identical honey-coloured mullets (the sort that Bono successfully sported at the time), seemingly spray-on stonewashed denim, tiny white leather pixie boots and burgundy satin tour jackets. Everyone looked like a roadie for Van Halen or one of those LA 'Hair Metal' bands that were all the rage back then. Cedar Rapids was the sort of place where you didn't dare chat anyone up because you weren't exactly sure what sex they were.

The band themselves were simply marvellous and got the crowd jumping up and down and hollering in the way that only Cedar Rapidians could truly jump and holler. My enjoyment was only tempered by the fact I was seriously bereft in both the honey-coloured mullet and the burgundy satin tour-jacket departments.

After becoming the most successful double act in American entertainment history, the duo went surprisingly quiet. One day they looked like two of the most famous men in the world, and the next they looked like a hairdresser from Weybridge and his dodgy-looking pal. After that, Daryl Hall released a couple of so-so solo albums, and

John Oates appeared with Harry Enfield in his legendary scousers sketch on television. (What do you mean, it wasn't him?)

They never went away in my car, though, and on any given weekday, as I carefully weaved my way through the London traffic, silently cursing the partially sighted cab drivers and overly caffeinated cyclists who endeavoured to interrupt my journey to Vogue House, I pushed the pedal to the metal and sang along to 'Maneater' or 'Private Eyes', drifting back to that balmy Saturday night in 1984 in Cedar Rapids.

No, they weren't cool, but what was cool anyway?

At *GQ*, we thought that – just occasionally – we knew.

Skunk Hairspray & Fermented Peas

Senses Working Overtime

With Damien Hirst, on the Rihanna shoot,
Brooklyn, 2013

WHEN ALASTAIR CAMPBELL WAS TONY Blair's press secretary and then director of communications, he was nothing if not partisan. Like all good political gatekeepers, he would brook no criticism and was immune to discussion. As Blair's white-knuckle major-domo, he oversaw New Labour's journey from ideological experiment to political omnipotence, earning a fearsome reputation and becoming a household name in the process.

What Campbell was selling was scripture, and you either took him at his word or you were banished – immediately – from the court. At the time (1997–2003) he was vilified by a press corps who found itself unable to manoeuvre around Downing Street or Whitehall without his tacit blessing. If, as a journalist, you were crazy enough to go against Campbell's wishes, or dared to contradict him publicly, his wrath would be enough to convince you never to do it again.

'Don't be a fuckhead,' he would say.

After all, one should never forget that Campbell was the original inspiration for Malcolm Tucker, the potty-mouthed director of communications-cum-Darth Vader of Whitehall in Armando Iannucci's *The Thick of It*, played brilliantly by Peter Capaldi.

Campbell's uncompromising attitude was one of the reasons I hired him to work for *GQ* in 2013. I had watched him eviscerate the *Daily Mail*'s deputy editor Jon Steafel one evening on *Newsnight* (as a response to Steafel trying to defend his paper's attempts to slur Ed Miliband's father, painting him as unpatriotic) and was immediately convinced this was the person we needed to hire to interrogate politicians for us. As we had successfully turned Piers Morgan into a TV star, we now needed another journalistic Rottweiler to attack politicians and big heads. On *Newsnight*, Campbell picked apart Steafel's half-hearted defence of the article with surgical precision, before adding that his newspaper was 'the worst of British values posing as the best.'

THE NEXT DAY I CALLED Campbell and arranged to meet him in a café near his home in north London – 'I don't want any of that Ivy nonsense,' he said, completely unconvincingly. 'Come up to where the real people live.' And so I went up to Hampstead. Where the real people live.

We both drew up a list of who he should interview, and one name appeared on both lists: Paul Dacre, the similarly foul-mouthed editor of the *Daily Mail*, Steafel's boss, and one of the most powerful men in the industry. As per usual, the *GQ* team then started approaching potential interviewees, including, obviously, Dacre.

Unsurprisingly, Campbell's column worked like a dream, and his *GQ* interview quickly became one of those things politicians didn't like doing, but felt they had to. Campbell's interviews always contained zingers that would generate media attention all over the world, whether he was interviewing politicians, sportsmen or royalty. Dacre, though, wasn't interested, unsurprisingly. He rarely agreed to interviews and was unlikely to put himself forward to be hanged, drawn and quartered by Campbell (the pair despised each other).

During one of my conversations with Alastair over the following weeks we agreed that, in addition to his monthly interviews, he should write a funny piece for the end of the year entitled 'The people who refused to be interviewed by me', which would include funny barbs about all the notables who had decided sensibly to body swerve his interrogation.

Then something happened. Quite quickly I picked up around the office that Alastair had been sending potentially abusive emails to Dacre, often late at night and sometimes in the early hours of the morning. I called Alastair up and said that, if he was sending them under his *GQ* umbrella, then I'd like to see them, to understand the tone, as I was worried he might be overstepping the mark. And so he sent them to me, and I was not amused. He was sending incredibly long, intricate messages to Dacre, which, if interpreted a certain way, might indeed be considered inappropriate, or even abusive. And while the idea of anyone successfully abusing Paul Dacre was somewhat ridiculous, I still needed to make sure Campbell was operating within the law (there was always the Editor's Code of Practice to consider, after all).

So, I asked him to stop. This resulted in an almighty row one day as I was about to go on holiday. The car was outside my house, full of my wife, my two daughters and our immaculately labelled bags, when Alastair decided to return my phone call. Perhaps my annoyance was compounded by my impatience (the clock was running), and so I didn't have any interest in compromise. I stood by the front door, giving as good as I was getting, eventually cutting him off. I won, after which Campbell was a markedly different person, at least with me. Dacre could lower himself into his coffin each night with a renewed sense of safety (poor lamb), and I wasn't going to get sued or hauled before a jury.

*

SHORTLY AFTERWARDS, I HAD ANOTHER huge row, this time with the staff. The issue was our One Direction covers, which none of them was keen on. They would often disagree with me over my choice of cover stars, as they frequently thought my suggestions were either too downmarket or esoteric. They didn't think we should have featured Simon Cowell or David Cameron; didn't think we should have done Boris Johnson, Jeremy Corbyn, Idris Elba or Borat. And they may have been right. (I have it on good authority that the unsold copies of the Borat issue were used as the landfill beneath the eastern section of London's Elizabeth line.)

I was mystified, however, by their reluctance to the One Direction idea. The group were a genuine global phenomenon, and in Harry Styles they had a proper star. I was convinced Harry had the potential to become as big as a Robbie Williams or a Justin Timberlake (and in the end became bigger than both). Ever since I saw my daughters' response to him on *The X Factor* I knew he was going to be an enormous star. He was gorgeous, he could sing, and he had character. So, I ignored the team and pushed ahead with the idea.

We were going to print five different covers, with an understanding – shared with One Direction's publicists – that we were going to have an even split, with each member of the band getting 20 per cent of the print run. I'm not sure who really believed that, though, as the final print run was definitely balanced in Harry's favour (around 60 per cent of the run). I commissioned Platon to take the pictures, as he was famous for shooting politicians and business icons in an extremely stoic way. I asked him to make the band members look as old as possible, turning them into men overnight. This made them more appealing to our readership, it created a news story, and it gave them a whole new look in the process.

The covers almost broke the internet when we released them in advance of the actual print issue. The group's fans took such exception to the cover line on Harry's copy – 'He's up all night to get lucky' – that we received death threats.

It's fair to say fame does strange things to people, even more so when a person is young. They get so used to acclaim that every accidental micro-aggression is seen as some kind of disloyal counterattack. Unless they are unusually grounded, they start to distrust people, especially strangers. Their acolytes, meanwhile, keep suspicion at bay by becoming overly enthusiastic courtiers, and by continually burnishing the truth. Fame can cause arrested development, which is obviously a problem if you become popular at eighteen.

I bumped into Harry Styles on holiday ten years after the axis of his world changed, and while it was obvious he'd grown inordinately in those ten years, he was charming, and as funny and as self-deprecating as he had been when I had first met him, right at the beginning. He was everything you hoped he'd be. A proper pop star, but a nice one.

FOR OUR TWENTY-FIFTH ANNIVERSARY ISSUE in 2013, I needed another memorable cover, one that would work at newsstands and on social, and which would be a testament to a quarter of a century of publishing. I started planning the issue nine months before it was due to be shipped, meticulously building the flatplan into something both distinctively contemporary and memorably celebratory. For the cover, we alighted on what we thought was a perfect storm, a Damien Hirst-designed image of Rihanna as Medusa, complete with real-life pythons. The shoot would take place in New York, the photographs would be taken by Mariano Vivanco, and – according to the budget, which our managing editor at the time, Mark Russell, thought we had inflated just to ruin his sleep patterns – was the largest ever for a *GQ* shoot.

Knowing Rihanna had a habit of treating timetables as though they were working documents open to interpretation rather than non-negotiable schedules, we turned up late to the shoot, only to find our Barbadian cover star had already been at the Brooklyn studio for over an hour – delivered by a tricked-out Escalade SUV (gleaming rims, panelwork as patent as an oil slick, and thick, tinted pap-proof windows). As I walked into the studio, the smell of industrial skunk made me feel as though I had just bumped into a group of particularly enthusiastic revellers at Glastonbury. But it was happening. Rihanna was being made up, Damien was chatting to Mariano, and what had started as a series of text messages two months earlier – Hirst to Rihanna: 'I'm not doing it'; Rihanna to Hirst: 'I'm a gonna kill you then' – was becoming a reality.

The two weren't exactly strangers, and when Rihanna first started having some success – in 2007, with her global hit 'Umbrella' – she asked her people to contact Hirst about buying a piece of his art. Apparently, she had already been given a Hirst by her mentor and label boss Jay-Z and wanted more. Hirst said she arranged to come to his studio five times, but never made it. 'It made me laugh, because that's precisely what I used to be like back in the glory days,' he said. 'I just kept missing appointments; going out on Friday night and turning up to meetings on Monday morning like a tramp, still off my head. I waited a few times for her, getting a taste of my own medicine.' Hirst said that he wanted to work with her because he considered her to be a role model, an unlikely one perhaps, but certainly more of a role model than David Cameron.

Halfway through our shoot, the snake handler arrived with two six-foot boa constrictors in a large white plastic container – a cool box with holes, basically. As she walked into the studio she stopped, somewhat alarmed.

'What's the smell?'

'Hairspray,' said one of the assistants, imaginatively.

'What, skunk hairspray?'

It was one of the biggest issues of *GQ* we ever produced and was so popular that the issue now changes hands for ridiculous sums. One website was still advertising the issue over a decade after it was published, even though they didn't have any copies left. 'Good condition. Massive. 514 pages. Very heavy issue.'

*

WE PRODUCED ANOTHER WALLOPING SUCCESS that year, starring one of the new breed of young, posh, British actors, Benedict Cumberbatch. We had been approached by a friend at one of the larger film companies to act as the media partner for an upcoming superhero movie. This was the sort of thing we did quite regularly, although this was on another scale altogether. The film company were going to hire one of the largest civic buildings in London, build a set that would have shamed the opening sequence of most sci-fi films, and had budgeted for an extravagant banquet and an after-party of Brobdingnagian proportions. There was going to a huge international media campaign, with global digital billboard advertising that was already being organised with military precision. From our side, all we had to do was shoot Cumberbatch for the cover of the magazine, marshalling our very best talent, write a fairly benign online review of the film, and then 'social the bastard to death'.

Simple.

On the night of the actual premier, there was one point where Cumberbatch and I had to come together on the red carpet for a photocall. He would be photographed dozens of times over a twenty-minute period, with his co-stars, the director, the producers and any other notables on the list. And then we had to lean into each other, smile, and go our separate ways. So far, the evening had been a swinging success, as the rooms were full, the atmosphere was positive and the campaign – just launched – was going swimmingly. Then, as our tuxedos touched on the red carpet, and we lit up for the camaras, Cumberbatch turned to me and whispered, 'So, he hated it then.'

'What?' I queried, while still trying to smile.

'Stuart, your reviewer. He said he hated it.'

And before I could remonstrate, we were separated by his minders, and he was shoved off to be photographed with his leading lady while I snuck off to the bar to try and process what has just happened. The review was already online, and so I called it up, and speedread it again. It was, I have to say, a rather fulsome review. Stuart McGurk had done a thoroughly professional job reviewing the film through a filter that contextualised it in a way that would be pleasing for everyone, not least its stars. So, I was baffled. Five minutes later, when I found one of the film's PRs to explain what had just gone down, she was equally confused. But then we found an adjective that, if you were an overly sensitive, pampered, finickity celebrity, you might just have taken as criticism. Not if you had been a normal person, you understand, but an actor. This reinforced what I'd known for quite some time, which was that you could never, ever anticipate what was going to annoy a celebrity. Was it irrational? Of course it was, but then adjectives can be very dangerous things.

OFTEN, WORK AND PLEASURE WERE indivisible. In 2014, Sofia Davis organised a couple of celebrity karaoke evenings with a live band at Abbey Road studios, in the 'big' room. They were hosted by myself and Samuel L. Jackson to raise money for Sofia's charity, One for the Boys. The cause aimed to bring attention to identifying the early stages of prostate and testicular cancer, which Sam Jackson sonorously espoused onstage on both nights. We sang a couple of duets, most memorably (for me, at least), Sam and Dave's 'Hold On! I'm Comin'', with me, as Sam enjoyed telling everyone, stepping in for Dave. To try and minimise the prospect of total embarrassment, Sam and Sofia came round for dinner so we could practise. Thankfully, after an hour or so debating the relative merits of Motown and Stax, Sam spent the rest of the evening congratulating Sarah on her cooking. I wanted to rehearse, but Sam said this wasn't necessary; easy for him to say, but leaving me extremely nervous about our impending duet. We simply decided to sing alternate verses and then come together on the choruses. At Abbey Road, we looked as though we were auditioning for a remake of *The Blues Brothers*.

Importantly, Jackson knew how to get a party started. Having thanked everyone for coming – everyone including Beth Ditto, Maisie Williams, Nicole Scherzinger, Cara Delavigne and Tinie Tempah – he said, calm as you like, 'Let's get this shit to stinking.'

*

EARLIER IN THE YEAR I'D been speaking at the Diageo World Class conference in Rio, where I spent three days talking about the vagaries of the luxury sector, and the various Western luxury brands that were 'now at 37,000 feet', i.e. cruising at altitude but soon to drop like a ruptured 747. Having never been to Brazil before, or indeed Rio, I was intrigued to see the place before the World Cup and the Olympics got hold of it, although I have to say in my three days there, I spent most of my time looking over my shoulder. The first thing I was given when I arrived at the airport was a Risk Matrix, a laminated piece of A4 paper that included an 'impact/likelihood' graph broken down into 'manageable, major and critical', spread across 'remote, possible and likely', and listing express kidnappings (where you are mugged, kidnapped and delivered back to your hotel in time for cocktails), carjacking, prostitution, purse snatchings and – bizarrely – employee binge drinking. I was told that on no account should I leave the hotel alone at night, and nor should I wear my watch. And we were staying right on Copacabana Beach, supposedly one of the major tourist destinations in the city. Consequently, I spent all of my time expecting to be abducted.

On my last day I had a few hours to kill before my flight, so I was given a car, although the driver said I was to sit up front next to him because, if I sat in the back, we would both be targets and no doubt robbed at traffic lights. As soon as I got back on the plane, I knew that in the future I wouldn't be thinking about Astrud Gilberto or the bossa nova whenever I imagined Rio; instead, I would be thinking how lucky I was I didn't have my Timex pinched.

One of the topics at the Rio conference had been the number of celebrities getting involved with drinks brands. Brad Pitt and Angelina Jolie bought a controlling stake in Château Miraval in 2008, Bruno Mars had his own rum, and Steven Soderbergh had spent a small fortune trying to convince people to drink Singani brandy. Jay-Z got into the champagne game because he thought he had no other choice. In the early noughties, he had helped widely popularise Cristal, often considered the best brand of bubbles. He referenced it in his songs and splashed it around in his music videos. But in 2006, Frédéric Rouzaud, then the MD of the Champagne Louis Roederer winery, the maker of Cristal, in his finite wisdom said something Jay-Z found innately racist.

When asked by *The Economist* if an association with hip-hop could hurt Cristal, Rouzaud said: 'That's a good question, but what can we do? We can't forbid people from buying it.' Of course, Rouzaud later issued a statement saying the company had 'the utmost regard for, and interest in, all forms of art and culture', but by then it was too late.

Jay-Z gave Cristal the finger.

'Those comments forced us to build our own thing,' he said, unsurprisingly.

His first move was to feature bottles of Armand de Brignac champagne – known as 'Ace of Spades' due to its label – in his 'Show Me What You Got' video. His second was to buy 50 per cent of the company.

When he decided to launch the brand in the UK, he asked me to co-host the party with him. Which, as the old *Fast Show* jazz character used to say, was nice.

The dinner was to take place at Automat, the Mayfair restaurant and event space, with a guest list that meant that, for at least one night only, all paparazzi leave was cancelled: Naomi Campbell, Lily Allen, Roger Federer, Matthew Freud, Mark Ronson, etc. Unusually, as his PR team were taking care of all the arrangements, my only task was pitching up at the Lanesborough at Hyde Park Corner in order to accompany Jay-Z to the launch. Which is when I experienced my first bout of hip-hop time.

And it was all my fault. When I arrived at the hotel to pick him up – dressed head to toe in Ede & Ravenscroft – he spied my pocket square, realised he wasn't wearing one himself, and promptly sent a flunky back to his room to pick it up. Which – obviously – took forever. It took so long it must have been hidden behind the ceiling tiles. Then, as the flunky failed to appear, Jay-Z then disappeared himself, 'sending a man to do a boy's job', as he said himself as he snuck back into the lift.

And for an hour that was the last I heard of him. I sat downstairs with his flunkies, none of whom appeared to be remotely bothered by their boss's disappearing act. Then, at nine-thirty, he reappeared, his pocket square cascading over his Tom Ford jacket, looking very much 'the full *GQ*'. In the car, as we discussed being 'dissed' by Noel Gallagher, who had said that Jay-Z shouldn't have been performing at Glastonbury ('The crazy thing is, "Wonderwall" is one of my favourite tunes'), his actual festival performance ('There were so many people I couldn't see the end of them') and his appearance on *The Jonathan Ross Show* ('People said he's tricky, but I got him good'), he suddenly burst into song, singing Coldplay's 'Lost!' at the top of his voice, causing his security guard to turn round from the front seat, wondering if his boss had suddenly – and rather convincingly – somehow morphed into Chris Martin. When we arrived at the restaurant, the paps acted as though Elvis was entering the building (well, Elvis accompanied by a tall, follicularly challenged Brit in a bright-blue Savile Row suit), drowning him in a blaze of flashbulbs.

KANYE WEST HAD HIS FAIR share of endorsements, too, with Fatburger, A Bathing Ape and Adidas, among others. And there was a period when he started hanging out at Paris fashion week, doing a fair amount of due diligence as he was thinking about launching his own clothing brand. One season he appeared, as if from nowhere, and was suddenly in the front row of every show. He muscled in on conversations, asked random questions, and acted like an overgrown schoolboy. He had made it his mission to find out about the fashion world, and we all helped as much as we could. I would be sitting in a café with the rest of the *GQ* team, in those forty-minute gaps that seemed magically to appear between shows, no matter what time they were scheduled for, and Kanye would breeze in, with a minder in tow, and begin asking questions about Tom Ford or Issey Miyake. He was perfectly good company, although he was taking it a lot more seriously than most of us.

Why?

Because after every show he went back to his hotel – could have been Le Bristol, could have been Hôtel de Crillon, could have been the George V – and change into a different outfit. One minute he would be in a yellow jumpsuit, the next in an orange tweed suit. You'd look around and he'd be dressed in double denim; ninety minutes later he'd appear to be wearing a kaleidoscopic beret and reflective sunglasses. He obviously liked wearing loud shirts, shirts than could be seen in different galaxies, different solar systems, shirts that demanded to be noticed, shirts that announced proudly to the world – well, OK, to Paris fashion week – that he had arrived, that he was HERE! HE WAS WORKING, AND HE WAS WEARING A PARTY SHIRT!

We all found his behaviour, as well as his clothes, terribly amusing, especially as he looked like a rent boy in mufti. I told him fashion was only about status, that instead of having labels inside our clothes, we should have price tags on the outside. That way I could take my jacket off in the middle of a business meeting so everyone could see the label on my sleeve: '£540', it would say. That way I could walk into a restaurant with '£3,400' plastered all over my jacket, or '£2,300' on my shoes and '£95' on my tie. And if you looked closely you could see '£2,500' on my watch. I suggested it might be quite sexy to find the words '£280' on your dinner date's knickers rather than Agent Provocateur. Of course, if you had spent most of the evening fantasising that her underwear had '£800' written all over it, then you might be a little disappointed, but I think he got my point.

I also gave him a crash course in fashion pronunciation. I explained that in the same way that true car enthusiasts always said Royce instead of Rolls (Royce was the engineer, after all), true fashionistas knew never to refer to Blahniks; it was always *Manolos*, stretching the last syllable as far as you could, possibly into the middle of next week.

To wit:

Christian name: Vivienne (Westwood), Tom (Ford), Calvin (Klein), Ralph (Lauren), Yohji (Yamamoto), Katharine (Hamnett), Luella (Bartley), Stella (McCartney), Giles (Deacon).

Surname: (Alexander) McQueen, (Alberta) Ferretti, (Tommy) Hilfiger, (Giorgio) Armani, (Nicole) Farhi, (Ozwald) Boateng, (Martin) Margiela, (Roland) Mouret.

One name: Valentino, Prada, Chanel, Gucci, Versace, Missoni, Moschino, Etro.

Both names: Paul Smith, Richard James, John Richmond, Margaret Howell, Antony Price, Donna Karan, Marks & Spencer.

Perhaps predictably, Kanye West turned out to be something of a loose cannon.

AS LONDON COLLECTIONS: MEN GATHERED steam, we took on more and more ambassadors, one of which was Lewis Hamilton. He too was thinking of launching his own line, and for a couple of seasons would regularly turn up at the London shows, sitting on the front row, attending parties and dinners, and generally getting involved. I gave him advice about when precisely to arrive at a fashion show. Someone of his magnitude should arrive a little late; not crazy late – not Naomi Campbell late – but late enough for there to be a buzz about your entrance.

Being a quick study, Hamilton took all this in, and started experimenting with various arrivals. He would sit in his limo and time his arrival to the minute. I suppose being a world-class racing driver helped in this respect. But he did this religiously, each time pushing it a little more to see how late he could be and still not miss the show. This turned out to be working extremely well, until one afternoon in Hyde Park, when Hamilton was so late he arrived at the Burberry show just as everyone was leaving.

I told him afterwards he shouldn't have made the last pit stop. To his credit, he laughed.

AS THE YEAR ENDED, WE started making plans for our annual Food & Drinks Awards, a diversion that had been enthusiastically embraced by the food and beverages industry. As well as celebrating the new and the pertinent, this was also an opportunity to investigate some of the finest restaurants in the world. This year it was the turn of Noma, René Redzepi's foraging beanery in Denmark, and I decided to go.

Cut to three weeks later and the first word of Danish I heard in Copenhagen was *kretiner*, which – perhaps unsurprisingly – means 'cretin'. This was directed at Oliver Peyton – again, unsurprisingly – as he had inadvertently stepped into a cycle lane outside the ultra-modernist Nimb hotel on Bernstorffsgade, and as I'd been wanting to say something similar to him since we'd arrived at Heathrow some three hours earlier, I felt my day was starting to look up.

Oliver and I had planned a trip to the world's best restaurant ever since Noma had leapfrogged the Fat Duck in 2010 to become the best restaurant in the world, as ranked by *Restaurant* magazine. Having been on various food tourism trips to Las Vegas, Florence, Milan, Paris, Tokyo, New York and Chicago, we had both become accustomed to devouring tasting menus and large bottles of stupidly expensive wine, and felt that it was time we did some similar due diligence on the food and wine at Noma.

Which is what we did.

Previously, my most memorable restaurant experience with Oliver happened in Alinea, the Michelin three-star eatery in Chicago. The food was exceptional, yet as anyone who had been would have been able to tell you, the atmosphere was decidedly anal, and the place felt a little like a library, as every 'aah', 'mmm' and 'ooh, isn't that nice?' was amplified around the whole room as if it were part of the menu. Which made the sudden appearance of what looked like a mobster with a 'real estate' girl on each arm even more incongruous than it ordinarily might have been. This man was in his late fifties, tremendously overweight, and chewing on an unlit cigar. He was jacketless, dressed in a scruffy polo shirt and chinos, and with a belly that looked as though it had been stolen from Buddha himself. He arrived around nine-thirty, and looked enormously pleased with himself, having secured a table at what was, at the time, undoubtedly Chicago's finest restaurant. We immediately had the impression that he had probably been trying to get a table since the place opened in 2005 (this was 2006), and had reluctantly been offered one when all obfuscation and diversionary tactics had failed, like the people who used to get the two-thirty bookings at the Ivy, back when the Ivy really was the Ivy.

Our mobster was the quintessential rube, ordering off-menu (asking for fries with everything), demanding champagne with every course, and generally making a spectacle of himself. He was sitting right next to us, and Oliver and I sat, quietly appalled, as he treated the place as though it were his own private dining room. After all, this was meant to be one of America's very best culinary experiences, and he was treating it like a theme park. Yet after half an hour or so, we started to admire the dismissive way he treated the oh-so-sniffy waiters and began enjoying the way he was determined to have a good time, almost in spite of the restaurant – which was being unbelievably uptight about the whole thing. After an hour or so we were sitting at his table, swapping stories, drinking various bottles of extremely good Amarone and treating Alinea like a restaurant rather than a church (as everyone else seemed to be doing). He even left us with an anecdote: 'So, one of you's Irish, and the other's English, right? Hey, you're two-thirds of a good joke!'

Both Oliver and I figured Noma would be different, and that if we were to bump into any mobsters with 'real estate' girls on their arms, we would be very surprised indeed. We had started our day in Copenhagen with lunch at Manfreds, in the Shoreditch-like Nørrebro district, where we ate fabulous small dishes of raw meats and leeks with sour cream and horseradish, all washed down with a selection of natural white wines, which were currently all the rage and were actually quite disgusting. We then retired to Nimb, for a completely unearned rest, to prepare for the evening's onslaught.

And what an onslaught it was.

Noma was housed in an old warehouse on the waterfront in the Christianshavn neighbourhood, in a fairly unprepossessing part of town, which added a sense of drama to our arrival. We were greeted like long-lost members of the maître d's family (everyone is given this treatment), and after various introductions, and a tour of the kitchens and prep areas, we were seated by a window overlooking the water, and the evening began. We started with champagne, followed by ants and sour cream. Nothing extraordinary about that, you might think, but these ants were alive, and you had to scoop them up from the cream with a piece of rye bread fashioned in the shape of a twig. The rest of the other twenty-seven courses were no less bewitching, although only one involved another live animal, a twitching shrimp that reminded me a little too much of *I'm a Celebrity . . . Get Me Out of Here*. ('Three courses in,' I tweeted, 'and still waiting for something dead.') Each small dish was presented on its own particular plate or podium, and they followed each other as though they were on a conveyor belt. And all were pretty amazing: fresh and fermented peas, aromatic tea, dried scallops and beech nuts, biodynamic grains and watercress, egg yolk and herbs, unripe plums and buttermilk . . . and towards the end of the meal we were even asked to fry our own egg (this, as they say, was worth the price of admission alone).

Oliver was so taken with the meal that, after only three courses he said, 'This is already the best meal I've ever had.'

Noma was the brainchild of the thoroughly charming René Redzepi, who, having shown us around, was there to guide us through each course. 'We've tried to make Noma as little like a restaurant as possible,' he said. 'The experience is not just about the food.' Ah, but the food. A lot of his recipes involved food that had been foraged from nearby woodlands, and so much of what we ate tasted of the forest. In fact, I think it's fair to say that Noma was the world's first edible garden centre.

René's staff were also terrifically obliging, running around as though they were all auditioning for jobs they had obviously already mastered with great ease. They came from all corners of the Earth, too, an Apple Generation of kids from everywhere from Valencia and

Chicago to Dublin and London. They were tremendously proud of Noma, and with very good reason.

I'd had the tasting menus at El Bulli, the French Laundry, Charlie Trotter's and the Fat Duck, and I have to say that I'd never eaten anything as fundamentally extraordinary as I did at Noma. If they only gave you ten courses instead of twenty-seven you would still think you'd eaten at the best restaurant in the world. You might not have eaten as much of the local forest, but you would be just as replete.

Towards the end of our feast, Oliver looked as though he were on the verge of impersonating Mr Creosote from Monty Python's *The Meaning of Life*, and this was a man who made most pencils look obese. 'I can't believe what we've just eaten,' he said, smiling. 'That was truly one of the greatest experiences of my life.'

I wasn't about to disagree, although my enthusiasm for the evening was tempered somewhat by having to endure Oliver's profoundly novel map reading as we tried to wend our way back to the hotel. I can't remember exactly how many times I shouted 'Kretiner' as we made our way back to Nimb, although any passing Copenhagener might have imagined it was the only word of Danish I knew.

Three Princes: Charles, William and Harry

A Royal Flush

Stealing the future King's *GQ* award,
Tate Modern, 2018

I FIRST MET PRINCE HARRY in 2011, when he was still very much a party boy. He had only recently recovered from the tabloid onslaught of being caught with his pants down (literally) in a Las Vegas hotel suite, playing air guitar, singing Michael Jackson's 'Beat It', using only a glove to cover his groin, as he handed his underwear to a stripper. He was playing strip billiards and things weren't going so well. The pants were later auctioned off by the (British-born) stripper – who worked as a dominatrix under the name of Lady Dominque – but not before they had been on display at Las Vegas's Erotic Heritage Museum.

When Harry was on, he was seriously on. A few years earlier, he was involved in a military fundraising auction near Sandbanks, in

Dorset. It was the kind of thing he did all the time back then. This had been an especially long evening of grandstanding and speeches from local dignitaries and a performance by an ageing rocker who had started getting used to going down the charts rather than up. It had been one of those nights that just dragged, but everyone was very appreciative. And then, as the waiters started clearing up, hoping to sweep the room in time for them all to get home at a respectable hour, a waitress dropped an enormous, paella-style tray of drinks, bang straight on to the marble floor, shattering over two-dozen glasses, most of which were still full of booze. The waitress looked completely distraught until Harry, his head barking at the moon like a rabid dog, screamed, 'Ooooohhh noooooo, yes, now the party has begun!'

Gallant, funny, bluff, he immediately defused the situation, making the waitress's day and making everyone feel at ease. He even managed to keep his trousers on.

Back then, pre-Meghan, that's the kind of guy Harry was.

IN 2011, IN A WORLD a long way away from Las Vegas, I met Harry and the Walking with the Wounded team as they prepared for an epic unaided trek. The charity – of which Harry was the patron – were sending a group of wounded British soldiers on an expedition to the North Pole; they would become the first amputees to reach the Pole unsupported, in an attempt to raise £2 million for charities focusing on the rehabilitation of injured British service personnel. The negotiations over the *GQ* cover photographs with Clarence House were exhausting and labyrinthine, but Harry's PR team calmed down a little when we told them we were intending to use David Bailey. Little did they know what he was like in person.

'Has Bailey been rude to you?' I asked Harry as I arrived on the set of our cover shoot at Stonefield Park in Chilbolton, Hampshire.

'Was he rude?' replied Harry, ruefully. 'Well, he tried to be. But I'm fairly sure I won.'

Bailey liked to test his subjects by being confrontational, and – no stranger to profanity – often tried to intimidate them simply by swearing at them.

'So, did he swear at you?' I asked the prince.

'Oh yeah, of course he did,' said Harry, smiling. 'We had all the Fs and the Bs and the cunty stuff, but then we swore back. A lot. You obviously learn to swear quite a lot in the army, and my vocabulary wasn't all learned in Buckingham Palace.'

Remarkably, Bailey actually seemed to have found the prince rather intimidating.

'I've been taking pictures since I was twelve, but I still get nervous before taking someone's picture,' said Bailey after the shoot, 'and I'm just as nervous with someone I know as with somebody I don't. In that respect, everyone's equal as far as I'm concerned. I just want to make everyone look the best I can or bring out their character as best as I can. But I wasn't biting my fingernails because Harry happens to be a royal!'

Bailey had shot Princess Diana, as well as Prince Charles, but this was a different commission altogether as the pictures I wanted Bailey to produce had to make Harry look iconic, monolithic. He had to look like a cover star, even though the bods at Clarence House weren't convinced they wanted him on the cover at all. Charles and Diana were already well-established icons by the time Bailey got hold of them. This was more of an act of reinvention. Harry was to be photographed with the men who were going to the North Pole with him, but – crucially, to maximise the publicity for the charity – he also needed to be photographed alone, too. And I wanted it done in a very particular way. I wanted Harry to look stoic, but approachable. Wanted him to look like a matinee idol, but a matinee idol who could take care of himself. Essentially, I wanted him to look like the perfect *GQ* cover star.

Being able to swear was just a bonus.

Harry had arrived at the studio with little fanfare but oodles of charisma. He was keen to meet his expedition teammates before doing anything else, and he embraced all of them, shaking them by the hand and slapping them on the back. They then spent the next twenty minutes joshing with each other and swapping army anecdotes, joking about what they had in store for Harry on the walk. It was immediately clear what huge respect the war heroes had for him, and he for them. When Harry tried on the padded jacket he would be wearing on the expedition, he pulled his hood up, partially covering his face, and started doing hip-hop poses. This was greeted with huge laughs from the soldiers but raised eyebrows from the Palace representatives.

GQ's photographic director James Mullinger took Harry through to meet Bailey, and they greeted one another like old friends. Harry seemed in awe of Bailey at first, and Bailey less so of Harry. As they started shooting, Harry began laughing and joking around, and at first Bailey bounced around with him (he was seventy-three at the time, but still quite agile when he chose to be). Every now and then Bailey would put his camera down, put an arm around Harry and whisper a filthy story in his ear. In each case Harry's eyes would theatrically pop out of his head before his head flew back and he burst into hysterics. These were genuine belly laughs, although they were obviously amplified for effect. What soon became clear was that while he was playing up as though he were in an amateur dramatic production, Harry was totally unguarded. This was a real, intimate moment and one that both of them perhaps enjoyed a lot more than they thought they might.

Bailey had been shooting for about twenty-five minutes when Harry decided he must be almost done. He began giving as good as he got and started winding Bailey up, mercilessly. 'You must have the shot by now,' he said, winking in our direction. 'How long does this bloody thing take? I thought you were meant to be good at this, Bailey. Aren't you a professional? They said you were. Come on, honestly, how long does it take to make us look gorgeous? You've got some seriously good-looking boys in front of you. You've got a room full of George Clooneys right here in front of you! Right here!'

Ever the charmer, Bailey responded with, 'It takes as long as I fucking say it takes.'

This was just banter, although some of the prince's team had started to look a bit slack-jawed.

Ten minutes later, Harry decided the shoot was over. 'OK, you've got fifteen seconds,' he said, and began counting down: 'Fifteen, fourteen, thirteen, twelve . . .' while Bailey just kept shooting, not reacting to Harry's countdown until he reached one. At which point Harry walked out of frame, leaving Bailey stranded, embarrassed, with both hands on his Rolleiflex.

People didn't walk out on David Bailey. I'd seen him deliberately intimidate prime ministers and world-famous pop stars, just because he knew he could get away with it. But people didn't step out of frame when they'd decided they'd had enough. It just wasn't done. It would have been the same with Mario Testino or Richard Avedon. Your job was to stand there and be shot.

'I don't think he's used to working with people like me,' said Bailey, rather unnecessarily, trying to make it look as though everything had gone according to plan.

HARRY WAS STILL GOOD COMPANY five years later, when I met him at Buckingham Palace. I had turned up at the designated time at SW1 1AA – invited along with the former *Evening Standard* editor Sarah Sands (who was then editor of the *Today* programme), BBC News supremo James Harding and a smattering of other journalists – to watch Harry unveil a documentary series produced for the umbrella mental health charity he supported with his brother William and sister-in-law Kate, Heads Together. The films included the likes of Professor Green, Freddie Flintoff, Adwoa Aboah and Alastair Campbell discussing their problems with mental health, adding support to a charity that aims to change the national conversation on mental health and wellbeing through a partnership with various independent charities with decades of experience in tackling stigma, raising awareness and providing vital help for people with mental health challenges. The films were amplified by Harry's revelations about his own struggles caused by the death of his mother, Diana Princess of Wales, revealing that he saw a counsellor, saying that he had purposefully shut down his emotions and then suffered two years of 'total chaos'.

Campbell used his Heads Together film to describe the psychotic nervous breakdown he suffered, his addiction issues and the chronic depression he had experienced over the years. The searing honesty with which he talked about his problems was at times shocking, and I suppose it was no surprise when Prince William wanted to use Campbell to help spread the word even further.

A few weeks later, an encrypted email appeared in one of my inboxes, containing Campbell's interview with Prince William, the one we would publish that spring. Never before had the prince talked with such honesty about the death of his mother, his attitudes towards the tabloid press or, indeed, his issues with depression. 'Practically everything in my charitable life in the end is to do with mental health, whether it be homelessness, veterans' welfare, my wife and the work she is doing on addiction,' he said. 'So much of what we do comes back to mental health. Also, if I think about my current job as a helicopter pilot with the Air Ambulance service in East Anglia, my first job there was a suicide and it really affected me. I have been to a number of suicides, self-harms, overdoses.'

He also talked about the imminent twentieth anniversary of his mother's death, which I felt was the real purpose of the initiative. 'I am not looking forward to it, no, but I am in a better place about it than I have been for a long time, where I can talk about her more openly, talk about her more honestly, and I can remember her better, and publicly talk about her better. It has taken me almost 20 years to get to that stage. I still find it difficult now because at the time it was so raw. And also, it is not like most people's grief, because everyone else knows about it, everyone knows the story, everyone knows her. It is a different situation for most people who lose someone they love; it can be hidden away, or they can choose if they want to share their story. I don't have that choice really. Everyone has seen it all.'

I'd arranged for William to see a transcript of the interview in case he said something he wanted to correct. This wasn't normal practice for us, but it was important he felt as comfortable as possible with the process. He only requested one change; that we delete the name of the tabloid newspaper (not the *Sun*, not the *Mirror* and not the *Star*) he blamed for the death of his mother.

Diana's death in 1997 was an example of how different the world was when it was ruled by print. Sarah and I were on holiday in the Dordogne, staying at Tony and Janey Elliott's house, and we travelled back to London the day after her death. As soon as we landed at Heathrow, I was desperate for a newspaper, but there was none anywhere, not in the airport nor any of the newsagents near where we lived. My strongest memory is of roaming the empty streets of the West End as though I was in a post-apocalyptic wasteland. There were no people and zero papers, although I eventually found a much-thumbed copy of the *Sunday Express* by Marble Arch tube. Still got it somewhere.

William knew we wanted to amplify his interview as much as possible, and so we started talking about the possibility of a shoot, some pictures that would help articulate his message around the world. So on Thursday, 20 April 2017, myself and two other *GQ* delegates, Jonathan Heaf and Paul Solomons, made our way to Kensington Palace to photograph the future king. Along with our photographer, Norman Jean Roy, and his two assistants, we walked quietly through the gatehouse, where we were effortlessly guided into the Duke and Duchess of Cambridge's private quarters. I had been asked to propose three names for the role of photographer, and we ended up lobbying for someone who we knew from experience could do the job without becoming overawed by the situation, someone who was going to take direction, and who understood that stealth was as important as composition. Having shot dozens of covers for us, we knew Norman was the person for the job.

We were all as relaxed as we could be in this situation, although we must have looked like the stiffest people in the room as soon as

William and Kate walked in. There were no formalities, no briefing on protocol before their arrival, just huge smiles and some quick yet overwhelmingly personable introductions – 'Hello, I'm William,' 'Hello, I'm Kate' – before we started chatting. It would be indelicate to discuss what we talked about, but while Norman busied himself with making sure our cover shot was going to be delivered precisely to our specifications, Paul, Jonathan and I suggested how we might spend the next couple of hours most productively. We spent the first fifteen minutes with the pair of them discussing previous *GQ* covers, most notably our recent Ed Sheeran cover, our David Cameron one, and the Damien Hirst/Rihanna cover we produced for our anniversary in 2013. They both wanted to know precisely what the pictures would look like, how they would be cropped, and whether or not there would be fashion credits. Kate knew a lot more about the process than we expected; she was also disarmingly flirtatious. We were all a little bit spellbound. 'She could flirt with a tree,' I said, when the royals were out of earshot. When she walked into the room while her husband was changing, it was almost as though she had a kind of Ready Brek glow.

The family pictures happened by accident, as both George and Charlotte were more than intrigued by the mini-circus unfolding around their father, a photographic session that looked for a while as though it was being art directed by the duchess herself, who appeared to have as keen a creative eye as anyone else on the shoot. The shoot happened so quickly, and was so easy to organise, that we had to pinch ourselves at times (a few days later, I got a text message from Paul saying, 'Did that really happen, or did I imagine it?'), and as the day went so incredibly smoothly, this was a testament to William and Kate's personal team as well as to the duke and duchess themselves. Considering the ridiculous hoops we were usually asked to jump through in order to slip into the orbit of even the most entry-level boldface names (you know who you are, you ghastly people), William and Kate's attitude was refreshingly casual, and somewhat transformative. Hollywood could learn a thing or two from our young royal family.

This entire project was produced by a very tight team; the rest of the editorial office, along with the publishing and sales departments, initially knew nothing about it. The story was produced in secret, not because we didn't trust our own teams – and the circle of trust grew slowly day by day, as others needed to be included in the process – but because the way in which magazines are produced meant that a rogue corrupted photograph or incomplete transcript of the interview might have found its way into the wrong hands. There was so much clandestine behaviour in Vogue House that for a few weeks I even felt as though my own conversations were encrypted.

AND THEN WE DID CHARLES. In September 2018, on a purpose-built stage in the Turbine Hall in London's Tate Modern, the then Prince of Wales received a special award at the *GQ* awards. At the twenty-first annual shindig, William and Harry's father opened by saying, 'First of all, I really wanted to apologise for being wrongly dressed. When they first announced I was winning the Men of the Year award, I felt sure it must have been some kind of ill-deserved fashion award. In fashion terms I'm like a stopped clock. I'm fashionable once every twenty-five years.'

I'd heard him say this before, but the crowd loved it. Never let it be said Charles can't judge a room. In front of six hundred of the most famous, most connected and most entitled people in the world, he played the cards of self-deprecation so deftly that for the next ten minutes he had the audience in his palms.

He also quickly got another gag in .

'I'm grateful to *GQ* for giving me a preview of my obituary.' Mocking the actual size of the gong, he said, 'I'm enormously grateful for this award and I see it's something I can throw at a burglar.'

I worked on the story myself, and spent the best part of six months accompanying him on various official jaunts and making many unofficial visits to St James's Palace. And everywhere he went, he shook hands; in one way, it was what he did for a living. He would keep up a constant stream of small talk, a fusillade of chat. Sometimes these were conversations he may not remember, but you could guarantee the person he was talking to would remember it for ever, making the onus rather more loaded. As he moved on to the next person in line, he'd often turn around and point to the person he'd just finished with, an emphatic gesture that appeared to imply that what had passed between them was of such importance that he wasn't going to forget it in a hurry. He would occasionally finish with one of his well-worn bon mots, such as 'as long as you don't get too many interruptions from people like me'.

When doing his rounds, Charles had a 'spontaneous' laugh, not unlike the one employed by Keith Richards. Now and then, Richards laughed for no apparent reason, almost as if the ridiculousness of his life had just occurred to him, wheezing and giggling at the preposterous nature of his good fortune. Similarly, HRH's face would occasionally explode into paroxysms of good-natured gurning, in the way it probably did fifty years ago when he mucked about with Spike Milligan and the rest of the Goons. It would be easy to assume that the laughs were designed to convince people he was having a good time and yet it looked to me like a double bluff, with the laughs disguising the fact that he actually was having a good time. But when he wasn't confecting the maximum of amusement out of everything around him, it would have been impossible not to allow himself a wry smile every once in a while.

One day, having travelled to the old BBC Television Centre in White City, west London, to open the latest outpost of Nick Jones's Soho House empire, he broke free from his minders and jumped into a lift with Jones as it made its way to one of the bars on the upper floors. Jones pointed out that he was giving him special dispensation today, as no one would normally be allowed into one of his clubs wearing a tie. 'I'll make a note of that,' said the prince, 'should I come back.'

All the Madmen

My Rape

Losing my virginity

WHEN WE FIRST MET JON Hamm's Don Draper in *Mad Men*, back in 2007, he looked like a billboard for his own charisma. It was 1960, peak Madison Avenue, and he was the king of his street – handsome as a statue, dressed to seduce, a master manipulator of men, women and messages. He was the *GQ* man incarnate – confident and well-groomed on the outside, a portmanteau of insecurities underneath. Designed and written as a character who could read other people but who couldn't read himself, Draper's motivations were at once both transparent and completely opaque. Which made him and the show he carried a more than perfect vehicle for all the things a *GQ* man might worry about – in 2007 as well as 1960. Draper was hypnotic, as were the rest of the chorus at the Sterling Cooper agency. Matthew

Weiner's show became that rare thing: a pop-culture phenomenon, as our writer Stuart McGurk said at the time, a watercooler show about the watercooler. It tackled the macro and the micro, from the trivialities of sex and success to legacy and mortality. I would eventually squeeze five covers out of *Mad Men* – January Jones, who played Betty, Draper's platinum-bobbed, repressed, Hitchcockian wife, in May 2009; John Slattery, who played the super-slick silver fox Roger Sterling, in October 2012; Jon Hamm twice, in October 2010 and September 2014; and Christina Hendricks, who played the pneumatic Jessica Rabbitesque Joan Harris, in August 2010.

I made sure they all came to our awards, too. Hamm came, when he was still drinking, and I took him to Soho House afterwards, where he spent most of the night sitting with David Beckham, performing a handsome-off. Slattery came too, the following year, as did Elisabeth Moss. January Jones came to one of the Elton parties we held at Cecconi's in LA, and was so cooperative she spent over an hour doing pictures. Nobody did this, but she was on the way up.

Mad Men was incontestably the best drama to come out of America since *The Sopranos*. Initially enjoyed for its surface smarts, its design sense (the early sixties never failed to look good on camera, small screen or not) and the fastidious men's clothes, the longer you watched, the longer you allowed yourself to be bewitched, the longer you realised this wasn't just a noirish soap dressed up as a fashion show. This was a world of impending change that echoed *Sweet Smell of Success*, *The Apartment* and *Days of Wine and Roses*, a world of adjustment, a world of turmoil.

The world of the three-Martini lunch that Weiner had been able to imagine with such skill was praised not so much for its flagrant sexuality as its exact opposite: the buttoned-up nature of the show made it even sexier. And it was all because of HBO. As the cable station turned it down, it eventually ended up on a small network – AMC – which meant any overt sexuality and profanity had to be toned down. *Mad Men* was all very clipped and was all the better for it.

Weiner worked as a scriptwriter and television producer for twenty years before *Mad Men*. He wrote the pilot back in 1999, sending it three years later as an example of his writing to David Chase, who was then looking for writers for *The Sopranos*. Chase promptly hired Weiner as a writer and executive producer, creating, among many other classic moments, the episode in which Tony Soprano murders his nephew Christopher. Weiner chose to focus on advertising as 'it was a great way to talk about the image we have of ourselves, versus who we really are. And admen were the rock stars of that era – creative, cocky, anti-authority. They made a lot of money and they lived hard.'

An obsessive, and a glutton for detail, Weiner wrote and produced each episode, directed as many as he could, and helped choose the actors, the furniture, the clothes and even the hairstyles. A show that deliberately moved uneasily from the generic Rat Pack tropes of the fifties to the social and cultural flashpoints of the sixties, *Mad Men* created its own orbit, its own generic world, its own merchandising. 'It's very *Mad Men*,' we said at the time. And we said it a lot.

For anyone who was a devotee of the show, it was difficult to forget the intensity of the last scene in the final episode. Having just disengaged from a group therapy session where a man called Leonard tells him about his dream of being left unwanted in a fridge, we see Don Draper meditating on top of California's Big Sur cliffs. As a cross-legged teacher carefully unfurls his mantra – 'The new day brings new hope. The lives we've led. The lives we've yet to lead. A new day. New ideas. A new you . . .' – a slight grin begins to curl its way over Draper's face. And as he does so, we cut to the opening frames of the famous 1971 Coke ad, 'I'd Like to Buy the World a Coke' (which was turned into a massively successful hit, 'I'd Like to Teach the World to Sing' by the New Seekers).

Was Don smiling because he had reached a new level of consciousness, having started finally to make peace with himself? Or was he happy because he'd just come up with the idea for the Coke ad? While Weiner was guarded about the meaning of the finale – 'The ambiguous relationship we have with advertising is part of why I did the show – why not end the show with the greatest commercial ever made?' – Jon

Hamm was in two minds about the flex of the scene. 'We see him in an incredibly vulnerable place, surrounded by strangers, and he reaches out to the only person he can at that moment, and it's this stranger,' he says. 'My take is that the next day, he wakes up in this beautiful place, and has this serene moment of understanding, and realises who he is. And who he is, is an advertising man. And so, this thing comes to him. There's a way to see it in a completely cynical way, and say, "Wow, that's awful." But I think that for Don, it represents some kind of understanding and comfort in this incredibly unquiet, uncomfortable life that he has led.'

Either way, the scene highlights the fact that by the early seventies, wellness – or at least what wellness was called before it became a genuine leisure pursuit – had been turned into an industry as well as a lifestyle. Self-awareness, self-discovery, homespun spiritualism, therapy, clinical psychology, New Age counterculture, Western esotericism, attempting to find peace in a frantic world or simply any general exploration of mind and body, by 1971 the Age of Aquarius had arrived (albeit a little early). If the sixties allowed anyone in the West to 'turn on, tune it and drop out' – opening the sluice gates to such an extent that literally all forms of expression and creativity, however marginalised, were validated by the media – by the beginning of the seventies some of the more transactional manifestations began to creep into society proper. This was what Tom Wolfe famously labelled 'the Me Decade', a focus on self, the analysis of self, and an increasing exploration of our psychic wiring. 'In one form or another they arrive at an axiom first propounded by the Gnostic Christians some 1800 years ago,' he wrote. 'Namely, that at the apex of every human soul there exists a spark of the light of God.'

Wolfe wasn't exactly being empathetic – that was never his beat – but empathy was a defining characteristic of the new ways in which personal development became so popular. By the noughties we were as interested in the wellbeing of others almost as much as we were in the wellbeing of ourselves, and were living in a culture where 'internal welfare' was not something to be embarrassed about, or shy away from. We were far more prepared to discuss our problems with friends and empowered enough to suggest help where we saw that some might be needed.

LIKE MANY PEOPLE I KNOW, I had been seeing a therapist on and off for years but had never felt the need to shout about it. The older I got, though, the past started to catch up with me. Mine had probably never left me. I spent most of my childhood being hit by my father, when he wasn't hitting my mother, that is. I was beaten relentlessly and repeatedly, hit so hard that for years I found it difficult to speak without stammering, finding it impossible to repeat my own name, 'don't' and Dylan both beginning with a D. For most of my life, all I could remember about the violence came in abstract, fuzzy images, and I managed to pretty much blank most of it out. It's called disassociation. When I became a teenager, I began treating it almost as a badge of honour, like having a criminal for a father, advertising what a tough time I'd had, an excuse for delinquent behaviour and appalling results at school. I'd occasionally tell other people about it, but not often. And then I just buried it, for years, just put it into another box, one I rarely ever looked at.

Through therapy, I gradually remembered more and more of the things that happened to me when I was a boy. The trauma of childhood was scooped out of me by therapy – and it was examined, recontextualised and eventually sent on its way. In a way, I was going in both directions at once, discovering things and then burying them. The more I delved into my past, the more I looked for explanations, the more I realised it was my father's own childhood (he too was beaten), his frustrations (sexual and professional perhaps), that would have led to much of his behaviour. Which although not an excuse was at least a signpost. There was also the not inconsiderable fact that back in the sixties, walloping your children was simply thought of as a way of keeping them in line.

Exploring my childhood obviously reflected on the family I was creating. Having children was never something I was especially interested in. My childhood had not exactly been a great template, and it wasn't until my future wife gave me an ultimatum that I forced myself to confront this. Sarah said that unless we were going to have kids then we had to separate as she knew she wanted them. And we had some. Two, in fact, and they changed my life in ways I thought unimaginable. As soon as Edie and then Georgia were born, everything became about them, and everything became because of them. From my perspective, I wanted to give them everything I hadn't had – principally a warm, nurturing environment that didn't involve me whacking them every five minutes – but what I got in return gave me an insight into family relationships I had never considered before. Having children gave me a purpose I had never entertained, imagined or, indeed, anticipated. Edie and Georgia were simply everything. Having a house full of noise and laughter was completely intoxicating. I used to think I enjoyed being by myself, but having children made me understand the opposite is true.

Of course, one of the joys was being able to spoil them, even if both Sarah and I went out of our way to say we weren't. One way I was determined to spoil them was through holidays, however, and this was for a very particular reason. I didn't want the girls getting to the age of sixteen or seventeen and start going off on motorbike holidays in Europe with spotty oiks in leather jackets (boys like I had been). I wanted them to have become so accustomed to fancy holidays that they would continue to come away with us. I wanted to keep them as they were. If I had understood anything about human nature, I would have known that in reality they would end up doing both.

Over the years there was some massive reappraisal, and some unlocking of boxes. I even told my therapist about being raped when I was seventeen. I was still living in High Wycombe when it happened. I had been out in London, by myself, exploring the West End clubs that I couldn't explore with anyone else as no one else appeared to be that interested, going to the punk venues in search of excitement. Having caught the last train, at Wycombe station I'd accepted a lift from someone I sort of knew, who was going to drive me home. We didn't go home, but instead went back to his flat to drink and smoke. He was friendly, maybe around thirty, and all I remember is the music he played – a succession of Paul Williams albums – and the drink. We were drinking spirits. Neat. Vodka, I think. The next thing I knew, I woke up, naked, in his bed, being raped.

My first thoughts were: this isn't right. And it hurts. I was seventeen and still a virgin, only now I wasn't. For a fleeting moment I thought, *Am I enjoying this?*, and then just as quickly the thought came bouncing back: no I am not. I was embarrassed, and told him to stop; which, after a while, he did.

But I had been raped.

I WASN'T SURE HOW TO process all this, and so I didn't. I shut up about it, hardly telling anyone. Occasionally I would mention it in my gauche, teenage way, almost showing off, in the same way I did a few years later when I was slashed across the back of the neck with a cutthroat razor after leaving that pub in King's Cross. As I grew up, I simply forgot about it, and hardly mentioned it to anyone. The reason I didn't talk about it was because I didn't think my way of dealing with it was particularly helpful or useful to other people who had suffered the same thing. I had managed successfully to put it in a box, but I didn't think that was an especially mature way of coping with it; not only that, but my indifference seemed to minimise people who had been in a similar situation and had been traumatised by it. While I realised I had successfully made it impossible for the rape to affect my life, I also knew this wasn't going to act as any kind of solace to anyone else. To admit that being raped hadn't had any discernible effect on my life felt somewhat disrespectful. So, I shut up about it and got on with my life. There may have been a bit of self-hatred for a while, some disgust at my body, but I think I was too strong for that. The whole thing felt unnecessary, like being beaten up by my father. It was just something else I wasn't going to bother with. Not at all. I was going to be fine. I didn't know where I was going, but I absolutely knew in my heart of hearts that I was going to get there.

In 2016, I went on a self-awareness course, something I had never considered before, not until my wife said I had to otherwise we couldn't stay together. Apparently, my behaviour was becoming so impossible (I was emotionally detached, never 'present' and unable to empathise or emote, plus I tended to go from nought to sixty in a nanosecond) that the family were walking on eggshells. So I did the Hoffman Process, and I loved it.

A personal development course with a difference, the Hoffman Process involves a variety of therapeutic techniques, including Eastern mysticism, deep meditation, a form of group therapy and a lot of physically expressive work. The process draws ingredients from various well-worn modalities including Gestalt, neuro linguistic programming, cognitive behavioural therapy, bioenergetics and some fairly extreme psychodynamic work. It has become, for many, a life-changing experience that can clinically remove negative habits. Many who finish the process become evangelical, and it has been compared by many to a form of rehab; I have friends who've been in places such as the Priory, the Meadows and Cottonwood in Arizona, and they all say that they did similar techniques. The practitioners tear you down and then build you back up again, teaching you tools and techniques to help you change the old behavioural patterns that might be preventing you from feeling fully alive, helping free you to make conscious choices that will improve your relationships with the people around you. It is intensive, and often transformational.

The salient belief of the Hoffman Process is the importance of childhood, or, more precisely, the emotional discovery of the truth about the unique history of our childhood. This is what the psychotherapist Alice Miller calls the drama of being a child. 'In order to become whole, we must try to discover our own personal truth,' she says, 'a truth that may cause pain before giving us a new sphere of freedom.' This is now a popular psychological belief, fast-tracked by John Bowlby's attachment theory, which believes that mental health and behavioural patterns are largely attributed to early childhood.

One night in 2017, I went along to an induction evening at Regent's University, in Regent's Park, in London, to see what all the fuss was about. I sat at the back of the room looking for all the world like a broadly drawn secret agent from the fifties, with my collar turned up, and my hat pulled down, convinced that no one was going to see me. And as I listened to half-a-dozen Hoffman graduates get up and discuss the course, telling us all how good it had been for them – and they were nothing if not passionate in their espousal – we were told time and time again that it's best if you don't know too much about it before you go, principally in case it scares you off.

How right they were. Six months later, I turned up at a small country house hotel on the south coast along with twenty-three other nervous inductees. To say we were all wary is a massive understatement, and while a few kind souls went out of their way to be nice to each other, most of us were grunting and staring at our shoes. We were then encouraged to walk into a room and take our seats in a circle, where we could all scrutinise each other. And this is largely where we stayed for the next week – of course, we were allowed to eat, sleep and use the bathroom, and occasionally to socialise, but broadly speaking this was where we stayed, going on a literal and metaphorical journey that I would imagine none of us on the course will ever forget. It all feels distant now, but I will never forget the experience itself. The Hoffman didn't involve a personality transplant, and I didn't start walking around with a sense of entitled transcendence, but what it gave me was a whole bunch of context.

I had previously been wary of personal development courses, as I figured they were either designed for those who couldn't make it on their own, or who had made it and were starting the slow descent to oblivion and wanted a way to cope with it. But then I'm rarely surprised by how shallow I can be sometimes. My narrative was a simple one. I loudly boasted that I was only on the course under duress, that my wife had made me go, and that I really didn't want to be there. I probably appeared terribly arrogant.

Technically the process doesn't involve group therapy, but as you need to be 'seen' while experiencing many of the emotions conjured up here, you are hiding (or not) in plain sight. The Hoffman Process is nothing less than traumatic at times, but you need to experience the trauma in order to cope with the euphoria that comes later. As I say, if you knew what the course involves then you probably wouldn't want to have anything to do with it, but rarely have I found a week so fulfilling as the one I spent on it. It is difficult to describe the intensity of some of the group work, and out of courtesy to the other people on the course I'm not going to tell. Suffice it to say that you are encouraged to go back into your childhood – *deeply* into your childhood – in a way that I didn't think was possible. Even though it is a process driven by emotion, intellectually it is fascinating.

As 'patients', if you like, we were carefully guided through the proceedings, and as we were working from seven-thirty in the morning to eight-thirty at night, and as it was an extremely busy programme (with various rituals occurring throughout the week), there was not much time for going off-piste (the only activity I found time for was watching the dawn break over the white cliffs of Dover). After a few days, I realised I was in fact being played, as the tsunami of emotions I was experiencing had all been carefully orchestrated by the three teachers in front of me. Everything I experienced was real, although each emotion had been carefully, methodically teased out of me.

During one session where I was forced to recall some of the more unpleasant memories of my early days, I not only remembered that I would be locked under the stairs after being punched, but also that a lot of the abuse I suffered must have been at a terribly early age. My brother, who is five years younger than me, didn't suffer any beatings himself, and although mine continued after he was born, for some reason they were more infrequent. I obviously found both pieces of information deeply troubling. I wasn't in therapy to wallow in self-pity, but it certainly caused me to think when my analyst said that if the abuse had taken place today, my father would have been in jail. As it is, he nearly was, having come close to killing a boy when he was at school.

You are encouraged to do a substantial amount of writing on the course, some of which you burn, and some you keep. Even the stuff I was told to burn, I copied, as I wanted to remember every moment, every rapidly written syllable. I also found the writing incredibly liberating, and having spent thirty years trying to hone my craft, writing as a form of expression was a revelation. You write and write and write and write . . . In one of the letters to my father (the letters you write are never sent), I found the following: '. . . but fuck I found you terrifying. Really, really fucking terrifying . . .'

We had to share a room, accept a shower rota and forgo all forms of electronic communication. No phones, no emails, no texts, no nothing. We were not allowed newspapers, magazines or books, and were discouraged from visiting the local town. Essentially, we were required to push the world away and focus entirely on ourselves. It took me a few days to acclimatise and get used to this new regime, but it slowly dawned on me that, having spent thirty-five years working for other people, and at no point during that time spending any real time on myself, I would be crazy not to accede completely.

We were also encouraged to step out of our comfort zones, to confront people, to look them squarely in the eye, openly discuss our feelings . . . and *share*. We had to stand up in front of everyone else and admit our fears and insecurities in the hope that by doing so they would eventually fall away. As one graduate said, the Hoffman Process scrapes you to the bone and publicly exposes you.

Looking back over the notes I made during the week, I came across the following: 'Trauma', 'abuse', 'destructive patterns', 'lack of guidance', 'perpetual anxiety', 'DISIDENTIFYING', 'Like being in a disaster movie or an Agatha Christie drama', 'wish I had done this years ago', 'transference', 'new behavioural expression', 'negative road map'. What was it like? Like an emotional rollercoaster in VR, AR and 3D – squared. A week of magical thinking.

The penultimate day was one of the happiest I've ever had, experiencing the kind of childlike glee I didn't know I was still capable of. If I had been asked to sing 'I'd Like to Teach the World to Sing', I would have sung it, gladly, without a care in the world. The process underscored yet again that life is short and needs to be enjoyed.

*

TWENTY-SIXTEEN HAD AN UNNECESSARILY POIGNANT ending. We all knew Adrian Gill had cancer, and we knew the signals were bad. Some of us had spoken to him and he was remarkably frank about the discovery. 'I've got the Full English,' he would say, referring to the way his cancer had spread from his neck to his lungs and also his brain. He had tumours everywhere. He and I messaged each other, and spoke on the phone, and then I literally bumped into him in one of our favourite restaurants, Colbert, in Sloane Square, one Saturday in the late autumn. Adrian was with his wife Nicola and their twins, and looked predictably awful: puffy, bloated, and a vague approximation of the man I knew. We hugged, chatted, and that was that.

He died shortly afterwards, aged sixty-two, the same age Christopher Hitchens was when he passed away. In *Dilettante*, Dana Brown's engaging memoir concerning his years as an assistant and then an editor at *Vanity Fair*, he writes affectionately about them both.

> Adrian always looked up to Christopher. I don't believe in the afterlife or heaven, but I hope there is one, if only so those two could have gotten to know each other over these past few years, talk about politics and art, poetry and culture and history. They'd agree on as much as they'd disagree on. They would debate, argue. They would giggle with laughter. It would be an eternal conversation that would no doubt attract a crowd, becoming the longest-running show in heaven. Maybe Adrian would have gotten Christopher to stop drinking. Or maybe Christopher would have gotten Adrian to start drinking again.

A few months earlier, when a mutual friend had asked him how he was, Adrian had replied that he had cancer. When our friend asked what kind, Adrian shot back with, 'The end of the road kind.'

Like a Postcard of a Golden Retriever

Edie and Georgia

Edie, Georgia and Sarah by Barry Lategan, London, 2003

SO, WE WERE IN SAN Francisco, Tony Bennett's city by the bay, and the four of us – me, Sarah, Edie (twelve) and Georgia (ten) – were just about to go out for a walk. This was at the end of October, a month when the West Coast's weather was notoriously unpredictable, as Indian summer turned into Hong Kong shower and back again at the drop of a San Francisco Giants baseball cap, and when the city started to lean into the pre-apocalyptic cyberpunk rain of *Blade Runner.* And since it had started to pour heavily (Albert Hammond once wrote a song called 'It Never Rains in Southern California', which was a bit like saying it never rains in Wales), I swapped my thin black loafers for my bulbous bright-blue trainers.

This was sensible, I thought, because although I almost never wore them outside the gym (why would I?), I didn't have any boots with me, and it didn't make sense to wear leather shoes in the wet.

Not such a big deal, right?

Wrong, apparently.

Now, I wouldn't have said my family were particularly judgemental, but just as we were due to leave the hotel room, my wife and my two daughters suddenly looked at my feet as though I were wearing pink fluffy carpet slippers. It was as if the Style Police had turned up en masse, masquerading as the three wise monkeys: See No Evil, Hear No Evil and Actually That's A Big Fat Lie As All Three Of Us Are Going To Be Extremely Evil Indeed.

'Er, OK, Papa, what are you wearing on your feet?' said Edie, with obvious amusement.

'What do you mean? I'm wearing trainers. Obviously.'

'Yes, we can see that, but why?'

'Have you seen the weather? It's pouring down!'

'Yes, but there's no way we're going out with you dressed like that.'

Suffice to say, as I refused to change, they wouldn't talk to me for the rest of the day and forced me to walk ten paces behind (I'm not making any of this up). Later, when they did, all they could do was laugh. We went up to Chinatown, down to the museums, over to Haight-Ashbury and in and out of Union Square, and whenever I tried to say something enthusiastic about where we were, either Sarah or one of the children would say, 'But what would you know? You're wearing bright-blue trainers and you look like a Smurf.'

And it was true. What *did* I know? After all, I was wearing trainers. Ever since I could remember, I had given men a hard time for wearing trainers for non-recreational purposes, for using them as fashion items, for celebrating them as examples of sartorial emancipation rather than ugly rubber things you fling on your feet when you fancy a run. In my eyes, training shoes had always made their owners look like children. And not in a good way, either. No, in my eyes training shoes had always been reductive, had always made their owners look like Teletubbies rather than masters of sartorial elegance.

Now, as Edie and Georgia got older, I'd become accustomed to them passing judgement on what I intended to wear to work in the morning. Not only was their sarcasm somewhat expected, but to me it was like water off a duck's back (or rather water off the back of an Alfred Dunhill bespoke brown mohair, two-piece, one-button suit with a two-inch shawl collar). When one of them said something about the unsuitability of my tie, or something like 'Bad shirt/jacket combo,' I could ignore it, safe in the knowledge that they were wrong, and I was right.

In this case, though, I knew they were right.

When I suggested that it was highly unlikely that either of the girls were going to bump into anyone they knew, they again shrugged and resorted to their (by now) default position: 'So what?'

As San Francisco was experiencing its own little monsoon, the Jones family took refuge in the Museum of Modern Art. And as we walked around the floors, discussing the pictures and laughing at the state of some of the other people who had come in out of the rain, I saw one particularly unsavoury character – a phenomenally badly dressed thirty-something chap, a weird homunculus with ratty ginger hair, a stained purple sweatshirt and the oddest pair of camouflage trousers (tight, turquoise) I'd ever seen. And the kicker?

Yup. He was wearing my shoes.

EVEN THOUGH SARAH BORE THE brunt of the work at home, I threw myself into parenthood. Life suddenly had two very distinct gears: work, and the girls. Sarah and I were obsessed about them, not just the operational issues, the guard rails and the care; but also the lore – what could we teach them in order to make them as perfect as possible? We were part of the generation who thought we could be totally prescriptive about children, who thought we could make the perfect cake as long as we used the right ingredients. The brutal reality hit us on a daily basis, although the counternarrative was the personalities they appeared to be developing without any help from us. They weren't just children, they were small people, and they had ideas about things we hadn't taught them at all.

When they were a lot younger (indeed, when I was a lot younger), I naively thought that I would be cool dad. Unlike my father and his father before him, I would be cool. I had a fancy job, had links to the fashion industry, was on nodding terms with half-a-dozen pop stars and could lay my hands on tickets for concerts, film premieres and the normal kind of stuff that most people in the media can access, should they choose to. Honestly, how difficult could it be to be cool dad? Cool Dad, even? In CAPS! COOL DAD!

But it wasn't long before I was disavowed of this. Edie had just had her fourth birthday when I was unceremoniously made aware that I wasn't cool at all, not by a long stretch of the imagination. No. While she liked the access, the spectacle of the cavalcade of strange people who regularly traipsed through the house (some of whom she recognised from television) and the occasional party she was allowed to attend, no, she didn't think I was cool at all.

I was, simply, a dad. Any dad. NOT EVEN IN CAPS. (My friend Stuart had a similar problem; his daughter Islay, a good friend of Edie's, had told him he wasn't ever allowed to use the word 'cool' because his relationship with it was so approximate.)

Once, late for school, Edie brushed by me in the kitchen, looked me up and down and said to no one in particular, although clearly directed at me, 'Brave.'

When Georgia finally reached the age when she could wear what she liked to school – which obviously meant her uniform was banished to that part of her wardrobe where she hid all the things she'd stolen from me over the years (David Bowie T-shirts, button badges, baseball caps, phone chargers – literally dozens of phone chargers) – she started wearing what she wore in the evening, with her friends.

One morning, as she passed me in the hall on her way out, I stopped her in her tracks.

'You're not going to like this,' I said, with my hands on my hips.

She gave me a sneer.

'What?' she said.

'Well, thirty years ago, probably to the very day, I was wearing exactly the same clothes as you . . .'

She then gave me an incredulous look, followed by a roll of the eyes and then a curt, 'Seriously?'

'Oh, yes,' I said, and proceeded to reel off the offending items: one blue nylon MA-1 flying jacket, one white T-shirt, one pair of Levi 501s, one logo belt (in her case Gucci, in mine, a 1986 Gucci knockoff), one pair of black Loake's loafers with rubberised soles and finally one pair of extremely white socks.

Predictably, Georgia said I was talking rubbish, pulled on her headphones and promptly stormed off to school.

That night, after some fairly furious rummaging, I produced photographic evidence of our sartorial clash, but after studying it for a good three seconds, she simply threw the picture back at me and went upstairs to her room.

'You look ridiculous,' she said by way of a parting shot. (This reminded me of the time I tried to explain that Drake's 'Hotline Bling' contained a sample from Timmy Thomas's 'Why Can't We Live Together'; when I played my daughters the original, they looked at me as though I was mad.)

Like her sister, Georgia thought she had the right to think of her parents as complete and utter losers. This was brought home to me when I took them to Spain on holiday when they were eleven and thirteen, while Sarah stayed at home to work. A week before we set off, the girls gave me a list of things I wasn't allowed to wear, at least not while I was in their company. This was quite a litany, and included flip-flops (unmanly, apparently), 'man jewellery' (gold watches, neck chains, earrings or 'unnecessary' bracelets), training shoes (they listed these twice), cycling shorts (although why anyone would want to wear cycling shorts on a beach holiday is beyond even me), and anything yellow, orange or 'hot pink' (which I thought was fair enough).

Having been given this list, I made the mistake of asking if there were other things I shouldn't wear or do and was then rewarded with a barrage of items that led me to believe they had been thinking about this for some considerable time. As their father, I was apparently not allowed to text OMG, LOL, Wicked or Respect. I was not allowed to wear fluorescent clothing, football shirts or baseball caps, nor hoodies, skinny jeans or anything by Abercrombie & Fitch, Hollister or Jack Wills (even though the thought of actually doing any of those things was preposterous). Oh, and according to my perspicacious progenies, Porsches were for old men, and Mini Coopers were not for men at all.

On the plane I was given further instructions about particular things I wouldn't be allowed to do in public, namely sing, dance or – my favourite, this – talk to anyone. The girls had been secretly briefed by their mother, and when I explained to them that there might be occasions when they needed to bathe, change their clothes, brush their hair and cover themselves in suntan cream, I was told they had already been informed that their father would be useless at policing such things and knew in this respect they'd have to fend for themselves. Because of this I became paranoid when either one of them went outside and covered them in so much factor 40 that they emerged from the villa each morning looking – and smelling – as though they were about to be surrounded by some par-boiled vegetables and put in an oven.

In truth, our three-amigo vacation was a revelation, and although they largely ignored my jokes with an Olympian disdain, expertly disengaged from conversation (using three words where twenty would normally do), openly mocked me ('Daddy, you've got moobs like Jagger . . .'), I discovered a lot, some of which was genuinely revelatory ('I like her first husband better,' said Georgia one day, referring to someone we know, 'even though I've never met him').

In the end, it rained every day, and so we spent every hour together, eating, laughing, sleeping, playing bridge (I lost, almost religiously) and generally enjoying ourselves in ways I don't think any of us previously thought possible.

SARAH AND I WOULD SOMETIMES bump into young parents at parties who would openly disparage their children, and bang on about how Tarquin, Bumblebee and Snaresbrook were ruining their social lives, and that they couldn't wait to bundle them off to boarding school. We never entertained this as we wanted to spend as much time with them as possible.

These parents would say things like, 'The trouble with children is that they are not returnable.' Or 'My husband and I are either going to buy a dog or have another child. We can't decide whether to ruin our carpet or ruin our lives.' They even said things like, 'I take my children everywhere, but they always find their way back home.'

We were not the sort of family who liked visiting places with kids' clubs, essentially because it meant we would never see our children, which was why we went on holiday together in the first place. I didn't see as much of my children as I'd like, and we always tried to plan holidays where we would be living out of each other's pockets.

We really did take them everywhere, even on trips where we could easily have left them at home. One summer we took them on a Zambian road trip with our friends Leatherman and Gillie. We were staying in their house in Lusaka and were going to drive from the Zambian capital all the way to Mfuwe, on the edge of the South Luangwa National Park, deep in the heart of Zambia – a 500-mile, ten-hour journey that was fulfilling in the most surprising ways. We had planned this for ages. It is one of the great road trips, up there with New York to Los Angeles, any section of the Pan-American Highway or one of the great European jaunts, such as Paris to the Italian lakes.

One morning Leatherman and I loaded up the Land Cruiser with guns, beer and children, and were on the road by 6 a.m. We were taking his boys while Sarah and Gillie were taking the girls. We were going to see who could get there first, and the girls had no interest in joining the losing side. They'd spent their lives in cars driven by both of us and had decided to go with the less neurotic pairing. They took great delight in telling us this, too.

The roads were so empty that we drove for over an hour before we saw another human being. We passed dozens of teenage boys wearing Chelsea tops selling charcoal by the side of the road, narrowly missing cows, goats, chickens and pigs as they darted across our path. Dirt tracks turned into tarmac and then back again when you least expected it. You needed to treat the roads with caution. Cars were still status symbols (there were cheap Japanese saloons everywhere, although you couldn't beat a Land Cruiser, as its two petrol tanks meant you could drive to Timbuktu and back again without filling up), and their drivers liked showing them off.

Roads were status symbols too, especially if they were tarmacked. There was money in them, you see. When a cross-country highway was finally greenlit, the farms it crossed suddenly turned out to be owned by local councillors. But then corruption, nepotism and needless bureaucracy were rife. A typical example of Zambian bureaucracy was a council official near the Luangwa Valley demanding tenants supply their fingerprints on an annual basis, 'in case they change'.

This was a place where distances were still measured by alcohol consumption. How long did it take you to get from Victoria Falls to Lake Tanganyika? Oh, about two-thirds of a bottle of Frangelico.

'There's no point using a TomTom,' said Leatherman, lighting up another cherry-flavoured cigar (a bizarre affectation, I have to admit), 'as all it'll say is "Turn left in 380 miles."'

Leatherman had a bad dose of muzungu malaria (the white man's hangover), having bumped into a case of red wine the night before, and so let me do most of the driving. Which was becoming something of a problem. For a while, I felt a little like Mad Max, the original road warrior, although after about twenty minutes I started to feel like a technician on a children's television programme. The cabin of Leatherman's Toyota was a vision of spaghetti hell, with a seemingly endless array of wires randomly crisscrossing the dashboard. Two were connected to the DVD player in the back – we were playing a succession of films to keep the children quiet – which was attached not to the back of our seats, but to a plank of wood with gaffer tape instead. The DVD player itself was covered in even more tape, in a vain attempt to keep the wires in place. Naturally, of course, they kept falling out, forcing me repeatedly to kneel backwards on my seat in vain attempts to fix it, as Leatherman negotiated the potholes – which I immediately rechristened inverted speed bumps – that the Zambian government use instead of tarmac. (One drunk Kenyan once told me that you can tell when a country got its independence, as that's when they stopped mending the roads.)

I was also having a problem with the Land Cruiser. Leatherman's car didn't appear to have a fourth gear, meaning I had to be rather deft when negotiating the gearstick. ('Ah, third to fifth,' he said, at one point. 'I like your style.') In reality, this meant me pressing the clutch while Leatherman found the elusive gear. Which, as you can imagine, was slightly dangerous when we were driving like Jenson Button in a souped-up tractor.

The road was long and often unnerving, especially as cars hurtled towards each other at 100 mph with only eighteen inches between them. There were several times on the journey when I thought a double-decker coach was going to nudge us into the tall grass. And considering the behaviour of the children, that might not have been the worst idea in the world.

We reached Mfuwe at 5 p.m. and celebrated with a beer in the cabin. As we looked round to check on the kids, we noticed that both of them had gaffer tape over their mouths. They had obviously been more inventive with their time than we had.

Gillie and Sarah had already arrived, and the girls were outside, eating cake and trying to keep it away from the monkeys who lived on the roof. On that trip they saw elephants, lions, leopards, impalas and even a chongololo, the giant African millipede. It goes without saying that – on this trip at least – the chongololo was afforded far more respect than I was.

BRINGING EDIE AND GEORGIA UP in the latter stages of the Information Age while trying to prepare them to enter the workplace wasn't a daily preoccupation, but it was certainly an existential issue. We wanted to instil values, although we relied upon real-life experiences more than anything else: do what we do as well as what we say. Both appeared to be following artistic avenues and were becoming adept at navigating the various tributaries of creative London. They surprised me daily, and each time they did, I felt as though I might burst with pride. I'd go to degree shows with Edie, or to galleries with Georgia, and was flabbergasted by the knowledge they'd accumulated. You properly become a parent when your children start teaching you, rather than the other way round. The seemingly endless discussions over the correct parameters of modern parenting appeared to me to revolve around how soon we should start treating our children like adults; instead, I fell back on common sense, which was possibly too authoritarian for modern tastes, but it seemed to work. I very quickly stopped being useful when they had difficult homework questions, but I knew I came in handy when they were writing theses. I was also good at standing guard like a postcard of a golden retriever.

Were we indulgent parents? Naturally. One evening, when the girls were probably around seven and nine, we had Jamie Theakston and Erin O'Connor around for dinner. Always curious to see who was cluttering up our dining room, Edie crept into the room, carrying the acoustic guitar she was currently trying to master. As she unsuccessfully attempted a Simon & Garfunkel song, I caught Jamie's eye; he had a gigantic thought bubble above his head: *Seriously? This is what I've got to look forward to?*

Both girls would eventually move out – Edie going to Goldsmiths and Georgia to UCL. After that, on any Saturday morning during term time, I could be found in our kitchen, in a pair of leather shoes, playing Paul Simon's 'Father and Daughter' on repeat.

Ed Fucking Victor and the Wolff at the Door

Mentor; Assassin

Ed, my transatlantic mentor, New York, 2016

SARAH POINTED OUT MY LIFE became a lot less rich when Ed Victor passed away, and she was right. He was my great friend, my mentor and not least my literary agent, and he died of a heart attack on 7 June 2017, while suffering from chronic lymphocytic leukaemia.

'I've always lived a life where people have said: "Look at him. Who does he think he is?"' Ed said once, unapologetically. 'And who I think I am, is someone living life to the brim.'

I have to say, few lived it with such dedication and vim, but what he loved more than anything were books, and the people who wrote them. 'What I'm dealing with is like crude oil,' he said. 'Creative writing in English can be made into anything, from Vaseline to rocket fuel. I can sell film rights, television rights, book rights. It's content, and people need content.'

I was one of his clients and knew him as an agent and friend for twenty years, but he had much bigger people on his list, people like Bono, Frederick Forsyth, Keith Richards, Damien Hirst, Erica Jong, Iris Murdoch, John Banville, Douglas Adams and the journalist Carl Bernstein.

(Bernstein came to our house in Hay for drinks once, during the annual festival. After an hour or so he let it be known he wouldn't be averse to being commissioned by me should I be interested. Interested? Obviously, I was interested. As I started to explain how the process might work, and what I might be interested in, he started his pitch. 'I would want £4 a word,' said Mr Watergate. No problem: I could worry about this later. 'And I only want to write travel stories,' he continued. 'Within reason, that might work,' I said, suddenly a lot less keen. 'And I only want to write captions, not actual articles,' he went on. 'Not actual articles?' 'No.' 'Ah,' I said, and wandered off.)

Ed would flatter his clients, telling many (maybe all of us) they had somehow made a deal with the devil, allowing them to squeeze more hours out of a day than mere mortals (i.e. people who weren't represented by Ed). He loved all his charges and divided them into those who took years to produce a book, and those – like me – 'who finish a book, drink a Diet Coke, and then start another'. Whenever I finished a book, I would call him up and say, 'Ed, I've had my Diet Coke, so what are we doing next?'

Ever self-aware, Ed said, 'People outside the literary world imagine books get bought and sold by a small group of people who all know each other, and all dine with each other and spend all weekend at each other's houses. And you know what? It's true.'

During a Hay Festival appearance, a member of the audience asked him how they could get their manuscript under his nose if they weren't part of his high-octane party circuit. Ed replied: 'You don't.'

I found him such a towering figure, both figurately and literally. There are few people who can walk into a room and then walk out again with a cheque for £10 million. He got more than a passing mention in Ava Gardner's autobiography, as she decided to go for Ed as her agent, rather than the more experienced Irving 'Swifty' Lazar. The clincher was when she was told by a friend that Ed didn't just like to make money for his clients, but that 'he liked to see the look of surprise in the author's eyes when he told them what the deal is'. Gardner replied, 'I like surprises, honey.' And so Ed was hired.

I suppose his excitement about life was predicated on his accomplishments as much as his confidence. He had earned the right to approach prime ministers, presidents and gangsters and ask them if they had ever considered the amount of money they could make if they allowed him to cut a deal for them.

Nicholas Coleridge first met Ed properly in Morocco, where he was staying at the Gazelle d'Or hotel near Taroudant, in the foothills of the Atlas Mountains. It was Eastertime, and the hotel was filled with discreet celebrities and their partners, sunbathing and reading their books round the pool: Michael Portillo, then a cabinet minister, Charles Saatchi, fashion photographer Terence Donovan; *Daily Telegraph* editor Charles Moore.

'Under normal circumstances, none of these people would have spoken to each other, terrified of invading each other's space,' said Coleridge. 'But then Ed took control . . . Every morning he would parade around the pool. "I have reserved a table for twelve for lunch under the olive trees. Would you care to join us?" Everyone agreed. Such was the power of Ed Victor. The lunches were magnificently enjoyable. Afterwards we all played Monopoly in the sunshine, which Charles Saatchi always won, with Portillo second. None of this would have happened without Ed. He was the greatest networker of all time. He made things happen.'

Ed acted like an old-school ruthless Hollywood agent, focusing on the deal as though it were a diamond, or a woman. Authors, he said, 'want a killer agent, a shark in the water, not a guy with an

MLitt'. Ed was both. Born in the Bronx but a committed anglophile, he married an Englishwoman, Micheline Samuels (later, as a writer, known as Michelene Wandor), before falling in love with the woman who became his second wife, the lawyer Carol Ryan (he was survived by two sons from his first marriage, Adam and Ivan; by his son with Carol, Ryan, and by three grandchildren).

He even went to more parties than I did. If I turned up at one and saw Ed, I knew I was in the right place. Not that he left it to chance, mind you. He was for ever making sure he was invited to the right events and looked dimly on those who weren't as dedicated as he was himself. Whenever we spoke on the phone, he'd ask me what I was up to that night. And when I said what I might do is walk across the park, go home and settle in front of the TV to watch a game of football or an episode of a programme he never had time to watch, he would berate me for having the temerity to miss a book launch, a premiere or a dinner party given by a mutual friend. He just couldn't understand why someone wouldn't want to go out as much as possible. The only night he'd stay in would be Friday. 'We'll have been out every night during the week,' he once said. 'We go out all the time, either in New York or London, as we live simultaneously in both cities, more or less. Our British home is in Regent's Park and we also have a beautiful house on Eastern Long Island outside New York. In each city we have completely different sets of friends and go to cocktail parties, theatre, dinners and opera.'

In anyone else's mouth, this might sound conceited, but Ed was all about celebration, and enjoying that celebration.

ED COULD BE WITHERING IN his appraisal, but always with a positive uplift at the end. Many's the time I sent him an outline for a book, or a hastily written idea in the hope that this was the one that Ed thought might make us both millions, and many's the time I'd get a brutal response by return.

'Dylan, this is a truly terrible idea. I suggest you get back on the sun lounger and pour yourself another glass of whatever it is you're anaesthetising yourself with!'

In this respect, he became a genuine mentor to me, a father figure, and while we laughed and smiled and gossiped and gandered, for me there was always a take-away, something Ed had probably said in passing, but which would stay with me long after he had moved on. He didn't pass on knowledge in order to show how smart he was, he did it almost by osmosis. He could bring great depth to seemingly asinine subjects and dismiss profundity for the hogwash it was pretending so hard to disguise. He was for ever the realist. 'People often wait too long to publish their memoirs because they don't want to admit it's all over for them,' he said. 'Lionel Bart [the composer and creator of *Oliver!*] came to me very late on, and when I said his memoirs were worth between £25,000 and £50,000, he didn't believe me because he'd been offered £2 million when he was younger. Eventually I got an offer of £37,500 and you know what he did? He turned it down.' He often said he applied three tests to determine a book's potential: 'Is the person fabulous? Is the work good? And is there a lot of money in it?'

When presented with a manuscript or an idea that held no interest for him (i.e. something that wasn't going to make him any money), he'd say, 'I gave them the second best answer – a quick no.'

He could be brutal. A mutual friend wanted Ed to meet a colleague who had spent years working for Martin Scorsese, but who wanted to change tack and write a novel. The three of them arranged to meet at the Ivy, where the colleague proceeded to tell Ed all about his book. Blunt, but charming, Ed said, 'In all honesty I don't have any interest in your novel, but do you think you could write a book about Martin Scorsese?' When the colleague said no, Ed's bluntness overpowered his charm. 'Well, it's been very nice to meet you, but sitting over there is my client Harold Pinter, so if you don't mind, I'm going to go over there and join him for lunch.'

And he did.

ED WAS A MAN WHO demanded a lot from life and seemed to know everything there was to know about getting the most out of it. He was never embarrassed about asking for substitutions on a restaurant menu, often to the point where he had actually ordered something the restaurant didn't offer (by which time it was too late for the waiter to do anything about it). Early in our friendship, when we were taking it in turns to take each other for lunch, he took me to the Ivy (when the Ivy was still the Ivy). At the end of the meal, after our coffee, Ed stood up and started walking out into the street.

'But, er, the bill . . . What shall we do about the bill?' I spluttered.

Ed stopped, turned around and looked at me as though I was the biggest rube on the farm.

'Dylan, I have an account.'

A number of years ago we were due to have a business meeting in New York, and while we were on the phone making arrangements, I casually mentioned I was taking some friends to dinner that night at Michael's, the famous midtown lunch spot.

Ed interrupted me and said, almost as he would if addressing a small child:

'But nobody goes to Michael's for *dinner*.' And he was right, as he was so consistently about so much.

Often Ed would call just to tell you what he had been up to, showing off about his extraordinary life. He would call, ostensibly to ask you how you were, but really to tell you what he'd been doing at the weekend. The monologue would go like this: 'So I just spent the weekend with Ruthie Rogers at her villa in the Tuscan hills with Gore Vidal, Bono, Mel Brooks, Candice Bergen and Alexander the Great. It really was the loveliest trip and I have to say they all made very good companions, and Ruthie really is the most sensational chef . . .'

He was a tremendous name dropper. Everyone knew it, and nobody cared. 'He almost always answered his phone,' says Alastair Campbell, 'but often to say he would "call you right back", on one occasion adding, 'I'm just getting on Cher's private plane, trying to get a deal done."'

Ed's name dropping was done in such a way that it made you collude in Ed's obvious enjoyment in mixing with the great and the good. In Ed's eyes – and in everyone else's – Ed was one of the great and the good too, so it wasn't as though he was pushing his face up against the glass and staring at people who were better and more accomplished. Ed was as accomplished as anyone he ever bumped into at a cocktail party, often more so. Yet he delighted in acknowledgement. I can still remember how excited he was when Keith Richards (whose autobiography *Life* he had sold to Little, Brown) gave him a new nickname.

'According to Keith I must now be addressed only as "Ed Fucking Victor".'

And for the duration of the publicity tour, and for a considerable amount of time afterwards, he was.

I once commissioned a freelancer to write a column on name dropping, and when it landed in my inbox a few days later, I was immediately handed a problem. The piece started something like this: 'The man who name drops with greater frequency than anyone I have ever met, who by rights should have a degree or PhD in name dropping, a man who finds it impossible to breathe without mentioning someone more famous than himself is of course the great literary agent, Ed Victor.' Having worried about this for several minutes I thought the best thing to do would be to send it straight to Ed, in order for him to share my concern. Literally two minutes after emailing it to him, Ed responded: 'Print it.'

Ed's conversation would be adorned with more boldface names than there were spots on the polka-dot ties he liked to wear so much. When he was asked what the funniest thing ever written about him was, he said, 'A profile by Will Self calling me the Olympic champion of name dropping.'

THE END CAME QUICKLY. I called Ed at the start of the year, while he was in Palm Beach (Ed and Carol had developed a rhythm of spending a third of their time in London, most of the summer in Long Island and a substantial part of the winter in Florida). I asked how he was in the rhetorical way we all do, and he said he'd had some worrying results from recent tests (a decade earlier he had battled leukaemia), and so was coming home to see his specialist. I saw him a week later, when he had been admitted to the London Clinic, where he was due to start a course of chemotherapy. I sat with Alastair Campbell and the publisher Gail Rebuck on the end of his bed, gossiping about the publishing world, and discussing the car crash of Brexit Britain. He was still planning trips, still criticising the government – Ed was always criticising the government, regardless of who was in power – and still trying to fit in lunches between appointments he surely knew were going to be difficult to fulfil. Ruth Rogers was sending over daily food packages from the River Café (and Ed, true to form, was still complaining about them: 'Why did Ruthie send me this pasta? She knows I like the other one. I'm going to have to speak to her . . .').

It was to be the last time I saw him.

Three days later, I called to see how the chemo had gone, only to find out he had been given a completely different treatment, and one that appeared to be working. He was as giddy as he ever was, and remarkably seemed as though he was going to make a full recovery. Perhaps predictably, my very last conversation with Ed went like this: 'You know the worst thing about all of this?' he said to me, without a hint of irony. 'I'm going to have to miss Damien's party in Venice.'

A few days later he developed pneumonia, deteriorating dramatically in the process, and the narrative arc developed accordingly. When he died, he was three months shy of his seventy-eighth birthday.

There was a tsunami of obituaries, with quotes from the literary great and good on both sides of the Atlantic. One of my favourites came from Sophie Hicks, who worked with Ed for many years, and whom I knew from sitting on the membership committee of the Groucho Club, an establishment Ed helped create. 'In my 25 years working with Ed, there were innumerable times when he would stop what he was doing and look up from his desk, or interrupt our lunch or suddenly pause during a walk through Bedford Square or Frankfurt or New York and with his Ed grin, say, "We are having so much fun, aren't we?" And we were. We really did.'

Having been invited by Carol to sit Shiva, she also invited me back a few days later to pick out something from Ed's wardrobe, his office, something for me to keep. I took a tie, because he was always so smart and it would be something to remind me of him whenever I wore it, and I took a photograph of him taken on his graduation day, when he still had a highway of green lights ahead of him.

A few years earlier I got a call from Ed one morning while I was at work. He seemed especially enthusiastic, and when I asked why he said he had some important news, and that he needed to ask my opinion about something. Barely able to contain his excitement, he told me that even though he knew he wasn't meant to say anything, as per protocol, he had just been awarded a CBE.

'Now, Dylan, I obviously know you've been given an honour yourself, and I just wanted to know how you used it. Do you use it on your letterhead, on your email, your business card, passport . . . just where do you use yours?'

I then explained that while I quite liked it when other people used it on my behalf, I almost never used it myself, as I thought it was a little ostentatious to do this. Ed didn't seem happy with this information, and simply carried on with his inquisition.

'OK, but how do most people use it? I mean, surely you must use it on your business cards?'

'No.'

'On your bank statements?'

'No.'

'On your website?'

'No.'

'How about on your Instagram account?'

'Never occurred to me.'

This rather protracted and unsuccessful conversation went on for another ten minutes or so, with Ed finding increasingly arcane and esoteric uses for his honour, in the hope I might buckle and admit that yes, I often use it when sending emails to important clients. Having known Ed for a long time, I could always tell when he'd had enough of a phone call (usually when one of his more important clients was on the line, usually Nigella Lawson or John Banville), and so I wasn't surprised when he brought this one to a close.

'You know what, Dylan? You've been incredibly helpful. And you know what I'm going to do? I'm going to use it on everything.'

I FIRST MET MICHAEL WOLFF in the early noughties at a Condé Nast conference in Venice. He was the star attraction, delivering a self-deprecating, motivational (and actually rather inspirational) talk on the back of his successful 1998 book, *Burn Rate,* which was about his failed experiment as a digital entrepreneur.

A Condé Nast conference in Venice sounds extremely glamorous, and in some respects it was. In other ways, it was incredibly stressful, having to make various presentations to our American owners, without sounding like we were taking over the world. The presentations I had to make over the years at these conferences were always a balancing act: on the one hand, I had to show that we were expanding our reach, and yet on the other I always knew the Americans expected the requisite amount of deference. I always thought New Yorkers (and not just the Condé Nast New Yorkers) looked at the rest of the world as though it were a version of the famous Saul Steinberg cartoon, with New York front and centre, and the rest of the world starting with little consequence on the other side of the Hudson River.

Every night in Venice there would be a cocktail reception before dinner. A perfunctory exercise in most countries, in Britain a cocktail party tends to be welcomed as an opportunity to line the stomach with copious amounts of alcohol before dinner. Each night as I walked into some fancy palazzo, I would be offered a champagne flute into which had been poured an inch of Prosecco. I would give the waiter a thin smile and say, 'Keep pouring. I'm English.'

There was also a certain amount of comedy, too, especially at breakfast time. I would make bets with other like-minded souls about which *Vogue* editor was going to come down to the dining room last. It was obviously bad form for these people to be anywhere on time, and so it was almost obligatory to be late, and the later the better, apparently. Not only were they all late, but they all seemed to be wearing sunglasses, something I've never understood. Sunglasses were designed for wearing outdoors when it's sunny, not indoors when you're eating. They all looked ridiculous, although the worst offenders were the editors from the smaller, newer territories, who assumed this was the only way to behave.

I have to hold my hand up here and admit that I have, on rare occasions, been guilty of similar crimes, but mainly in my teens and never for forty-five minutes. I sometimes (only sometimes, you understand) wore them in fashion shows, but only to keep myself from being blinded by the Klieg lights, and to stop everyone else from seeing how hungover I was.

There are very few people who can get away with it. Jack Nicholson. Brad Pitt. Stevie Wonder. Senior sales executives dressed as the Blues Brothers for a fancy-dress party. And that's just about it. No one else really has a plausible excuse.

I once bumped into Jack Nicholson in the early nineties at a party for *Vogue* at San Lorenzo, the formerly Eurocentric trattoria in London. He arrived by chauffeur-driven Porsche, of all things, resplendent in his trademark Reservoir Poodles ensemble: crumpled suit, black suede shoes, white shirt and impenetrable black Wayfarers. He loped down the stairs, puffing incessantly on a beleaguered Marlboro Light, where he inadvertently joined the queue for the buffet, immediately behind me. Assuming it would be rude not to, I engaged him in conversation, and, for approximately six minutes, we discussed the quality of the champagne, the long night ahead and the pros and cons of various members' clubs in London (the Groucho won hands down, principally – according to Jack – 'because you can walk around on your hands and knees, and no one bats a damn eyelid').

Then, as he finished surveying the sumptuous but strictly vegetarian fare laid out in front of him, he slowly turned his head to mine, lowered the sunglass by the merest fraction and whispered in his unmistakeable drawl, 'Are the women here as bad as the food?'

MICHAEL WOLFF WAS A TERRIFIC, if slightly laconic, speaker, and I loved him. We stayed in touch and would see each other occasionally when one of us was in London or New York. He always made a point of visiting Savile Row to stock up his wardrobe and was always the best-dressed diner at the Wolseley in Piccadilly whenever we ate there. I was told by people I respected (including my boss) not to trust him, not to tell him anything I wouldn't want anyone else knowing and certainly never to hire him.

So obviously I hired him.

Michael started working for *GQ* in 2010 when he was still writing for *Vanity Fair*, although I think both of us knew that his time there was nearing its end. Michael was getting sick of Graydon and I'm fairly sure Graydon was getting sick of Michael. My friend knew he was on shaky ground when he went into Graydon's office one afternoon to pitch a story about David Cameron, who was still in opposition but very much in the ascendancy. Graydon listened for a while, then closed his eyes and said, 'Michael, what do you know about Hollywood? James Cameron is really not your beat. Stick to New York gossip and you'll be fine.'

Michael and I would gossip about everything – media, politics, Hollywood, society – but I rarely asked him about the status of his professional relationships, not least because he was always falling out with people. True to form, he fell out with the *Guardian*, left *Vanity Fair*, and I assumed that one day he would probably fall out with me, too. Heigh-ho, I thought, what the hell. He was a terrific journalist, always good company – he hosted a dinner party for me at his apartment once in New York and I was more than impressed by the number of media luminaries he managed to corral (even though Joanna Coles, then riding high as the editor of *Cosmopolitan*, had decided as a matter of policy to disagree with everything I said) – and he wrote like an eiderdown dream.

Michael would skewer anyone I asked him to: *Rolling Stone*, Tina Brown, *Vice*, the *Guardian*, the *New York Times*, Jeff Bezos, Rupert Murdoch, Uncle Tom Cobley. If you dared to stick your head above the parapet then at some point you'd see Michael on the other side of the drawbridge, about to launch a bloody great water cannon at you for a profile in the pages of our magazine.

Nothing was wasted, either. When he texted or emailed, his messages were short. Michael, like many journalists, was paid by the word, and he didn't like working for free. I interviewed him a couple of times at the Hay Festival, and he was practically mute before and after his stage appearances; he wasn't going to perform unless the paying customers could see him.

He could be cruel, but then that was part of his toolkit. In 2011, friends of the Manhattan restaurant legend Elaine Kaufman were fuming over our profile – 'Hell's Kitchen' – in which Michael called her 'grotesque'. He compared the late restaurateur to 'a low-class madam or public-house wench vastly past her prime'. Wolff said the food at her Upper East Side eatery was 'inedible' and the dining room 'an annex of Page Six'. Most of the bile directed at Wolff came, predictably, from the *New York Post*, a Murdoch paper.

One of his favourite tricks was to gesticulate with his face rather than actually speak, giving what he wasn't saying an extra shade of tension, and giving you the feeling that everything he said was somehow being listened to by those (and there were many) who wanted to bring him down. He was never less than fascinating company, and especially so when he was regaling you with stories about prominent boldface names – much of which was wholly unrepeatable.

That's saying something when you consider how much he was willing to share in his bracingly well-informed columns. His access to the inside track was precisely why, despite covering such seemingly well-trodden ground, he always kicked up such a stir. When the dandy hitman turned his gimlet eye on Alan Rusbridger for his 2014 piece 'The Guardian at the Gate', about the paper's attempt to break America, he got under the skin of the story as only he could. His knowledge of the paper's internal politics, his ability coolly to appraise the characters involved (the American website's editor was 'a dishevelled figure always in need of a cigarette in non-smoking Manhattan') and his witheringly unequivocal analysis made it an instant must-read.

For that matter, I still encounter people who bring up a piece he wrote for me in 2013, 'The Damnation of St Christopher', about Christopher Hitchens's transformation from socialist showman to moral sage. It outraged Hitchens's devotees (obviously). One website decried 'Michael Wolff's shameful hatchet job on Christopher Hitchens' – but was, predictably, unable to dispute his thesis. It's rare for a columnist to make news but make news he did.

He fell out with many of the people he wrote about. After Michael's piece about former *Vanity Fair* and *New Yorker* editor Tina Brown, for instance, she refused to ever speak to him again, which, considering that they both stayed at Claridge's when they visited London, resulted in some rather embarrassing encounters in the lobby. Ed Victor hosted a dinner for Harry Evans in New York around this time, and when I arrived, late from a meeting, I instinctively went to kiss Tina Brown, only to be met with a mouth full of hair as she rebuffed my advances. I had completely forgotten that six months earlier Michael had eviscerated her in the pages of my magazine. Tina, it was only business.

FAMOUSLY, MICHAEL FELL OUT WITH Donald Trump, too. Trump's bizarre ascension to the White House was initially benchmarked as a vote against the apparent liberalism of the Obama administration, and for a while everything that surrounded Trump was framed in this way, as an understandable, if unacceptable, reaction to what had gone before. Even those who were appalled by his electoral success – basically everyone you'd ever met – begrudgingly understood why it had happened.

Trump's presidency started to be defined by his behaviour almost as soon as he took office, as any misplaced idealism we may have expected from him was swiftly clouded by a swirl of feverish tweets, angry TV appearances and the start of what would be a never-ending fusillade of denials. Here was the petulant president. The ultimate narcissist. Trump wasn't so much in office as in abeyance, unable to do anything other than respond angrily to the fury and profound disbelief which surrounded him, and which immediately started to define his presidency.

Michael's reporting on Trump paid dividends, as his remarkable bestselling book *Fire and Fury: Inside the Trump White House* and its sequels *Siege: Trump Under Fire* and *Landslide: The Final Days of the Trump Residency* have shown. With unprecedented access, Wolff told the inside story of the most controversial presidency of our time, unravelling a period that was fraught with tension, fear and speculation. Wolff's material – which was corroborated later in the year by Bob Woodward's own *Fear: Trump in the White House* – revealed an administration already in meltdown, telling a tale that was by turns stormy, outrageous and never less than mesmerising. Wolff provided a wealth of new details about the chaos in the Oval Office, including what Trump's staff really thought of him, what inspired Trump to claim he was wire-tapped by President Obama, why FBI director James Comey was really fired, why chief strategist Steve Bannon and Trump's son-in-law Jared Kushner couldn't be left in the same room together, what the secret to communicating with Trump was, and – bizarrely – what the Trump administration had in common with the movie *The Producers*.

When Michael wrote his biography of Rupert Murdoch, *The Man Who Owns the News*, in 2008, he was celebrated and vilified in equal measure. He took repeated kickings from the Murdoch press. Various people associated with the Murdochs on both sides of the Atlantic encouraged me to stop using him – some quite vociferously, and one quite aggressively – but in my mind, this was the sort of contentiousness that made him a great journalist. This was business,

I told my friends who were trying to make me fire him, not pleasure. Actually, it was pleasure as well, but mainly it was business.

Michael was, without doubt, the very best gossip in the business. Of course, by dint of its very nature, gossip is a slippery beast: the easiest way for conjecture to become fact. But isn't that why we gossip in the first place? I was first told by Michael that he was writing a book about Trump at the beginning of 2017. I was in New York for a dinner, and Michael and I were having breakfast in a midtown hotel, just around the corner from Trump Tower. As we ate, it gradually dawned on me that he was claiming to have been granted access to the White House, where he would be spending the first 100 days of the new presidency.

I nearly spat out my Eggs Benedict, Double Down Truffle Fries, Reformation Power Drink and mouthwash coffee.

When I asked how he had pulled off this extraordinary feat, he replied it was something he had been trying to wangle for some time, and no, he couldn't quite believe it either. And when I questioned whether anyone in the West Wing had actually ever read anything he'd written, and whether they were actually mad, he gave me a classic Michael Wolff look, making a face with his eyebrows and mouth without saying a word, the gist of which was plain to see: *Yup, they are damned fools, but let's keep that between ourselves for a while, shall we?*

Over the next few months, I would receive emails, often at strange hours of the day, giving me titbits about what was going on in the Oval Office. I would be lying in bed reading when my phone would light up and there would be a message from Michael that said something like, 'Tony Blair has just walked into the White House' (which was weeks before the story of Blair's visit hit the press). He told me other things, too, but these will remain between me and Michael. After all, I need to keep on his good side (and he needs to stay on mine).

I saw him a few times just before Christmas 2017, and remarkably he seemed relatively sanguine about the publication of the first Trump book. Michael had given *GQ* its own exclusive extract (which we quickly had to put online when the story broke), and he talked in some detail about the launch. The UK publication of the book was initially planned to coincide closely with the anniversary of the inauguration, but its incendiary content forced an earlier simultaneous release.

When leaked passages of *Fire and Fury* appeared in the *Guardian*, which had obtained an early copy from a bookseller in New England, and an extract ran in *New York* magazine, it set social media ablaze. Every news outlet ran the story, and seemingly everyone was delighting in the gory details. Well, everyone apart from Trump himself.

His press secretary Sarah Sanders immediately brushed it off as 'trashy tabloid fiction', and Trump declared that his former chief strategist Steve Bannon – one of Wolff's interviewees – had 'lost his mind'. The White House wanted to block the book's release, so Trump's lawyers wrote a stern letter to the publisher, Henry Holt, demanding that it 'immediately cease and desist from any further publication, release or dissemination', citing 'numerous false and/or baseless statements'. Wolff, however, was steadfast. He responded that he had recordings, that he had notes and – contrary to what Trump was claiming – he had had access to the president.

'I authorized Zero [*sic*] access to White House (actually turned him down many times) for author of phony book,' Trump said in response. 'Full of lies, misrepresentations and sources that don't exist.'

Honestly, who could have wished for better marketing?

The publisher moved the publication date forward 'due to unprecedented demand'. The BBC posted photographs of Washingtonites queuing up at midnight to read it first, as if it were the release of the new Harry Potter. The author posted a message on Twitter: 'Here we go. You can buy it (and read it) tomorrow. Thank you, Mr. President.'

This was more than a coup, it was a coup d'état.

As swiftly became clear, his book was one of the defining chapters of Trump's first year in office. The *New York Times* observed that Wolff was, right then, the most famous journalist in the world. And rightly so.

Elsewhere, Wolff was called – disparagingly – a 'media provocateur', and yet he became one of the era's most trenchant and astute commentators, not just on new media, but on the old newspaper and

TV behemoths, those dinosaurs who Wolff came to bury. When media organisations queue up to call you 'pathetic', 'disgusting', 'twisted', and write articles based on 'zero evidence', then you know you must be doing something right.

There were always certain stories that he couldn't do. There were two or three organisations that I always thought would make good features for *GQ* but, like all of us, Michael had his favourites, his arrangements. There were relationships that he needed to foster in order to keep his job, plates that he needed to keep spinning in order to carry on being Michael Wolff. This in itself was something of an art. If the work of a journalist is a combination of guile and craft, initiating and keeping relationships is something altogether more sophisticated, and something that Michael was always remarkably good at. Still is.

Not least because he has fallen out with more people than you can shake a stick at. And Michael certainly has a very big stick.

I HAD SOME HISTORY WITH Trump, as in 2000, when *GQ* was still quite ribald in parts and had a fairly demonstrative libido, we had photographed Trump's then girlfriend, the twenty-six-year-old Slovenian supermodel, Melania Knavs, in a preposterous fourteen-page naked profile shoot by Antoine Verglas on Trump's customised Boeing 727 (even the seat buckles were 18-carat gold) at La Guardia airport. She was wearing handcuffs, wielding diamonds and holding a chrome M1911 pistol. The shoot was called 'Sex at 30,000 Feet'. We had been bombarded by requests from Trump's office to shoot Melania. Given that she was obviously so keen to be featured in *GQ*, we came up with a rather kitsch and camp story for her to feature in. The whole thing was deliberately vulgar, in the way that you could be deliberately vulgar in 2000. There were more levels of irony in those pictures than there are in a layered chocolate mousse cake, and we all thought they were hilarious. Trump loved the pictures so much he demanded some original prints be couriered to his office, and so we framed the cover and a selection of prints and sent them as soon as we could.

'She's popular, she's brilliant, she's a wonderful woman,' Trump told us, with uncharacteristic understatement. At the time, the property magnate was the Reform Party presidential candidate, and Trump said he was 'going to do everything I can to see that regular Americans can fly as high as their wings will take them'. Melania, perhaps already relishing the prospect of a future pressing the flesh on state occasions, said, 'I will put all my effort into it, and I will support my man.'

It appeared the First Lady was rather proud of the images, because the White House website listed the cover shoot as one of Melania's greatest achievements. When Trump took office, the White House website underwent something of an overhaul. As part of a string of alterations, including the removal of all references to climate change, profiles of the president's key personnel were uploaded to the 'Administration' tab. If you scanned Melania's official biography you would have found, in among the puffs for her many charitable roles, philanthropic interests and of course her jewellery business, a fulsome celebration of her topless appearance on a private jet brandishing a decorative handgun. It was almost as though the metaverse had been invented by *Spy* magazine, a diabolical delve into the ludicrous and the kitsch.

In 2016, one of the Verglas images was used by the anti-Trump super (PAC) political action committee Make America Awesome, along with the strapline 'Meet Melania Trump. Your Next First Lady' in a crude attempt to dissuade potential voters in the community. Trump was furious – furious! – accusing his opponent Ted Cruz (incorrectly) of being the source of the attack, and threatened to 'spill the beans on [Cruz's] wife'. In response, Cruz called the property mogul a 'snivelling coward' and said he should 'leave Heidi the hell alone.'

Then the *Washington Post* reported that the photoshoot might have helped Knavs secure permanent residency in the United States under a visa programme designed for Oscar winners, Olympic athletes and nuclear physicists. Only those with 'extraordinary abilities' or who had demonstrated 'sustained national and international acclaim' are able to secure an EB-1 visa, created under the US Immigration Act of 1990, which Melania was granted in late 2001. It was in 2000 that she applied for such a visa, when her notable achievements were the aforementioned *GQ* shoot, appearances on runways at fashion shows and a spot in the swimsuit edition of *Sports Illustrated*. In 2001, she was granted one of only 3,376 EB-1 visas, a fraction of the 1 million green cards issued that year.

Famously, in 2000 Trump featured in an episode of *The Simpsons* in which creator Matt Groening depicted the Donald as the US president. When the unthinkable happened, and Trump actually became president, Groening delivered a disturbing verdict on Trump's first 100 days in office. In the minute-and-a-half clip, White House press secretary Sean Spicer has killed himself, Trump's hair is so evolved it can wipe a tear from his eye, Ivanka Trump has been appointed as the ninth Supreme Court Justice, and back home in Springfield Marge has run out of Prozac anti-depressants while Grandpa Simpson is being deported. But what caught our eye was what happens at the six-second mark. With the camera zooming in on the White House corridor, not only do viewers see a portrait of the president, but they also catch a glimpse of an image taken from our photoshoot.

When I was called by someone from the *Hollywood Reporter* and asked if we would feature another similar shoot with Melania given the opportunity, I said that 'in all seriousness, I think we'd rather photograph Donald in the nude.'

And I meant it.

In 2008, I had also sent Piers Morgan to interview Trump in his palatial new home in Beverly Hills. Trump was sixty-two, tanned, fit and suitably pumped to give Piers a guided tour of the immediate neighbourhood. 'I'm buying it all, house by house,' he bragged. 'And I'll make a ton of money out of it when I'm finished.' Piers found him fascinating. Earlier in the year, he had taken part in *The Celebrity Apprentice* show in the States, and Trump eventually chose Morgan as his winner – but not before branding him in the live finale, perhaps correctly, 'ruthless, arrogant, evil and obnoxious'. He spent a month filming the series in New York and saw 'Mr Trump' (as they all called him) every day. 'Unbelievably self-confident (I'd never met anyone who exudes an air of such stunning belief in his own abilities), razor-sharp, funnier than I expected and extremely clear-headed and decisive.'

Piers was out on his own on this occasion, as his usual instinctive bullshit detector appeared to have deserted him. Worryingly, he responded well to Trump's brashness, and enjoyed his boorish behaviour. Rereading the interview today, in a conversation full of Trump's usual inanities, he claimed George Bush would go down as the worst president in history. When asked about Barack Obama he said, 'I think he would have had a much easier chance of winning if he had chosen Hillary Clinton as his running mate, definitely. But obviously he doesn't like her, and I don't believe the Clintons like him.'

You could already sense the way in which he had started to bend his political narratives, plucking random thoughts seemingly out of the air, and then amplifying them simply to see how far he could go. Self-awareness, though, was in desperately short supply.

I privately wondered how long it might take for the public to become inured to Trump, but I figured it just could never happen. The levels of toxicity in the White House were impossible to cap. The fumes could be smelled wherever you went. For the same reasons I knew Melania would never grace the cover of US *Vogue*, so I knew that Donald Trump would never have a British *GQ* cover.

'Standard! Standard!'

Read All About It

With Sadiq Khan at the Hay Festival, 2023

LOCKDOWN SEEMS LIKE AN AGE away now, but as the country shut down because of the coronavirus in 2020, life just stopped. This interruption was always going to wreak havoc with the publishing industry, and our little part of it was no exception. Our website continued to pump out an enormous amount of material, and we vastly increased the number of regular daily meetings we had about both editorial and commercial propositions (our affiliate business was on fire), but with print it was challenging, to say the least. If you were a subscriber (print or digital), then your experience would have been unaffected, but if you were the kind of person who idly picked up a copy of the *Spectator*, *Evening Standard*, *Private Eye* or *GQ* on your way through Paddington station, then the interruption was fundamental: it would precipitate a massive change in consumer (as well as commuter) patterns that will take an age to reverse, if indeed they ever do.

Operationally, it caused problems internally, too. While we quickly acclimatised digitally (unsurprisingly our numbers became almost vertical), producing the monthly print magazine became more difficult. All events were obviously cancelled, advertising didn't so much as fall off a cliff as jump, and many of the stories we had planned were no longer possible. The team, as usual, were magnificent, and we managed to carry on even though we were sequestered at home in almost fifty different locations. For much of the first lockdown I was working from my home office halfway up a Black Mountain in Hay-on-Way, Wales. And while the weather outside was unanticipatedly glorious, I spent all day on Zoom calls, with my team, with the commercial team, with management, and increasingly with the American arm of the company. This meant the day would start at 8.30 a.m. and end twelve or fourteen hours later. The Americans, bless them, didn't seem to understand that the time difference meant people in Europe had their working days lengthened, not shortened, because of COVID.

The team were mostly brilliant (disappointingly, I could tell which staff members had taken their foot off the pedals, even though I couldn't see them), inventive, smart and caring about their fellow staff members. I spent as much time offering pastoral care to the team as I did arguing with management about the unprecedented (and unnecessary) budget cuts. We spent every day conjuring up ways to fill the magazine without resorting to publishing petrol receipts or stories that had been destined for the spike. Because we commissioned so much, and because we always commissioned so far in advance, we had a huge backlog of material, although after a while even we started to run out of stories.

Jonathan Heaf excelled himself, regularly checking in with the staff, marshalling our freelancers, and ingeniously coming up with a weekly Instagram chat show, *GQ Happy Hour*, that he produced completely alone. A complete self-starter, Jonathan presented the show, scripted it and organised his own guests (I think he even managed to have the odd cocktail, too). These included Anthony Joshua, Jack Whitehall, Johnny Marr, Mark Ronson, Rufus Wainwright, Karen Elson, Fat Tony, James Bay, Emily Ratajkowski and more. I was in awe of Jonathan as he was smart, tenacious and completely up for whatever anyone threw at him. He had true *GQ* DNA. He was tough, which was probably more important than anything.

In the summer of 2020, George Floyd was murdered by Minneapolis police officer Derek Chauvin, who knelt on his neck for nearly ten minutes having just arrested him. Floyd was being arrested for allegedly using a counterfeit bill, although the crime – if there ever was one – soon disappeared from any argument. Begging for his life and repeatedly saying, 'I can't breathe,' Floyd died soon afterwards, the victim of one of the worst acts of police brutality in history. Or at least one of the worsts acts of police brutality captured on a smartphone. Film of the killing went viral immediately, resulting in a massive, global sense of outrage and public protest. The global outcry was a fillip for organisations such as Black Lives Matter, resulting not just in a series of protests both in the US and abroad, but also in a massive redressing of the media in terms of discrimination and representation.

Magazines in particular came in for some serious scrutiny, as an industry that had not always been as scrupulous in its espousal of Black celebrity as it might have been, was put under the spotlight. At *GQ*, we had always been colourblind in that respect and had celebrated people for their relevance and their commercial appeal rather than anything else. In the eight years from 2013 until 2021, for instance, thirty-five of our cover stars were people of colour, approximately 30 per cent (we gave Adwoa Aboah her first cover, in October 2017, a full fat month before *Vogue*). Men's magazines also came under attack because of the way the #metoo movement had swept through the entertainment industry; again, by the end time this much-needed redress started affecting the industry, our libido had been recalibrated substantially. By the end of the decade, we had for some time simply been a general interest magazine with nice trousers.

And as the pandemic peaked and troughed, dogfights over free speech, cancel culture, race and science took hold. Commissioning comment pieces became more and more problematic, as opinions on any contentious subject seemed to be rushing towards opposite poles, making it difficult to take a position without being framed as someone espousing the exact opposite opinion. Nuance was evaporating and being contrary simply made you look flippant. False equivalences started popping up everywhere, like unwanted moles, while everyone attempted to avoid being accused of bias. Journalists were being encouraged to normalise some politicians while abnormalising others, block booking arguments as though they were competitive sports. On social media, sophistication didn't play well.

THAT YEAR'S *GQ* AWARDS SHOW was a predictably different proposition, not just in terms of its format – we hosted a digital presentation, a series of specially interlinked films – but because there was a central imperative, a desire to applaud those who had genuinely contributed to society during a time of great upheaval and appalling strife.

It had been such a cataclysmic year in so many ways, and yet there had been those who had contributed to the culture in ways we perhaps wouldn't have imagined twelve months previously. That year we celebrated *Star Wars* actor John Boyega because of his involvement in the Black Lives Matter movement in the summer, and especially for the moving speech he made in London's Hyde Park in July. Patrick Hutchinson stepped up to the podium, too, acclaimed for his behaviour during the BLM protests on the South Bank, carrying a white counter-protestor to safety amid a heated confrontation within the crowd. The photograph of this act of bravery was seen all over the world. For our Heroes event at the end of the year we wanted to put Hutchinson and the man he carried to safety together for a filmed fireside chat. Sadly, it didn't happen; his counter-protestor would only do it if we paid him, which we weren't prepared to do.

We also celebrated Piers Morgan, who spent 2020 calling the government to account and being rewarded by a cabinet boycott in the process. He had been especially withering about the health secretary, Matt Hancock, articulating the frustrations of an entire nation. Piers was also the first person to call me when it was announced in the summer of 2021 that I was going to be leaving *GQ*. Condé Nast had decided they were going to consolidate their global offer, and base pretty much everything in New York from now on. So, in the space of just a few months, the London office was largely dismantled. From now on it would be a satellite operation, meaning there was no room for me or my team. And when this was announced, Piers was immediately on the phone offering his advice.

'Mate,' he said, as his virtual arm reached out across my shoulders, 'I've only got one word of advice for you, and it's this: wait. Trust me, I've been in this situation a lot, and I've always found it's best not to make any rash decisions, not to rush back into the fray, and to take a step back and take a good hard look at the situation. And wait.'

LEAVING CONDÉ NAST AFTER SUCH a long time was disorienting, largely because my support system evaporated. It was less to do with the instant downgrading of status, and much more to do with the loss of things such as my personal assistant, car account, expense account, mobile phone and credit cards. In the space of three months, perks I had taken for granted for twenty-two years just vanished: the Range Rover, Sky, unlimited phone calls, my email address, private medical care, the lot. As my exit process took nearly nine months, I was prepared for a lot of it, but not all of it. My lawyer couldn't believe the torturous and convoluted way Condé Nast's lieutenants were dealing with the exit, and yet every misstep only served to underscore how much the company had changed. It was time to go.

My exit agreement took months to arrange, and yet the final actuality was perfect. The day it happened I was joining a group of friends who had started meeting for lunch after lockdown, but before the world had properly opened up. The lunch club was started by Paul McGuinness (who I started to think should change his name to Legendary), and included John Reid from Live Nation, the BBC's head of music, Jan Younghusband, impresario Nick Allott, film director Molly Dineen and music industry veteran Nick Stewart. On this occasion, we were meeting on the terrace of the River Café, which was then enjoying something of a renaissance due to the fact that most of its business was conducted outside.

As I sat down my phone flashed, and it was my lawyer.

'It's starting,' he said, 'so don't go anywhere. They want to do it now, and the contract will need to be signed by six p.m. Don't move.'

So, I didn't.

After much haggling, three long hours and a completely unnecessary disagreement over a forthcoming flight to LA which appeared to be irredeemable, I finally signed at exactly the same time I was signing my portion of the River Café bill. John and I then went on a pub crawl, moving from Hammersmith to Hyde Park with methodical precision.

WHEN I LEFT CONDÉ NAST, a few months later, I decided a rest was as good as a change, and I immediately started to take things easy. Piers's paternal thoughts were actually exactly the same as mine, and waiting is what I had already decided to do.

First, I went on a very long holiday, taking the family away to a lush, expensive island on the other side of the world. In the autumn, I made half-a-dozen programmes for the BBC and had another half-a-dozen scheduled for the end of the year. And then, when I figured I probably had enough on my Alan Partridge-sized plate, I got commissioned to write another book; so, I spent six months asking dozens of people what it was like working with Andy Warhol. I also helped turn Soho House into a digital global media brand, reconfiguring their internal structure. Then, having been approached by a friend of mine, Maggie Todd, who had worked at Disney for over a decade, I formed a film company, Beacon Films.

Then something extraordinary happened, at least I thought so. Out of the blue, I was paid a visit by an old friend of mine, Guy Fletcher, a veteran songwriter, who had a suggestion he thought I might find interesting. Guy was one of our most successful songwriters, and had written classics for Elvis Presley, Aretha Franklin, Ray Charles, Cliff Richard, the Hollies and Frankie Valli to name a mere smattering. His suggestion was certainly a strange one: would I like to write a musical?

Guy's idea was to produce a musical based on the work and life of Jimmy Webb, the man whose 'Wichita Lineman' had such an effect on me as a boy, and the song that Bob Dylan once called the greatest ever written. Both Guy and Jimmy Webb himself wanted me to write the 'book' (the show's story), and was this the kind of thing that might interest me?

Having established that I had absolutely no expertise in this (nor, indeed, any experience), both Guy and Jimmy were adamant that I was the person for the job; I had previously written an ode to 'Wichita Lineman' for Faber, and it was this that had made them think I might be appropriate. Having thought about the idea for longer than I might have done (I reckon it took me three minutes), I dived right in.

And so we started meeting once a week, every week, trying to wrestle down a first draft of the show. I loved the whole thing. Loved working with Guy, loved attempting to put words into our characters' mouths, and loved working with what is undoubtedly one of the great collections of songs in the world ('MacArthur Park', 'By The Time I Get to Phoenix', 'Up, Up and Away', 'Didn't We', 'All I Know', 'Galveston', etc.). I compared the process to building a house, something else at which I had no experience or expertise. You found your land, you designed where you wanted everything to go, you built the foundations, and then tinkered and tinkered until you ended up with hopefully the thing you wanted. All the time wearing hardhats, of course.

The process was ostensibly quite simple. Guy would come to my house, and we would sit opposite each other at my large kitchen table (it wasn't exactly Putinesque, but it was big enough for a heated exchange if we disagreed about something). Then I would make tea (biscuits tended not to appear until the afternoon). Then we started. Working with Guy was something of a dream because he was a stickler for the truth and whenever I started on another flight of fancy, and started suggesting that we conflate events or alter the chronology of Jimmy's story, he would look carefully down his nose, gently cross his arms and say, 'No, I really don't think we want to do that, do we, Dylan?'

AROUND THE SAME TIME, I was approached again about editing the *Evening Standard*. The negotiations took nine months – when I discussed the offer with Sarah, she said, 'Look, you get up at five a.m. to read the papers anyway, so you may as well get paid for it' – and I eventually started in April 2023, finally editing the paper that had so enlivened me when I moved to London in 1977. My task was a simple one: energise the paper, marshal the team, restructure my part of the organisation and get us ready for digital transformation. Which is what I did. It was enormous fun being back in an office, being surrounded by the energetic hum of clever people doing clever things. The last newspaper I had worked on was the *Sunday Times*, but the rhythm of a daily was completely different. The adrenalin was like caffeine, although I probably needed to stop drinking quite so much tea.

My first week included a variety of front pages – Prince Harry (twice), Rishi Sunak looking more like a baseball mascot than the baseball mascot he was standing next to, and Donald Trump, the gift that kept on giving. One of the things I enjoyed most was the assembly of the comment pages; my favourite headline in my first week was the one we used for a piece by Anna van Praagh: 'I wasn't breastfed as a child and I'm perfectly clever.' The paper needed reinventing and required help to draw attention to itself again after lockdown. I changed the front pages, focusing on single issue stories, and tightened it up inside. One of the first things I did was encourage a new set of columnists, from Michael Wolff, Rachel Johnson, Tracey Emin and Fat Tony to Tomiwa Owolade, Martha Gill and Nimco Ali, as well as my friends James Cowan (an ex-General who was an expert on global military strategy) and Guto Harri (the Welsh writer and broadcaster who was still tight with Boris Johnson), while focusing editorially on London, Westminster and the arts. I'd been using Rachel as a columnist for years on *GQ* as she was funny, trenchant and fast. One of the columns I could never get her to write was the HLD List ('Hung Like A Donkey'). At one point at *GQ* I even offered her £5 a word (which would have worked out at about £7,500 for forty minutes work). But she was understandably nervous. 'Go on,' I said. 'It's not like anyone is going to sue.' The list included Michael Fassbender, Jon Hamm, Mick Hucknall, Tommy Lee, Michael Gove ('A baby's arm holding an apple'), Boris Johnson, Andrew Roberts, Daniel Craig, Jay-Z, David Beckham ('Like a tractor exhaust pipe'), Matthew Freud, Liam Neeson ('It was like an Evian bottle fell out of his pants'), Jamie Foxx, William Hague and Alain de Botton.

The other thing I loved was discussing the daily cartoon with our resident illustrator, Christian Adams. Our conference began at 8 a.m., split into three sections – (1) audience, news, pictures, video, sport and business; (2) 'Londoner's Diary', features, arts, lifestyle, fashion, podcasts; (3) comment, leaders – and Christian would loiter on a chair just outside the conference room, and then dash off to his drawing board as soon as he had an idea. Sometimes he'd be there for quarter of an hour, but usually he'd darted off by the end of the news briefing. And, bar the occasional argument, his analysis of which two ideas should be fused together for the cartoon were invariably right. I also inherited a brilliant managing editor, Jack Lefley, who ran an incredibly tight ship. He left most of our meetings muttering, 'I'll have a word.' And he did.

Then there was Robbie Smith, our comment editor. I called Robbie into my office one afternoon and told him Tracey Emin was very unhappy about the headline he had run on one of her pieces, and she wanted to meet him.

The colour started to drain from his face.

'Oh,' said Robbie, 'what do you think she wants?'

'Oh, I think I know exactly what she wants,' I said. 'And I know what she's going to do. She's going to tear you a new one. Very long and very deep.'

At this point the rest of the colour in his face completely disappeared, leaving him almost transparent.

One of the first people I met at the *Standard* was our brilliant sports editor James Major, who, like many probably viewed me with some suspicion. This wasn't helped by our first conversation in the office. When he asked me which football club I supported, I told him that I supported the most popular team in London. 'Oh great', he said. 'Arsenal? Tottenham? Surely not Chelsea?'

'No,' I said, 'Manchester United.'

There was also our terrific picture editor Elliot Wagland, who, having discovered that I didn't like pictures of animals in the paper, seemingly made it his life's work to try and shoehorn in as many as possible whenever I went on holiday.

Then there was Ethan Croft, our diary editor, the oldest 25-year-old I'd ever met. Ethan was such a fogey that even his elbow patches had elbow patches.

The *Evening Standard* was one of the city's great institutions. Sure, the protracted nature of lockdown hadn't helped the business much, but we soon developed a new business model that didn't rely so much on commuters, and it was exhilarating teasing out ways in which we could genuinely thrive. My strategy was linear: first we would turn our front pages into posters, focusing on single issues; then we would tighten up the paper, making it more colourful, more urgent, and slowly replacing news with comment; then we would relaunch the website. I was the lucky beneficiary of some exemplary and expensive digital work, and when we eventually launched standard.co.uk it was a roaring success. Traffic increased by 30 per cent within six weeks.

In a heartbeat I became a creature of habit. I found myself at 6 a.m. every morning pouring myself into a pair of Ralph Lauren jeans, a foxed Tommy Hilfiger white shirt and a navy-blue jacket. At lunch, I ate the same Pret sandwich (cheese and pickle) and drank a completely unnecessary Diet Coke. I then spent twenty minutes answering the emails I'd ignored since breakfast. Weirdly – and I think all journalists are like this – whenever I got a spare five minutes, I didn't call my friends or go for a walk, I simply found another newspaper to read. I started to read more papers now than I ever had; not because I was back working on one, but because it had become something of an addiction; in fact, it was such a habit I almost stopped reading novels. I was a fan of both Tom Wolfe and Noel Gallagher, two unlikely bedfellows who shared an unlikely soundbite: 'Why would I read a novel?' they were both quoted as saying – 'It never happened so it's not true.' I knew what they meant.

Friends asked me how I transitioned from a monthly to a daily, and my answer became immediate: easily. We had spent the best part of a decade building a digital proposition that was the most successful in Condé Nast, and the daily composition, architecture and inventory of a multipurpose website had been my priority for much of my time at *GQ*. (When George Michael died, for instance, on Christmas Day 2016, there were three of us – myself, George Chesterton and Jonathan Heaf – in London, the Brecon Beacons and France, writing obituaries at six in the morning and building picture packages for the rest of the day; our coverage was quicker and better than any national newspaper's.) So, in that respect there was little difference. The nuance of interpretation and presentation was what was different, the constant evolving of a news story, and the way in which a narrative could change in seconds, often completely altering the emphasis. You saw this every day as a customer, and as a producer, it helped – weirdly – to have been a consumer of newspapers for fifty years.

This wasn't an enterprise fuelled by waggish exuberance, either, but rather expertise. I was driving my job at the *Standard* with a lifetime's experience, which meant it was far more of a job than a lifestyle. Which was also a benefit. If lockdown had taught us anything it was that time is even more precious than we thought it was. From now on, I would spend my evenings with friends, sleeping or at important work events; the 70 per cent of stuff I did before COVID – the parties, the openings, the unnecessary dinners, the this-might-be-useful events – were downgraded to the second tier of importance. 'I would love to come,' I would deadpan, 'but I'm fairly certain there's something I want to watch on television that night.'

There were tentpole events, though, and the paper brought post-COVID glamour back to London with the 67th Evening Standard Theatre Awards, held at Claridge's in November 2023. The *Standard*'s proprietor, Evgeny Lebedev, filled the hotel's ballroom with the cream of industry talent: Elton John and David Furnish, Ian McKellen, Nicole Scherzinger, Boy George, Paloma Faith, David Tennant, Tom Hiddleston, Sam Mendes . . . It was that kind of evening. It very much felt like a post-activism event, a night dedicated to the performative arts and little else. And it was all the better for it.

KEEN TO THROW MYSELF INTO work, I started interviewing as many people as I had time for. Pete Townshend. Gilbert & George. Van Morrison. Keir Starmer. Back in 2017–18, when we photographed and interviewed Jeremy Corbyn for a *GQ* cover, I was heavily criticised for saying that his team made the process just as difficult as dealing with a Hollywood celebrity, and for having the temerity to say that I found the Labour leader a little underwhelming in person. As the Conservative Party battled on a daily basis with an electorate who appeared to be tiring of them after thirteen years in power, his successor Starmer – a centrist without Tony Blair's jazz hands – started to look like a seriously viable option. Since becoming Labour leader in April 2020, the serious-minded but charisma-challenged Starmer had had a galvanising effect on his party: his greatest achievement so far had been turning Labour into a party that actually looked fit for purpose. Not only was Corbyn completely unelectable, it seemed that he had also set Labour back decades, managing to turn Britain's only genuine political alternative into a marginal circus show. Starmer had calmed the unions, largely purged the party of its anti-Semitic narrative and moved it to the centre ground. All politicians make an initial pitch for attention, and Starmer's was competence. And competence is one of the most powerful tools you have as a political party. In politics, sustaining attention isn't the means, it's the point, the politician's way of justifying themselves. As such, the pitch is almost always the hard sell – intense, elemental sensation, immediately delivered. Starmer's sell was, 'I can do this. Just watch.'

Like all politicians, in the flesh he looked like his newspaper caricatures, with a large concrete head, big, buggy, slightly rabbit-caught-in-the-headlights eyes, and an earnest disposition. In other respects, he was exactly as I expected him to be, i.e. rather more charismatic than he is on television. Never happy discussing his private life, he had become extremely eloquent talking about his relationship with his mother, Jo, a lifelong Labour supporter, who suffered from Still's disease – a rare form of arthritis that can destroy the joints – and who died in 2015, just weeks before Starmer was elected MP for Holborn and St Pancras. 'It was really tragic,' he said. 'She would have loved to have seen that. But she was so ill by then. She couldn't move, she couldn't use her hands, so she had to be fed. She couldn't speak, couldn't communicate. I would have loved her to have been there, but she was in a terrible way. In a terrible, terrible place.' When I asked him what her illness and his experience of being around that illness taught him, he looked down at his hands, and almost whispered. 'Courage,' he said. 'Courage and resilience.'

This was something I could have imagined my mother saying about her own experience, her own survival. The older she became, the more strident she was, gradually turning the tables on my father. After various periods of separation, they were back together, steadily wearing each other down in a terrible war of attrition. By the end, she had the upper hand, treating my father almost as a carer. When she died, aged eighty-one, it was time, as it so often is.

My father died exactly a year after my mother, like her, in Cheltenham General Hospital. He had recently been moved into a care home and seemed to be doing fine until he fell and slipped into a coma from which he never recovered. Four days later he was dead. Because we always fought when I was young, I was sort of leaving for good when I left home at sixteen. After one final confrontation with my father, I decided I wanted out, and so that was it. We stayed in touch, he would occasionally help me financially, and I sometimes went home for Christmas, but ours was a troubled relationship. It got better over the years – it couldn't get any worse, and so had to get better – and we learned to spend time together without ever acknowledging the past. (When he visited me at the office, he would always take pictures on a cheap disposable camera, to show my mother.) Those early years stayed with both of us, however, in ways that we never bothered to articulate. At least not to each other.

After a while, our relationship seemed to become like the relationships that many fathers have with their sons: he would berate me for not achieving what he thought I was capable of, often referring to what I did as 'rubbish'. Yet I could tell he was secretly proud of me; he just couldn't, wouldn't, find a way to tell me. We didn't spend much time together, but whenever I casually mentioned I'd been somewhere or met someone he admired, he was rapt. I don't think he could quite believe that I'd done the things I said I'd done; he didn't think I was making it up, he just couldn't imagine how I found myself in these situations. There is a part of me that thinks he would have liked to have known those people too; and that, maybe if we had been closer, there might have been a possibility. But our relationship seemed locked in the psychological dynamics of the past, where he was always playing the father, and I pretended to be his son, even though we both knew each role was ridiculously inappropriate. Whenever we met, we talked about something else: trivial things, inconsequential things, things that didn't have borders or a subtext that would hurl us instantly back to when he used to punch me in the face.

He once asked my brother why I had started to write about my experiences of being hurt when I was growing up.

'What did he expect?' I said.

As he got older, he became what I thought was an easy read. He would feign illness, and deliberately exaggerate any symptoms he might have. Mike was a huge man – tall, heavy, strong – but he seemed to enjoy appearing weak and submissive. I always found this playacting ridiculous, as well as the narrative he tried to spin about not knowing what he was doing when he hit me.

One Christmas, towards the end of his life, he came to stay with us at our cottage in Wales. After one particular dinner – he'd pointedly not offered to help clear the table or wash up – he attempted a heart-to-heart with me. He started talking about the indiscretions that had caused so much unrest at home. When he came home from work, only to be confronted by my mother because he had obviously been with another woman, she would throw a pan or a kettle at him and he would hit her in the face.

'The thing is,' he said to me, as the two of us were sitting at the kitchen table, 'I didn't have any affairs and there was one really important reason why. The thing is . . . I had a small penis, so it was never going to happen. It would have been out of the question.'

Apart from the fact that it still felt very strange for him to be talking about his cock in front of me, I knew what he was saying was a lie. He didn't have a small penis; far from it, in fact. He wasn't exactly a member of the HLD club, but why was he deliberately going out of his way to disguise what no longer needed disguising? We were at the denouement of our relationship, not the beginning, so what was he trying to achieve? Why was he now going out of his way to fabricate a story that had been inadvertently responsible for me not being able to say my own name for five years? I had been witness to other faux declarations over the years, when he had gone out of his way to explain his behaviour, but it rarely rang true. So, I guess this was just another clumsy attempt to exonerate himself. Even so, I felt sorry for him rather than anything else. He could be extraordinarily perceptive when he chose to be, so when he acted dumb it didn't chime. And that annoyed me.

I dropped the conversation, but he had had a couple of drinks and was obviously keen to talk. He asked me what I was up to, and I explained the book project I was involved with, a book about the increasing cultural importance of David Bowie's appearance on *Top of the Pops* in 1972, when he performed 'Starman'. Keen to move on from his faux admission, I went into detail, describing the colour, the clothes, the lights, the way in which the decade had suddenly come alive.

Dad let me bang on for a while, and then, when I paused for breath, quietly said, 'You know we had a black and white television, don't you?'

I'd been seen.

ONE OF THE ACCIDENTAL BUT perhaps inevitable by-products of ageing is finding out which clichés are actually true. And so regardless of what decisions you make along the way – seemingly monumental or apparently incidental – a lot of life is determined for you. This was the case with our relationship: after a while, it was always going to be this way.

When my father died, my brother Dan and I went to empty his room. His death had left me strangely unaffected, although spending a day dismantling what was left of his life was the hardest thing. The day had its comic moments, as my brother and I divided his meagre belongings like a couple embarking on a divorce. ('No, it's OK, you can have the wagon-wheel coffee table. The Phil Collins CD? Actually, you can have that too if you like . . .') The process was as much of a bonding exercise as a cathartic one.

But it was the briefcases under the stairs that threw me. My father had always been a keen collector of my work, and whenever a photograph of me appeared in a newspaper, or whenever I'd written something for a magazine – no matter how small – he had found it, cut it out and pasted it into a scrapbook, had it mounted on cardboard or even, sometimes, framed. Oh, these foolish things. He had honoured my brother in a similar way, covering the walls of his room with photographs of Dan getting another promotion or military medal; but you can write a lot of columns in thirty years, and my father had seemingly collected them all. I'm no slouch when it comes to archiving my own work, yet my father had found and kept articles, features and reviews I'd long since forgotten about.

His bookcases were full of my books – sometimes three or four copies of the same one – including a couple I'd written or contributed to early in my career, which I was so embarrassed about I didn't even have myself.

Just when I thought I'd found everything of mine he'd collected, I discovered four metal briefcases that were full of cuttings from a newspaper I had worked on back in the nineties. There they were, all my cuttings, carefully glued into A4 booklets, each one with the date of its appearance scribbled in dark-blue ink in my father's spidery writing. There was even a photograph of me with Bowie, crudely cut out from a copy of *Hello!*.

All I could do was stare. His obsession didn't border on anything other than love and regret. Ever since I started to appear in print, he had collected me. Collected my life. A life he had inadvertently help build. Maybe he had collected them because he thought that one day they would run out, that one day there wouldn't be anything else to collect. But there it all was, scraps of a life told through scraps of a talent. He had collected my life as I was attempting to control it.

My brother didn't need to ask which one of us was going to keep these files, and, in an act of something more than brotherly love, he just started carrying them out to my car. I've still got the boxes at home, pushed under the stairs in my house. I never look at them, but then I don't need to.

My father had done that for me.

Acknowledgements

Andreas Campomar, Edie Jones, Georgia Jones, Gordon Wise, Sarah Walter.

Image Credits

All images from author's personal collection unless otherwise stated.

Integrated images:
P31 – Photograph by Terry Smith, Camera Press London; P109 – Gie Knaeps/Getty Images; P169 – David M. Benett/Getty Images; P223 – FG/Bauer-Griffin/GC Images/Getty Images; P263 – Anton Emdin, GQ Condé Nast; P299 – Richard Young; P341 – Mariano Vivanco; P359 – David M. Benett/Dave Benett/Getty Images for Hugo Boss

Picture sections:
Section 1: P1 bottom – Whizzer and Chips, Archie & Goal; P2 bottom – NME, David Bailey, Street Life; P3 bottom – Punk, Ritz; P4 middle – Boulevard; P5 – i-D; P7 – The Face, Arena; P8 top left – Terry O'Neill; P8 middle – Observer; P8 bottom – Sunday Times Magazine

Section 2: P1 – GQ Condé Nast; P3 bottom right – Richard Young; P8 middle left and bottom – Evening Standard

Index

host the greatest Karaoke Night EVER!
including the official recording of the charity single for
ONE FOR THE BOYS
United Against Cancer™
Thursday 25th Sept 2014 - 7pm
Abbey Road Studios, 3 Abbey Rd, London NW8 9AY
RSVP sofia@onefortheboys.com
request the honour of the
at a private dinner to ce
LONDON COLLECTIONS MEN
Tuesday 18 June 20
7.30pm cocktails, 8.30pm seat
Annabel's
44 Berkeley Square
LAND-ROVER
SAVE THE DATE
Spas Roussev & Dylan Jones
Invite you to an intimate dinner
our of Tina Brown to celebrate the Royal Wedding
WEDNESDAY 27TH APRIL AT 8.30PM
HARRY'S BAR
26 SOUTH AUDLEY STREET
LONDON
GQ
SOHO HOUSE
DYLAN JONES, NICK JONES AND REVEL GUEST
IN ASSOCIATION WITH LAND ROVER
INVITE YOU TO A PARTY AT CABALVA HOUSE
TO CELEBRATE THE 25TH ANNIVERSARY OF THE HAY FESTIV
WHITNEY-ON-WYE, HEREFORDSHIRE HR3 6EX
SUNDAY 3RD JUNE
DRINKS AND DINNER FROM 8 PM
RSVP
hayparty@sohohouse.com
THIS INVITATION IS STRICTLY NON-TRANSFERABLE. PLEASE BRING THE INVITATION
PRINTED BY SMYTHSON
Royal Academy of Arts
Dylan Jones, Tracey Emin RA and Nick Jones
Request the honour of your company for
The Committee Dinner
After the Summer Exhibition Preview Party
Wednesday 30 May 2012
The Cast Corridor, Royal Academy Schools
RSVP by Monday 23 May 2012
To: Deborah Mellor, 020 7300 5702
deborah.mellor@royalacademy.org.uk
Seated Dinner at 9.00pm
This invitation may not be transferred and must be presented to gain entry
Ford
Dylan Jones
Editor of British GQ
Tel: 323 656 1010
to meet Dylan Jones, the Editor of British GQ
and his team at the Penthouse at the Chateau Marmont
on Sunday 1st May
Drinks from 6.30 until 9.30pm
Please RSVP to:
Danielle Radojcin Tel: 44 207 152 3793
or
Virginia Banks Tel: 310 276 5802
invite
LONDON FASHION WEEK MEN'S
Dylan Jones and David Beckham
have the pleasure of inviting
to a private dinner to celebrate London Fashion Week Men's
Monday 7 January 2019 7pm reception, 7.45pm dinner
Brasserie Of Light at Selfridges Duke Street entrance,
400 Oxford Street, London W1
RSVP GQDinner@condenast.co.uk
Invitation is non-transferable. If after acceptance you find you are
MOËT & CHANDON
CHAMPAGNE
BELVEDERE
VODKA